To my wonderful wife, Sheila. Your patience and support during the writing process has been phenomenal. Sometimes the work is long and keeps me away from you, even when I am in the same house. Thanks for everything. Love always.

– Steve Hughes

Packt.com

Subscribe to our online digital library for full access to over 7,000 books and videos, as well as industry leading tools to help you plan your personal development and advance your career. For more information, please visit our website.

Why subscribe?

- Spend less time learning and more time coding with practical eBooks and Videos from over 4,000 industry professionals

- Improve your learning with Skill Plans built especially for you

- Get a free eBook or video every month

- Fully searchable for easy access to vital information

- Copy and paste, print, and bookmark content

Did you know that Packt offers eBook versions of every book published, with PDF and ePub files available? You can upgrade to the eBook version at packt.com and as a print book customer, you are entitled to a discount on the eBook copy. Get in touch with us at customercare@packtpub.com for more details.

At www.packt.com, you can also read a collection of free technical articles, sign up for a range of free newsletters, and receive exclusive discounts and offers on Packt books and eBooks.

Foreword

I respected Steve's knowledge and technical depth long before I met him and as we have worked together, the root of his success is evident. Steve is a person worth listening to and learning from. He helps with a giving heart to truly enable others. His passion for lifting others up is evident in the labor of love that is this book.

Much learning is now done in smaller chunks or digital bites that allow us to solve problems quickly and move on. This is a great enabler and accelerator for our journeys. There are subjects, however, that can get deep quickly and require a more comprehensive approach to truly master them.

We need people and resources committed to combining industry-leading experience with theory, practicality, and hands-on approaches that explain, enable, and enlighten us to a new set of solutions and possibilities.

Analysis Services is close to my heart because, like many of you, I have banged my head on the keyboard because a query would not perform, or a hierarchy would not work properly or worse yet my model just would not support where I needed to take the solution. I have been blessed to work alongside some of the most brilliant minds in our field. I'm honored to learn from them at every step and you have an incredible opportunity with this book to learn from one of the best.

Enjoy this book. Take notes in the margins, dog-ear the pages, or highlight in your e-reader. There will be plenty you will want to revisit.

My best wishes for your success.

Adam Jorgensen

Vice President, Professional Services - Data & Analytics

3Cloud

Contributors

About the author

Steve Hughes is the director of consulting and an enterprise architect at 3Cloud. He has worked extensively on Microsoft SQL Server Analysis Services multidimensional models throughout the years, followed by working with tabular models including Power BI and Power Pivot implementations. He is passionate about using data effectively and helping customers understand that data is valuable and profitable. He has worked in many industries, including healthcare, finance, manufacturing, transportation, and utilities. He is a Microsoft Certified Professional with multiple Microsoft Azure and Data Platform certifications.

I want to thank Edward Jankowski (my father-in-law), Adam Jorgenson (friend and boss), and Terry Hughes (my father) for their examples of excellence in technology and work.

About the reviewers

Dan English is a data and AI cloud solution architect at Microsoft in Minneapolis, MN. He has been developing with Microsoft technologies since 1996 and has focused on data warehousing and business intelligence since 2004. He has helped run and present at user group events such as the Minnesota SQL Server user group and the Microsoft Minnesota BI user group, along with SQLSaturday events. He holds a Bachelor of Science degree in business administration from Minnesota State University, Mankato. He and his wife, Molly, live in Minnesota and have two children, Lily and Wyatt.

Alan Faulkner is an IT professional with more than 20 years of progressive technical experience. He specializes in business intelligence, data warehousing, and database architecture. With the advent of the cloud, Alan architects data solutions based on Azure technologies as well. His experience across disparate industries, applications, and tools provides efficient delivery of flexible and scalable data architectures. Alan holds a B.S. degree in Computer Information Systems (CIS) from DeVry University. He participated in the Microsoft SSAS Maestro program during its short-lived tenure and has written about Analysis Services on his blog, FalconTek Solutions Central.

Packt is searching for authors like you

If you're interested in becoming an author for Packt, please visit authors. packtpub.com and apply today. We have worked with thousands of developers and tech professionals, just like you, to help them share their insight with the global tech community. You can make a general application, apply for a specific hot topic that we are recruiting an author for, or submit your own idea.

Table of Contents

Section 2: Building and Deploying a Multidimensional Model

3

Preparing Your Data for Multidimensional Models

4
Building a Multidimensional Cube in SSAS 2019

5
Adding Measures and Calculations with MDX

Section 3: Building and Deploying Tabular Models

6

Preparing Your Data for Tabular Models

7

Building a Tabular Model in SSAS 2019

8

Adding Measures and Calculations with DAX

Section 4: Exposing Insights while Visualizing Data from Your Models

9

Exploring and Visualizing Your Data with Excel

10

Creating Interactive Reports and Enhancing Your Models in Power BI

Section 5: Security, Administration, and Managing Your Models

11

Securing Your SSAS Models

12

Common Administration and Maintenance Tasks

Other Books You May Enjoy

Index

Preface

SQL Server Analysis Services (**SSAS**) continues to be a leading enterprise-scale toolset, enabling customers to deliver data and analytics across large datasets with great performance. This book will help you understand MS SQL Server 2019's new features and improvements, especially when it comes to SSAS.

First, you'll cover a quick overview of SQL Server 2019, learn how to choose the right analytical model to use, and understand their key differences. You'll then explore how to create a multi-dimensional model with SSAS and expand on that model with MDX. Next, you'll create and deploy a tabular model using Microsoft Visual Studio and Management Studio. You'll learn when and how to use both tabular and multi-dimensional model types, how to deploy and configure your servers to support them, and design principles that are relevant to each model. The book comes packed with tips and tricks to build measures, optimize your design, and interact with models using Excel and Power BI. All this will help you visualize data to gain useful insights and make better decisions. Finally, you'll discover practices and tools for securing and maintaining your models once they are deployed.

By the end of this MS SQL Server book, you'll be able to choose the right model, and build and deploy it to support the analytical needs of your business.

Who this book is for?

This Microsoft SQL Server book is for BI professionals and data analysts who are looking for a practical guide to creating and maintaining tabular and multi-dimensional models using SQL Server 2019 Analysis Services. A basic working knowledge of BI solutions such as Power BI and database querying is required.

What this book covers?

Chapter 1, Analysis Services in SQL Server 2019, introduces Analysis Services and the steps to install the tools used in the rest of the book.

Chapter 2, Choosing the SQL Server 2019 Analytic Model for Your BI Needs, presents multidimensional and tabular models of Analysis Services and provides reasons to choose between them.

Chapter 3, Preparing Your Data for Multidimensional Models, outlines how to organize data into star schemas to support multidimensional models.

Chapter 4, Building a Multidimensional Cube in SSAS 2019, covers the necessary steps to build the multidimensional model, complete with facts, dimensions, and partitions.

Chapter 5, Adding Measures and Calculations with MDX, illustrates how to expand a multidimensional model with measures and calculations created with MDX and how to query a multidimensional model with MDX.

Chapter 6, Preparing Your Data for Tabular Models, covers the steps required to build a Power Pivot model in Excel and prep data for work with tabular models.

Chapter 7, Building a Tabular Model in SSAS 2019, shows how to build tabular models using standard refresh, Direct Query, and Power Query, and how to import a Power Pivot model to create a tabular model.

Chapter 8, Adding Measures and Calculations with DAX, elucidates the steps to query a model with DAX and expand the model using DAX to create measures, columns, and calculated tables.

Chapter 9, Exploring and Visualizing Your Data with Excel, highlights the use of Excel to visualize the data from the models after the models have been created.

Chapter 10, Creating Interactive Reports and Enhancing Your Models in Power BI, focuses on the use of Power BI to create modern reports using both multidimensional and tabular models.

Chapter 11, Securing Your SSAS Models, engages in imparting knowledge and implementing various patterns to secure multidimensional and tabular models.

Chapter 12, Common Administration and Maintenance Tasks, provides steps to manage models by helping in understanding the backup and restore operations, scaling options, and performance techniques.

To get the most out of this book

This book is designed for those of you who are experienced working with data and analysis in their business. Most readers should have some experience with Excel or Power BI. Analysis Services is the next level of data analysis that uses the power of SQL Server 2019. This book will give you hands-on guidance, from installing tools to the basics of maintenance and operations.

Software/hardware covered in the book	OS requirements
SQL Server 2019 Analysis Services	Windows 10, Windows Server
SQL Server 2019 Database Engine	Windows 10, Windows Server
Excel	Windows 10, Windows Server
Power BI Desktop	Windows 10, Windows Server

In the first chapter of the book, we will walk through the installation of the SQL Server tools. However, you should plan to get Excel and Power BI Desktop downloaded so that you build reports and visualizations on the models you will create in the later chapters.

If you are using the digital version of this book, we advise you to type the code yourself or access the code via the GitHub repository (link available in the next section). Doing so will help you avoid any potential errors related to copy/pasting of code.

Download the example code files

You can download the example code files for this book from GitHub at `https://github.com/PacktPublishing/hands-on-sql-server-2019-analysis-services`. In case there's an update to the code, it will be updated on the existing GitHub repository.

We also have other code bundles from our rich catalog of books and videos available at `https://github.com/PacktPublishing/`. Check them out!

Download the color images

We also provide a PDF file that has color images of the screenshots/diagrams used in this book. You can download it here: `https://static.packt-cdn.com/downloads/9781800204768_ColorImages.pdf`.

Conventions used

There are a number of text conventions used throughout this book.

`Code in text`: Indicates code words in text, database table names, folder names, filenames, file extensions, pathnames, dummy URLs, user input, and Twitter handles. Here is an example: "In my case, the account name is `NT Service\MSOLAP$DOWSQL2019TAB`."

A block of code is set as follows:

```
USE [Master]
CREATE LOGIN [NT Service\MSOLAP$DOWSQL2019TAB] FROM WINDOWS
WITH DEFAULT_DATABASE=[master], DEFAULT_LANGUAGE=[us_english]
GO
```

Bold: Indicates a new term, an important word, or words that you see on screen. For example, words in menus or dialog boxes appear in the text like this. Here is an example: "Once you have the user in place, choose **Impersonate Service Account** and click **Connect**."

> **Tips or important notes**
> Appear like this.

Get in touch

Feedback from our readers is always welcome.

General feedback: If you have questions about any aspect of this book, mention the book title in the subject of your message and email us at `customercare@packtpub.com`.

Errata: Although we have taken every care to ensure the accuracy of our content, mistakes do happen. If you have found a mistake in this book, we would be grateful if you would report this to us. Please visit `www.packtpub.com/support/errata`, selecting your book, clicking on the Errata Submission Form link, and entering the details.

Piracy: If you come across any illegal copies of our works in any form on the internet, we would be grateful if you would provide us with the location address or website name. Please contact us at `copyright@packt.com` with a link to the material.

If you are interested in becoming an author: If there is a topic that you have expertise in, and you are interested in either writing or contributing to a book, please visit `authors.packtpub.com`.

Reviews

Please leave a review. Once you have read and used this book, why not leave a review on the site that you purchased it from? Potential readers can then see and use your unbiased opinion to make purchase decisions, we at Packt can understand what you think about our products, and our authors can see your feedback on their book. Thank you!

For more information about Packt, please visit `packt.com`.

Section 1: Choosing Your Model

We kick off the book with an introduction to SQL Server 2019 and the process to install and configure the data engine, the Analysis Services engines, and the sample databases. When starting to work with **SQL Server Analysis Services (SSAS)**, the developer or architect needs to choose the proper model to use. This section will clarify what SSAS is and the key differences between the models.

This section comprises the following chapters:

- *Chapter 1, Analysis Services in SQL Server 2019*
- *Chapter 2, Choosing the SQL Server 2019 Analytic Model for Your BI Needs*

1
Analysis Services in SQL Server 2019

As you prepare to build your analytic models in SQL Server, you need to understand the basics about **SQL Server Analysis Services** (**SSAS**) including the purpose of the overall platform, with a basic understanding of the product. We will be exploring the origin of SSAS and its evolution into what we use today.

Upon completion of this chapter, you should understand where SSAS fits into the overall data analytics ecosystem. In this chapter, we're going to answer the following key questions about Analysis Services:

- What is SQL Server Analysis Services anyway?
- Why use SQL Server Analysis Services?
- What's new in SQL Server Analysis Services 2019?
- What are the tools used with SQL Server Analysis Services?
- One last thing – our sample data

In preparation for the rest of the book, the final section of the chapter discusses the tools we use. We will provide links and instructions for the installation procedures to prepare for the various examples and development used throughout the book. We will also walk through the restoration of the SQL Server database used to support our Analysis Services examples in later chapters.

What is SQL Server Analysis Services anyway?

SSAS is distributed as part of the SQL Server *stack* of tools. This stack has included a variety of tools over the years:

- **SQL Server Management Studio**
- **Data Transformation Services**
- **SQL Server Integration Services**
- **SQL Server Reporting Services**
- **Data Quality Services**
- **Master Data Services**
- **Data Virtualization with PolyBase**
- **Big Data Clusters**

Some of these options have been part of SQL Server for years, such as Integration Services, but some are brand new to SQL Server 2019, such as Big Data Clusters. Analysis Services has been in the product line for a long time, having been added in 1998.

SQL Server Analysis Services is not SQL Server

This statement may seem odd, but it is important to understand the place that Analysis Services has in the SQL Server stack and related **Microsoft Business Intelligence** (**MSBI**) ecosystem. As the list earlier in the chapter calls out, Analysis Services and many other products have been included in the purchase of SQL Server but are not a **relational database management system** (**RDBMS**).

The only component of SQL Server that has no official title is the **relational data engine**. It is simply referred to as *SQL Server*. SQL Server directly refers to the capability to store data in tables and use **Transact-SQL** or **TSQL** to interact with the data. Relationships, indexes, views, and stored procedures can be used in this engine and are commonly used for transactional systems and data warehouse solutions.

Analysis Services is designed to optimize data for analysis and reporting. Relational systems specialize in managing large amounts of transactions with good performance. Analytic solutions such as Analysis Services are designed to aggregate and query large amounts of data efficiently. While design methodologies such as star schemas are designed to optimize relational systems for analytic workloads, these schemas still require significant optimization within relational systems to match the performance of analytic solutions.

Relational versus analytic workloads

Relational workloads are typically normalized in relational database systems. Normalization involves using a lot of related tables to keep the data changes to a minimum. They are optimized to load data. Analytic workloads are denormalized using large flat tables with minimal relationships. This keeps the work of reading the data to a minimum.

The key takeaway here is that SQL Server refers to the relational database engine. Analysis Services is a separate data storage solution that is optimized for analytic and reporting workloads.

SQL Server Analysis Services through the years

SSAS has a long and interesting history. Personally, I started working with Analysis Services with its first release in 1998. Microsoft did not reinvent the wheel; they acquired another company to accelerate their introduction into analytic server tools or **Online Analytical Processing (OLAP)** servers. They started the process in 1996 and acquired Panorama Software's development team to begin the development of their new OLAP server product called OLAP Services 7.0, which was shipped with SQL Server 7.0 in 1998.

OLAP Services was a multidimensional database solution. Microsoft rebranded this to Analysis Services with its SQL Server 2000 release. They made significant changes to the multidimensional server and supporting technology in the 2005, 2008, and 2012 releases. The multidimensional server was designed to work with large-scale data on spinning disks. As hardware continued to improve, optimizations for the platform changed and we saw the shift to more memory-optimized solutions.

Enter **Power Pivot** with SQL Server 2008 R2 and **Excel** 2010. This is a significant turning point in the Analysis Services story. The **Vertipaq** compression engine was introduced to the MSBI set of offerings. While technically a part of SSAS, Power Pivot was released to Excel first. This columnar-based in-memory solution laid the groundwork for **tabular models** in Analysis Services, which is now the preferred option for working with Analysis Services.

Check out the following timeline. It illustrates the key points in the history of Analysis Services and related technologies:

Figure 1.1 – Over 20 years of Microsoft Analysis Services history

Microsoft has focused most of its attention on the tabular model technology in the most recent releases of Analysis Services. This technology is the heart of the Power BI products and is the only model type supported as a native Azure technology.

We will walk through the value of both types of models in Chapter 2, *Choosing the SQL Server 2019 Analytic Model for Your BI Needs*. Let's take a step back and look at why you would consider using Analysis Services to support your workloads today.

Why use SQL Server Analysis Services?

Now that you understand where Analysis Services fits into the SQL Server stack and the Microsoft BI ecosystem, why would you choose to use Analysis Services? Traditionally, Analysis Services was the best option to organize data for easy and performant analysis of data at scale. I have used Analysis Services to optimize data warehouses built on a variety of relational technologies including Microsoft SQL Server and Oracle. Analysis Services is *source agnostic*. If you can connect to the source, you have a use case for Analysis Services if you want more efficient analytics and reporting.

Optimized for reporting and analytics

This is the primary reason OLAP servers were introduced to the market. Earlier, we called out relational solutions and their optimization for efficient transaction handling. However, many of the optimizations for transaction handling conflict with reporting needs. One key example is the complexity of a relational solution.

The following diagram shows the complexity of relational design. The number of tables and joins required for reporting and analytics hinders the performance of report writers and queries:

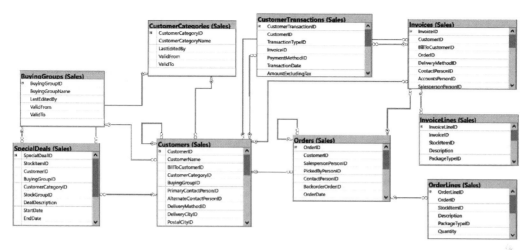

Figure 1.2 – Relational diagram of the Wide World Importers sales schema

As you can see in the preceding diagram, relational models make heavy use of foreign keys and related tables. Ralph Kimball introduced **dimensional modeling** and the **star schema** concepts to help optimize read techniques with relational systems. This resulted in simpler, flatter (denormalized) schemas such as the following diagram, which is the best design to support multidimensional model design:

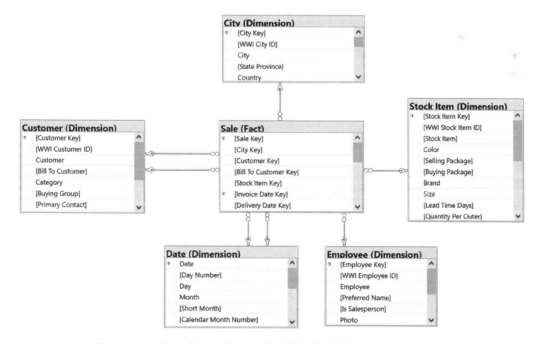

Figure 1.3 – Star schema diagram for Wide World Importers sales facts

While the star schema and dimensional models improved the ability of relational systems to extract reporting data, they were still bound to relational rules and languages. OLAP servers were introduced to further optimize the data for end user consumption. This resulted in even simpler, user-friendly options. The following example shows a pivot table in Excel that is directly connected to an Analysis Services model. This makes the data accessible and easy for users to analyze and create reports without deep technical skills:

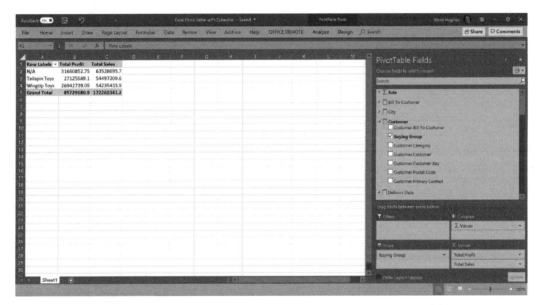

Figure 1.4 – Excel pivot table connected to an Analysis Services model

Let's see the relation of Analysis Services with Excel.

Works great with Excel

This leads to one of the primary reasons that Analysis Services has become a beloved delivery platform for users and IT organizations. Once data is delivered in Analysis Services, it can be easily consumed by Excel. When a user connects to an Analysis Services model, they are able to interact with the data and build what they need from the underlying database without coming back to IT for additional support.

Organized with end users in mind

The other reason that has to be considered is that the data is organized to support the business, not database or code efficiencies. Well-designed OLAP solutions use business-friendly names for the data. OLAP solutions typically hide system fields as well making sure the data in the OLAP database is relevant.

Here is a list of key user-friendly features in OLAP databases:

- Proper spelling and grammar, using spaces, capitalization, and punctuation.

- Hidden system values such as primary keys, surrogate keys, and system names.

- Relationships built in so the user does not have to determine how the data is related; it is related in the model itself.

- Pre-existing common calculations such as totals or averages, which respond correctly to filtering or slicing.

The following table shows how reporting queries becomes simpler as the database engine and structure is more focused on an aggregated and report-friendly structure:

Comparing Queries Returning the Same Results	

Relational, normalized, SQL	SELECT SUM(sil.ExtendedPrice) AS [Total Sales]
	    , SUM(sil.LineProfit) AS [Total Profit]
	    , ISNULL(sbg.BuyingGroupName, 'N/A') AS [Buying Group]
	FROM Sales.Invoices si
	INNER JOIN sales.InvoiceLines sil ON si.InvoiceID = sil.InvoiceID
	INNER JOIN sales.Customers sc ON si.CustomerID = sc.CustomerID
	LEFT OUTER JOIN sales.BuyingGroups sbg ON sc.BuyingGroupID = sbg.BuyingGroupID
	GROUP BY sbg.BuyingGroupName

Relational, star schema, SQL	SELECT SUM(fs.[Total Excluding Tax]) AS [Total Sales]
	    , SUM(fs.Profit) AS [Total Profit]
	    , dc.[Buying Group]
	FROM fact.Sale fs
	INNER JOIN Dimension.Customer dc ON fs.[Customer Key] = dc.[Customer Key]
	
	GROUP BY dc.[Buying Group]

Multidimensional, OLAP, MDX	SELECT {[Customer].[Buying Group].[ALL].children} ON ROWS , {[Measures].[Total Profit], [Measures].[Total Sales]} ON COLUMNS FROM [Wide World Importers DW]

Figure 1.5 – How reporting queries becomes simpler

Each of these queries returns the same results:

Total Sales	Total Profit	Buying Group
73037043.78	31660852.75	N/A
62654262.56	27125589.10	Tailspin Toys
62352133.11	26942739.05	Wingtip Toys

As you can see, making data more consumable for users is one of the key reasons to use Analysis Services. When considered in combination with OLAP-friendly tools such as Excel, Power BI, and Tableau, the use of OLAP servers is even more compelling.

What's new in SQL Server Analysis Services 2019?

The focus of this book is on using SSAS 2019. What has Microsoft added to the product in its most recent release? Because Analysis Services is effectively broken into two types of databases – **multidimensional** and **tabular** – we will talk about the changes to each separately.

Multidimensional models in 2019

This is the short list. Microsoft has not made significant changes to multidimensional capabilities in Analysis Services since the SQL Server 2012 release. Even that release focused on the new **xVelocity In-Memory Analytics Engine (aka Vertipaq)** that would support tabular models. Microsoft considers the multidimensional model in Analysis Services mature and is not adding major features at this point. The focus is on bug fixes and various performance enhancements to the engine. The key takeaway here is that multidimensional models still have a place but are not receiving any significant updates. The following is from Microsoft's documentation:

> *Multidimensional mode and Power Pivot for SharePoint mode are staples for many Analysis Services deployments. In the Analysis Services product lifecycle, these modes are mature. There are no new features for either of these modes in this release. However, bug fixes and performance improvements are included.*

Source

```
https://docs.microsoft.com/en-us/analysis-
services/what-s-new-in-sql-server-analysis-
services#sql-server-2017-analysis-services
```

Tabular models in 2019

While multidimensional models are considered mature, Microsoft is continuing to make significant investments in tabular model technology. Since its release in 2012 until now, major changes have happened with tabular models.

> **Compatibility levels**
>
> When working with tabular models, you need to understand **compatibility levels**. Microsoft introduced compatibility levels to allow new versions of Analysis Services to be **backward compatible** while enabling significant changes to supported features. When creating a tabular model, it is recommended to use the most current compatibility level. However, if you have an existing model and want to upgrade to the latest SQL Server version, you can set your compatibility level to what you are currently running until you have a chance to update the level and test it with the new features. The compatibility level is set when creating a new project in **Visual Studio**.
>
> SQL Server 2019 supports the 1500 (SQL Server 2019), 1400 (SQL Server 2017), and 1200 (SQL Server 2016) compatibility levels. The features released with SQL Server 2019 are included in compatibility level 1500.

Here are some of the key updates included with SQL Server 2019 Analysis Services (compatibility level 1500):

- Query interleaving
- Calculation groups in tabular models
- Governance setting for Power BI cache refreshes
- Online attach
- Many-to-many relationship support

Let's look at each of these changes in terms of *what* they are and *why* they matter.

Query interleaving

Query interleaving allows you to set how queries are handled based on query length and performance. Tabular model queries are handled in a *first-in, first-out model (FIFO)* by default. This means that a long-running query could make shorter queries run for longer if they follow that query in the queue. By enabling this feature, shorter queries can be executed during a long query run. This feature is only available for import models, not **Direct Query**. However, if you have a high-concurrency tabular model solution (lots of users or complex queries), this feature could improve performance for your users and reduce CPU pressure on the server.

Calculation groups

Calculation groups are used to group related calculations, which users often work with at the same time. This is really helpful with large complex models with many different calculations for the users to navigate. Microsoft calls out that **Time intelligence** will benefit from this significantly. For example, you can create a calculation group that has **Current**, **Month-to-Date (MTD)**, **Quarter-to-Date (QTD)**, and **Year-to-Date (YTD)** and call it *xTD*. When the user views the deployed model, they will see a calculation group as a single column they can add to their visual, which displays all four of these calculations as applied to a base measure such as Revenue. This feature has been added to improve usability in complex models.

Governance settings for Power BI cache refresh

The Power BI service caches data for dashboards and reports to improve performance and user experience when using live connections with tabular models. However, in some cases, this can cause a significant amount of queries with the possibility of overloading a server. This setting will override background refresh policies set on the client, preventing performance issues on the server.

Online attach

Currently, updates to tabular models require the model to be taken offline while deploying changes to the model. This results in downtime for the model. This feature allows model designers to deploy model changes live. This is similar to the shadow copy feature with multidimensional models, which supports the same online deployment.

The process currently is supported using **XML for Analysis (XMLA)** (more about that later). However, for tabular models, you will need to account for double the model's memory footprint during the online attach operation. The effective result is that during the attach process, both the new model and the old model will be in memory during the process. Once the process has completed, the old model will be removed. During the operation, users can continue to query the model and will start using the new model once it is loaded.

Many-to-many relationship support

Many-to-many relationship support has always been an issue with tabular models. This change allows relationships to be created between two tables where the relationship may not be unique. For example, if you have a fact table that is aggregated to the month, you will now be able to use the month value from a date table that has daily granularity. This allows cleaner, simpler models that are easier to use. Next, we will look at the tools that are used with SSAS.

What are the tools used with SQL Server Analysis Services?

Because SSAS is part of the SQL Server stack, many tools can be used to support both products. Microsoft has made a significant push to consolidate tooling over the years. As a result, we have two key tools used for building and interacting with models – **SQL Server Management Studio (SSMS)** and **Visual Studio**. In the following sections, I will discuss what role each plays and where to get the tools to match the work we are doing in the rest of the book. We will also walk through the installation of both Analysis Services modes.

SQL Server 2019 Developer edition

Let's start with installing SQL Server 2019 and both Analysis Services modes. We will be using the Developer edition of the SQL Server products. Because we will be using data stored in SQL Server to support our models, you will be installing three instances of SQL Server – one relational, one multidimensional, and one tabular. The relational and multidimensional instances will be installed during the same installation. The Developer Edition is the functional equivalent of the Enterprise Edition.

You can find the latest version of SQL Server 2019 Developer edition by searching for SQL Server 2019 Developer in your preferred search engine. The current location for all SQL Server downloads is `https://www.microsoft.com/en-us/sql-server/sql-server-downloads`. You should download the Developer edition as shown in the following screenshot. It is a free developer option for you to use while learning SSAS:

Developer

SQL Server 2019 Developer is a full-featured free edition, licensed for use as a development and test database in a non-production environment.

Figure 1.6 – Downloading the Developer edition

We do have the ability to install two of the instances simultaneously. Next, we will install the database engine and multidimensional mode as described. Once those are complete, we will install another instance to support the tabular mode.

Installing SQL Server 2019 database engine and SQL Server 2019 Analysis Services multidimensional mode

For the most part, we will follow a normal installation process for the database engine and Analysis Services in multidimensional mode. I will use the following set of screenshots to highlight decision points through the process:

1. After you launch the installation for the first time, you will need to select the **Custom** installation type. **Basic** does not include the option to install Analysis Services:

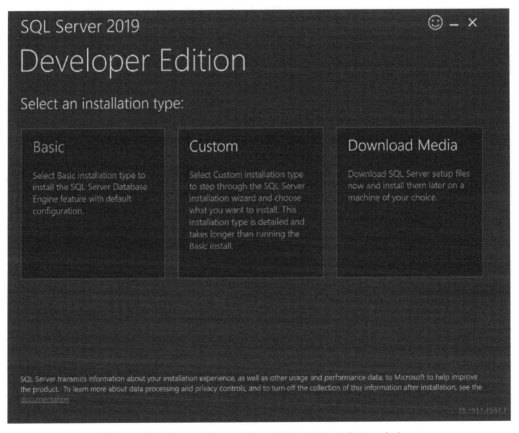

Figure 1.7 – Choose Custom from the initial installation dialog

> **Production installations**
>
> The instructions provided here are intended for **development** and **experimental** installs. Please refer to the latest best practices from Microsoft regarding production workload installations.

2. You will need to select the **Installation** tab on the left, then select **New SQL Server stand-alone installation or add features to an existing installation** option:

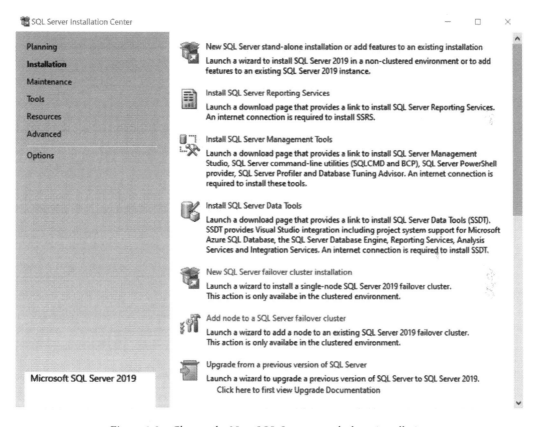

Figure 1.8 – Choose the New SQL Server stand-alone installation

3. You will start the installation process. You can select the default options until you get to the **Product Key** screen. On this screen, you should select the **Developer** edition for your free key. This will allow you to use all the features available in SQL Server Enterprise edition:

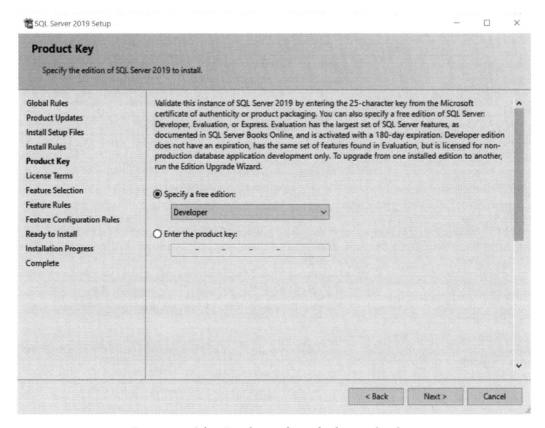

Figure 1.9 – Select Developer edition for free product key

4. The next stopping point is **Feature Selection**, as shown in the following screenshot. I encourage you to review all the options available to you with SQL Server 2019. There are a lot of non-database features included in SQL Server, such as support for **machine learning** and **data virtualization (Polybase)**. If this is the first time you have installed SQL Server in some time, you should note that **SQL Server Reporting Services (SSRS)** and **SQL Server Management Studio (SSMS)** are not included here. Both of these products should be downloaded separately. We will walk through Management Studio for our purposes shortly.

We will need **Database Engine Services** and **Analysis Services** for our installation. That will allow us to create instances of SQL Server and SSAS during our installation:

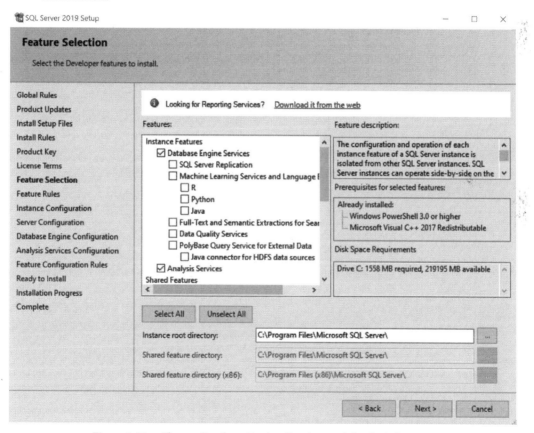

Figure 1.10 – Choose Database Engine Services and Analysis Services

5. The next section of interest is **Instance Configuration**. If you have been around SQL Server for a while, you have likely installed the **Default instance** many times. I am recommending you use the **Named instance** option. We will have two instances of Analysis Services when we are done. Using the **Named instance** option will help you keep these clearly separate:

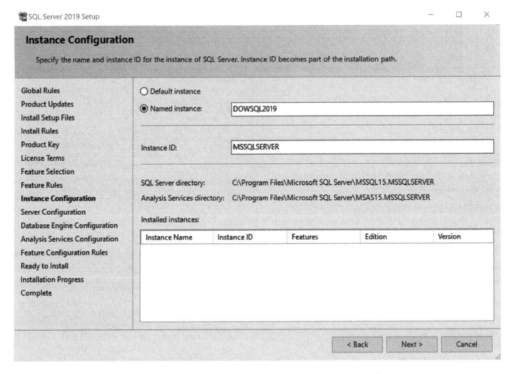

Figure 1.11 – Select Named instance and provide a unique name for your instance

Two names or three names

The current installation path we are following will result in two instance names. The first instance name will be used for both Database Engine Services and Analysis Services – Multidimensional Mode. We will go through the install process again to install Analysis Services – Tabular Mode with a different instance name. If you want to identify all of your instances separately, go back a step and unselect **Analysis Services**. This will allow you to create **Database Engine Services** with a unique instance name. You will need to follow the steps in the tabular mode installation instructions to add an instance for multidimensional mode as well. Refer to the setup instructions in the following sections for the Multidimensional Mode installation. This is your choice and will not affect examples used in the remainder of the book.

Remember that the name you choose here will be used by both the Database Engine Services instance and the Analysis Services Multidimensional Mode instance.

I am choosing to keep the default settings for **Server Configuration**. In a production installation, you should use service accounts configured for this purpose. Service accounts are created by your security team and are typically the more secure option for production environments. You may choose to do this for your developer install here if you choose to:

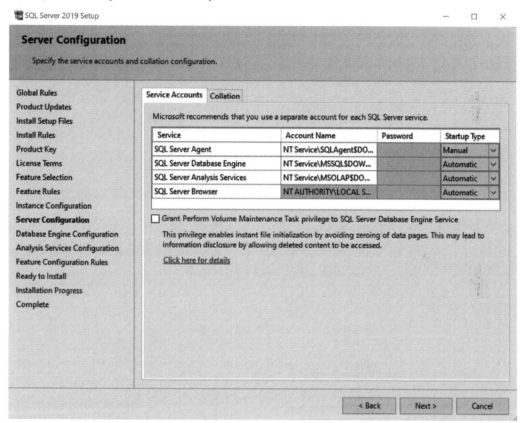

Figure 1.12 – Set custom accounts here if preferred

6. The next section covers **Database Engine Configuration**. I almost always set up mixed mode when doing development or testing work. This allows me to have an System Administrator user as well as to set up local database users if needed. I would not recommend this for most production scenarios. Using an Active Directory account is more secure for production servers. In our scenario, I would also recommend adding your current Windows user account to the SQL Server Administrators group:

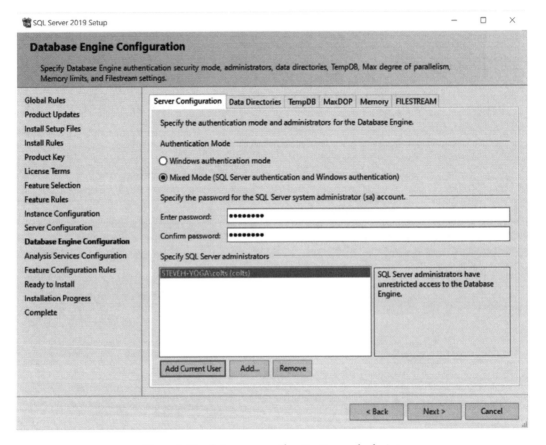

Figure 1.13 – Set up your authentication and admins

7. Now click on the **Data Directories** tab. This is a preference for you as well. You are welcome to keep the default options here. I typically create a data directory off of a drive – in this case, C – to hold data files. If you have multiple drives, you should select the fastest drive for your SQL Server data. Take note of your backup directory as you will need to use that later in the chapter:

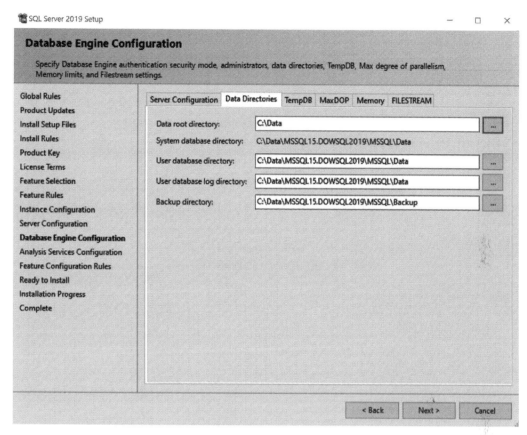

Figure 1.14 – Choose the location for your data directories

I will not be customizing the rest of the install. Feel free to browse the other tabs to review additional options you can set during installation.

8. The next screen is **Analysis Services Configuration**. It is similar to the previous two screens we worked with. However, you will notice that Analysis Services does not have a mixed mode option. It only supports Windows or Active Directory security.

We will be installing **Multidimensional and Data Mining Mode** in this instance. While I don't have a screenshot of the data directories, I would recommend you choose your fastest available hard disk for this instance as well:

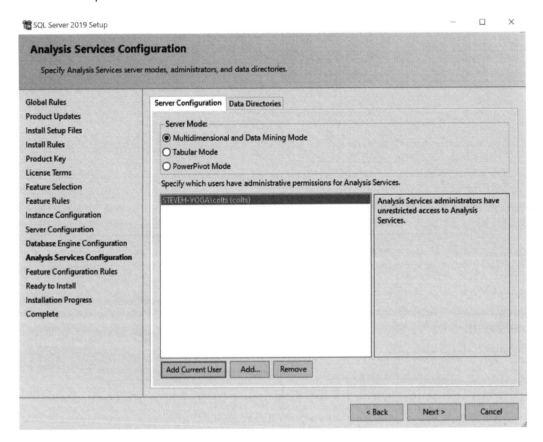

Figure 1.15 – Select multidimensional mode and add your user as an admin

You have completed the configuration settings at this point. The next few dialogs will show you what you have chosen to install, and you will be able to see your installation progress. You will see the following dialog when you have successfully completed your installations:

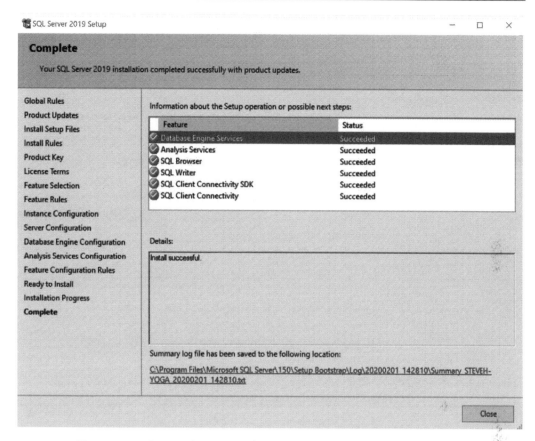

Figure 1.16 – Congratulations! You have successfully installed SQL Server 2019

Let's now look at the installation of SSAS using tabular mode.

Installing SQL Server 2019 Analysis Services tabular mode

Now, we will install another instance of Analysis Services using the tabular mode
as follows:

1. Typically, the **Installation** dialog box is still open at this point (assuming you did
    not close it). If it is not open, you will want to run the installation media for SQL
    Server 2019 again.

You will choose the new SQL Server stand-alone installation option as we did in the previous section:

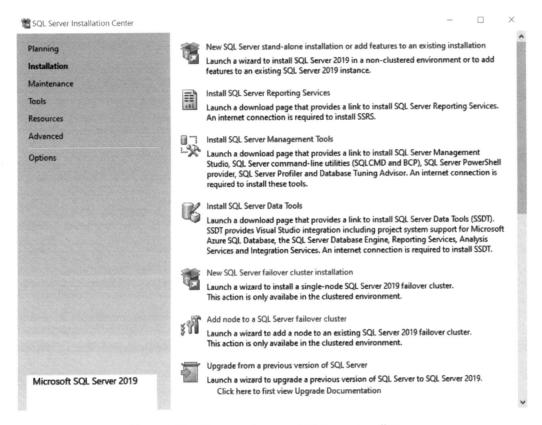

Figure 1.17 – Choose to do a new SQL Server installation

2. You can use the default settings until you get to the **Installation Type** dialog. Do not choose to add features. You must perform a new installation. The reason for this is that you cannot add another Analysis Services instance to your current instance:

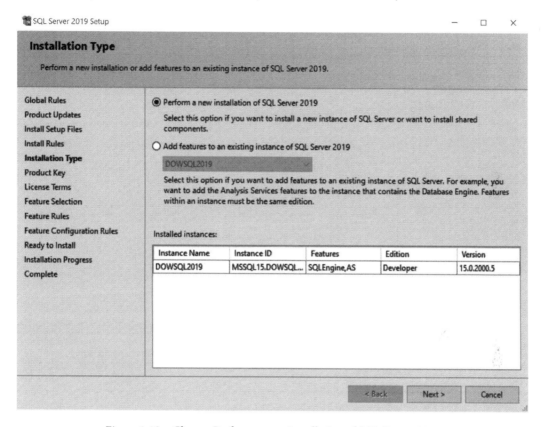

Figure 1.18 – Choose Perform a new installation of SQL Server 2019

3. As you move through the next few dialogs, you will choose the development free option once again. When you get to the feature selection, you should only select the **Analysis Services** option. We are only planning to install an additional Analysis Services Tabular Mode instance:

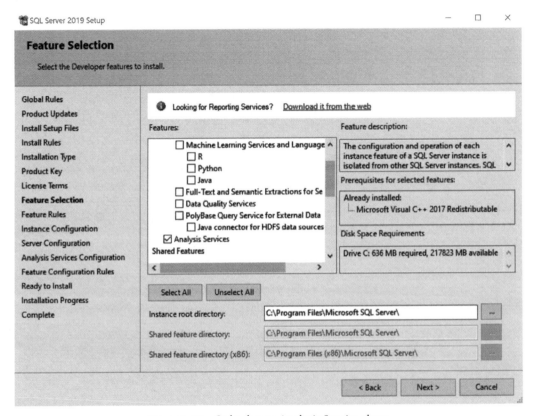

Figure 1.19 – Only choose Analysis Services here

4. Once again, I will recommend a named instance for this installation as well. As you can see, we do not have a default instance, so that is still an option here. Your existing instance name is shown in the table for your reference:

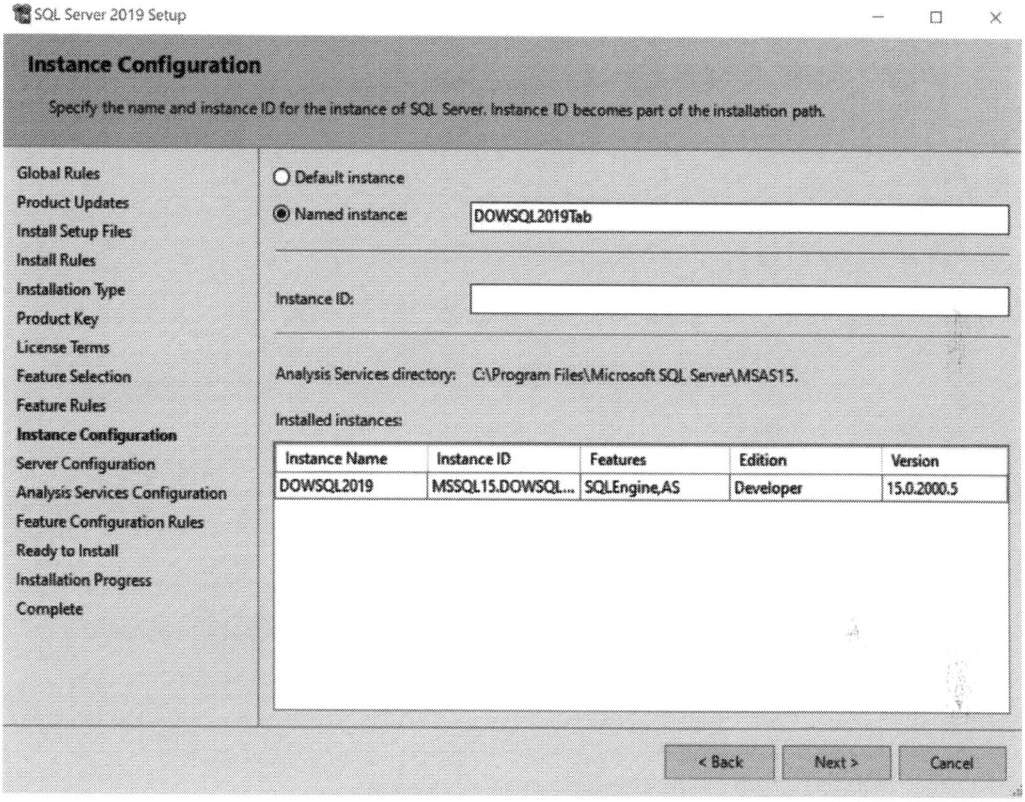

Instance Name	Instance ID	Features	Edition	Version
DOWSQL2019	MSSQL15.DOWSQL...	SQLEngine,AS	Developer	15.0.2000.5

Figure 1.20 – Create a new named instance

5. The next step is **Analysis Services Configuration**. In this case, you will select the **Tabular Mode** option. As with the other installation, you can specify your **Data Directories** and set your current user as an administrator for this instance:

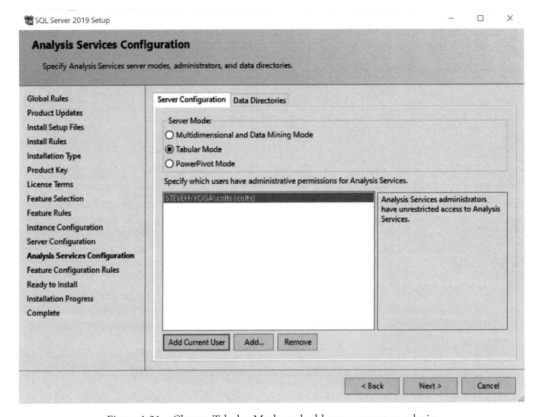

Figure 1.21 – Choose Tabular Mode and add your user as an admin

6. Complete the installation process and you should see the following **Complete** dialog with only **Analysis Services** in the **Feature** list. Congratulations, you have successfully installed the three instances of SQL Server 2019 to be used throughout the book:

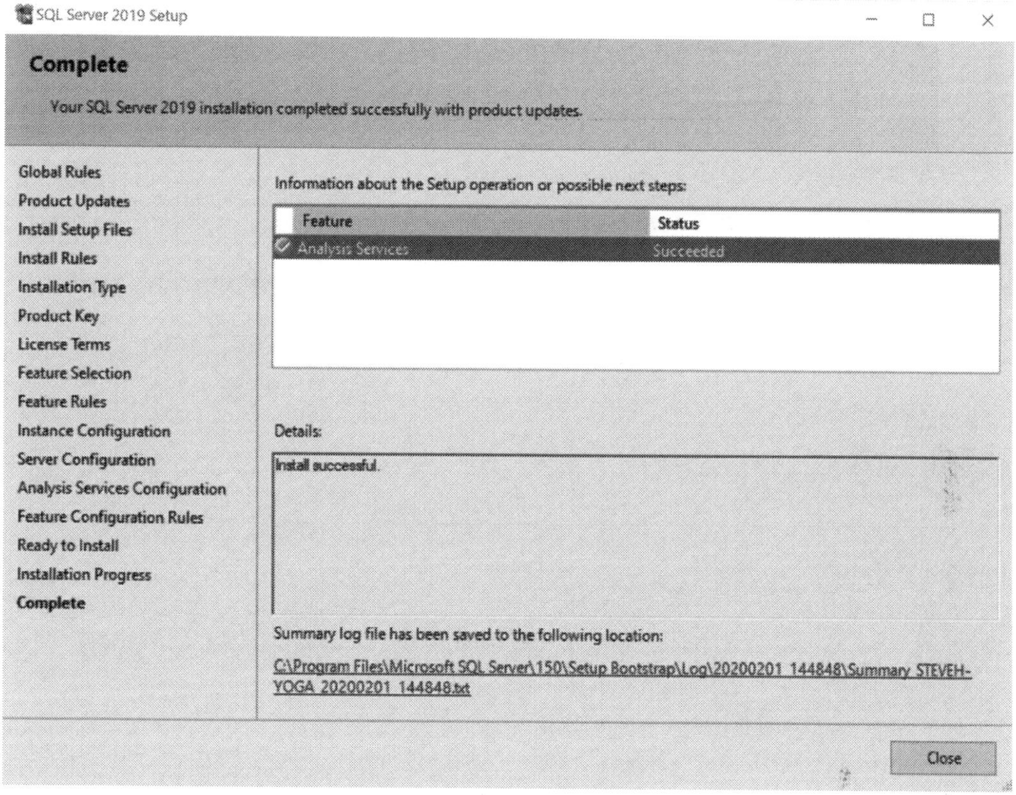

Figure 1.22 – Congratulations! You have successfully installed your Analysis Services – Tabular Mode

Now that we have successfully installed Analysis Services for tabular models, let's see how to manage installations.

Managing installations

Once installed, you will find that SQL Server tends to be very resource hungry. My recommendation is that you turn the services off when you are not using them. The following scripts are PowerShell and will allow you to turn them on and off as needed. In order to use these scripts, you will need to put the instance name in the locations where `[[INSTANCE NAME]]` is in the code. Replace all that text with your instance name. If that does not work, you will need to find the service name in the services list in Windows.

There are two scripts here – the first will disable the service and turn it off. This will prevent it from restarting if you reboot your PC. The second script will turn on the services. I saved these files as SQLServerOn.ps1 and SQLServerOff.ps1. I execute them by opening a PowerShell window as an administrator. At the prompt, you type the following:

```
$ "<<YOUR PATH HERE>>\SQLServerOff.ps1"
```

You will need to replace <<YOUR PATH HERE>> with the location you stored the file at. Now to the scripts themselves. This script will disable the services and power down the service:

```
Set-Service 'MSSQL$[[INSTANCENAME]]' -StartupType Disabled
Stop-Service -Name 'MSSQL$[[INSTANCENAME]]' -Force


Set-Service 'MSOLAP$[[INSTANCENAME]]' -StartupType Disabled
Stop-Service -Name 'MSOLAP$[[INSTANCENAME]]' -Force


Set-Service 'MSOLAP$[[INSTANCENAME]]' -StartupType Disabled
Stop-Service -Name 'MSOLAP$[[INSTANCENAME]]' -Force
```

I saved this script as SQLServerOff.ps1. Once this is run, these services will not restart on reboot. The next script will re-enable the services. I chose to enable with a manual StartupType in order to prevent a restart in the event of a reboot. You can choose **Automatic** if you prefer:

```
Set-Service 'MSSQL$[[INSTANCENAME]]' -StartupType Manual
Start-Service -Name 'MSSQL$[[INSTANCENAME]]'


Set-Service 'MSOLAP$[[INSTANCENAME]]' -StartupType Manual
Start-Service -Name 'MSOLAP$[[INSTANCENAME]]'


Set-Service 'MSOLAP$[[INSTANCENAME]]' -StartupType Manual
Start-Service -Name 'MSOLAP$[[INSTANCENAME]]'
```

This script is saved as SQLServerOn.ps1. Remember to execute this with a PowerShell command window open in administrator mode.

> **Enabling PowerShell execution**
>
> By default, PowerShell execution is secured. If you have not enabled PowerShell execution on your PC, you will be unable to run a script you have created. To enable PowerShell to run locally created scripts on your PC, you will need to open a PowerShell window and run the following script:

```
Set-ExecutionPolicy RemoteSigned
```

Next, we will get familiar with SSMS.

SQL Server Management Studio (SSMS)

A few versions back, Microsoft removed SSMS from the SQL Server media. This allowed them to make changes to the tool independent of the version of SQL Server released. This made it significantly easier for users to get Management Studio, eliminating the need to run the SQL Server installation process. At the time of writing, the latest version of Management Studio is 18. You should install the latest version to make sure you have all the capabilities we will go through in the book.

Installing SQL Server Management Studio

The installation link for SSMS can be found on the same page as SQL Server 2019 Developer edition. It is usually located near the bottom of the page with all the supporting tools, as follows:

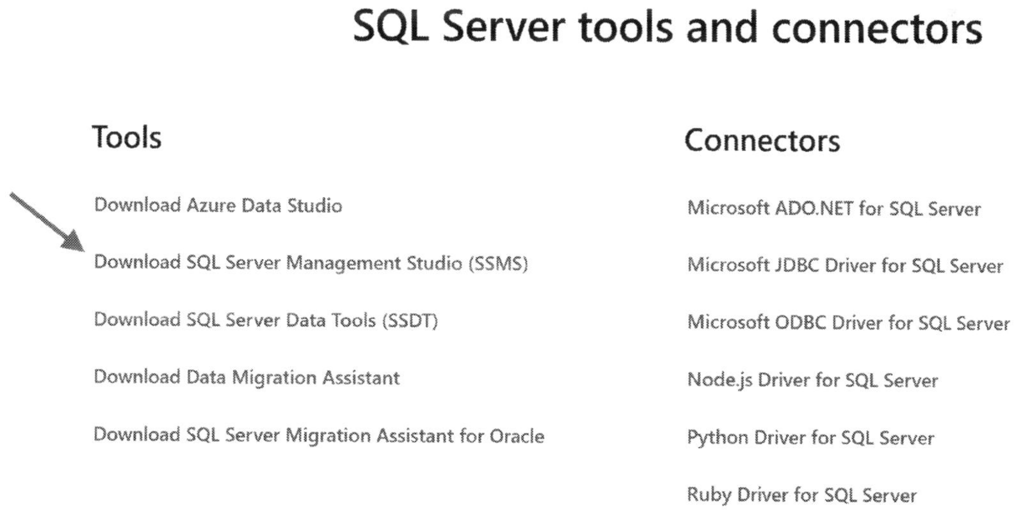

SQL Server tools and connectors

Tools	Connectors
Download Azure Data Studio	Microsoft ADO.NET for SQL Server
Download SQL Server Management Studio (SSMS)	Microsoft JDBC Driver for SQL Server
Download SQL Server Data Tools (SSDT)	Microsoft ODBC Driver for SQL Server
Download Data Migration Assistant	Node.js Driver for SQL Server
Download SQL Server Migration Assistant for Oracle	Python Driver for SQL Server
	Ruby Driver for SQL Server

Figure 1.23 – Choose SQL Server Management Studio

When you select the SSMS link, you will be redirected to the Microsoft Docs page with instructions and details about the current version of Management Studio. Download and install SSMS. This is a simple install with no options that impact the work we will do in the book. As noted in the following install dialog, this book will be using **RELEASE 18.4**:

Figure 1.24 – Installation screen for SQL Server Management Studio – release 18.4

Next, let's learn more about Visual Studio.

Visual Studio with SQL Server Data Tools (SSDT)

Visual Studio and SQL Server have had many different working combinations over the years. While I included SSDT in this section's heading, Visual Studio 2019 is set up differently. Prior to the current version of Visual Studio, SSDT was a separate installation that you installed after selecting your Visual Studio version. As a reminder, we will be using Visual Studio 2019 for the examples and illustrations in this book:

Figure 1.25 – Choose Download SQL Server Data Tools for this section

---

Previous versions of Visual Studio

SSDT is still a valid install with Visual Studio version 2017. However, SQL Server 2019 components including the latest **Compatibility Level** are not supported. You may need to keep Visual Studio 2017 and related tools to support the current project. Visual Studio 2017 and Visual 2019 can be installed side by side.

Installing and configuring Visual Studio with support for Analysis Services 2019

The first decision you will need to make is what edition of Visual Studio you want to use. If you have a Visual Studio subscription, a corporate license, or a personal license, you likely have options to install Visual Studio 2019 Professional or Visual Studio 2019 Enterprise. If you are starting out and this is truly a learning experience for you and you don't want or need to purchase a license for Visual Studio, the best option is likely the Community Edition.

For the purposes of this book, I will be using the Community Edition of Visual Studio 2019. You can find this edition for download at `https://visualstudio.` `microsoft.com/downloads/`. Let's get it installed and configured.

As part of the installation, you will need to select one or more workloads. While you are welcome to choose other workloads for the installation, for our purposes, you need to select **Data storage and processing** in the Visual Studio installation dialog.

Once the installation is complete, launch Visual Studio. Under the **Get started** options, choose **Continue without code**. The next step is to install the extensions to create Analysis Services projects.

Adding Visual Studio Extensions for Analysis Services 2019

Now that you have Visual Studio 2019 open, you need to install the extensions used to support Analysis Services development:

1. First, let's open the **Manage Extensions** dialog. You can open this by selecting the **Extensions** option in Visual Studio and selecting **Manage Extensions**:

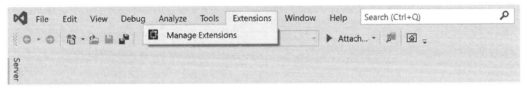

Figure 1.26 – Open Manage Extensions in Visual Studio 2019

2. Once you select **Manage Extensions**, the following dialog will open. You will need to open the following menu sequence: **Online > Visual Studio Marketplace > Tools > Data**. This will filter the list of options to data-specific extensions. Choose **Microsoft Analysis Services Projects** and then click **Download**. This will start the process to download and install the extension:

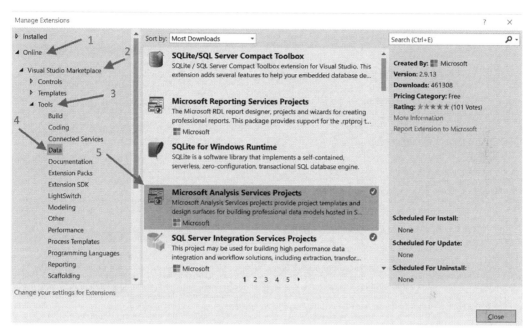

Figure 1.27 – Choose the Microsoft Analysis Services Projects download

3. Once the install is complete (it may require you to close Visual Studio), you should be able to create a new project and see the Analysis Services project types in the options:

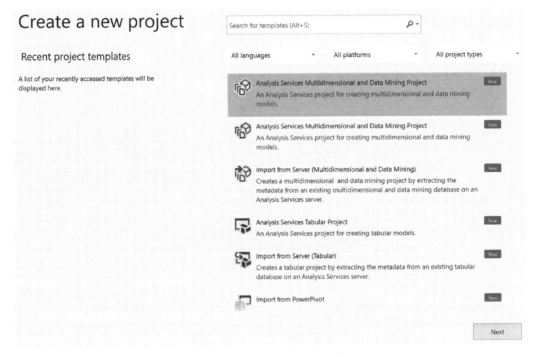

Figure 1.28 – Congratulations! You can create Analysis Services projects

You will need to restart Visual Studio to complete the installation process. Once you have restarted Visual Studio, you are ready to create Analysis Services models and deploy them to Analysis Services 2019.

One last thing – our sample data

This is the final preparation piece before we build the Analysis Services models. We will be using the latest Microsoft sample database from **Wide World Importers**. The Wide World Importers data warehouse sample is a star schema database. While a number of cool features have been added and can be explored in the data warehouse, our focus is on source data for our Analysis Services models.

You can find the World Wide Importers sample databases on GitHub: `https://github.com/Microsoft/sql-server-samples/releases/tag/wide-world-importers-v1.0`. For our purposes, you only need the `WideWorldImportersDW-Full.bak` file. If you are interested in the features for the transactional database, which is the actual source for the data warehouse, you can also download `WideWorldImporters-Full.bak`. If you get both samples, you will need 10 GB of storage for the databases and a minimum of 1.5 GB of RAM to support them.

> **The sample databases use the latest features of SQL Server 2019**
>
> This is a warning for if you choose to install both databases on your server. Both use in-memory features, which could cause performance issues on your computer. These features are meant to highlight some of the latest features but can be resource-intensive. If this is a concern, you should not restore the transactional database at this time.

Once you have the backup file downloaded, I would recommend you move the file to the `Backup` folder located where you selected during the install process. This folder will be easily discoverable from SSMS during the restore process. This is not required, but I find it a good practice in most cases.

Restoring the data warehouse backup

Let's restore the database now:

1. Open up **SQL Server Management Studio**.

2. Connect to your SQL Server 2019 database instance.

3. Right-click on the **Databases** folder and select **Restore Database...**:

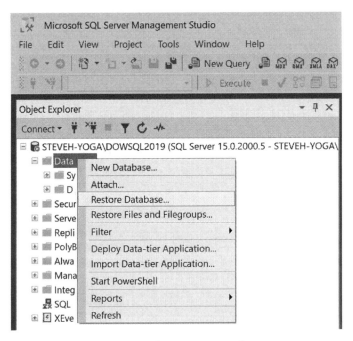

Figure 1.29 – Select Restore Database...

4. In the **Restore Database...** dialog, choose **Device**.

5. Then use the ellipses button to open a dialog box that will allow you to choose the WideWorldImportersDW-Full.bak file. Click **Add** to find your backup file.

6. Once selected, your dialog should be filled in similar to the following:

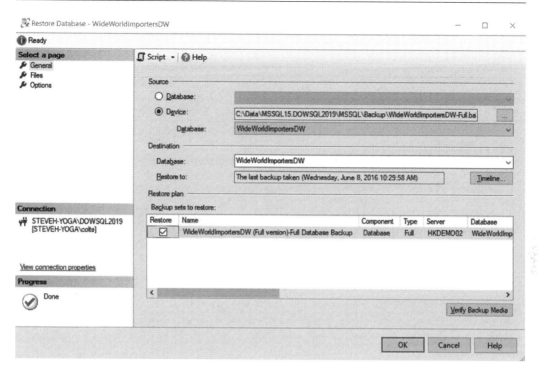

Figure 1.30 – Your dialog box should look like this

7. Next, select **OK**. This will take some time, but you should see the restored database in Management Studio when the process is complete.

    You can also use a script to restore the backup as shown here. You will need to replace {YOUR PATH HERE} with the location of your files:

```
USE [master]
RESTORE DATABASE [WideWorldImportersDW]
FROM  DISK = N'{YOUR PATH HERE}\MSSQL\Backup\
WideWorldImportersDW-Full.bak'
WITH  FILE = 1,
MOVE N'WWI_Primary' TO N'{YOUR PATH HERE}\MSSQL\DATA\
WideWorldImportersDW.mdf',
MOVE N'WWI_UserData' TO N'{YOUR PATH HERE}\MSSQL\DATA\
WideWorldImportersDW_UserData.ndf',
MOVE N'WWI_Log' TO N'{YOUR PATH HERE}\MSSQL\DATA\
WideWorldImportersDW.ldf',
MOVE N'WWIDW_InMemory_Data_1' TO N'{YOUR PATH HERE}\
MSSQL\DATA\WideWorldImportersDW_InMemory_Data_1',
DOWNLOAD,
```

```
STATS = 5
GO
```

Whichever option you choose to use, this will result in a restored database for us to use in later chapters.

Summary

At this point, we are ready to start working with Analysis Services in SQL Server 2019. You have successfully installed the tools we will be using and uploaded the sample data. Along the way, you were able to learn some of Analysis Services' history and how the introduction of Tabular Mode and the VertiPaq engine disrupted the multidimensional database world.

In the next chapter, we will evaluate the right times to choose one mode over the other. As you noticed during the installation, they are not the same product and they come with their own strengths and weaknesses. Once we look at the reasons to choose one option over the other, we will begin the process of creating models in both, starting with multidimensional and moving to tabular. We will look at some common reporting tools to interact with these models and wrap up with some advanced techniques. Remember, if you follow the exercises in the book, you will create models in both modes in Analysis Services and understand which fits your business needs better.

2
Choosing the SQL Server 2019 Analytic Model for Your BI Needs

Before we jump into detailed hands-on work with both types of models in **SQL Server Analysis Services (SSAS)** 2019, we'll look at some of the key differences in the products. This chapter will refer to specific examples later in the book to point to more specific details. The goal of this chapter is to help you understand that the models are different, but both – multidimensional and tabular – are still valuable and can have a place in the solutions you create.

In this chapter, we will walk through a short recap of how we got to two models in SSAS. Then, we will dig into the key strengths and weaknesses of the models. Besides the strengths and weaknesses, there are other differences that should be considered when choosing a model. Some of those differences are more technical in nature and others are specific to business problems. Keep in mind that you and others in the industry may agree or disagree with the importance of some of the differences based on specific experiences or needs, but that is fine.

The goal of this chapter is to give you some key thoughts so that you can make an educated and informed choice on the direction you want to go with your analytics model. We will call out locations later in the book that highlight the topics so that you can get hands-on with the details.

In this chapter, we're going to cover the following main topics:

- Understanding how we got here – two modes

- Discovering multidimensional model strengths and weaknesses

- Discovering tabular model strengths and weaknesses

- Understanding other differences that matter

- Choosing the mode for business-specific reasons

Technical requirements

There are no technical requirements for this chapter. This chapter is focused on deciding the model type.

Understanding how we got here – two modes

In *Chapter 1, Analysis Services in SQL Server 2019*, we delved into the history of Analysis Services in SQL Server. As you can see, multidimensional mode has been around for over 20 years now. Tabular mode was introduced to SQL Server in 2012. But why bring in tabular? As the analytics industry has continued to grow, the technology has also improved. In particular, **column-oriented database technology**, which optimized memory consumption, was one of the biggest industry changes. It introduced technology in the Microsoft database space called **VertiPaq**. This column-based storage technology changed how we think about analytics and introduced Power Pivot in Excel and tabular mode in SQL Server.

When Microsoft introduced tabular mode, Microsoft **Business Intelligence** (**BI**) architects in the industry had mixed feelings. At that point, we had built complex business solutions on multidimensional models and were very skilled at managing and improving the solutions. Multidimensional models were not perfect, but they were easy for users to use once deployed and were key to supporting *ad hoc* analysis in Excel and other similar tools. Tabular models lacked many of the sophisticated capabilities that were well-established in multidimensional models.

One additional feature that was introduced with Power Pivot and tabular model technology is the ability to mash up data easily. For the first time, users had easy access to tools that enabled them to do data modeling and shaping.

Welcome to SQL Server 2019! With the latest release, Microsoft has closed much of the gap between the features and even went beyond multidimensional capabilities in some cases. If you search for model comparisons on the internet, you will find many of the comparisons are from 2016 or before. Let's start by looking at the strengths and challenges of the multidimensional model.

Discovering multidimensional model strengths and challenges

When multidimensional models were introduced, they were difficult for most report developers to wrap their heads around. They were not relational in nature and we had to think differently about structures. In order to create a good multidimensional model, we now need to understand dimensional modeling and denormalization (we dive into details on this in *Chapter 3, Preparing Your Data for Multidimensional Models*). However, the results were high performing, ad hoc-capable analytics databases that were simple for users to consume.

This section will focus on the strengths and challenges specific to multidimensional models. While not necessarily an exhaustive list, these strengths and challenges will influence your model choice. These are not listed in any particular order because they may apply differently to your specific technical or business needs.

Strengths of the multidimensional model

In this section, we will discuss the *key strengths* of the multidimensional model.

The multidimensional model is mature

When discussing model types in Analysis Services, the age or maturity of the multidimensional model is often stated as one of its strengths. This is still a strength in many ways. In particular, the product *does not change* a lot from release to release (this could be seen as a weakness as well). Stability is a key factor in data solutions, as changes to the server could prevent upgrades due to instability in the release or features that break existing functionality.

The other advantage that maturity brings is the *availability of resources* to support developing solutions. Multidimensional model development and operations are well documented. Developers that are new to the multidimensional model will find that much of the best documentation can be over 5 years old. However, this documentation is still effective as the product has not had major changes for a while. A great example of this is the *Analysis Services Performance Guide for SQL Server 2012 and SQL Server 2014* from Microsoft, which was last updated for the 2014 release but is still very relevant to the current version of Analysis Services (link to the document: `http://download.microsoft.com/download/D/2/0/D20E1C5F-72EA-4505-9F26-FEF9550EFD44/Analysis%20Services%20MOLAP%20Performance%20Guide%20for%20SQL%20Server%202012%20and%202014.docx`).

Scaling for large datasets

Multidimensional models are built on the filesystem, unlike tabular models, which are built into memory. Because of this difference, multidimensional models can scale to very large, multi-terabyte sizes. Some models have exceeded 20 terabytes in size. Typically, models that will be measured in terabytes should be considered good candidates for multidimensional models. While memory capabilities continue to grow, the expense becomes an issue as memory is still more expensive than high-performing storage solutions.

Analysis Services compression considerations

One of the key reasons to use SSAS is **data compression**. Multidimensional models typically see **3x** compression, which means that relational data used in the model will be effectively three times smaller in multidimensional models. As with any database solution, this compression level will vary based on the data and tuning. For example, more aggregations in multidimensional models will increase the size required to store the data. Tabular models have a much higher compression rate at **10x**. Because of this disparity in compression, you will need to consider the impact of compression when planning an Analysis Services solution.

When evaluating very large models in multidimensional databases, you must make sure that your storage solution is designed to support the model. If storage is not optimized for or cannot be optimized for multidimensional models, this may not be the best option. Refer to the *Performance Guide* mentioned previously for details on optimizing storage.

Using actions to enhance the user experience

This is one of the coolest features in multidimensional models, which has not been implemented in tabular models yet (I'm not sure whether it is in the plan for a future feature in tabular models). We create actions in *Chapter 5, Adding Measures and Calculations with MDX*, and demonstrate them in Excel in *Chapter 9, Exploring and Visualizing Your Data with Excel*. Actions allow the developer to create a more interactive or elegant solution directly in the cube with data in the cube.

For example, we have used actions to allow users to see details in a **SQL Server Reporting Services** (**SSRS**) report with the filters filled in with data in the cell that is selected. Others have used this to create links to websites, such as product details. This allows the multidimensional model to focus on the data required for analytics while still creating an enhanced experience for users, who can find additional content or information related to what they are working with.

Building complex relationships and rollups

This strength involves a couple of topics that support specific business scenarios, such as a **chart of accounts** or **organization chart**. Both business scenarios are designed with **parent-child relationship** or **self-join** structures. For example, the relational data for an organizational structure likely has an employee key and a manager key. The manager key is actually an employee key from the same table, which is a self-join. This join type is not supported in tabular models but is easily supported in multidimensional models. In *Chapter 4, Building a Multidimensional Cube in SSAS 2019*, we cover how to create these dimensions and the properties in the model design that specifically support that structure.

In the same section, we cover the basics of **custom rollups**. Custom rollups are particularly helpful when working with financial models. We often want to display expenses as a positive number in the reports but want to subtract it from income in the rollup. This type of aggregation is possible in multidimensional models using **unary operators**. When these operators are implemented, users are able to easily create reporting and perform analysis in a format they are used to seeing in financial reports. This is one of the key reasons that multidimensional models should be considered for financial analytics.

Solving 'what if' scenarios with write back

The ability to write back to Analysis Services has long been considered a strength of the multidimensional model. While this is not covered in detail in this book, this capability is important to understand. This feature is typically used to handle *'what if'* scenarios, such as budgeting and forecasting.

The write back capability in multidimensional models retains and updates data modified in the process. Typically, these changes are written to a database and are included in analytics and reporting. We have seen that write back is also used to support some budget versus actual scenarios as well. Write back support is one of those features that most solutions don't require, but when it is required, it is frustrating to deal with workarounds. (While not built into tabular models, some third-party solutions exist to support write back capabilities in tabular models.)

Forces good data modeling techniques

We are calling this a strength because of peers in the industry who miss the formal design process that was required. With tabular models and related technologies, such as Power BI, **self-service** is the next great thing. Power BI and even tabular models can use **Power Query** and **M** to collect data from any data source and model that data as they see fit for their reporting purposes. This often leads to **dataset spreadmart**. Datasets are spread all over with inconsistent data modeling, transformation, and calculations. Excel spreadsheets were the first tool to see this issue in the business, but now we see it with Power BI, Tableau, and similar self-service tools.

Multidimensional models just don't work that way. You must have a solid star schema built on dimensional modeling techniques to create the cube. In *Chapter 3*, *Preparing Your Data for Multidimensional Models*, we walk through the modeling process and the design decisions that go into creating a great multidimensional model. While some may consider this a weakness as it requires more time and technical development, the end result is highly trusted. Traditionally, multidimensional models designed by the technical teams were modeled well, properly maintained, and secure and compliant. Tabular models are the end of the self-service life cycle that leads to the same result in many cases. However, multidimensional models start with these requirements in mind.

Now that we have reviewed the strengths, let's look at some key challenges with multidimensional models.

Multidimensional model challenges

In this section, we will review some key challenges of the multidimensional model.

Difficult implementation of distinct count

One of the measures that is always requested by business users is **distinct count**. Distinct count measures are key to understanding data and are often used in reporting. However, since its inception, multidimensional models have not handled distinct counts very well. This is due to the fact that distinct count measures cannot be easily aggregated in multidimensional models, making the measure perform very poorly in queries.

That issue is resolved by creating a separate measure group, as we call out in *Chapter 4, Building a Multidimensional Cube in SSAS 2019*. The problem with this solution is that developers and the business have to make trade-offs or decisions around which distinct count measures they want to include in order to keep the cube reasonable for size and operations.

MDX can be difficult

MDX is not **SQL**. Sure, it has SELECT, FROM, and WHERE, but that is where the similarities end. Because the data is stored and queried multidimensionally, the traditional understanding of how tables and relationships work doesn't apply. This distinction causes most great SQL developers to struggle with MDX. When the code gets more complex, this becomes worse.

In *Chapter 5, Adding Measures and Calculations with MDX*, we introduce MDX to you and get you through the basics. However, large books have been written to support MDX developers throughout the years. The complexity and the limited use cases for the language have made it a primary reason for many to shy away from using multidimensional models.

Small changes require full reload

Of all the multidimensional model challenges, this is by far the most significant. Small changes can effectively *break* the cube, which will force the cube to be rebuilt or fully reprocessed. While full processing can be a best practice for smaller cubes and multidimensional models, as noted in *Chapter 12, Common Administration and Maintenance Tasks*, larger cubes can take hours or even days to fully rebuild and reload. This lack of flexibility has been an issue for developers and administrators of cubes for years.

The problem is that the actual storage of data, design of aggregations, and index designs are all impacted with a change as simple as adding an attribute to a dimension. There are many options to help reduce or manage processing time, but design changes to the model will cause a greater impact. These changes must always be weighed against the time required to publish the change and reload the data.

Now that we have reviewed some key strengths and challenges of multidimensional models, let's look at the strengths and challenges of tabular models.

Discovering tabular model strengths and challenges

Tabular models are the not-so-new version of analytic models in SSAS. They have been around for nearly 10 years now and are a key product in Microsoft's future of business intelligence tools. As discussed in *Chapter 1, Analysis Services in SQL Server 2019*, they are built on VertiPaq technology, which leverages memory and column compression to create a great analytics platform. Like multidimensional modes, tabular models have strengths and challenges that we want you to know about.

One key consideration of our list here is that we only cover **compatibility level 1500**. Tabular models have been through a lot of change since 2012, including with this release (see the new features in *Chapter 1, Analysis Services in SQL Server 2019*). Some of the features in the current release eliminate some key challenges that have existed in tabular models since they were released. One such weakness is no support for **many-to-many** relationships. Depending on your compatibility level, you may not see support for other features, such as **ragged hierarchies**, **translations**, and **calculated tables** (which support role-playing functionality).

If you are working with an older version of tabular models or have your compatibility level set lower than 1500, some or all of these features may not be available to you. Refer to the *What's New in SQL Server Analysis Services* page located here for details on what is available to you: `https://docs.microsoft.com/en-us/analysis-services/what-s-new-in-sql-server-analysis-services?view=asallproducts-allversions`.

While this is not an exhaustive coverage of the strengths and challenges of tabular models, this list should help you make decisions about which model is the best option for your implementation.

Strengths of tabular models

Tabular models are newer, and bring a new set of strengths for us to consider.

Everything is a table

This is an interesting strength. In multidimensional design, we work with measure groups and dimensions. However, that concept does not exist in the same way. Whether it is a dimension or a fact table, it is merely a table in tabular models. This gives the designer flexibility to create different types of models to support business needs. The other area where this is a key differentiator is in managing changes in the model.

In a multidimensional model, as we noted previously, a small change can cause the *entire* model to be rebuilt and reloaded (fully processed). However, when a similar change is made to a table in a tabular model, only that table is impacted. For example, if you add a field to a table, you will need to refresh that table, but the entire model does not need to be processed.

Another concept that extends this strength is that the fields in a table are also treated the same. This means that you can create a measure on a field such as Amount and slice on it as well. This capability is not at all available in multidimensional models.

DAX is typically easier for users

Data Analytic Expressions, or **DAX**, is often viewed as *simpler* for all users and developers to learn. The reason behind this is that DAX is designed to work like **functions in Excel**. The goal of DAX was to make it easier for Excel users and developers to transition to a new function language.

That simplicity comes at a cost. While DAX lends itself to many of the same capabilities of MDX and Excel functions, it is still an expression language that is not designed for complex scenarios or simple querying. It is true that Excel users will find the transition easier than a transition to SQL or MDX, but the opposite is true for SQL or MDX developers. Microsoft has made significant improvements to DAX with every release. DAX is getting more support for *set-based* operations, which is where it is significantly weaker than SQL or MDX.

Developers who have been working with Power BI or tabular models for a few years have been able to make significant progress with DAX. For example, in Power BI, **quick measures** include community-created measures to support some optimized DAX calculations. You can use these quick measures to learn some of the more complex DAX calculations. We have a good DAX primer in *Chapter 8, Adding Measures and Calculations with DAX*. This is a good way to get started with DAX.

Mashing up data with Power Query

Because tabular models are built on the back of **self-service** capabilities, they include **Power Query** to support pulling data from various data sources. Power Query is intended to be a lightweight data mashup tool for *retrieving* and *shaping* data prior to loading it into a model.

In some situations, this can expedite the creation of tabular models and get them delivered to the business for consumption more rapidly. Power Query allows developers to work with a variety of data sources beyond relational databases. This capability lets them mash the data together, which can eliminate the need for a relational data warehouse. We will be creating a tabular model using Power Query in *Chapter 7, Building a Tabular Model in SSAS 2019*.

This should not be considered as a replacement for a standard **extraction, transformation, and load (ETL)** process using tools such as **SQL Server Integration Services (SSIS)**. Power Query, while simple and flexible, struggles to perform in large enterprise solutions. We expect it to continue to improve as Microsoft continues to invest but be wary of using this as your sole ETL solution. You should also not use this to replace the traditional data warehouse. There are still many benefits to having the transformed or shaped data stored in a warehouse, including access to reporting tools or analysis by open source analytic tools, such as Azure Machine Learning.

Extending tables with calculated columns

One unique feature in tabular models is the ability to create a **calculated column**. This feature allows you to calculate a column based on the context of the row. This has a couple of key uses. One is that we can calculate values based on what is in the row. For example, if we wanted to include an amount field that is calculated to increase the amount by 10 percent (10%), we can add a column that uses a DAX expression such as `10% Increase in Sales:='Sales'[Sales Amount] * 1.1`. This will create a column that can be used like a standard column. Measures can be created against or, for instance, can be used to filter data.

Another great use for this feature is to create calculated key columns that can be used to establish relationships between data from different sources. For example, if the product key for red balloons in the inventory data source is `Red Balloons - 0909`, which signifies product and lot, we could separate the column for the lot ID so that it could be related to the manufacturing table of products that uses the lot number for the key.

You can explore more options using calculated columns in *Chapter 8, Adding Measures and Calculations with DAX*. We use calculated columns to add a column to count a specific item that we use in another calculated measure.

Using data source capabilities with DirectQuery

DirectQuery allows you to work with sets of data beyond the size that can be supported in tabular models due to memory restrictions. DirectQuery also allows you to take advantage of underlying data source servers to return results. Tabular models can serve as a **semantic layer** and send queries back to the supported data sources. Some analytics can be served better when run on the host servers. We will create a tabular model with DirectQuery in *Chapter 7, Building a Tabular Model in SSAS 2019*.

Distinct count is a simple expression

This is a huge deal with tabular models. Distinct count measures are painful to work with in multidimensional models. However, in tabular models, the `DISTINCTCOUNT` function works great on a column in your table. This is likely due to the column-oriented storage used in the underlying engine. If you need many distinct count measures, tabular models are the best choice.

Challenges with tabular models

Newer, tabular models have a different set of challenges.

Model size is limited to memory capacity

One of the key design decisions is around the size of the model you are creating. Because tabular models are stored in memory, you need to understand the potential impact to the server memory you will experience when your model is fully deployed and in use. A typical rule of thumb is that you need enough memory to support the size of your model twice over (size x2) for normal operations. However, if you don't use a separate server for processing (see *Chapter 12, Common Administration and Maintenance Tasks*, for details on scaling out your tabular server), you should plan for three or four times the size of your data. You do not want to run out of memory on your server.

This is only a weakness in that it realistically caps the size of your model to the amount of memory on the server. This has limited scale due to cost as memory size increases. There are a couple of options to work around this weakness:

- You can use multiple models to deliver solutions. Reduce the functional area of your models. This is less convenient for your users but will let you use multiple servers to support the analytics environment.

- The other option is the next strength listed as well – use DirectQuery for large models. However, you will need to convert your model to DirectQuery.

> **Composite models in Power BI**
>
> While beyond the scope of this book, Power BI has advanced capability that uses a combination of refreshed data and DirectQuery data to address large models called **composite models**. We bring this up here because while this functionality is not currently available in Analysis Services, it is likely on the roadmap for future releases. If this is the functionality you require, be sure to look at the composite model capability in Power BI as one way to support larger models.

The only other option beyond the tabular model options in Analysis Services is the option to use multidimensional models for large analytic solutions. Microsoft will continue to improve scaling options, but you should always keep in mind that memory is the key hardware constriction for tabular models.

Subpar design experience in Visual Studio

This is a challenge that is very frustrating for those of us who develop either model type in Visual Studio. The tooling for multidimensional models is very robust and has not changed significantly since 2016. However, the tabular model design in Visual Studio can be an exercise in frustration. This is magnified by the simplicity of creating similar solutions with Power BI and Power Pivot in Excel. First, you cannot design the tabular model without a workspace server (we will set that up in *Chapter 7*, *Building a Tabular Model in SSAS 2019*. There is also a discussion there on the best approach for your development. You cannot design without data available in the model).

Another frustrating issue with Visual Studio is that the tools we use for development have not been updated or optimized for high-resolution monitors. Because almost all laptops and most other systems use higher resolutions, dialog windows and other areas of the development environment will appear tiny or boxes will only show half of the height. Throughout this book, you will see some *zoom-ins*, which are done because of this issue. It seems clear that this issue will not be resolved soon, so you need to plan for this when designing your Analysis Services models.

Code is contained in a single file

This challenge is focused on the design and development of tabular models. In Visual Studio, the model is stored in a single file, .bim. Multidimensional projects store the various objects in different files, such as cubes, dimensions, and so on. This allows development teams to work on various areas in multidimensional models. Tabular models are effectively limited to one developer at a time due to merge issues. The following figure compares the file structures in the **Solution Explorer** windows of each model project type:

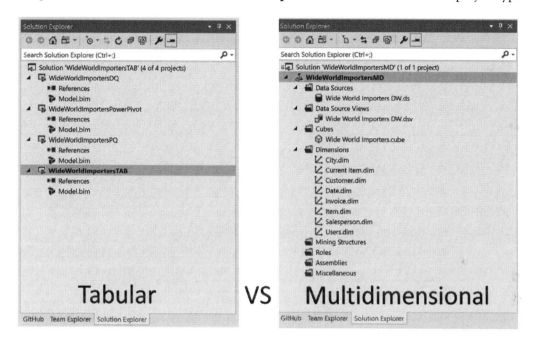

Figure 2.1 – Tabular versus multidimensional project file structures

While this will not impact small development teams, the frustration of limited development capacity could impact a business intelligence team's ability to deliver in team settings.

The following table summarizes the technical strengths and challenges of the two types of models in SSAS:

Multidimensional Model		Tabular Model	
Strengths	Mutltidimensional mode is **mature**.	**Strengths**	Everything is a **table**.
	Scaling for **large** data sets.		DAX is typically **easier** for users.
	Using **actions** to enhance user experience.		**Mashing** up data with **Power Query**.
	Building complex **relationships** and **rollups**.		Extending tables with **calculated columns**.
	Solving "**What if**" scenarios with **write back**.		Use data source capabilities with **DirectQuery**.
	Forces **good data modeling** techniques.		**Distinct count** is a simple expression.
Challenges	Difficult implementation of **distinct count**.	**Challenges**	Model size is limited to **memory capacity**.
	MDX can be **difficult**.		**Subpar design experience** with Visual Studio.
	Small changes require **full reload**.		Code is contained in a **single file**.

Figure 2.2 – Comparing the strengths and challenges of the two models

As you can see, both models have technical strengths that will influence your choice of model. This is not an exhaustive list, but it will hopefully help you with your decision. In the next section, we will explore some additional differences in implementation patterns.

Understanding other differences that matter

Besides the strengths and challenges called out previously, in this section, we will see the differences in how a feature is implemented or how a capability is accomplished with each of the models. The differences between the model types may or may not impact your decision on the model you will choose. The importance of these topics is to understand the differences and the effect those differences may have on your model design.

Partitioning

Partitioning is the process of *separating a table into sections* to improve performance or maintainability. Before we dig into the differences, you can find more about implementing multidimensional model partitions in *Chapter 4, Building a Multidimensional Cube in SSAS 2019*, and implementing tabular model partitions in *Chapter 7, Building a Tabular Model in SSAS 2019*.

So, both model types support partitions. In both models, partitioning larger tables can improve the processing time. Partitioning allows you to process the partitions independently so that you can reload smaller amounts of data, which reduces load time accordingly. This means that if you need to reduce the time it takes to bring the latest data into a model of either type, partitioning will do that for you. Now, what is different?

Where partitioning supports improved processing in both models, it only improves query performance in multidimensional models. Partitions in multidimensional models are used by the query engine and underlying indexes and aggregations to limit the amount of data being returned. This is significant because multidimensional models are stored and pulled from storage, not memory. The lesson here is: do not use partitions to improve query performance in tabular models.

The other key difference is that in multidimensional models, partitions are only applied to measure groups or fact tables. Because all tables in tabular models are tables, every table can be partitioned in a tabular model, even tables that function as dimensions. This can be helpful for large dimensions where most of the change is on a specific set of members. For example, a large product dimension could be partitioned between discontinued and current items. You could then process the current item partition only, which would reduce processing time and resource needs.

As you can see, partitions are an important part of the design process. However, you need to consider why and how you plan to implement partitions in your model.

Role-playing dimensions

Role-playing dimensions have been a part of data warehouse and cube design for years. For a detailed look at dimensional modeling and role-playing dimensions, check out *Chapter 3, Preparing Your Data for Multidimensional Models*. Role-playing dimensions refer to those dimension tables that may have multiple relationships with a fact table. The most common example is the date dimension. In a sales fact table, you have multiple dates that are relevant for analysis, such as order date, invoice date, shipping date, and delivery date. Depending on the user of the solution, they may want to perform analysis on any one or more of these dates.

This functionality is built into the multidimensional model natively. You can add multiple relationships to the table in the data source view (*Chapter 4*, *Building a Multidimensional Cube in SSAS 2019*), and then create multiple dimensions on the table. This allows the fact table to be sliced or filtered by either date. One key design consideration is that it is good to have a *master date* dimension that is used across multiple fact tables. This makes analysis easier when comparing different measure groups. For example, you might consider the master date for sales facts to be the order date, and the master date for the inventory to be the inventory date. You could have a date table that is used for both. This allows you to compare the current inventory at the time of the order date easily.

With the inclusion of calculated tables in tabular models, you can now create the equivalent of a role-playing dimension (we create calculated tables in *Chapter 8*, *Adding Measures and Calculations with DAX*). Prior to this feature being added, you had to add the table multiple times, which complicated the data model and made designing for role-playing dimensions more difficult. Calculated tables are just that: calculated. This allows you to bring one table into the model and create calculated tables for additional roles. Keep in mind that only the primary date table can be marked as the date table.

OLAP versus relational concepts

We have touched on this difference in a number of topics. The crux of this difference is that multidimensional modes were designed for **Online Analytical Processing** (**OLAP**) databases. Dimensions and facts are the normal design pattern. When traditional BI architects move to tabular models, they see that this is no longer true. Tabular models are built on relational concepts. There are strictly two dimensions – columns and rows. This simplifies the model and is much easier for people familiar with Excel or relational databases to comprehend the model.

Multidimensional models and OLAP models are built with the concepts of cells with intersecting dimensionality. One of the ways we often see this being handled is by implementing star schemas and dimensional models to be used by tabular models. While that structure is not required, there are definitely advantages to using that design. It simplifies the overall model and follows a known design pattern that can be supported by many BI practitioners.

Hardware requirements

As you have seen in previous topics in this chapter, these models have different hardware needs. We are using *hardware requirements* generically. The same problems must be resolved whether the model is deployed directly on servers (bare iron), on virtual machines locally (VMware or HyperV), or on virtual machines in the cloud (Microsoft Azure or Amazon Cloud Services).

Multidimensional models require more overall performance considerations as the data is retrieved from disk. Tabular models only use the hard disk to store metadata and data when the server is shut down. When working with SSAS in multidimensional mode, we recommend that you use solid-state hard drives. Multidimensional models are stored as many small files and the storage should be optimized for random reads for the best query performance.

Both systems require substantial memory for querying and processing. Multidimensional models use the memory capacity to optimize queries through various caching mechanisms. For example, there is a section in *Chapter 12, Common Administration and Maintenance Tasks*, that covers warming the multidimensional model to support better initial query performance. However, with tabular models, memory is the most important consideration. The entire tabular database must be loaded into memory and around three to four times the size of the database will be required to properly support a tabular model. Memory or RAM is one of the most consistent needs in Analysis Services models.

After memory, both modes need to have high-speed CPUs with onboard caching to support query and processing operations. Because both model types use parallel processing techniques, more cores are preferred. As user count and query concurrency increase, more memory and CPU will be required to maintain optimal performance.

Once you have reached the peak of performance with the hardware capability, we recommend scaling out Analysis Services. Scaling up or increasing hardware capacity only solves some of the issues that you may experience with your deployments. We recommend that you scale out as opposed to scale up. There are additional considerations for scaling out your solutions. You can find more details on scaling out in *Chapter 12, Common Administration and Maintenance Tasks*.

Finally, you should never put instances of both models on the same machine (bare iron or virtual). These servers need to be tuned for different use cases. The biggest area of contention will be memory, but the CPU will also be taxed when run on the same machine. When working with tabular models, you must consider the memory constraints for running multiple models on the same instance. As noted previously, you need to account for the size of the database and an additional three or four times that size for tabular models. Too many models on the same machine will cause significant memory contention and cause the servers to no longer respond to requests.

Now that we have the key differences between the solutions, let's look at some business considerations.

Choosing the model type for business-specific reasons

Now that we have reviewed many of the technical differences between the models, let's look at how specific business needs may influence your decision. This section of the chapter is a blend of business needs and technical fit. We will wrap this section up with a combined matrix to help you determine the best fit for your business and technical leads.

Rapid development and change

Businesses change often and quickly. As they change, reporting and analytic needs change as well. The amount and the frequency of the change directly impact which solution is a better fit. Tabular models are by far the better option to support frequent changes. They are simpler to construct and more flexible to supporting change.

The primary factors for this recommendation include the ability to retrieve and shape data using **Power Query**. This allows developers to change and include data from more sources in the model. Multidimensional models require a solid star schema, which involves more complex ETL solutions as well. This design requirement also slows down the ability to handle business changes quickly. The more complex multidimensional solution has caused frustration for business and technical teams alike. One of the ways it has been handled throughout the years is by trying to include as much as possible in a cube.

Tabular models allow you to work with tables as *individual* entities. Change to a single table can be handled in an *isolated* fashion, which allows the model to flex more rapidly to accommodate changing business needs.

Cloud readiness

As the importance of cloud and hybrid solutions continue to increase, it is important to understand where SQL Server 2019 and its Analysis Services models fit. SQL Server 2019 is built with a variety of hooks for hybrids solutions, such as big data clusters or stretch databases in Azure SQL. So, where does Analysis Services fit into this scenario?

Azure Analysis Services is built on the same technology as Power BI and tabular models. This means that tabular models are much easier to migrate to Azure when you are ready for a full cloud solution. Multidimensional models are not natively supported structures in Azure and require virtual machines.

> **Cloud support for tabular features**
>
> While tabular models are supported in Azure Analysis Services and Power BI Premium, not all features in SQL Server 2019 Analysis Services are available in the online servers. We highly recommend that you do not commit to a purely cloud solution until you have tested the features you are using. In most cases, you will not have feature issues. The other area to consider is the size of your model. At the time of writing, Azure Analysis Services models are limited to 400 GB.

While the support for multidimensional models is missing, other technical or business reasons may make them a better solution. If that is the case, you can support multidimensional deployments to the cloud using virtual machines. You can also use virtual machines to support larger tabular models or use features not currently available in true cloud deployments.

Complex analysis

As noted in various preceding sections, multidimensional models have a significant amount of maturity. This includes support for complex analytical scenarios. One such scenario concerns financial analysis including balance sheets, charts of account, and other financial statements that change signs as the data is rolled up. There is currently no simple, built-in functionality to support this type of reporting in tabular models. For example, you can set the rollup using a **unary** operator as a property within a chart of accounts dimension. Beyond this, other complex scenarios are more easily solved with MDX and multidimensional models. When deciding on the model type, it will be important to understand which model is better equipped to handle your most complex problems.

Client tools

Because tools that work with Analysis Services typically support either model type, this is usually not an issue. What is important to understand is how those tools interact with Analysis Services and the potential tuning complications. In many cases, the tools are sending MDX to both models. Analysis Services has the ability to use this for both model types, but you should understand the tooling so that you can make an informed decision. **Power BI**, for example, supports both model types well with **Live Connection** capabilities. **Excel** is best equipped for MDX, which it has been doing for years.

While any tool is likely to have issues with generating the most efficient queries, understanding the language the tool uses will help you determine tuning issues along the way. By knowing which tools you plan to use, you may find that a model is better suited to meet your needs.

Summary

As you can see, there are many different aspects to consider when choosing a model. As you continue through this book, you will see some of the strengths and challenges in action.

The remainder of the book is focused on hands-on experiences working with both types of models. *Chapters 3–5* focus on building out a multidimensional model. In *Chapters 6–8*, you will build and expand on various types of tabular models. The rest of the book will use the models you create to build reports and exercise advanced features such as security and scaling. Let's get started with multidimensional models in SSAS 2019. In the next chapter, we will start by preparing data for use with multidimensional models.

Further reading

Here is some additional reading to help you along with your decision-making process.

In this chapter, we covered technical differences, implementation differences, and business impacts to consider when making your model choice. For the current feature comparison list, refer to Microsoft's documentation here: `https://docs.microsoft.com/en-us/analysis-services/comparing-tabular-and-multidimensional-solutions-ssas?view=asallproducts-allversions`.

Section 2: Building and Deploying a Multidimensional Model

This section will cover creating a multidimensional model with **SQL Server Analysis Services 2019** and will expand on that model with **Multidimensional Expressions** measures. Once completed, the model will be deployed to a development server.

This section comprises the following chapters:

- *Chapter 3, Preparing Your Data for Multidimensional Models*
- *Chapter 4, Building a Multidimensional Cube in SSAS 2019*
- *Chapter 5, Adding Measures and Calculations with MDX*

3
Preparing Your Data for Multidimensional Models

Multidimensional models are the original OLAP structures supported in **SQL Server Analysis Services** (**SSAS**). Starting out as OLAP services over 20 years ago, the tooling is now considered mature by Microsoft and is not planned for any major updates in the foreseeable future. Throughout the years, Microsoft has made significant improvements to Analysis Services and its support for multidimensional models. This includes changes to support dimensional models or star schemas. Today's version of Analysis Services continues to lean heavily on that data modeling pattern.

This chapter focuses on preparing your data. To properly build a multidimensional model, your data should be shaped using dimensional modeling techniques. You will be introduced to dimensional modeling theory, design practices to support those models, and other techniques to support using cubes with SQL Server. Without this data preparation, you will struggle to build cubes that are efficient and performant.

In this chapter, we're going to cover the following main topics:

- A short primer on dimensional modeling

- Designing and building dimensions and facts

- Loading data into your star schema

- Using database views and data source views

- Prepping our database for the multidimensional model

- Let's get started!

Technical requirements

In this chapter, we will be using the **WideWorldImportersDW** database from *Chapter 1, Analysis Services in SQL Server 2019*. You should connect to the database with **SQL Server Management Studio** (**SSMS**). We will be creating views at the end of this chapter in preparation for building multidimensional models in *Chapter 4, Building a Multidimensional Cube in SSAS 2019*.

A short primer on dimensional modeling

The foundational architecture for successfully building multidimensional models in SQL Server is the **dimensional model** or **star schema**. As Microsoft continued to improve Analysis Services, one of the key elements was embracing dimensional model design as a key element to building cubes. The marriage between dimensional modeling and Analysis Services eventually resulted in a book by the Kimball Group, which combined their concepts with the Analysis Services implementation – **The Microsoft Data Warehouse Toolkit**. In this section, we will introduce you to the basics of dimensional model design.

Understanding the origin of dimensional modeling

Ralph Kimball is considered the father of the dimensional model. He founded the Kimball Group in the 1980s and coauthored all the books in the **Toolkit series**. The Kimball Group authored multiple books, conducted thousands of training sessions, and supported the growth of dimensional modeling until it closed its doors in 2015. You can find out more about the Kimball Group on their website at `https://www.kimballgroup.com`.

Dimensional modeling exists today in response to the need to simplify reporting for end users and report writers. By the time dimensional modeling was introduced, relational database theory was mature and **relational database management systems (RDBMS)** were optimized to support those normalized data models. The key design principles for normalization are as follows:

- Eliminate duplicate data.

- Make sure all the data in the table is related.

Highly normalized structures involve multiple tables with relationships between them. These databases could be normalized based on **normal forms**. The most common designs today for transactional systems are in the third normal form.

Let's look at the first, second, and third normal form rules:

- Remove duplicate columns or fields from the table (**First normal form rule**).

- Create separate tables for related columns and assign a unique primary key (**First normal form rule**).

- Remove common data elements from a table that apply to multiple rows (**Second normal form rule**).

- Create relationships between these tables using foreign keys (**Second normal form rule**).

- Remove all columns not directly related to the primary key (**Third normal form rule**).

While normalization supports high-performing transactional business needs, it adds a significant amount of complexity when you're trying to build a report on the information. In some cases, dozens of tables may be required to build out a meaningful report in mature, normalized solutions. Furthermore, the database engines built by vendors such as Oracle and Microsoft were designed to optimize this type of interaction with the data.

The complexity of normalization is the impetus for dimensional models and the denormalization of data. This is not a simple design choice. In order to effectively improve the ability and performance of RDBMS solutions so that they return large amounts of aggregated data, specific design considerations were made to support the systems where the data was located, as well as the needs of the business.

For this new model to be successful, it needed to lean on the capabilities – and account for the weaknesses – of the platforms it would be deployed on. The star schema design, with its dimensions and facts, did just that. Indexes and caching capabilities were considered in the design, as well as the simple use of data. While there are hundreds of nuances and variations in the design principles, the core result was an elegantly simple design that could be supported by the systems available when it was created.

Now, we will look at a number of key concepts around dimensional modeling that impact our multidimensional design. Understanding these concepts is important when it comes to prepping your data for a successful multidimensional model or cube.

Defining dimensional modeling terms

Dimensional modeling has its own vernacular. Some of the language carries forward into the cubes themselves. Here are some core terms you should know:

- **Dimension**: Something you can *slice* a metric by. The key word here is *by*; for example, I want to know the sales *by* country, *by* month, *by* salesperson. That statement would result in three likely dimensions – geography, date, and employee.

- **Fact**: A fact is measurable. It may be able to be summed, averaged, or otherwise aggregated. It is the target of the dimension. A sales fact table could likely have revenue, quantity, and taxes as measures or facts.

- **Star Schema**: This is the design of the dimensional model. It looks like a star since it has fact tables at the center and the *arms* of the star as the dimensions. The following is an example of a star schema:

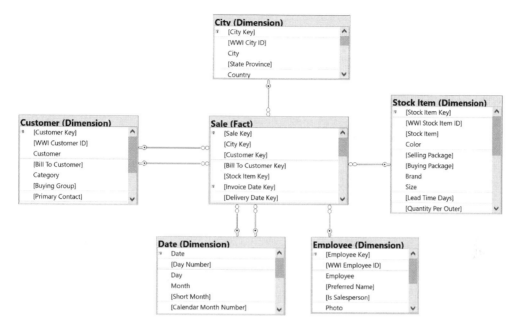

Figure 3.1 – Star schema example from Wide World Importers Data Warehouse

- **Grain**: The grain of a fact table is effectively the lowest level you can drill to in the data. This is usually defined by combining the dimensions in the table. For example, if the fact table has a daily grain by salesperson, it would aggregate the sales for the salesperson to the day. This would likely add another fact to the table with the count of sales for the day.

- **Surrogate Key**: These keys are used with the dimensions. Because most data warehouse solutions combine data from multiple source systems, they often have separate keys for the same dimensional item. For example, a CRM solution may have a product ID, which is different from the inventory system. In dimensional models, we strive to have only one product dimension to help related data from various facts in a single solution. Surrogate keys allow us to create a generic key that will be used to represent the same item from multiple systems. This is key to making **conformed dimensions**, which will be covered in the next section.

Many more terms exist in the world of dimensional modeling, and there are books and other resources that dig into the details. We'll cover a couple more key concepts around dimensional modeling next.

Key dimensional modeling concepts

Dimensional modeling includes some key concepts that have set it apart from traditional relational database modeling techniques through the years. Those concepts must be considered when you're designing your multidimensional model.

Conformed dimensions

Conformed dimensions are one of the key simplifying concepts in the dimensional model design process. Data warehouse solutions often pull data from various source systems. These systems usually handle specific business needs. Continuing with the sales example we used previously, products could exist in the customer relationship management, inventory, and point of sale systems. This would result in three keys and different attributes related to a product in each solution. As the star schema is built out, having one product dimension to support all data will be the key to success within the model. In the following example, I will walk through these three sources and how we could create the conformed dimension.

Product source definitions

The following definitions show the three sources and their product attributes, as well as an example of our Wonderful Widget product:

- **Customer Relationship Management (CRM) Product:**

  a) **Product ID**: `WW123`

  b) **Product Name**: `Wonderful Widget`

  c) **Product Description**: `Wonderful Widget that everyone loves`

  d) **Product Color**: `<<empty>>`

- **Inventory Product:**

  a) **Product ID**: `4321`

  b) **Product Name**: `Wonderful Widget`

  c) **Product Source**: `Joe's Amazing Emporium`

  d) **Product Storage Requirement**: ¼ `pallet`

- **Point of Sale (POS) Product:**

  a) **Product ID**: 8712.12

  b) **Product Name**: Wonderful Widget

  c) **Product Price**: $12.00

  d) **Product Cost**: $8.44

  e) **Product SKU**: WW1223-001-009

Conforming a product

As you can see, we have different IDs and names. Part of conforming a dimension is understanding what the business wants to see on your reports, as well as making sure that the product dimension has the right information from the sources. Here is one way we could choose to make the product dimension conform with the source we chose:

- **Product SID**: 79, Surrogate key, not related to any source

- **Product SKU**: WW1223-001-009, from POS

- **Product Name**: Wonderful Widget, from Inventory

- **Product Description**: Wonderful Widget that everyone loves, from CRM

- **Product Cost**: $8.44, from POS

- **Product Price**: $12.00, from POS

- **Product Source**: Joe's Amazing Emporium, from Inventory

Not all the fields we specified previously were required for our data warehouse. One of the keys to good design in this case is related to the cost of storage and performance. When the dimension is loaded, a staging area will likely support the lookups in order to match the keys and updates. By conforming the dimension, we can collect facts into fact tables that can share this dimension, thus making report design simpler and standardized.

Slowly changing dimensions

As you likely noticed, product cost and price attributes likely change over time and can affect calculations throughout the life of a data warehouse. The concept of **slowly changing dimensions** (**SCD**) covers this design issue. There are many types of slowly changing dimensions. The most common implementations that can be supported in a cube are as follows:

- **SCD Type 0**: In this case, we never change the dimension attribute, even if a change comes from the source.

- **SCD Type 1**: We replace the dimension attribute with the latest value from the source. We retain no history of its previous value. In our product example, the name and SKU are great candidates for this. Typically, we only care about the current name and SKU for our business.

- **SCD Type 2**: We add a row with the updated attribute and retain its history. This is the most complicated to effectively implement here (there are more complicated SCD types, but they are not in the scope of this book). In order to support the SCD Type 2 attribute, you need to add fields to your dimension table. This typically includes **Date Valid From**, **Date Valid To**, **Current**, and in some cases **Deleted**. This combination of attributes supports using the correct value at the time the data was valid.

> SCD Type 2
>
> In my experience, many businesses want the ability to do this, but also do not want it to affect their reporting. I have commonly created a *current* version of a dimension to support consistent reporting. The SCD Type 2 dimension was used when historical support was required. It is typically more complicated to build reports using Type 2 because a user often sees the changes as bad data if they are not aware of whether the historical support is in place. Use SCD Type 2 only when needed to support a specific business case.

The enterprise data warehouse bus matrix

In the late 1990s, Ralph Kimball introduced the **Enterprise Data Warehouse Bus Matrix**, or simply the **Bus Matrix**. It is a simple and elegant way to describe the relationship between dimensions and facts within a dimensionally modeled data warehouse. There are multiple articles on its implementation if you are interested in reading up on them. Here is an example of a bus matrix that is reflective of our current example solution; that is, Wide World Importers:

Dimensions	Movement	Order	Purchase	Sale	Stock Holding	Transaction
City		X		X		
Customer	X	X		X		X
Date	X	X	X	X		X
Employee		X		X		
Payment Method						X
Stock Item	X	X	X	X	X	
Supplier	X		X			X
Transaction Type	X					X

Figure 3.2 – Bus matrix for Wide World Importers

The bus matrix is implemented in Analysis Services. By designing your underlying database in a dimensional model, you will find it easy to translate that design into your multidimensional model.

Common issues in relational dimensional models

With all the effort that's put into dimensional models, why do we need tools such as Analysis Services? Great question!

RDBMS systems were not specifically designed to support OLAP workloads. The star schema was designed to take advantage of the strengths within an RDBMS, while at the same time simplifying the model for the business. However, relational systems designs were still focused on meeting transactional demands, not reporting demands. Small high-speed transactions are the focus, not large volumes of data, which are aggregated as required for reporting.

SQL Server columnstore indexes

Microsoft released its new **columnstore index** functionality in SQL Server 2012. This technology has been improved significantly as SQL Server has matured today. Columnstore indexes use the same technology as SSAS tabular models to increase the performance of reporting by storing data in a column-wise pattern. While most normalized systems reduce duplication in tables with related tables, columnstore indexing reduces how many duplicated values can be stored in columns, thus improving performance and improving how the data is compressed. It is ideally suited to support denormalized schemas, such as the star schema.

While improvements have been made to the RDBMS products through the years, SSAS was designed from the ground up to support aggregations and reporting. Multidimensional models support large amounts of data that's highly compressed and optimized for returning aggregated results.

Another reason that SSAS was introduced was to eliminate the use of SQL in writing reports. Integration with Excel made SSAS a favorite tool for business analysts all over the world. They are able to connect to the cube and then use drag and drop features with pivot tables and pivot charts to do a quick analysis of the data, without writing SQL or requesting data from the IT team. This simplified data analysis considerably.

Planning dimensions and facts

Now that the basics around dimensional modeling concepts have been covered, the next step is planning the dimensions and facts for your data warehouse. The following principles need to be kept in mind:

- Know what problem you are trying to solve. You need to know what the business is trying to understand. Your design should understand the various business areas that need to be analyzed.

- Understand the grain. As we noted previously, it is important to know what the grain of each of the fact tables will be. Do you need to support multiple grains? For example, let's say a sale has a total and a date when it occurred. However, if the sale or invoice consists of multiple items, you may need to track your sales at the purchase level (one fact table) and your line items in the sale in a different fact table.

- Build out your bus matrix. You need to understand your facts and dimensions. This will continually change throughout your implementation but understanding your first fact and its dimensionality will help you add facts and know when you need to add dimensions. We often know a few dimensions we need right away, such as customers, products, dates, or locations. Plan your core conformed dimensions out so that you can start the build quickly and expand the capability of your solution with your business needs.

At this point, I will lay out a word of caution: too much time spent in the design process will be counterproductive. Businesses are typically very impatient. If you try to solve everything at the beginning, you will never build anything. Always try to identify how you can make the wins you need iteratively. You should always be delivering more to the business so that they can see your progress and support your efforts as you build out the solution.

Designing and building dimensions and facts

Because our focus is on building a multidimensional model in SSAS, the next few sections will be relatively short, but focused on what you need in order to build out a good star schema using SQL Server 2019.

Column names – business-friendly or designer-friendly?

Without trying to start a war about whether you should have spaces in your column names, I want to call out that this is merely an option. In SQL Server, you can use truly business-friendly names in your tables and columns. Most, if not all, DBAs will argue that this is not a best practice. In order to properly do this, the database object names must be enclosed in brackets. While the name might appear in a nice format on the resulting report, the SQL syntax becomes more complex.

The reserved word conundrum

In every RDBMS system, reserved words exist. This commonly includes words such as **NAME**, **EXTERNAL**, **GROUP**, **BULK**, and **USER**. SQL Server has well over 100 of these words. This means that something such as a product name needs to have a fully descriptive name, not just *NAME*. While you can potentially use reserved words in your table designs, this is not a best practice and should be avoided.

Let's design the product dimension from the work we did previously. We will create the table using both types of syntax and then show you what the query would look like.

Here is the script for the table with spaces in the names:

```
CREATE TABLE [Dimension].[Product] (
     [Product SID] INT NOT NULL
     ,[Product SKU] NVARCHAR(15) NOT NULL
     ,[Product Name] NVARCHAR(100) NOT NULL
     ,[Product Description] NVARCHAR(500) NULL
     ,[Product Cost] DECIMAL(18,2) NOT NULL
     ,[Product Price] DECIMAL(18,2) NOT NULL
     ,[Product Source] NVARCHAR(200) NULL)
```

Here is the script for the table without spaces in the names:

```
CREATE TABLE [Dimension].[Product] (
     [ProductSID] INT NOT NULL
     ,[ProductSKU] NVARCHAR(15) NOT NULL
     ,[ProductName] NVARCHAR(100) NOT NULL
     ,[ProductDescription] NVARCHAR(500) NULL
     ,[ProductCost] DECIMAL(18,2) NOT NULL
     ,[ProductPrice] DECIMAL(18,2) NOT NULL
     ,[ProductSource] NVARCHAR(200) NULL)
```

While some data professionals like using underscores in their designs, I typically only use that syntax style to clarify a use or something similar. For example, I use them to clarify that a field has a special use. The surrogate key for the product dimension could be ProductKey or Product_Key. However, I would not use underscores to replace spaces – Product_Short_Name versus ProductShortName. The point of this is that you should settle on a naming convention for your solution and that it should be understandable and simple. The focus should be for others, not you. A data warehouse designed for you may make it easy for you to maintain, but not something the business wants to use.

Now, let's look at those queries against the tables we created previously. The first query does not require brackets for the object names:

```
SELECT ProductSID, ProductSKU, ProductName
FROM Dimension.Product
```

The second query does due to the spaces in the names:

```
SELECT [Product SID], [Product SKU], [Product Name]
FROM Dimension.Product
```

If you are going to have report writers and business users interacting with your data, I recommend that you don't use spaces. It will be easier to train report writers to handle SQL correctly than to deal with the multitude of issues that will likely be generated using brackets.

One other thing about naming conventions that you should take into consideration is that some developers and database designers using *dim* and *fact* as prefixes for the tables. Others use schemas to accomplish the same result. Once again, this is a preference, not a rule. Pick the pattern you want to implement and stick with it. Our example database, **WideWorldImportersDW**, uses schemas – `Dimension` and `Fact` – to clarify the tables.

Dimension tables

Dimension tables should be planned to support the conformed dimension logical design you have. Continuing with the product theme, the product dimension table should have the following fields:

- `Product_SID`: Surrogate key, identity column, clustered index
- `ProductSKU`
- `ProductName`
- `ProductDescription`
- `ProductCost`
- `ProductPrice`
- `ProductSource`
- `Product_ValidFrom`
- `Product_ValidTo`
- `Product_Current`
- `Product_Deleted`

This design supports SCD Type 2 functionality. Following the design we have in place, this dimension supports SCD Type 2 for cost, price, and source. The rest of the attributes support the SCD Type 1 design, which overwrites on update. The primary key is the surrogate key in our design. Traditionally, SQL Server developers use identity columns (auto-incrementing integers) for the surrogate key. In SQL Server 2019, the recommendation is to use sequences to auto-populate the key. To wrap up the design, we will add a clustered index to the primary key and cover indexes that support our expected query patterns.

A little bit of information about indexes

Indexes are used to optimize searches and queries in databases. In this section, we mentioned two common types of indexes used in relational databases that support data warehouses. The first is the clustered index. A clustered index is used to order the data in a table. The second is the covering index. A covering index is used to organize data so that you can specifically support queries against a table. Overall, indexes are used to improve the performance of queries in databases.

The rest of the dimensions for any data warehouse you are working on should follow the same basic principles laid out here.

Fact tables

Fact tables typically have metrics and dimension keys. Be aware that this is a fairly simple design. In many cases, fact tables will have additional, non-measurable fields. Our example is a simple design to highlight design patterns. The fact table in our case includes a key for the table, which is effectively a row number. Foreign key constraints are added to each of the dimension keys used in the fact table.

With SQL Server 2019, additional techniques can be used to further improve the design and implementation of the fact table. For example, in our example data warehouse, a similar table, `Fact.Sale`, was built with a clustered columnstore index instead of a standard clustered index, but only on the primary key fields. The primary key for this table has a unique index applied as well. The rest of the fact tables will use similar design patterns.

Indexing strategies

While indexing strategies are not a primary concern when working with multidimensional models, they have to be considered when completing the star schema. The key impact this has on Analysis Services is data refresh. As data volumes grow, indexes will be required to optimize processing performance for the cube. When designing the star schema initially in SQL Server 2019, the following indexes should be applied to support the expected workload.

Organizing the tables with **clustered columnstore indexes** will improve the overall performance of processing. This is primarily because a denormalized database design such as a star schema lends itself to many duplicated values in the columns of the tables. This duplication is optimized through compression and memory support and results in better performing queries on larger tables in particular. A key consideration is that the compression and related performance for clustered columnstore indexes is realized on partitions larger than one million rows. If your table has less than one million rows, performance may not be helped as much.

If clustered columnstore indexes are not a good fit for your table, start by creating a standard **clustered index** on the table. Using the key is the best way to keep the load to the table efficient, but if the data is bulk loaded using a date value or similar pattern, consider expanding the clustered index so that it includes that value. Clustered indexes represent the physical storage order of the table. As such, if the key value is constantly loaded out of order, the table will become fragmented. For dimension tables, using the unique, typically sequential, key for the clustered index makes the most sense.

Traditionally, **non-clustered indexes** have been at the heart of performance improvements in data warehouse solutions. When designing the star schema, non-clustered indexes are initially used with the foreign keys in fact tables. (Foreign keys are used to match data between tables.) As query performance is evaluated and common patterns for queries are identified, **covering indexes** are added to tables. Covering indexes have multiple columns in the index. Some columns are ordered, while others are included. This improves read performance in the data warehouse and helps with loading the cube when the indexes are set up to support processing Analysis Services databases.

Plenty of indexing techniques and patterns have been used through the years to support relational databases that have star schemas. Analysis Services uses these optimized databases to process the data in the model. However, these same databases may also be used for reporting or other data analytics purposes. When applying indexes to databases, always consider competing workloads.

Foreign key

Because the work is being done on a relational database platform, enforcing relationships is considered a best practice. Most data warehouses will include this in the design. However, if you experience performance issues during the loading process, you may find significant gains when removing the constraints. I would only recommend this if you need to improve load performance and you can validate that constraint checking is part of the issue. The constraints should be kept if your load process may have orphan records due to load inconsistencies.

These are just a few design considerations you should think about when building your solution so that it supports a multidimensional model. Next, I will walk through some of the loading options you can consider.

Loading data into your star schema

Now that you have your star schema designed, what's next? You need to build a plan so that you can load data from the source systems and get them properly in place in your star schema. In this section, I will give you some pointers to get you going. This is not an exhaustive or complete loading strategy but should help you understand the basics you need to plan.

Staging your data

I recommend that you plan to stage your data in a database prior to loading it into your star schema. The process of lookups and standardization can add significant load on the system that you are loading from. By having a staging database or a staging schema, you can load data from various source systems with minimal transformation. Then, using the resources dedicated to the process, the data can be loaded from staging to the star schema without there being any negative impacts on the source. How often you stage data can be managed based on the needs of the source system.

SQL Server data loading methods and tools

SQL Server has a number of methods and tools you can use to load data into a star schema. I will reference the two most common methods – ETL and ELT – and the most common tools – **SQL Server 2019 Integration Services** (**SSIS**) and SQL – used to load star schemas.

When working with any type of data warehouse solution, **ETL** and **ELT** are the most commonly referenced patterns. Let's take a look at what each of the letters in ETL and ELT stand for:

- E: Extraction, the process of pulling data from a source system
- T: Transformation, the process of manipulating and shaping data for use
- L: Load, the process of loading data into a destination system

The order of the letters – ETL and ELT – describe when and where the data will be transformed or shaped. ETL is the most traditional solution. This typically involves a specialized tool such as SSIS to be used between the two datasets.

In an ETL solution, to load the star schema from staging, SSIS will connect to the staging dataset, bring the data into the tool, use steps in the tool to manipulate the data, and then load the manipulated data into the star schema. The following is an example of an SSIS package that loads a dimension into the star schema:

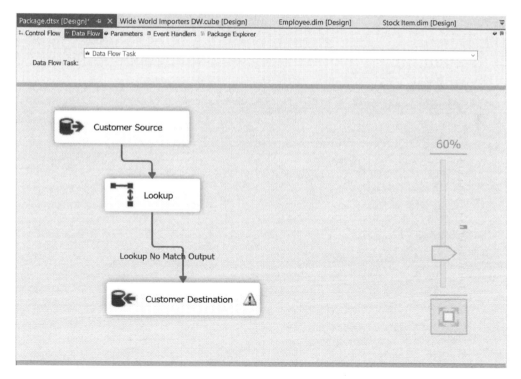

Figure 3.3 – Sample data flow task in an SSIS package

The key here is that the most significant transformation work is conducted while the data is in the process of being loaded into the star schema. SSIS and similar tools flow data through and use memory and temporary storage to make changes required to the data along the way.

ELT moves the transformation workload to the destination. This technique has come into fashion more recently as developers seek to use the processing power and capabilities of the destination system to transform data. In this pattern, data is moved from the source to the destination first using the data movement tool of choice (for example, SSIS). Once it has been moved, jobs are initiated that typically use SQL and stored procedures to transform the data into the star schema. If you have your staging database on the same instance or if you're using a schema for staging, this is a popular choice. This allows development teams to focus on fewer coding languages, which helps with ongoing maintenance and staffing.

There is not a right or perfect design choice. More mature solutions have a combination of these techniques, with the goal of being the best option for the job at hand. Whichever path you choose, this section should have given you a basic understanding of the primary options you can use to move and shape your data into the star schema, which is used to support multidimensional models.

Using database views and data source views

So far, the focus has been on prepping the star schema in the relational database so that you can build out the multidimensional model. This section will focus on a design decision that impacts database design, but also impacts how you work with Analysis Services itself. As part of building out a multidimensional model, data source views are created in Analysis Services to serve as the mapping between the relational and multidimensional models:

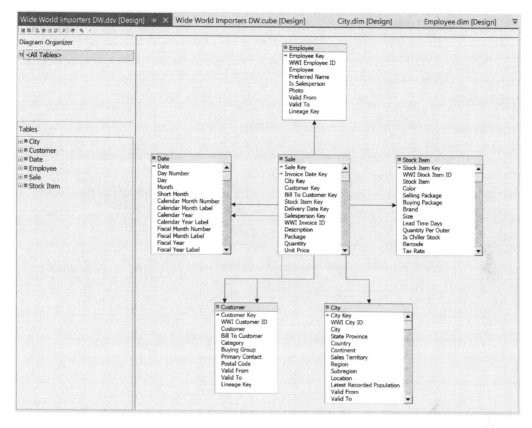

Figure 3.4 – Data source view in SQL Server 2019 Analysis Services from Visual Studio

We will now look at the pros and cons of data source views.

Data source views – pros and cons

Data source views (DSVs) are an integral part of a multidimensional model project. This is where the source data is modeled for the multidimensional model. In the preceding screenshot, the star schema can be clearly seen. The preceding model has been pulled directly from the underlying SQL Server database with no modifications. The key to the preceding statement is *no modifications*. In my opinion, this is the best way to implement the data source view. However, it is not the only way.

DSVs support the creation of custom tables, fields, and relationships. The end goal is star schema shaped data that can be easily used by the multidimensional model.

Why would you modify the shape of the data here? Some designers make changes here because it is convenient. Changes are made here for the purpose of cube design and do not require any other intervention. Convenience is not a good reason to make changes here. Often, those changes are not well-documented or easy to discover. When the source changes, care must be taken to ensure the DSV also handles these changes. If not, cubes will not process, which creates frustration with the end users or consumers of the cube when it is not available.

The best reason to shape the data in the data source view is when developers cannot easily change or modify database views, as this helps support the star schema model in the underlying database. If this is the reason, then I recommend that you make it the pattern for ongoing work. You will not be able to take advantage of better view design techniques from the database, but it will allow you to make the changes needed to support multidimensional model design. Be aware that complex data source views can significantly impact model processing (loading the data). I recommend only using DSVs when this is the case. The preferred option is to push the view design to the relational database, where management and performance are better.

Database views as an interface layer

The preferred practice is to use database views as an **interface layer**. There are two principles to take into account – flexibility and protection.

Database views allow you to be *flexible* in your design. Views can be used to support calculations, aggregations, and column design. In a view, a calculation can be added that will reduce the calculation workload in the cube. For example, the following measures are part of the sales fact: **Total Sale**, **Total Sale with Tax**, and **Total Sale with Shipping and Tax**. They use **Total Sale**, **Total Tax**, and **Total Shipping** as base metrics. These can definitely be calculated in the cube using **multidimensional expressions** (**MDX**). However, they will not be pre-aggregated and will degrade performance. If these are precalculated in the view, they will not need calculations to be created in the cube.

This example already works to support *aggregation* optimization in the cube. Another example is that **SUM** typically performs better than **COUNT** in a cube. If each row counts as **1**, then adding a column with the value of **1** to the view allows the cube to optimize the aggregation using a sum rather than counting the rows.

Finally, by using a view to cover all tables used in the multidimensional DSV, changes can be made to optimize the underlying tables while guaranteeing there's an *interface* for the relational model that does not change. This protects the cube from unintentional breakage when you're changing the underlying schema to optimize the database or to change functionality. For example, if a source system changes the way a date is formatted, the view can modify the format so that it matches what is expected in the cube, thereby preventing processing issues. This method also prevents issues caused by core changes in the underlying database, such as fields being added or removed and object name changes (tables or columns).

I recommend using views as the interface or abstraction layer as it will protect the cube from disruption and lead to better user satisfaction. Optimization and aggregation support are helpful as well, but protection is more important.

Prepping our database for the multidimensional model

Everything in this chapter is about prepping the underlying data and database in order to support a multidimensional model. This section presents a hands-on implementation of the views to support the multidimensional model we are going to create.

Wide World Importers Sales

The focus of this book is on **Wide World Importers Sales**. In particular, the **Fact.Sales** table will be used as the heart of the schema. The following dimensions are part of our model design:

- **City**: `Dimension.City`
- **Customer**: `Dimension.Customer`
- **Bill To Customer**: `Dimension.Customer`
- **Invoice Date**: `Dimension.Date`
- **Delivery Date**: `Dimension.Date`
- **Item**: `Dimension.Stock Item`
- **Salesperson**: `Dimension.Employee`

A total of six tables will be used in the multidimensional model. These tables already exist in our data warehouse, so the next step is to create views that will support the multidimensional model build in the following chapters.

Role playing dimensions

While only five dimension tables support the sales of the star schema, seven dimensions are in the design. Date and customer tables are used twice each in this design. Dimension tables used more than once in a schema are referred to as **role playing dimensions**. These dimensions use the same data but represent different business relationships in the data. Date is one of the most common role-playing dimensions. In the Wide World Importers Sales fact, both an invoice date and delivery date are used. The underlying shape and content of the date table for both dimensions are identical, but the business purpose or role of the relationship is different. This technique allows data warehouse teams to manage the data while making it available for many purposes.

The data warehouse designers choose a few techniques we have described:

- Using business-friendly names for database objects.

- Using common naming with spaces included in table names and field names.

- Using square brackets [] when referring to objects in the schema. As a best practice, square brackets will be used in all the code to keep the pattern uniform, whether they are needed or not.

- Using database schemas to differentiate fact tables, dimension tables, and staging tables. The [Fact], [Dimension], and [Integration] schemas are already in place and used in the data warehouse. The integration schema supports staging tables and other ETL support tables.

Here are a few other design techniques to be aware of:

- **Key** is used for primary and foreign key fields.

- Foreign key constraints are in place with matching non-clustered indexes.

- SCD Type 2 is in place for the City, Customer, Stock Item, and Employee tables:

    a) The [Valid From] and [Valid To] fields specify the range.

    b) If [Valid To] is 9999-12-31 23:59:59.9999999, the record is current.

    c) No current flag is in place.

- [Lineage Key] is used throughout to identify the load information.

- [Fact Sale] has a dual field primary key – [Sale Key] and [Invoice Date Key].

- The primary key is not clustered.

- [Fact Sale] is built with a clustered columnstore index.

- Unicode (for example, nvarchar) types are used for text fields.

- The date dimension uses the date type for its primary key.

I wanted to call attention to these as these are design details to be aware of. Now that you have a basic understanding of the data in the data warehouse, the next section will describe some considerations for creating our views.

Creating the views for the multidimensional model

Now that we know what is in our model, let's plan out what the views will be. The views that will support our model should be isolated from other views or objects in the database. This is done using a database schema.

Database schemas for the data warehouse

Schemas serve various purposes in the data warehouse. The Wide World Importers data warehouse comes with schemas that support design, such as Fact and Dimensions, as well as schemas that support various functional areas, such as **Sequences**, **Application**, and **Integration**. I have used schemas to separate functional areas and apply appropriate security for those areas. I commonly create at least two schemas when implementing multidimensional models – **Reports** and **Cube**. Reports supports our ability to build reports directly from the database. It allows report designers to build against views as opposed to the underlying tables. Cube is used to support multidimensional models. While these may have significant overlap, they can be matched functionally to their purpose and create that interface layer. This helps protect database designers and consumers from change that is often required to support business and technology changes.

We will add a schema to hold the views for the multidimensional build called Cube. Use the following code in SSMS to create the schema in **WideWorldImporterDW**:

```
USE WideWorldImportersDW;
GO
CREATE SCHEMA [Cube];
GO
```

Next, we need to create the views. We are going to implement two views for the dimension table with SCD Type 2 implemented that have historical changes in place. One view will carry the *Current* label and will only have the current representation of the dimension value. The other view will contain all the data. Currently, some of the tables have no change history. In our design, we will only create `Current` views for dimensions with change history. If other dimensions start to have historical changes, a current view can be added to the dimension to support the business needs.

> **Why have a current view?**
>
> While business users want us to track change, typically, they want to create reports with the most current information. They are often unable to properly query SCD Type 2 dimensions since they often appear as more than one row. This can impact calculations as well. I have found it necessary to include both in the design of the cube as the business needs the capability of both options.

For each of the dimensions, a `Current` flag will be added for the SCD Type 2 dimensions. This will be used to help identify the current state easily in the resulting report.

The fact table will get a count column. As we previously noted, this will allow for better aggregations in the cube.

An `Invoice` dimension view will then be added. This will be based on the `Sales` fact table and allows us to group and count invoices, as well as sales that represent lines on the invoice. This will also have an `Invoice Sales` fact table to support the metrics at the invoice level. This addition will support more capability within the cube while not impacting the underlying database table design.

The following sections lay out the views that will be created to support the cube and are organized based on the underlying database table. Do not use `SELECT * FROM TableName` in your views. If a column name changes, you can support that properly if the columns are called out in the view.

City dimension view

The `City` dimension table has SCD Type 2 support but has no historical changes that are needed for our analytic models. Only one view will be created for `City` to support the multidimensional model:

```
CREATE OR ALTER    VIEW [Cube].[City] AS
    SELECT [City Key]  ,[WWI City ID]
      ,[City]  ,[State Province]
      ,[Country]  ,[Continent]
      ,[Sales Territory],[Region]
      ,[Subregion],[Location]
      ,[Latest Recorded Population]
   FROM [Dimension].[City];
```

Customer dimension view

The City dimension table has SCD Type 2 support but has no historical changes in place. One view will be created – Customer:

```
CREATE OR ALTER    VIEW [Cube].[Customer] AS
SELECT [Customer Key]  ,[WWI Customer ID]
      ,[Customer]  ,[Bill To Customer]
      ,[Category]  ,[Buying Group]
      ,[Primary Contact],[Postal Code]
   FROM [Dimension].[Customer];
```

Date dimension view

The Date dimension table does not have SCD Type 2 support. No additional fields have been added at this time:

```
CREATE OR ALTER    VIEW [Cube].[Date] AS
SELECT [Date],[Day Number]
  ,[Day]  ,[Month]
  ,[Short Month]  ,[Calendar Month Number]
  ,[Calendar Month Label]  ,[Calendar Year]
  ,[Calendar Year Label]  ,[Fiscal Month Number]
  ,[Fiscal Month Label]  ,[Fiscal Year]
  ,[Fiscal Year Label]  ,[ISO Week Number]
  ,CASE WHEN GETDATE() = [Date] THEN 1 ELSE 0 END AS [Today]
FROM [Dimension].[Date];
```

Salesperson dimension view

The Employee dimension table has SCD Type 2 support and has historical changes in place. Two views will be created – Salesperson and Salesperson-Current. The Current flag has also been added to these views. These views will be filtered by the [Is Salesperson] flag and that column will be removed from the view. The Photo column will also be removed since, currently, there is no data in that column.

Based on the name pattern, the name will be split into Last Name and First Name to allow flexibility in the reporting display, including a Last Name, First Name format. By making these optional in the views, we can handle changes here. An assumption has to be made at this point. We assume that the first name is followed by a space and that, in most cases, this will leave the rest of the characters in the last name. The design of the columns reflects this assumption:

```
CREATE OR ALTER   VIEW [Cube].[Salesperson] AS
SELECT [Employee Key] ,[WWI Employee ID]
  ,[Employee] ,[Preferred Name]
  ,SUBSTRING([Employee],CHARINDEX(' ', [Employee])+1,
LEN([Employee])) AS [Last Name]
  ,SUBSTRING([Employee],1,CHARINDEX(' ', [Employee])) AS [First
Name]
  ,[Valid From] ,[Valid To]
  ,CASE WHEN [Valid To] > '9999-01-01' THEN 1 ELSE 0 END AS
[Current]
  ,[Lineage Key]
FROM [Dimension].[Employee]
WHERE [Is Salesperson] = 1;
```

The Salesperson-Current view will be shorter as the key and SCD information will be removed. Here is the script for that view:

```
CREATE OR ALTER VIEW [Cube].[Salesperson-Current] AS
SELECT [WWI Employee ID]
  ,[Employee] ,[Preferred Name]
  ,SUBSTRING([Employee],CHARINDEX(' ', [Employee])+1,
LEN([Employee])) AS [Last Name]
  ,SUBSTRING([Employee],1,CHARINDEX(' ', [Employee])) AS [First
Name]
FROM [Dimension].[Employee]
WHERE [Is Salesperson] = 1 AND [Valid To] > '9999-01-01';
```

Stock Item dimension views

The Stock Item dimension table has SCD Type 2 support and has historical changes in place. Two views will be created – Item and Item-Current. The Current flag has been added to the standard view, not the current view. The Photo field has been removed in these views because all the values are NULL:

```
CREATE OR ALTER   VIEW [Cube].[Item] AS
SELECT [Stock Item Key]
      , [WWI Stock Item ID] , [Stock Item]
      , [Color] , [Selling Package]
      , [Buying Package] , [Brand]
      , [Size] , [Lead Time Days]
      , [Quantity Per Outer] , [Is Chiller Stock]
      , [Barcode] , [Tax Rate]
      , [Unit Price] , [Recommended Retail Price]
      , [Typical Weight Per Unit] , [Valid From]
      , [Valid To]
     ,CASE WHEN [Valid To] > '9999-01-01' THEN 1 ELSE 0 END AS
[Current]
      , [Lineage Key]
   FROM [Dimension].[Stock Item];
```

The Item-Current view is shorter as the key column has been removed, along with all of the SCD support columns:

```
CREATE OR ALTER VIEW [Cube].[Item-Current] AS
SELECT [WWI Stock Item ID]
      , [Stock Item] , [Color]
      , [Selling Package] , [Buying Package]
      , [Brand] , [Size]
      , [Lead Time Days] , [Quantity Per Outer]
      , [Is Chiller Stock] , [Barcode]
      , [Tax Rate] , [Unit Price]
      , [Recommended Retail Price]
      , [Typical Weight Per Unit]
FROM [Dimension].[Stock Item]
WHERE [Valid To] > '9999-01-01';
```

Sales fact views

The Sales fact table will be used in multiple views to support our multidimensional model. Not only will the fact table be expanded, but an aggregated view for invoices will be created as well. To round off the support for the new fact table, a new invoice dimension will be added as well. These tables will be defined in the upcoming sections.

[Cube].[Sales]

The Sales view is a match with the [Fact].[Sales] table grain. Effectively, this view represents the line items on an invoice. This table will include a Sales Count field, which will have a value of 1. Additionally, several ID fields will be added to this table to support Current dimensions that have been created in addition to the Key fields. The relationships will be built to support Current with the unique source key:

```
CREATE OR ALTER   VIEW [Cube].[Sales] AS
SELECT fs.[Sale Key] ,fs.[City Key]
,dc.[WWI City ID] ,fs.[Customer Key]
,dcu.[WWI Customer ID] ,fs.[Bill To Customer Key]
,dbc.[WWI Customer ID] as [WWI Bill To Customer ID]
,fs.[Stock Item Key] ,dsi.[WWI Stock Item ID]
,fs.[Invoice Date Key] ,fs.[Delivery Date Key]
,fs.[Salesperson Key] ,de.[WWI Employee ID]
,fs.[WWI Invoice ID] ,fs.[Description]
,fs.[Package] ,fs.[Quantity]
,fs.[Unit Price] ,fs.[Tax Rate]
,fs.[Total Excluding Tax] ,fs.[Tax Amount]
,fs.[Profit] ,fs.[Total Including Tax]
,fs.[Total Dry Items] ,fs.[Total Chiller Items]
,1 as [Sales Count] ,fs.[Lineage Key]
FROM [Fact].[Sale] fs
INNER JOIN [Dimension].[City] dc
  ON dc.[City Key] = fs.[City Key]
INNER JOIN [Dimension].[Customer] dcu
  ON dcu.[Customer Key] = fs.[Customer Key]
INNER JOIN [Dimension].[Customer] dbc
  ON dbc.[Customer Key] = fs.[Bill To Customer Key]
```

```
INNER JOIN [Dimension].[Stock Item] dsi
  ON dsi.[Stock Item Key] = fs.[Stock Item Key]
INNER JOIN [Dimension].[Employee] de
  ON de.[Employee Key] = fs.[Salesperson Key];
```

[Cube].[Invoice]

This will serve as a simple Invoice dimension. While not complex, the two-field dimension will be helpful us perform some calculations across the solution as we build it out:

```
CREATE OR ALTER   VIEW [Cube].[Invoice] AS
SELECT fs.[WWI Invoice ID] ,fs.[Invoice Date Key]
FROM [Fact].[Sale] fs
GROUP BY fs.[WWI Invoice ID] ,fs.[Invoice Date Key];
```

[Cube].[Invoice Sales]

Finally, this view will serve as a fact table with aggregated values that can be used at the Invoice level. A number of fields related to the line items have been removed. A field for Sales Count has been added here, which is a count of the Sales rows that make up the Invoice line. Invoice Count was added to support better aggregation performance:

```
CREATE OR ALTER   VIEW [Cube].[Invoice Sales] AS
SELECT fs.[WWI Invoice ID] ,fs.[City Key]
,dc.[WWI City ID] ,fs.[Customer Key]
,dcu.[WWI Customer ID] ,fs.[Bill To Customer Key]
,dbc.[WWI Customer ID] AS [WWI Bill To Customer ID]
,fs.[Invoice Date Key] ,fs.[Salesperson Key]
,de.[WWI Employee ID]
,SUM(fs.[Total Excluding Tax]) AS [Invoice Total Excluding
Tax]
,SUM(fs.[Tax Amount]) AS [Invoice Tax Amount]
,SUM(fs.[Profit]) AS [Invoice Profit]
,SUM(fs.[Total Including Tax]) AS [Invoice Total Including
Tax]
,SUM(fs.[Total Dry Items]) AS [Invoice Total Dry Items]
,SUM(fs.[Total Chiller Items]) AS [Invoice Total Chiller
Items]
,1 AS [Invoice Count] ,COUNT([Sale Key]) AS [Sales Count]
```

```
FROM [Fact].[Sale] fs
INNER JOIN [Dimension].[City] dc
  ON dc.[City Key] = fs.[City Key]
INNER JOIN [Dimension].[Customer] dcu
  ON dcu.[Customer Key] = fs.[Customer Key]
INNER JOIN [Dimension].[Customer] dbc
  ON dbc.[Customer Key] = fs.[Bill To Customer Key]
INNER JOIN [Dimension].[Employee] de
  ON de.[Employee Key] = fs.[Salesperson Key]
GROUP BY fs.[WWI Invoice ID] ,fs.[City Key]
  ,dc.[WWI City ID] ,fs.[Customer Key]
  ,dcu.[WWI Customer ID] ,fs.[Bill To Customer Key]
  ,dbc.[WWI Customer ID] ,fs.[Invoice Date Key]
  ,fs.[Salesperson Key] ,de.[WWI Employee ID];
```

This concludes the views that we need to create to support the multidimensional project in the next chapter. These views support two star schemas using two fact tables with conformed dimensions, as described in the bus matrix. The following screenshots illustrate the two star schemas we've created (these diagrams only include view names, keys, and relationships so that they can be easily viewed here):

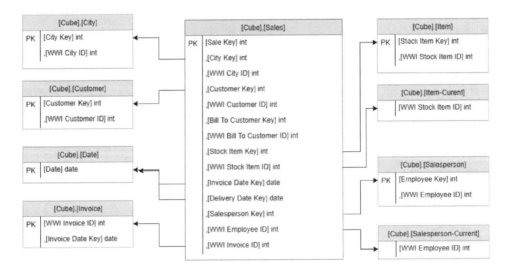

Figure 3.5 – Sales star schema based on views (key fields only)

Here's the next one:

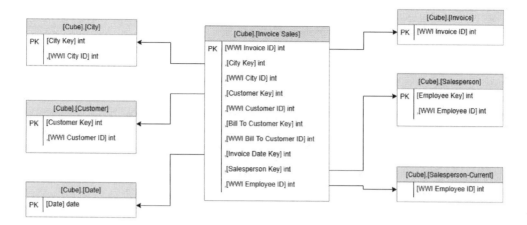

Figure 3.6 – Invoice Sales star schema based on views (key fields only)

This concludes the data preparation we need to do for our multidimensional models. As you can see, star schemas are needed to move on to the next step, which is creating the cubes.

Summary

In this chapter, we walked through the various techniques, patterns, and tools that you can use to prepare your data for the multidimensional model. This chapter was wrapped up with you learning how to create the views that will be used to create the multidimensional model in the next chapter. In this chapter, you learned about the basic skills required to create a quality dimensional design and the principals behind it. This implementation is not only used for building SSAS models, such as for reporting databases, but is also required for multidimensional models. This results in an updated star schema that will be used in the next chapter to create those models.

In the next chapter, the focus will be on creating the multidimensional model using Visual Studio 2019 and deploying the model to SQL Server 2019 Analysis Services. Remember that we'll be building upon what we've learned here to create a great cube in Analysis Services.

4

Building a Multidimensional Cube in SSAS 2019

In this chapter, we will create and deploy a multidimensional cube in SQL Server 2019. We will use the existing data in the `WideWorldImportersDW` database that we uploaded in *Chapter 1, Analysis Services in SQL Server 2019*. This data has already been organized using dimensional modeling techniques. As you work through this chapter, you will learn how to create the Analysis Services project and build out a functional cube. Once it has been built out, we will deploy it and review more advanced techniques that will automate cube processing.

In this chapter, we're going to cover the following main topics:

- Creating an Analysis Services project in Visual Studio
- Adding dimensions and hierarchies to the project
- Adding cubes and measure groups to the project
- Let's get started!

Technical requirements

In this chapter, we will be using the `WideWorldImportersDW` database from *Chapter 1, Analysis Services in SQL Server 2019*. You should connect to the database with **SQL Server Management Studio** (**SSMS**). You will be using the schema and views you created in *Chapter 3, Preparing Your Data for Multidimensional Models*. If you are starting with this chapter, you will need to apply the view from *Chapter 3, Preparing Your Data for Multidimensional Models*, to the `WideWorldImportersDW` database before we start.

This chapter will also require the use of **Visual Studio 2019 Community Edition** to create the Analysis Services project.

Creating the Analysis Services project in Visual Studio

Analysis Services databases are created in Visual Studio. In this section, we will create the project and connect to the database views we created previously. This will create a data model in Analysis Services that will serve as the basis for the rest of the work we'll do in this chapter. Let's get started:

1.   Start by opening Visual Studio:

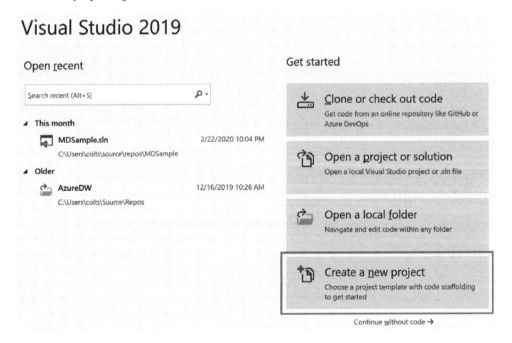

Figure 4.1 – Creating a new project in Visual Studio

2. Choose **Analysis Services Multidimensional and Data Mining Project** and click **Next**:

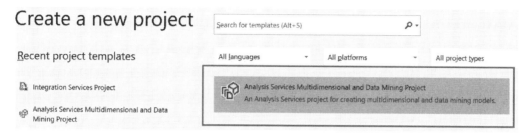

Figure 4.2 – Creating an SSAS multidimensional project

3. You now are ready to **Configure your new project**. You will be asked to fill in the following properties associated with your project:

a) **Project Name**: WideWorldImportersMD

b) **Location**: This will be the location where you want to store the project

c) **Solution Name**: WideWorldImportersSSAS

> **Naming your Visual Studio project and solution**
>
> There are a couple of comments to be made on the names. We can put this project and the tabular project we'll create later into the same solution. This will simplify the process as we can add a project in later sections.

4. Click **Create** when you are done.

Congratulations! With that, you have created the project. If you are new to Visual Studio, now is a good time to review the **integrated development environment** (**IDE**). When you have a new project, the two key features you need to know about are the design surface and the **Solution Explorer**. In the following screenshot, we have highlighted the design surface (**1**) and the solution explorer (**2**):

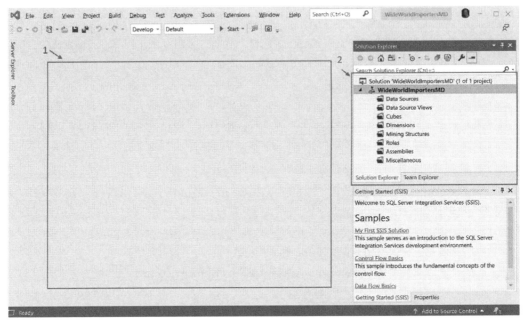

Figure 4.3 – Blank canvas for a new project in Visual Studio 2019

As we continue the process of getting the project ready so that we can build out our first cube, we will be working with the solution explorer, which will add tabs or pages to the design surface.

The next few sections will cover the base items that will support the entire project. First, we will create the connection to the `WideWorldImportersDW` database that we created. Then, we will create the data model, which will be the basis for cube development.

Adding the SQL Server database connection to the project

SQL Server Analysis Services (**SSAS**) supports connecting to many different data systems. For our hands-on example, we will be connecting to SQL Server 2019 and the `WideWorldImportersDW` database.

Database connections are created in the **Data Sources** section of **Solution Explorer**. Let's get started:

1. Right-click on the `Data Sources` folder in **Solution Explorer**. This will open a menu where you can choose to create a **New Data Source…**, as shown in the following screenshot:

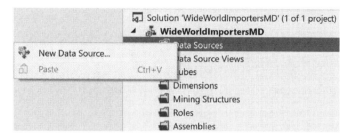

Figure 4.4 – Creating a new data source from the Solution Explorer

2. Click **New Data Sources…** to open the **Data Source Wizard** screen.

3. Click **Next** on the screen that appears.

4. On the next screen, select **How to define the connection** and change the selection to **Create a data source based on an existing or new connection**. Then, click the newly exposed **New** button. This opens the **Connection Manager** screen.

5. Set the following **Connection properties** on the **Connection Manager** screen:

    a) **Provider**: Choose **Native OLEDB\SQL Server Native Client 11.0**.

    b) **Server Name**: Enter your server name here.

    c) **Authentication**: I am using Windows authentication. However, you may need to use SQL authentication and the username and password if you have issues with Windows authentication. You can use the username and password you created when installing SQL Server in *Chapter 1*, *Analysis Services in SQL Server 2019*. This is not an uncommon experience when performing local development with SSAS.

    d) **Connect to a Database**: You can either select the `WideWorldImportersDW` database from the list or type it in. Either option works.

6. We recommend that you click the **Test Connection** button to verify that the authentication works and that the connection is good. Click **OK** after testing the connection.

7. Now, you should be back in the connection wizard with your newly created connection in the **Data Connections** list already selected. If it is not selected, select it now.

> **What if you have more connections in your list?**
>
> It is possible to have more connections show up in your **Data Connections** list. This usually occurs if you have other Visual Studio projects that have used similar connection processes. Be sure to connect the connection to the `WideWorldImportersDW` database before proceeding.

8. Once you have selected the correct connection, click **Next**.

9. You should now be on the **Impersonation Information** dialog of the **Data Source Wizard** screen. This allows you to select the authentication options you will use when loading data into the SSAS database once it has been built. For our purposes, select **Use the credentials of the current user**. This is useful for the local development and deployment we will be using. However, other options are better choices for production deployments. The option you choose for a production deployment will depend on the security and authentication methods that have been implemented within your organization.

10. Give the data source a name (the default is fine) and click **Finish**.

Congratulations! With that, you have created the data source. This is now in the `Data Sources` folder. Now, we are ready to create our data source view.

Adding the DSVs to the project

Data source views (**DSVs**) serve as the translation layer between the source of your data and the SSAS model. In *Chapter 3*, *Preparing Your Data for Multidimensional Models*, we created views in the database to serve in a similar capacity. Why both?

DSVs in SSAS serve as an abstraction layer from the underlying data source. This means that data not in a DSV cannot be accessed by the multidimensional model. If you want to use the data for design, it has to exist in the DSV.

> **Database schemas and security**
>
> In the previous chapter, we created a schema and added the views that will support our model build. It is a good practice to use a specific user or system account in production deployments. When combined, these two activities limit access to the schema and data for the model. If you implement this during design, you can create an **Active Directory** group and give it permissions to the schema. This will limit access to data for developers as well.

DSVs become more important when the multidimensional model designer has no access or influence on the underlying database. As an example, multidimensional models are often created to make data in data warehouses more accessible. This includes non-Microsoft database systems such as Oracle.

In situations where the data warehouse team and the business intelligence team are not the same, multidimensional model development can be significantly hindered if database views cannot be easily created. In a case such as this, a DSV can help with the process. It allows you to add the table and then make changes to support the multidimensional model design.

As we work through this section, we will be creating our core DSV based on the Cube schema we created in *Chapter 3*, *Preparing Your Data for Multidimensional Models*. However, we will also add a couple of tables using the DSV directly with the tables. We will then illustrate some changes that can be made in the DSV, such as using a relational view.

Creating DSVs from relational views

The following steps will help you create a DSV from the Cube.Customer view in the Cube schema. Let's get started:

1. Right-click the Data Source Views folder in **Solution Explorer** and select **New Data Source View…** to open the respective wizard, as shown in the following screenshot:

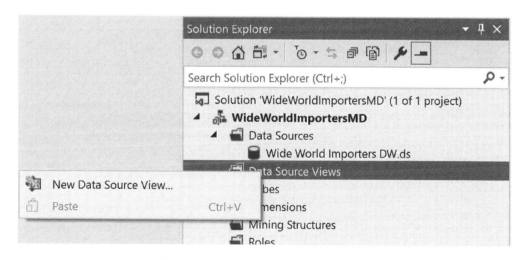

Figure 4.5 – Creating a new data source view

2. From the welcome screen, click **Next** to get started.

3. In the **Select a Data Source** dialog, you can select an existing data source or create a new one. We created the data source in the previous section, so it should be in the list of **Relational data sources**. Select the data source you created in the previous section and click **Next**.

4. The **Select Tables and Views** dialog lists the available tables and views you can add to your DSV. In the **Available objects** list, you can see all the tables and views you have access to from the data source. If you have implemented security for your developers, which limits the schemas or objects they can see, this will be similarly filtered. Also, you are unable to select any other types of database objects. The list is limited to tables and views. The schema name is in parenthesis after the table or view name.

5. You should also see a **Filter** field, which is located under the **Available objects** list. This feature is particularly helpful when working with large lists of tables and views. It filters for the word or words listed there. Try it out using *cube* to see the list become limited to those items in the Cube schema.

6. You can move the entire list of remaining objects to the **Included objects** list by clicking the >> button between the lists. You can also move objects one at a time using the > button or remove them from the **Included objects** list using either << for all selected or < for one at a time. If you are following along, your wizard dialog should look as follows:

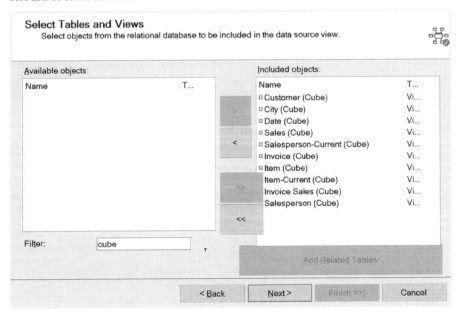

Figure 4.6 – Select Tables and Views window

> **Adding related tables to the Data Source View Wizard**
>
> The option to **Add Related Tables** is the button below the **Included objects** list. This button will add all the tables related to the table you add. For example, if we selected the Sales (Fact) table and then clicked the **Add Related Tables** button, it would add the Employee (Dimension), Customer (Dimension), Date (Dimension), Stock Item (Dimension), and City (Dimension) tables to the **Included objects** list. This does not work when using relational views. While it can be inconvenient to use relational views, using views is still a better practice in most cases. We do not recommend trading development convenience for maintainability.

7. Once you have moved all the Cube schema objects to the list of **Included objects**, click **Next**.

8. Give your DSV a name. The default name uses the same name as the data source. This is fine for our use, but feel free to change it to something that means more to you. Once you've done this, click **Finish** to close the wizard.

Double-click the DSV you just created to open the **Design** view for the DSV. As shown in the following screenshot, we do not have any relationships between our tables. This is what we will look at next:

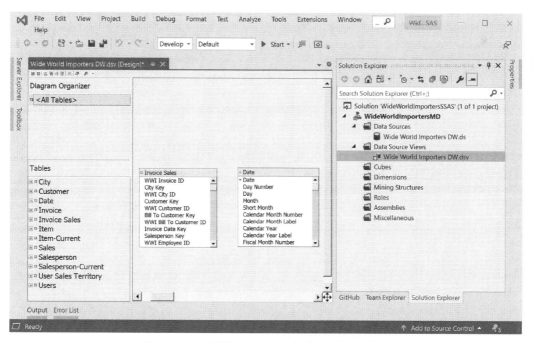

Figure 4.7 – DSV Design view before relationships

We will be adding diagrams for each fact table we included. The diagrams help us keep the views organized around themes. We will also add relationships to finalize our DSVs for the next steps.

Before we start the next section, let's do a quick refresher on our data model. We have created eight dimensions, two of which are *current*. We have also created two fact tables. The `Sales` fact view matches the `Fact.Sale` table in the data warehouse and the data is at the line item level. The `Invoice Sales` fact view aggregates the date in `Fact.Sale` to the invoice number level. Therefore, we will create two diagrams that have some dimension table overlap – **Sales Diagram** and **Invoice Sales Diagram**.

Creating the Sales diagram and its relationships

1. Create a new diagram by right-clicking on **Diagram Organizer** in the top-left corner of the DSV **Design** window. Click **New Diagram**, name it `Sales Diagram`, and hit *Enter*.

2. You will now have a blank diagram window. We will now drag the tables we want to include in this diagram. Let's start by dragging the `Sales` table onto the diagram design surface.

3. Next, we'll add the dimensions we want to include; that is, `City`, `Customer`, `Date`, `Item`, `Item-Current`, `Salesperson`, and `Salesperson-Current`. When you drag them in, place them around the `Sales` table, as shown in the following screenshot:

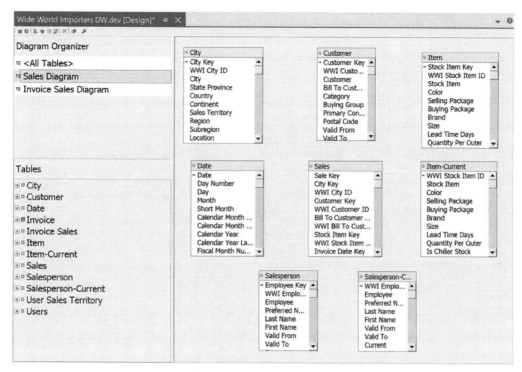

Figure 4.8 – Sales diagram with dimension tables

4. You can create relationships in the diagram in two ways:

a) The first way is to drag the column from the `Sales` table and drop it on the matching column in the dimension table. For example, you can drag `City Key` from `Sales` to `City Key` on `City`.

b) The other option is to right-click the `Sales` table and choose **New Relationship**.

Both of these techniques will open the **Specify Relationship** dialog. If you drag and drop the column, the columns will be filled in. In that dialog, you can update the source and destination tables that will be used in the relationship. The **Source (foreign key)** table is the fact table. In our case, select `Sales` from the drop-down list. The **Destination (primary key)** table is the dimension table. In this case, select `City` from the drop-down list.

5. For both **Source Columns** and **Destination Columns**, choose **City Key**. This will build the relationship between the two tables. If you have the source and destination tables in the wrong order, an error will occur. You can use the **Reverse** button to switch the tables so that they're in the correct relationship direction. Once you've done this, click **OK**. You should see the following output when this step is complete:

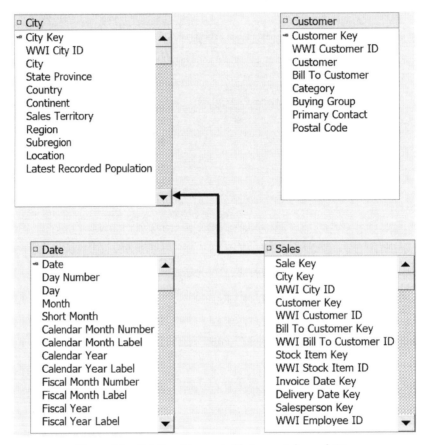

Figure 4.9 – Relationship created between Sales and City

To complete this diagram, repeat the previous process and create the remaining relationships. Use the following list to create the remaining relationships. The first two lists are followed by the *action to be taken* after they are created. The list is organized as follows: *Source table, key field > Destination table, key field*. Here is the first list:

- `Sales, Customer Key > Customer, Customer Key`

- `Sales, Stock Item Key > Item, Stock Item Key`

- `Sales, WWI Stock Item ID > Item-Current, WWI Stock Item ID`

When creating this relationship, you may be prompted to create a **Logical Primary Key** in the `Item-Current` table. Agree to this change by clicking **Yes** in the dialog that opens as follows:

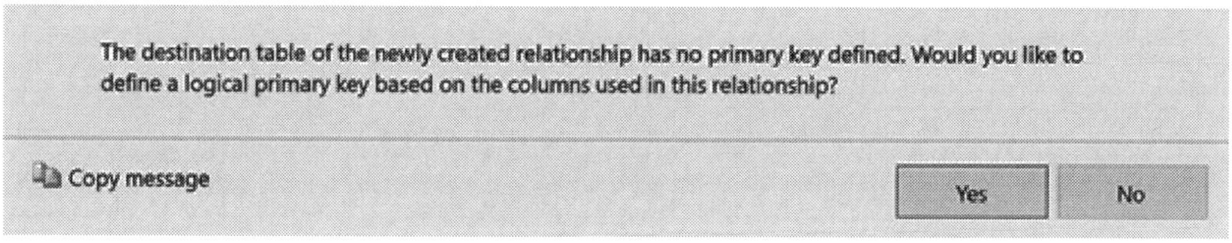

> The destination table of the newly created relationship has no primary key defined. Would you like to define a logical primary key based on the columns used in this relationship?
>
> 📋 Copy message | Yes | No |

Figure 4.10 – Prompt to create a logical primary key in your DSV

Here is the second list:

- `Sales, Salesperson Key` > `Salesperson, Employee Key`
- `Sales, WWI Employee ID` > `Salesperson-Current, WWI Employee ID`

When creating this relationship, you will be prompted to create a **Logical Primary Key** in the `Salesperson-Current` table. Agree to this change by clicking **Yes** in the dialog that opens.

Here is the third list:

- `Sales, Invoice Date Key` > `Date, Date`
- `Sales, Delivery Date Key` > `Date, Date`

> **Role-playing dimensions**
>
> A role-playing dimension is a dimension that has multiple relationships with the fact table. From a data warehouse implementation, it is more space-efficient to create separate relationships from the same table. In our design, the date is used for `Invoice Date` and `Delivery Date`, which have distinct relationships but use the same dimensional data. This type of relationship happens often in a data warehouse.

Now that the relationships have been created, your `Sales` diagram is complete. It should look as follows:

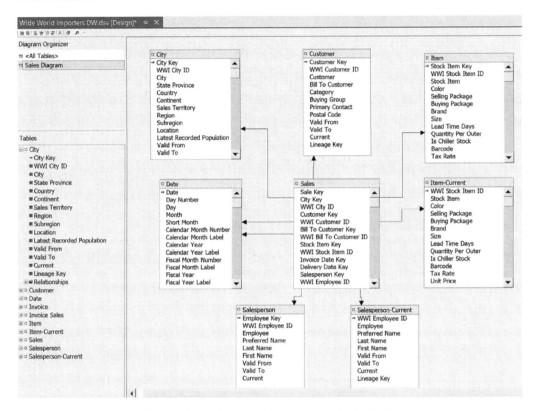

Figure 4.11 – Completed Sales diagram in the DSV

Next, we'll create a diagram for Invoice Sales and its relationships.

Creating the Invoice Sales diagram and its relationships

Next, we need to create the `Invoice Sales` diagram. This process is similar to the one we followed for the `Sales` diagram. Here is the list of relationships you will need to complete. The following list contains *Source table, key field > Destination table, key field*:

- `Invoice Sales, Customer Key > Customer, Customer Key`

- `Invoice Sales, City Key > City, City Key`

- `Invoice Sales, Salesperson Key > Salesperson, Employee Key`

- `Invoice Sales, WWI Employee ID > Salesperson-Current, WWI Employee ID`

- Invoice Sales, Invoice Date Key > Date, Date
- Invoice Sales, WWI Invoice ID > Invoice, WWI Invoice ID

The resulting Invoice Sales diagram should look as follows:

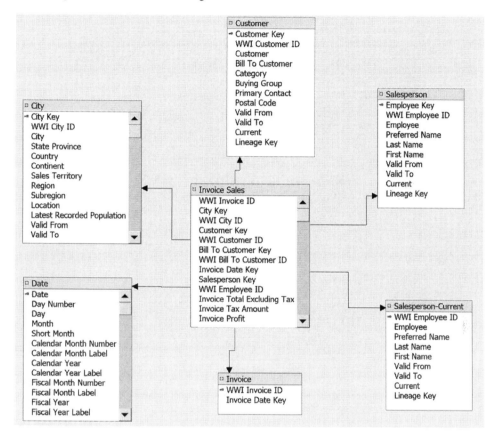

Figure 4.12 – Completed Invoice Sales diagram

We will now review the DSVs.

Custom DSVs

Before we move on to building out the dimensions and measure groups, we need to review some additional capabilities available in our DSVs. We are going to update an existing table and add some additional fields to it. To do this, we will replace the table with a **New Named Query**. Let's get started:

1. Open the **Data Source View Design** window.

2. Right-click on the **Invoice** table name in the **Tables** panel. Here, you'll see the **Replace Table** option. Expand that menu and choose the **With New Named Query … ** option, as shown in the following screenshot:

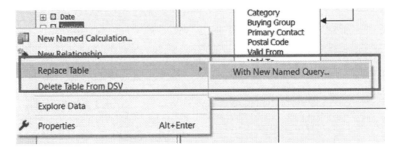

Figure 4.13 – Creating a new named query to replace an existing table

3. This will open the **Create Named Query** dialog. We will be changing the SQL section at the bottom. This is highlighted in the following screenshot:

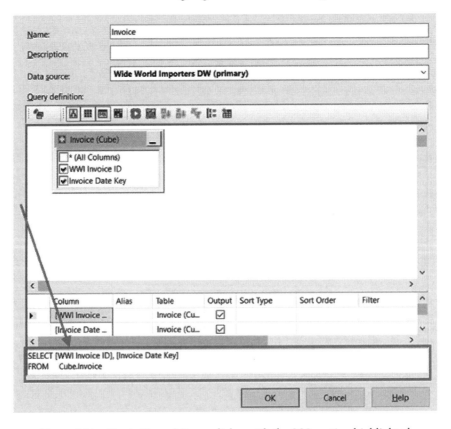

Figure 4.14 – Create Named Query dialog with the SQL section highlighted

4. Replace the query in the dialog with the following code:

```
SELECT [WWI Invoice ID]
, [Invoice Date Key] as [Invoice Date]
, CAST(DATEPART(year, [Invoice Date Key]) AS VARCHAR) +
'_'
    + CAST(DATEPART(month, [Invoice Date Key]) AS
VARCHAR) AS [Invoice Month]
, DATEPART(year, [Invoice Date Key]) AS [Invoice Year]
FROM Cube.Invoice
```

5. Click the green **Run** button in the **Query definition** section to update the query. This should return the rows and update the dialog. When you can run this without errors, click **OK** to close the dialog.

6. You will now see the additional fields in the DSV model. Because we did not change the key column and we replaced the existing `Invoice` table, the relationships stayed intact.

Now that we have created the **Data Source View**, we can start adding dimensions.

Adding dimensions, attributes, and hierarchies

In SSAS, dimensions are comprised of a group of attributes and hierarchies that define the dimension. Before we get into how, we need to discuss three key topics; that is, **dimensions**, **attributes**, and **hierarchies**:

- **Dimensions** are the slicers we use in our cubes to filter and segment our data for analysis. We defined our dimensions in *Chapter 3, Preparing Your Data for Multidimensional Models*.

- **Attributes** are the various related items in our dimension. For example, if we use the `City` dimension, the attributes include `City Name`, `City Key`, `Country`, `State or Province`, and `Last Recorded Population`. These are the fields we added to our DSV.

- **Hierarchies** help us organize our attributes. A hierarchy gives us a clear drill path into our data. In our `City` dimension, we will create a `Geography` hierarchy that consists of `Country`, `State or Province`, and `City` in that order. The goal of hierarchies is to be able move through our data in a well-understood fashion.

Now is a good time to remind you that multidimensional databases have been around for many years. As a result, they have been modified significantly and have a wealth of capabilities that are outside the scope of this book.

In the next few sections, we will create our dimensions through the use of the **Dimension Wizard** window. This is the most efficient method to do this. Once the dimensions have been created, we will create the hierarchies and attribute relationships. This is the most basic development task required to create dimensions. The remaining sections will call out specific, more advanced techniques that can be used improve the usability and performance of the dimensions. Let's get started.

Creating dimensions with the Dimension Wizard

Let's begin with creating dimensions with the dimension wizard with the help of the following steps:

1. The first step is to make sure we have the project open and can see the **Solution Explorer** window. Right-click the Dimensions folder in your Analysis Services project. You will see the option for **New Dimension…**, as shown in the following screenshot. Click that to launch the wizard:

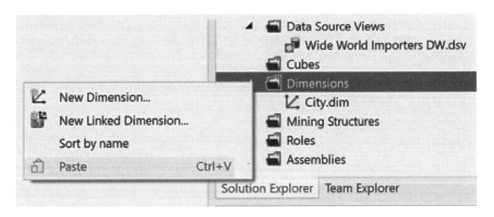

Figure 4.15 – Launching the Dimension Wizard from Solution Explorer

2. Now that you have the **Dimension Wizard** window open, you can click **Next** to move to the first action screen – **Select Creation Method**.

3. You will see a list of options for creating dimensions. Because we are using a full data warehouse and we have created our DSV, we will use the default option; that is, **Use an existing table**. With that selected, click **Next**.

Other dimension creation methods

As shown on the **Select Creation Method** screen of the **Dimension Wizard** window, you can create dimensions by generating tables. Two of the options are designed for situations when you need a Date dimension by generating a table in the DSV or underlying data source. While convenient, we typically recommend against this process. The reason for this is that most of the time the wizard does not generate the attributes you need in your model. Most data warehouses, such as ours, have a date dimension created to support this functionality. The third option uses a generic template to create dimension tables. For example, you can create a customer dimension using the **Customer Template** option. However, you will still need data to support this. If you are looking for design examples for various business needs, this may be a good way to experiment. Typically, you will follow the pattern we have been using and create a relational star schema to support multidimensional model design.

4. In **Specify Source Information**, select **Data source view**, **Main table**, and **Key columns**. For our first run with the wizard, we will select Customer for our main table. You will see that if keys are defined in the DSV, they will populate the **Key columns** section. Confirm that Customer Key is listed in the **Key columns** section and then click **Next**.

5. Next, we'll select the attributes we want to include in our dimension. This page lists all of the attributes or fields from the Customer table in the DSV. You have three options for each attribute. By selecting **Attribute name**, you are choosing to include it in the dimension. The next option is **Enable browsing**. This option will set the property that makes the attribute available in client tools. Finally, you can choose an **Attribute type**. The next few steps will walk through these in detail.

Choosing your dimension attributes

Every field can be chosen as an attribute. Here are some of the key considerations when choosing an attribute:

a) Does the business need the attribute? System values are typically not necessary for development. Examples commonly include lineage IDs and other fields designed to support the load process.

b) Is the field used at all? Just because the name sounds good does not mean it is a candidate for an attribute.

c) The primary consideration is that the attribute needs to have value to the business or is necessary for a calculation. Don't include the attribute just because it is there.

6. We will use all the attributes except `Valid From`, `Valid To`, `Current`, and `Lineage Key`. This will be a common practice for all our dimensions as we build them. For the customer dimension, leave **Enable browsing** selected. We do not need to change our **Attribute type**. Your screen should look as follows:

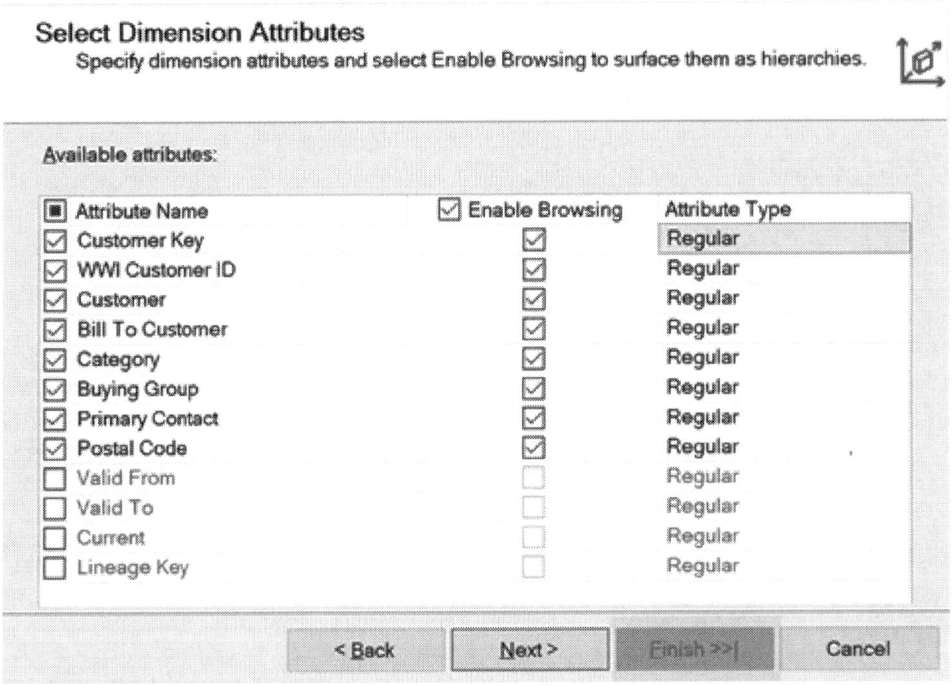

Select Dimension Attributes
Specify dimension attributes and select Enable Browsing to surface them as hierarchies.

Available attributes:

Attribute Name	Enable Browsing	Attribute Type
Customer Key	☑	Regular
WWI Customer ID	☑	Regular
Customer	☑	Regular
Bill To Customer	☑	Regular
Category	☑	Regular
Buying Group	☑	Regular
Primary Contact	☑	Regular
Postal Code	☑	Regular
Valid From	☐	Regular
Valid To	☐	Regular
Current	☐	Regular
Lineage Key	☐	Regular

< Back   Next >   Finish >>| Cancel

Figure 4.16 – Customer Dimension Wizard with attributes selected

7. Click **Next** to preview the dimension. If everything looks correct, click **Finish** to close the wizard and create the `Customer` dimension.

Congratulations! You have created the first dimension in your multidimensional model. You should now see the **Design** tab for your dimension open in Visual Studio. Now, we need to add our remaining dimensions. For each of the dimensions, you will go through similar steps to what we followed here. We have listed each dimension here, along with any changes you should consider while creating them:

*   `City`: The wizard does not have **Enable browsing** selected for **Location**. Location is a geography data type that is not supported in SSAS. We recommend that you do not include that attribute. In the **Attribute type** section, you will see that there is a **Geography** list of types. Go ahead and set **Attribute type** for `City`, `State Province` (`State` or `Province`), `Country`, and `Continent`. You should also set the dimension as a **Geography** type. This increases support in visualization tools.

- `Item`: No changes from the pattern are required for this dimension.

- `Current Item`: We are changing the name of this dimension, which is based on `Item-Current` in the last step to `Current Item`. This will be more understandable for our users.

- `Salesperson`: We are using the `Salesperson-Current` table for this dimension, not the `Salesperson` table. There are changes to the `Salesperson` dimension that we need to bring into the multidimensional model, which means we will have only one `Salesperson` dimension in use.

- `Invoice`: Change the name of `WWI Invoice ID` to `Invoice Number`. This can be done on the **Selection Dimension Attributes** page of the wizard by double-clicking the `WWI Invoice ID` name.

- `Date`: `Date` needs to have its **Attribute types** set. When you click the dropdown list, you will find `Date`, which expands into date categories and specific types for those categories, as shown in the following screenshot:

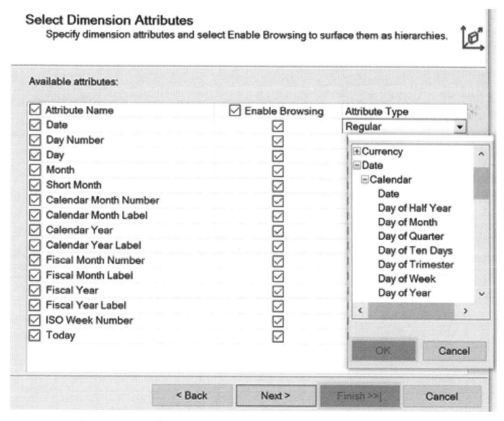

Figure 4.17 – Selecting attribute types for the Date dimension attributes

Here is the completed dialog box for your reference. You will also find attribute types for the standard calendar dates, fiscal dates, and ISO:

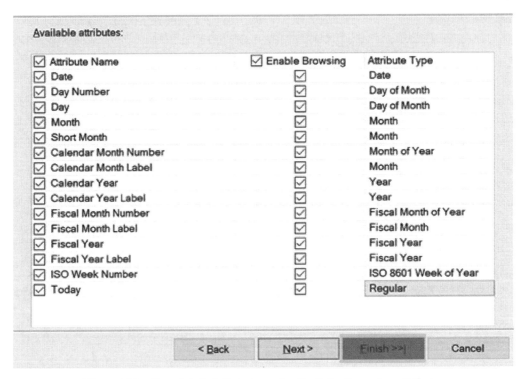

Figure 4.18 – Completed attribute types for the Date dimension attributes

You should see all your dimensions in the `Dimensions` folder in **Solution Explorer**. You should also have all the dimension **Design** tabs open in Visual Studio.

> **Using the Business Intelligence Wizard to set attribute types**
>
> We could have used the **Business Intelligence Wizard** on both the `City` and `Date` dimensions to set the attributes. The Business Intelligence Wizard is designed to support tasks such as attribute types. Because we did this while creating the dimension, it is not necessary. If you want to view the wizard, right-click the `Date` dimension and choose **Add Business Intelligence**. Select **Define Dimension Intelligence** to view the mapping you just completed. This works with the `City` dimension as well. This is just one other option you can use to set the attribute types for your dimension.

Combining the key and name attributes

Before we start working on the hierarchies, we need to combine the dimension key with its name. This is important as we do not need the surrogate key available in the hierarchy or to users as it is meaningless. This process will result in the name or other meaningful attributes being visible to the users while the data is optimized using the key in the background. Let's begin:

1. Go to or open the **City dimension Design** page.

2. Click on the `City` attribute in the **Attributes** pane.

3. In the **Properties** pane, find the **Source** section and change **KeyColumns** from `City.City` to `City.City Key`. When you choose to change this, the **Key Columns** dialog will open. In that dialog, remove the `City` column first, and then add the `City Key` attribute. This will result in `City.City Key (Integer)` being in the property.

4. Change **NameColumn** to `City.City (WChar)`.

5. Find the **Usage** property in the **Basic** section and change it from **Regular** to **Key**.

6. Delete the `City Key` attribute from the **Attributes** pane.

This will set the `City` attribute as the key column for the `City` dimension. We have highlighted the areas you need to be concerned with in the following screenshot:

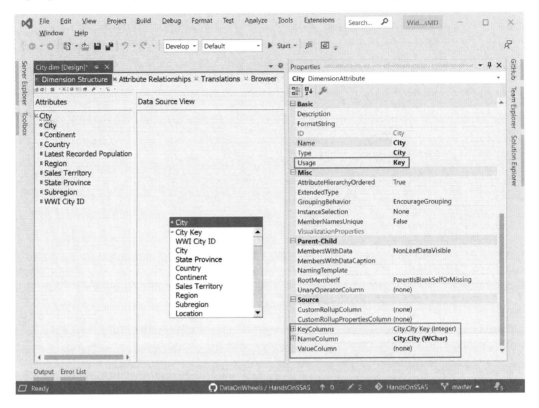

Figure 4.19 – Changing the dimension key

This process should be completed for each dimension, before you add the hierarchies. The following is the list of keys and names for the remaining dimensions that need to be modified (not all the dimensions need this update):

Dimension	Changes
Current Item	*Remember that the "Current" dimensions use natural keys, not surrogate keys.* *Remove:* WWI Stock Item ID *New Key Attribute:* Stock Item • **KeyColumns:** WWI Stock Item ID • **NameColumn:** Stock Item
Customer	*Remove:* Customer Key *New Key Attribute:* Customer • **KeyColumns:** Customer Key • **NameColumn:** Customer
Date	*No changes are required. The key is a date value. This is the only dimension we have that uses the "name" as the key.*
Invoice	*No changes required. There is no concept of an invoice name in this dimension. This is the only dimension we use a key value (Invoice Number) as the name.*
Item	*Remove:* Stock Item Key *New Key Attribute:* Stock Item • **KeyColumns:** Stock Item Key • **NameColumn:** Stock Item
Salesperson	*Remove:* WWI Employee ID *New Key Attribute:* Employee • **KeyColumns:** WWI Employee ID • **NameColumn:** Employee

Figure 4.20 – Dimension and hierarchy definitions

> **Reminder**
> Be sure to save your work on a regular basis.

Adding hierarchies to your dimensions

Hierarchies are key to good design in all business intelligence models. However, in multidimensional models in SSAS, they are even more important. They enhance the user experience, improve performance, define aggregation levels, and refine storage patterns for the data.

Let's dig into some basics about hierarchies that you should know about. First, we need to differentiate between **natural** and **unnatural or artificial** hierarchies:

- A **natural** hierarchy is a set of attributes in a dimension that are related in a pattern from the smallest to the largest group. For example, a common natural hierarchy is date. We know that a year has four quarters, each quarter has 3 months, and that each month has between 28 and 31 days. The following diagram illustrates the pattern we look for in natural hierarchies:

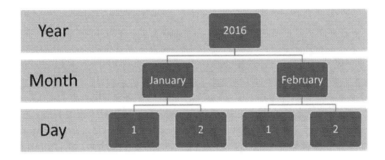

Figure 4.21 – Sample date hierarchy

- An **unnatural or artificial** hierarchy is when the attributes are not related in a *natural* pattern and can have inconsistent group sizes throughout. These hierarchies are typically helpful to the business for analysis but are not organized well in the data. A clothing dimension provides a clear example of this type of hierarchy.

The natural hierarchy might contain Type (outdoor, indoor), Style, and Product or the item of clothing. However, the business may want to create an artificial hierarchy using different attributes, such as Color and Size. The business now wants a hierarchy that uses the following pattern: Season, Style, Color, Size. The following diagram illustrates the imbalance between natural and artificial hierarchies based on the data:

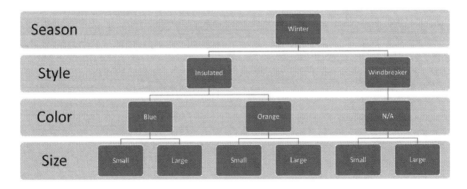

Figure 4.22 – Unnatural or artificial hierarchy of clothing

This is not ideal as it cannot be optimized for SSAS. While it is possible to create these in SSAS, it is typically not recommended. This is particularly true now that tools such as Power BI can handle those requirements easier in their design tools. We will be creating natural hierarchies in our dimensions in the next section.

Creating and updating attribute hierarchies

Once a dimension has been created, every attribute is created as a two-level hierarchy. The levels are **All** and the attribute itself. As we discussed previously, this is to support aggregations and storage. When measures are added later, each attribute will be aggregated at the **All** level and the individual attribute level. In some cases, this is what we want. However, we typically do not deal with most attributes in isolation, which is why we create hierarchies.

We will start with the City dimension. Go to the **Design** tab for the City dimension. If you have closed your tabs or Visual Studio, reopen the project, expand the Dimensions folder, and double-click the City dimension to reopen the **Design** tab. You should be looking at a screen similar to the one shown here:

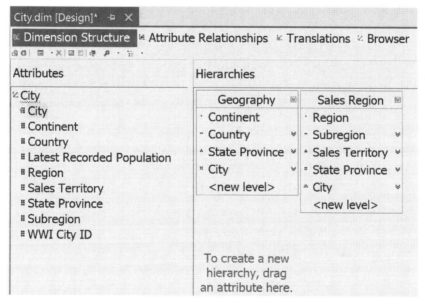

Figure 4.23 – Dimension design window with the Attributes and Hierarchies panes highlighted

We will be working with the **Attributes** and **Hierarchies** panes to create our hierarchies. Typically, we should know the hierarchy options through data or business analysis. In this case, we will be creating two hierarchies:

- **Geography**: This hierarchy will have a standard pattern for supporting continents to cities.

- **Sales Region**: This hierarchy will support the sales territories as defined by Wide World Importers.

We will create each hierarchy using the following steps:

1. We will start with the `Geography` hierarchy. Drag the `Continent` attribute onto the **Hierarchies** pane. This will create a new hierarchy with `Continent` as the first level.

2. Rename the hierarchy `Geography`. You can do this by clicking **Hierarchy** in the new hierarchy table or by changing the name in the **Properties** window, which can usually be found on the right-hand side of the screen, under **Solution Explorer**.

3. Next, drag the `Country` and `State Province` attributes onto the hierarchy you just created in that order. You should target the **<new level>** row in the `Geography` hierarchy. Don't worry if you drop it in the wrong place; you can move the levels around by dragging them up or down as needed.

4. Finally, add the `City` attribute as the lowest level. As the key or leaf level, this is where the relationship will be made with the fact table, as defined in the DSV.

5. Now that the `Geography` hierarchy is complete, we can create the `Sales Region` hierarchy by dragging the `Region` attribute onto an empty area of the **Hierarchies** pane.

6. As we did previously, rename the hierarchy by clicking into the header and giving it the name `Sales Region`.

7. The rest of the attributes to add are `Subregion`, `Sales Territory`, `State Province`, and `City` in that order.

Staying in the `City` dimension, you might have seen the warnings in the hierarchies letting you know that the attribute relationships are not in place. That is the next area of focus for our dimension build-out.

Adding attribute relationships

Attribute relationships in SSAS support additional query and storage optimizations. SSAS uses the defined relationships to consolidate processing operations, which makes loading data into a multidimensional model (processing) and querying data in the model more efficient. SSAS optimizes storage by using more compression when attribute relationships are defined.

When we created the hierarchies, SSAS assumed that the relationships could be optimized based on the relationships in the hierarchies. Let's add the relationships that support the hierarchies we have created.

When you open the **Attribute Relationships** tab on the City dimension's **Design** window, you will see that all the attributes that have been added to our hierarchies have been mapped to City. The remaining attributes are considered direct attributes that have a 1:1 relationship with City:

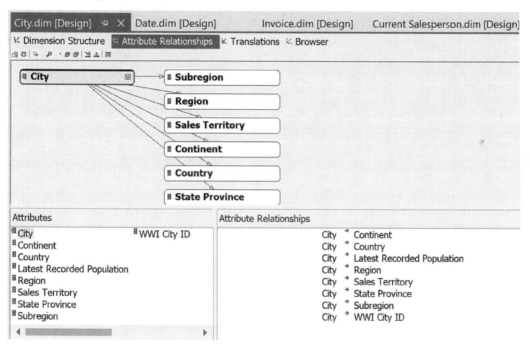

Figure 4.24 – City dimension attribute relationships before applying hierarchy mappings

You can change the mapping in a couple of ways. The easiest and sometimes the most frustrating option is to drag and drop. You can create the relationship between `Country` and `State Province` by dragging `State Province` onto `Country`. The resulting relationship is `State Province > Country`. If you do this the other way around, you will need to fix the relationship. You can also adjust or create the relationship by right-clicking on the attribute relationship in the pane on the right, under the mapping window. This will open the following dialog, where you can add or create the relationship you need:

Figure 4.25 – Edit Attribute Relationship dialog

Whichever pattern you choose, you should end up with a set of relationships that match the hierarchies we created.

> **Flexible versus Rigid attribute relationships**
>
> The default type of relationship for attributes is **Flexible**, which assumes that the relationship could change over time. This is the default and most flexible option, as the name suggests. However, this is less efficient if **Rigid** is a valid option. **Rigid** assumes the relationship will not change over time. A great example of a **Rigid** relationship is in the **Date** dimension. Years have quarters, quarters have months, and months have days. This will not change. However, an employee dimension could see people promoted to managers. This would require the **Flexible** relationship type to support the movement of attributes and their relationship over time. Be aware that if you choose **Rigid** and a change does occur, the model load may fail as a result.

Here is what the attribute relationships should look like when they are mapped correctly:

Figure 4.26 – City dimension attribute relationship configured correctly

Building out the rest of the hierarchies

You need to have followed the preceding steps for each of the dimensions we have created. Let's take a look at the hierarchy definitions for each of the remaining dimensions. Remember to create the hierarchy and then update the attribute relationships for each of these dimensions. We have included the attribute relationship image for each dimension as a reference.

> **Hierarchy and dimension names must be unique in the multidimensional model**
>
> When designing a multidimensional model, it is common to have names repeated in the design. When working with hierarchies and dimensions, your hierarchy names need to be unique within the model; otherwise, you will get a build error. For example, the Current Item and Item dimensions have the same structure, while the Brand hierarchy we are creating will need to be named differently to prevent conflicts. We will also use Customer Hierarchy in the Customer dimension to differentiate the hierarchy from the dimension.

Here is the attribute relationship for the Current Item and Item dimensions:

- Current Item dimension:

  Hierarchy Name: **Current Item Brand**

  Hierarchy Levels: **Brand** > **Stock Item**

- `Item` dimension:

Hierarchy Name: **Item Brand**

Hierarchy Levels: **Brand** > **Stock Item**:

Figure 4.27 – Current item and item dimensions attribute relationships

Here is the attribute relationship for the `Customer` dimension:

- `Customer` dimension:

Hierarchy Name: **Customer Hierarchy**

Hierarchy Levels: **Category** > **Buying Group** > **Bill To Customer** > **Customer**:

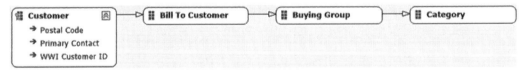

Figure 4.28 – Customer attribute relationships

Here is the attribute relationship for the `Date` dimension:

- `Date` dimension:

Hierarchy Name: **Calendar**

Hierarchy Levels: **Calendar Year** (**Calendar Year Label** attribute renamed `Calendar Year`) > **Calendar Month** (Calendar **Month Label** attribute renamed `Calendar Month` in the hierarchy) > **Date**

Hierarchy Name: **Fiscal**

Hierarchy Levels: **Fiscal Year (Fiscal Year Label)** attribute renamed `Fiscal Year` in the hierarchy) > **Fiscal Month (Fiscal Month Label** attribute renamed `Fiscal Month` in the hierarchy) > **Date**

Hierarchy Name: **ISO Week**

Hierarchy Levels: **ISO Week Number > Date**:

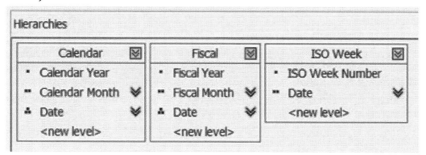

Figure 4.29 – Date dimension hierarchies

Once you've created the hierarchies, you should set the relationships up like so:

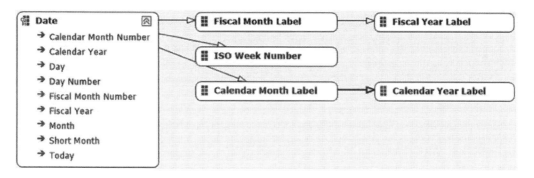

Figure 4.30 – Date dimension attribute relationships

Here is the attribute relationship for the `Invoice` dimension:

- `Invoice` dimension:

Hierarchy Name: **Invoice Hierarchy**

Hierarchy Levels: **Invoice Year > Invoice Month > Invoice Date > Invoice Number**:

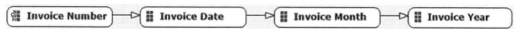

Figure 4.31 – Invoice dimension attribute relationships

Here is the attribute relationship for the `Salesperson` dimension:

- `Salesperson` dimension – *no hierarchies or updates to attribute relationships required*

Now that we have all the dimensions built, along with their hierarchies, we can load and preview the data. The next section describes how you can process your dimensions, which will load the data into SQL Server 2019 Analysis Services.

Processing the dimensions

Processing in SSAS multidimensional models is the method of loading the data into the multidimensional database. At the end of this chapter, we will dive into processing techniques in more detail. The focus of this section is processing our dimensions. We will walk through processing the `City` dimension in this section. By doing this, you will be able to apply these steps once more so that you can process the rest of the dimensions. Some of the setup here is for the entire project and will be repeated in the processing section at the end as well.

Prepping your project for processing

The following steps only need to be done if you have not already set up the deployment properties for your project. For these steps to work, SSAS in multidimensional mode should be running:

1. Right-click on the project name in **Solution Explorer** and select **Properties** from the menu.

2. This will open **Property Pages** for the project. You will see the **Configurations Properties** page and three sections called **Build**, **Debugging**, and **Deployment**.

3. In the **Build** section, set **Deployment Server Edition** to **Developer**.

4. In the **Deployment** section, set **Server Name** to the server you have running in multidimensional mode. In most cases, **Localhost**, the default option, will not be correct if you set your environment up with named instances, as recommended in *Chapter 1, Analysis Services in SQL Server 2019*.

5. Click **OK** to apply these changes.

   Your project should now be ready to deploy to Analysis Services. Let's take a look:

6. Right-click on the `City` dimension and select **Process…**.

7. This step only applies if you have made changes to the project since the last time it was processed. You will see a message that states **The server content appears to be out of date. Would you like to build and deploy the project first?**. Select **Yes** to continue with the build and deployment.

8. Once the project changes have been built and deployed, you will see a **Process Dimension** dialog box. We will spend more time on processing options later in this chapter. For this section, leave the default settings as is and click **Run** to continue.

9. Once this has completed, you can close all the open windows.

10. Now, go to the **Browser** tab in the `City` dimension's **Design** tab to explore the hierarchies you've created. You will also see the other hierarchies, which are single levels under the **All** level.

Solving impersonation issues while processing

One of the most common and annoying issues with SSAS in a development, non-enterprise network environment is due to impersonation. You may recall when we created the data source at the beginning of this chapter that we used **Use the credentials of the current user** for impersonation. This impersonation has served us well for development and my work for you as well.

In my setup, this did not work when processing because the current user is the *SSAS NT Service* account, which is running the service. This is a default service that was user created when my account was set up. To work around this issue, I added that user account to my `WideWorldImportersDW` database in the `db_datareader` role. If you have issues with processing, you can use this option. I would not recommend this for production use. A system account with the appropriate permissions should be used to manage this scenario. We will discuss this in detail in *Chapter 11*, *Securing Your SSAS Models*. If you want to implement the solution I used quickly, run the following scripts in **SQL Server Management Studio** when it's connected to your **SQL Server Data Engine** instance.

First, you will need get your service account name from our **Services console** or **SQL Server 2019 Configuration Manager**. In my case, the account name is NT Service\ MSOLAP$DOWSQL2019. Here are the scripts you need in order to add this user to your data warehouse:

```
USE [master]
GO
CREATE LOGIN [NT SERVICE\MSOLAP$DOWSQL2019] FROM WINDOWS WITH
DEFAULT_DATABASE=[master], DEFAULT_LANGUAGE=[us_english]
GO
```

```
USE [WideWorldImportersDW]
GO
CREATE USER [SSASMDSys] FOR LOGIN [NT SERVICE\
MSOLAP$DOWSQL2019]
GO
USE [WideWorldImportersDW]
GO
ALTER ROLE [db_datareader] ADD MEMBER [SSASMDSys]
GO
```

Depending on your environment setup, this option may not work. In some cases, using a Windows account may work. These issues typically affect development environments that are not connected to an **Active Directory** domain. If you are connected to a domain, service accounts will support a more cohesive solution.

Processing the rest of the project

Now that we have successfully processed the City dimension, you can choose to process everything we have created so far by right-clicking the project name and selecting **Process All**. This will confirm everything is working. If you have any errors, fix them and process everything again. You can also choose to process them one at a time so that you can deal with issues on a smaller scale. You must remember that the process queries the source database and replaces the data with new data. When working with larger multidimensional models, this can be a time issue. If your development environment is not very powerful, you could even experience issues with our project.

Whether you process the entire database or one object at a time, a processing log is displayed at the end. This provides the processing time and row counts for all the dimension attributes and hierarchies that have been processed. You should take a moment to explore the log to see the details of the work you have done. You should also browse the dimensions to see how the data will be presented in end user tools. This is an excellent way to handle issues early in the design process.

Updating our dimensions

If you have taken the time to browse the data, you may have noticed some issues with our dimensions. The obvious issue is ordering dates. We would like them ordered by date, not name or label. We will fix that order in this section, as well as the order for the Salesperson dimension.

Another issue is with the `Customer` dimension. `Bill To Customer` and `Customer` have duplicate values in the `Customer` hierarchy for the head office of both *Tailspin Toys* and *Wingtip Toys*. These are the two customers that are currently available in our data. We will implement **ragged hierarchy** principles here to hide duplicate values. Let's get started with fixing the sort order in our dimensions.

Fixing dimension and hierarchy orders

By default, dimension and hierarchy attributes are sorted by the key in the attribute. You can sort attributes by other attributes in the dimension. Let's fix one so that you have an example to work with. We will start with the **Date** dimension. SSAS knows how to sort dates properly, so the lowest level, **Date**, is sorted correctly. However, we need to fix the **Month** levels. Both the **Fiscal** and **Calendar** hierarchies have issues with the **Month** level sorting. The **Year** and **Date** levels are fine. Let's get started:

1. Open the **Date** dimension's **Design** window.

2. Click on the `Calendar Month Label` attribute in the **Attributes** panel. This is the attribute that's used in the **Calendar Hierarchy Calendar Month** level.

3. In the **Properties** panel, we need to add `Calendar Month Label` to the **NameColumn** property.

4. Next, we need to add the `Calendar Month Number` attribute to **KeyColumns**. In this dialog, `Calendar Month Number` needs to be on top of the list. This effectively makes the key a combination of both.

5. In the **Properties** panel, find the **OrderBy** property. **OrderBy** should be set to **Key**.

6. Process the dimension and browse the change. (You may need to click the **Reconnect** button at the top of the **Browser** window to refresh your results.)

7. Repeat this process for the `Fiscal Month Label` attribute.

We can also change our `Item` and `Salesperson` dimensions so that they use **Name** instead of **Key** for the sort order. Let's walk through changing the `Salesperson` dimension:

1. Open the `Salesperson` dimension's **Design** window.

2. Select the `Employee` attribute in the **Attributes** panel.

3. In the **Properties** panel, locate the **OrderBy** property.

4. Change this from **Key** to **Name**. `Salesperson` will now be sorted by **Employee** (which is the full name) instead of the `WWI Employee ID` value that's used in **Key**.

5. Process the dimension and review the results.

6. Repeat this process with the `Current Item` and `Item` dimensions on the `Stock Item` attribute.

You can apply the same pattern if you have other attributes you would like to change the order of.

Ragged hierarchies

Ragged hierarchies are used when a hierarchy has levels that are skipped or end early. This happens often in geography dimensions, for example. If you have customers in Europe and Canada, you may have different levels of hierarchy.

Let's look at a Canadian hierarchy:

- **Country**: Canada
- **StateOrProvince**: Ontario
- **City**: Dinorwic

Now, let's look at a customer hierarchy in Norway:

- **Country**: Norway
- **StateOrProvince**: NONE
- **City**: Oslo

How is this handled in the data? Often, we repeat the city name in **StateOrProvince** if it is not in the underlying data or structure. So, Olso would look as follows in the hierarchy:

- **Country**: Norway
- **StateOrProvince**: Oslo
- **City**: Oslo

The issue with this is that no one wants to see this in their report tools. We can remove the second Oslo in the hierarchy by selecting the **StateOrProvince** level in the hierarchy and changing the **HideMemberIf** property for the level to **OnlyChildWithParentName**. This will make the unused level invisible to the report tools.

Let's put this to use with our `Customer` dimension. We know that `head office` for both Wingtip Toys and Tailspin Toys is repeated in the `Bill To Customer` and `Customer` levels of `Customer Hierarchy`. Here is how we resolve this issue:

1. Open the `Customer` dimension's **Design** window.

2. Select the `Customer` level in `Customer Hierarchy`.

3. In the **Properties** pane for that level, change **HideMemberIf** from **Never** to **ParentName**. This will hide that level when both levels have the same name.

Impact of ragged hierarchies

In the geography example, we introduced an artificial level that will have no data associated with it. This means that Oslo levels will return the same values , no matter which level we viewed. However, with our example, data may exist at the `Customer` level for either head office. This means we will not see the specific order of data for the head offices if it exists. We will leave this in place in our model to demonstrate ragged hierarchies. However, you will need to evaluate the user experience to ensure you display the data as expected to your users.

Using Parent-Child relationships

We do not have an example of Parent-Child relationships in our model. However, as you continue to develop your skills with multidimensional design, you will find that implementing this type of relationship is fairly easy. Two of the most common examples are chart of accounts (general ledgers) and employee reporting structures. Often, that data has an unknown number of levels in it. This results in the underlying table having both a key and a parent key. The following is a partial screenshot of the properties window for a dimension with the various properties that support Parent-Child dimensions:

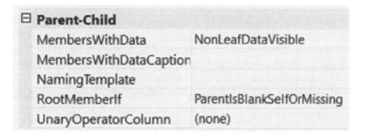

Figure 4.32 – Parent-Child properties

The two key properties to consider are **RootMemberIf** and **MembersWithData**. **RootMemberIf** helps SSAS determine where the *top* of the hierarchy is. For example, if the top level of your corporate hierarchy is the president and the parent key is null, then you would use **ParentIsBlankSelfOrMissing**.

MembersWithData helps determine if we display data at intermediate levels. In our previous example, you may have `President > Vice President > Director` in your hierarchy. You have the option to show data at intermediate levels, which assumes you have data at those levels. In some cases, the only data that matters is at the leaf level. We encourage you to experiment with this property to confirm you have the user experience you need.

One last callout that is unique to multidimensional models is **UnaryOperatorColumn**. When working with a chart of accounts, the aggregation and signs change as you traverse the hierarchy. For example, expenses are represented as positive numbers until they are at the same level as revenue. Unary operators specify how to aggregate and sign data in the model. This information will have to be part of the dimension table and can be specified here. This is a very powerful implementation and one of the reasons financial analytics are often easier to implement in multidimensional models.

Cleaning up dimension hierarchy lists

We have done a lot of work with our dimensions already. However, there is one more cleanup task we need to implement to make the user experience better for our users. This task involves removing or hiding attributes that are not required in the dimensions.

For example, the `Date` dimension should only have the hierarchies exposed. As shown in the **Dimension Browser** tab, all the attributes that are not used in the hierarchy are exposed to the users. This is not a great user experience as those attributes are not very valuable when they're not contained in a hierarchy:

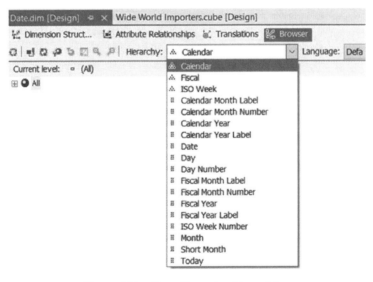

Figure 4.33 – Date dimension hierarchies

You can remove these hierarchies from the list by hiding them. Let's take a look at how to do this:

1. From the **Dimension Structures** tab, select an **Attribute** you want to hide.

2. In the **Properties** pane, find the **AttributeHierarchyVisible** property and set it to **False**.

Complete this task for every attribute in the **Date** dimension you want to hide. We will plan to hide all of them, leaving only the hierarchies we explicitly made visible to users. Hiding these hierarchies only affects the user experience. We can still use these attributes when creating hierarchies or custom calculations.

This concludes our work on dimensions. Next, we will be adding measure groups to see how dimensions slice and dice our data.

Adding cubes and measure groups

In multidimensional models, cubes typically map to fact tables in our data source. They have relationships to all the relevant dimensions and contain measures that can typically be aggregated. Before we dig into creating our cubes and measure groups, let's talk databases and cubes.

In multidimensional models in SSAS, a database generally refers to the overall structure of the SSAS model. When SSAS was first introduced, only one measure group was supported, so the entire structure was referred to the common term *cube*. As the product matured, the structure became more complex. When we talk about the multidimensional model, we are usually referring to the database. The model or database is made up of dimensions, cubes (which contain multiple measure groups), the DSVs, and data sources. In SSMS, you will see a similar structure to Visual Studio. The project in Visual Studio is the equivalent of the database in SSMS. That being said, *cube* can also refer to the entire database, even though cubes are specific structures in the model and used by users and developers alike.

Measure groups in SSAS are typically organized around fact tables and share a common set of dimensions. This pattern follows the dimensional model paradigm and is why it is important to have star schemas to support multidimensional models.

Creating the cube and measure groups

In this section, we will create our cube so that it contains our measures. Follow these steps:

1. In **Solution Explorer**, right-click the **Cubes** folder and select **New Cube…** to open the **Cube Wizard** window.

2. Click **Next** on the opening screen.

3. Select **Use existing tables** on the **Select Creation Method** screen, and then click **Next**.

4. On the **Select Measure Group Tables** screen, select the `Sales` and `Invoice Sales` tables, and then click **Next**.

5. On the **Select Measures** screen, click the `Sales` and `Invoice Sales` checkboxes to unselect all the measures.

6. Under `Sales`, select the following measures to include: `Quantity`, `Unit Price`, `Tax Rate`, `Total Excluding Tax`, `Tax Amount`, `Profit`, `Total Including Tax`, `Total Dry Items`, `Total Chiller Items`, and `Sales Count`.

7. Under `Invoice Sales`, select the following measures to include: `Invoice Total Excluding Tax`, `Invoice Tax Amount`, `Invoice Profit`, `Invoice Total Including Tax`, `Invoice Total Dry Items`, `Invoice Total Chiller Items`, `Invoice Count`, and `Sales Count-Invoice Sales`.

8. Once the measures have been selected, click **Next**.

9. On the **Select Existing Dimensions** screen, select all the dimensions if they have not been selected already. Click **Next**.

10. On the **Select New Dimensions** screen, deselect any options here. We do not need to add any suggested dimensions. Click **Next**.

11. Change the name of the cube to **Wide World Importers** and click **Finish**.

You should now see the Wide World Importers Cube's **Design** window. Congratulations – your first cube with two measure groups has been created! You should see something like the following in your Cube **Design** window:

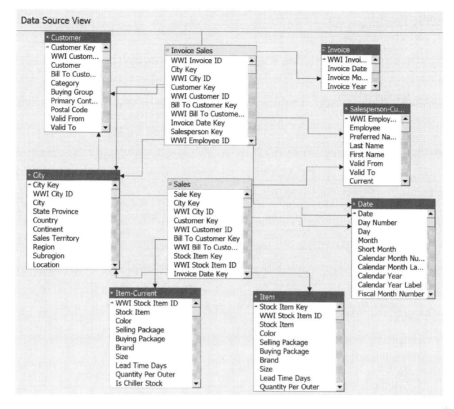

Figure 4.34 – First view of the Cube Design window

The rest of this section will explore the tabs in the Cube **Design** window. While we may not change each section here, the goal is to make sure you understand their purpose and can implement what you need to deliver specific solutions in your business.

Before moving on to the next section, process the project and resolve any errors.

Reviewing the cube's structure and modifying measures

The specific panes in the **Cube Structure** tab are **Measures**, **Dimensions**, and **Data Source View**. You can add or modify measures in the **Measures** pane. If you click a measure, you can review the properties for that measure, including its aggregation, format, and source. In the **Dimensions** pane, you can add a dimension or go to the **Design** window for a dimension from that pane. If you need a new dimension or need to remove or add a dimension to the cube structure, you can do that here. The other cube pane is **Data Source View**. This is the visual diagram of the underlying structure that supports the cube and its measure groups.

Modifying measures

Now, we are going to modify some measures. Cubes present measures based on the settings here. The primary focus will be on the aggregation functions and their formats. Let's modify the `Quantity`, `Total Including Tax`, and `Tax Rate` measures in the `Sales` measure group. You should update these for each measure in both measure groups before leaving this pane. These examples should help you understand the basics.

Modifying the Quantity measure

The `Quantity` measure is the quantity of items ordered. We will review the key attributes and add a format string in these steps:

1. Select **Quantity** under **Sales** in the **Measures** panel.

2. In the **Properties** panel, find **AggregationFunction** and confirm it is **Sum**.

3. Next, find the **FormatString** property and set it to `#,##0.00;-#,##0.00`. Then, remove `.00` from both to set this properly for integers, which is the data type for **Quantity**. The resulting format string should be **#,##0;-#,##0**.

With that, you have just formatted the **Quantity** measure. If you prefer to use parentheses for negative numbers, the format string would be **#,##0;(#,##0)**.

Modifying the Total Including Tax measure

The `Total Including Tax` measure is the total sales amount for the order, including tax, as the name suggests. We will review the key attributes and add a format string in these steps:

1. Select `Total Including Tax` under `Sales` in the **Measures** panel.

2. In the **Properties** panel, find **AggregationFunction** and confirm it is **Sum**.

3. Next, find the **FormatString** property and set it to `$#,##0.00;($#,##0.00)`.

Modifying the Tax Rate measure

The Tax Rate measure is the tax rate that's applied to each line. We will review the key attributes and add a format string in these steps:

1. Select Tax Rate under Sales in the **Measures** panel.

2. In the **Properties** panel, find **AggregationFunction** and change it to Average of Children. This will result in the average being used for the dimensions selected. It will change depending on the filters and slicers used in a query. While true for all measures, it important to remember that an average aggregation typically cannot be added to other measures because the math becomes an issue. When using averages as an aggregation, you will need to confirm it is returning the results you expect.

3. Next, find the **FormatString** property and set it to #,##0.00;-#,##0.00.

You should be able to use these patterns to update the remaining measures in both measure groups. There are other aggregations that can be used here, including Count, Min, Max, and even None.

> **Distinct counts in multidimensional models**
>
> **Distinct count** aggregations should only be used in their own measure groups. This is recommended to prevent adverse performance on queries that do not require this measure. If you need to add a distinct count, you should add a new measure group and select **Distinct Count** for the aggregation type. Then, you should select the attribute to perform the distinct count on. This will create a new measure group in the cube that will manage the distinct count measure. Refer to Microsoft's and other community documentation for additional information on managing distinct count aggregations in multidimensional models.

Reviewing dimension usage

This tab highlights the importance of the **Bus Matrix** we referenced in *Chapter 3, Preparing Your Data for Multidimensional Models*. This tab visualizes the actual implementation of measures with the dimensions. Here is what you should expect to see on this page if your cube has been organized correctly, as per the steps outlined in this book:

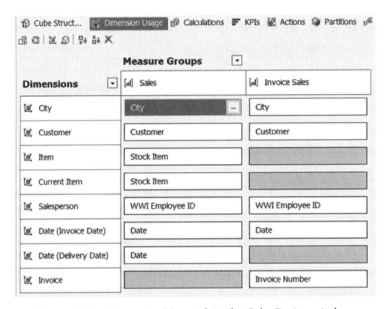

Figure 4.35 – Dimension Usage tab in the Cube Design window

Now that we have the dimensions set up, we can add more capabilities to our model.

Reviewing calculations and KPIs

The next two tabs are the focus of *Chapter 5, Adding Measures and Calculations with MDX*, where we'll dig into MDX and calculations. For now, you can skip these.

Creating an action

Actions are a great feature available in SSAS cubes. An action will allow you to drill through to details, open a report, or open a URL based on where you are in the data. It uses the data available to build out the action.

> **Note**
> Be aware that actions are not supported in all end user tools. For example, they are supported in Excel, but not in Power BI.

We will add a **drillthrough** action to our cube, as follows:

1. In the **Actions** tab of the Cube **Design** panel, right-click the **Action Organizer** pane and select **New Drillthrough Action**.

2. This will add the new action to the **Action Organizer** pane. You will see the properties for the action in the middle pane.

3. Rename the action `Drill to Details`.

4. Next, we need to select our drillthrough columns. In the **Drillthrough Columns** section, select the `Item` dimension table and choose all the fields.

5. On the next line, select **Measures** and choose the `Quantity` field.

6. On the next line, select `Invoice Date` and choose the `Date` field.

7. Process the cube. With that, your action should be in place. If you want to test it, you can use Excel to connect to the database and try it out. We will dig into using Excel in *Chapter 9*, *Exploring and Visualizing Your Data with Excel*.

Reviewing our partitions

On the **Partitions** tab, you will see the default partitions that have been created for our measure groups. Partitions physically separate the data in our measure groups into different buckets. These can be used to reduce processing time and effort for measure groups. While our cube does not require these since processing performance is fine in single partitions, let's walk through adding year partitions to the `Sales` measure group.

Our `Sales` measure group contains data from 2013 through 2016. We will create four partitions:

- `2013 and previous`
- `2014`
- `2015`
- `2016 to Current`

We will use the Partition Wizard to help us create our partitions. In production environments, you need to plan on creating new partitions as new data comes in. Some of those techniques will be covered later in this book. Let's get started:

1. Select **Source** in the `Sales` partition (line 1) and click the ellipsis (**...**) to open the **Partition Source** dialog box.

2. Change **Binding Type** to **Query Binding**.

3. Add `[Sales].[Invoice Date Key] <= '12/31/2013'` to the **WHERE** clause at the end. This will filter the current partition for dates from 2013 and earlier.

4. Rename the partition `Sales 2013`.

5. In the **Properties** pane, find **EstimatedRows** and set it to `61000`. You can check the row count in SSMS by querying the source table with the same filter. When using partitions, this helps the aggregation wizard make better choices about aggregations.

6. Click **New Partition…** to launch the **Partition Wizard** window in order to create the next partition.

7. Click **Next** on the opening screen.

8. Select the `Sales` table on the **Specify Source Information** screen and click **Next**.

9. On the **Restrict Rows** screen, select **Specify a query to restrict rows**. This will open a query like the one we saw when we modified the first partition. Add `[Sales].[Invoice Date Key] BETWEEN '1/1/2014' and '12/31/2014'` to the **WHERE** clause. **Check** your work and click **Next**.

10. Leave the default values as is and click **Next** on the **Processing and Storage Locations** screen.

11. Rename the partition `Sales 2014`. Choose **Design aggregations later** and click **Finish**.

12. Follow the same process for the `Sales 2015` partition.

13. Set **EstimatedRows** for the `Sales 2014` partition to `70000`.

14. Set **EstimatedRows** for the `Sales 2015` partition to `75000`.

15. For the `Sales 2016 to Current` partition, use `[Sales].[Invoice Date Key] >= '1/1/2016'` in the **WHERE** clause. Set **EstimatedRows** for this partition to `35000`.

When you are done, your **Partitions** tab should have the following partitions for the `Sales` measure group:

Item	Partition Name ▲	Source	Estimated Rows	Storage Mode	Aggregation Design
1	Sales 2013	SELECT [Cube].[Sales].[Sale Key],[Cube].[Sales].[City Key],...	61000	MOLAP	AggregationDesign
2	Sales 2014	SELECT [Cube].[Sales].[Sale Key],[Cube].[Sales].[City Key],...	70000	MOLAP	AggregationDesign
3	Sales 2015	SELECT [Cube].[Sales].[Sale Key],[Cube].[Sales].[City Key],...	75000	MOLAP	AggregationDesign
4	Sales 2016 to Current	SELECT [Cube].[Sales].[Sale Key],[Cube].[Sales].[City Key],...	35000	MOLAP	AggregationDesign

New Partition…   Storage Settings…

Figure 4.36 – Sales measure group partitions

We did not change the **Storage Mode** option. This option enables support for **Relational Online Analytical Processing (ROLAP)**, which is used for direct relational querying from the cube. This is typically done to support real-time techniques so that we can view data changes as they occur. **Multidimensional Online Analytical Processing (MOLAP)** is typically the best option to choose for performance reasons. This is the default option and how multidimensional models are stored. Aggregations will be covered in the next section.

Process your model and resolve any errors. Next, we will add aggregations to our model.

Reviewing and creating aggregations

Aggregations are used to improve the query performance of your model. A balance has to be struck between too many aggregations, which can bloat the size of the model and ultimately hurt your processing and query performance, and too few aggregations, which keeps the cube smaller but makes performance an issue. When first creating a cube, the best plan is to let the Aggregation Design Wizard help you design them. Once you have deployed the model and there has been a lot of usage, you can use the **Usage Based Optimization** wizard to target aggregations to improve the user experience directly. For our model, we will use the Aggregation Design Wizard to create our initial aggregations.

Let's add aggregations to our `Sales` measure group:

1. Expand the `Sales` measure group on the **Aggregations** tab.

2. Right-click on **Unassigned Aggregation Design** and pick **Design Aggregations** to launch the wizard. Click **Next** on the opening screen.

3. You will see the partitions we created in the previous section. Select them all and click **Next**.

4. On the **Review Aggregation Usage** screen, you will see all the dimension attributes that can be targeted for aggregation. **Default** allows the wizard to decide on the amount of aggregation to use. The other settings should only be used if you have familiarity with the usage patterns and can provide guidance to the wizard. For our example, we will leave the defaults in place. Click **Next**.

5. The **Specify Object Counts** screen lets you enter estimates for the counts for all attribute and measure groups. Alternatively, you can click **Count** and the wizard will count them all. If you have any performance issues due to the size of the data, networking, or compute, you should enter the estimates yourself. Our dataset is small, so having the wizard count should not be an issue. Click **Count**. Once it's done this, you can expand the dimensions to see the counts. Click **Next** when you are done.

6. The next screen is **Set Aggregations Options**. The wizard will estimate and build an aggregation design based on the options selected. **Storage** will likely not be an issue for us. **Performance Gain** is a decent option for us to use here. I like to let it run and click **Stop** when it starts to slow down (meaning it is finding fewer options). You can choose any of these options. We are going to use the **I click Stop** option. Select that option, and then click **Start** to kick off the wizard. You can stop it whenever or let it run until it is done. The following screenshot shows where I stopped my wizard. Yours will likely look a bit different:

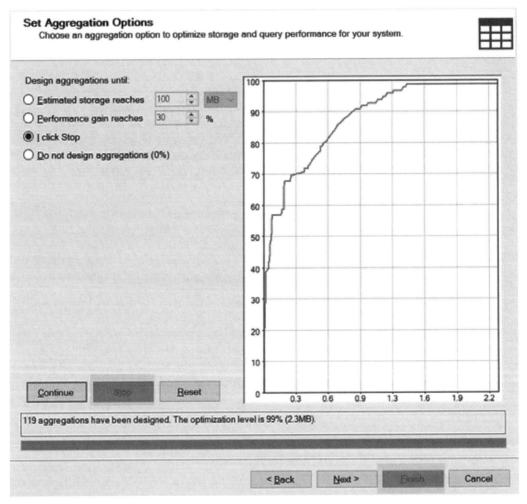

Figure 4.37 – Aggregation Design Wizard completed with 99% optimization using 2.3 MB of storage

7. Click **Next** to move on to the final step.

8. Give the aggregation design a name, such as `Initial Sales Aggregation`, and choose the **Save aggregations but do not process them** option. Click **Finish**.

We can repeat this process for the `Invoice Sales` measure group. If you take a look at the **Specify Object Count** screen, you should notice that the counts are partially filled out based on the work we did with the `Sales` measure group. Now, process your project.

Reviewing and creating a perspective

Perspectives are like views in SQL Server databases. They allow you to create analytic views, which can make browsing the cube or creating reports easier. Let's create a simplified view of our `Invoice Sales` data:

1. Right-click in the empty space of the **Perspectives** tab. Choose **New Perspective**.

2. You will see that a new perspective has been added next to the **Object Type** column. Rename the perspective `Invoicing`.

3. Deselect the `Sales` measure group.

4. Deselect the `City`, `Current Item`, `Item`, `Delivery Date`, and `Salesperson` dimensions.

5. Only select `Customer Hierarchy` in the `Customer` dimension and `Invoice Hierarchy` in the `Invoice` dimension.

6. Only select the `Invoice Total Including Tax` and `Invoice Count` measures from the `Invoice Sales` measure group.

7. Save and process your model.

Reviewing translations

Translations allow you to supply a specific language for the names of dimensions, measures, and other viewable objects. You can also manage translations for dimension attributes on the **Translations** tab. You can do this for each dimension.

Browsing our cube

We have been building out a lot of functionality, and you have likely already used this to view your changes. We recommend processing the cube one more time to make sure all your changes are in place:

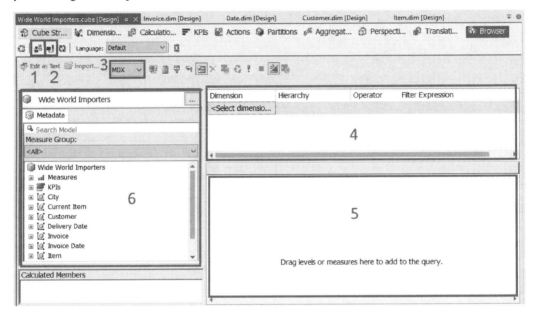

Figure 4.38 – Opening the cube browser

Here are some key things to be aware of in the browser:

1.   This is the **Change User** button. You can choose which user experience you want to see. This is related to securing your cube data and can involve filtered objects and data.

2.   This is the **Reconnect** button. Use this after processing your model so that you can see the latest changes.

3.   This dropdown is how you toggle between **MDX** and **DAX**. In most cases, you will use **MDX** when working with multidimensional models.

4.   This area is the filter area. You can drag a dimension here to limit the results of the query. Add a date filter here. Drag the Invoice Date dimension to this area. Leave **Operator** set to **Equal**. In **Filter Expression**, select **CY2014**. This will filter the results to invoice dates in calendar year 2014.

5. This is the metadata area. From here, you can drag measures, KPIs, and various dimension components, including the full dimension, hierarchies, and attributes, to the query area. You can also change the metadata view by selecting a different cube or perspective at the top. Click the button next to **Wide World Importers** at the top of the metadata and change the view to the **Invoicing** perspective.

6. This is the query area. You drop items from the metadata area here to build the query. You will see the results as you build. You need at least one measure and one dimension to see data here. Drag Bill To Customer from Customer Hierarchy, Invoice Count, and Invoice Total Including Tax to the query area. The results are filtered for CY2014. You should see the following output. Click the link in the query area to execute the query:

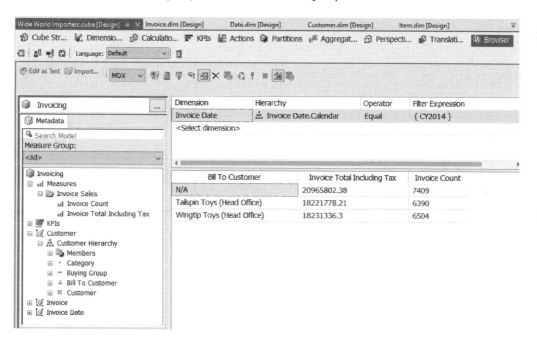

Figure 4.39 – Sample query using the cube browser

This concludes the build portion of the multidimensional model.

Summary

At this point, you have successfully created an Analysis Services multidimensional project. You have added dimensions and cubes to the project. You have also deployed your project as an Analysis Services database and processed that database so that you can load it with data. You now have a cube that supports basic analytics, which means you can browse the cube right now using tools such as Excel or Power BI. We wrapped up our build and deployment by browsing the data we deployed to the cube.

In the next chapter, we will continue to expand the cube by adding calculations and KPIs to it. We will also explore our data using SSMS and MDX.

5

Adding Measures and Calculations with MDX

Now that we have the cube built, the time has come to enhance it with MDX. **MDX**, or **multidimensional expressions**, is the language used to query a multidimensional model and build calculations in the cube. In this chapter, we will introduce the core concepts of MDX for building measures, calculations, and queries. While MDX has some similar syntax and structure to SQL, the implementation and results are not similar. We will use MDX to expand the functionality in the cube with measures, calculations, and KPIs. Measures and calculations can be used to standardize business metrics for all users. **KPIs**, or **key performance indicators**, are used to visualize performance and trending against specified goals.

In this chapter, we're going to cover the following main topics:

- Introducing MDX basics – SELECT, FROM, WHERE
- Adding calculations and measures to your cube
- Adding KPIs to your cube
- Exploring more MDX expressions

Technical requirements

In this chapter, we will be using the **WideWorldImportersMD** Analysis Services database from *Chapter 4, Building a Multidimensional Cube in SSAS 2019*. You should connect to the database with **SQL Server Management Studio**. You will be using the SSAS database and the cube created in *Chapter 4, Building a Multidimensional Cube in SSAS 2019*.

This chapter will also require the use of **SQL Server Management Studio** to execute the queries and build out most of the MDX examples. **Visual Studio 2019** will be required to add calculated measures and KPIs to **WideWorldImportersMD**.

Introducing MDX basics – SELECT, FROM, WHERE

MDX serves two primary purposes when working with multidimensional data – querying data and enhancing the cube. In this section, we will walk through the basics of building a query with measures. We will be working in SQL Server Management Studio for this section. You will need to have your cube processed in order to create the queries.

Understanding multidimensional query concepts

SQL is a *tabular* query language. It returns data in columns and rows. A multidimensional model has more depth than columns and rows. This means you can have rows, columns, and other dimensions. Conceptually, every data point in a measure group is intersected by every level on every dimension in the cube. This will allow you to navigate the model in different ways. While MDX has the same core language construction as SQL, it adds expressions that support navigating data multidimensionally. Now you know why they are called cubes. Let's evaluate some of these key concepts and syntax.

Dimensions

We created dimensions in the previous chapter when we built the cube. Dimensions are the building blocks for MDX. For example, if we build a calculation for average sales, a dimension defines the context for the average. Dimensions slice and filter the data to build the context for the measure and aggregation. What are average sales by month for each customer? In this request, sales are the measure. Month and customer are the dimensions. Average sales are measured in the context of the date and customer dimensions.

> **The Measure dimension**
>
> One unique characteristic of a multidimensional model is that the measures in a measure group are also organized as a dimension called **Measure**. The **Measure** dimension has a single level, so there is no concept of drilling into the **Measure** dimensions by itself.

Levels

Hierarchies define the levels in a dimension. Because of this, MDX supports levels within hierarchies of a dimension to drill up and down the levels in the dimension. For example, you can use MDX to determine the values at `Year`, `Month`, and `Day` levels within the `Date` dimension. Revisiting our current cube, we have defined many hierarchies that will be implemented with levels in our MDX code. As we have been looking at our `Date` dimension, it is important to understand that dimensional data can be represented with multiple hierarchies and, as such, have different ways to view the data in code, as shown in our current `Date` dimension. The following screenshot shows the **Date** dimension hierarchies:

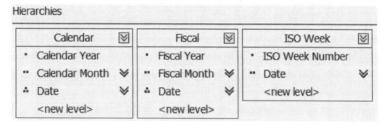

Figure 5.1 – Calendar hierarchies

As you can see in our **Date** dimension, we have three hierarchies. We can traverse the **Date** dimension using those hierarchies. You will also notice that the lowest level is **Date**, which represents a shared leaf or lowest level. Logically, you can use this relationship in the levels to do comparisons between the **Fiscal Month** and **Calendar Month** levels in the hierarchy. This type of level traversal is one of the unique features in MDX.

> **Every hierarchy has an ALL level by default**
>
> Every attribute and user-defined hierarchy contains an `ALL` level by default. This is effectively an unfiltered level that allows you to build measures and queries with MDX without having to explicitly reference every dimension. In most cases, this will not impact your designs, but it is important to understand that this exists. In some cases, you may have a business need to change the default value for a dimension. This is rare. When this occurs, you will have to account for the new default value's impact on your calculations.

Members

Members are the actual values or names for specific items in a level. Keeping up with the `Date` dimension, we already called out the `Year`, `Month`, and `Day` levels. The members representing individual items in each level would be `Year = 2019`, `Month = March`, and `Day = 3/15/2020`. Levels contain all the members within the level and understand the relationships between those members.

Using levels and members together, the model understands that the `Date` dimension has user-defined hierarchies that have specific levels. It can navigate between members in a dimension based on the relationships between levels.

Tuples and sets

Tuples represent the intersection of members. A tuple represents the *address* of a location within a multidimensional model. Let's look at our example of average sales from the previous section. It used two dimensions – `Date` and `Customer`. A tuple is a grouping of members that acts as the address for the value we plan to act upon. In our example, we were seeking the average by month and customer. To be more specific, we want to see this for June 2019 for Customer1. This would result in a tuple such as the following: `([June 2019],[Customer1])`. At this intersection of dimensions, we want to see the average sales.

> **Tuples implicitly include all dimensions in the address**
>
> One of the most difficult concepts when working with MDX and multidimensional models is that every measure is intersected by every dimension and hierarchy, whether you include it or not. As mentioned previously, this is typically the ALL level. In our preceding example, the tuple could be expanded to include `([All Fiscal],[All Product], [All Item], [June 2019], [Customer1])`.

Sets are a group of tuples that can be used to determine a set of combined values between related tuples. For example, you may use a set of tuples if you wanted to get the average sales for June and July in our example. That set could be expressed similar to this: `{ ([Customer1],[June 2019]), ([Customer1],[July 2019]) }`. This would give us the average sales for Customer1 across June and July for 2019.

When working with MDX, many of the expressions return a set to allow you to perform a calculation. Set expressions allow you to get all the children of a specific level or even related members within the dimension.

Square brackets, curly braces, and parentheses

This section is key to understanding MDX. Let's call it the punctuation of MDX. I have used the various formats in the preceding examples. Let's clarify them here:

- **Square brackets** [] are used to encapsulate the names of the design elements and members. In SQL, you do not need to use square brackets if the name has no spaces. However, a well-designed cube will actively use spaces to make the cube more user-friendly. First, when working with design elements, we should use square brackets: [Calendar Year]. This level contains all the years as members. In our Date dimension, the Calendar Year level of the Calendar hierarchy contains the following levels: [CY2013], [CY2014], [CY2015], [CY2016], and [Unknown].

- **Parentheses** () are used to encapsulate tuples, as shown previously. However, parentheses are also used with functions and math as is typical for most expression languages.

- **Curly braces** {} are used to encapsulate sets within MDX.

- **Periods or dots** . are used to build definitions for members and to build out functions. In our cube, we have a customer called Tailspin Toys (Sylvanite, MT). That customer is represented in MDX as [Customer].[Customer Hierarchy].[Customer].&[2]. This is the definition for that member: Dimension.Hierarchy.Level.Member. If we wanted to discover the parent or the next level up, we would express that as [Customer].[Customer Hierarchy].[Customer].&[2].Parent. This will return the parent level value for us. We can continue to move up the tree by asking for the next parent level as well: [Customer].[Customer Hierarchy].[Customer].&[2].Parent.Parent. This is how periods are used to both define the member as well as build out functions in the expressions.

Properties

We have covered a lot of details for navigating your cube with MDX. Every design element has properties that can be referenced as needed. The most common properties are Key, Name, and Value. Key is required and is typically displayed by default. In the previous example, the customer member was represented as &[2]. The ampersand (&) signifies that the value we see is the key. You can pull up the Name property by using .Name or the Value property by using .Value. These properties are helpful when refining a report or when you have a value you want to use in a calculation that you do not include in the aggregated data. You define the properties during the dimension design.

Putting it together

MDX uses familial relationship language to describe the relationships of data and design in the model. Examples include functions such as Descendants, Ancestors, Children, Parent, and even Cousin. We will use a number of these expressions to show the strength of MDX as it successfully performs complex calculations. By looking at these relationships as family trees, you should be able to better visualize how the model stores the data and allows you to traverse the tree to produce those calculations.

Understanding query structure

When you look at a typical query, whether SQL or MDX, you see the core structure of SELECT, FROM, WHERE. However, in a cube, these do not operate the same. Let's break down the core structure to understand it better:

- SELECT is used to define the content you want to show. In MDX, you should tell it where you want that data to go. Is it on the column, row, or a different dimension? This is where we start to struggle understanding MDX. You can actually return a number of dimensions with your data. The issue is that most tools only visualize rows and columns. In a query, you specify ON COLUMNS or ON ROWS. You should also know that ON 0 is equal to columns and ON 1 is equal to rows.

- FROM is used to define the cube you are querying. In all of our examples, this will be [Wide World Importers].

- WHERE is used to slice or filter the data across a set definition. The set is used to define the filter for the query, such as the month you want to see the data. This is used to effectively create a sub cube or subsection of the cube to apply the rest of the query to.

Building your first query

Enough discussion about the *what*; time to dig into *how*. We will be using **SQL Server Management Studio (SSMS)** to create a query. The process to create a query is as follows:

1. Open SSMS and connect to your SQL Server Analysis Services database:

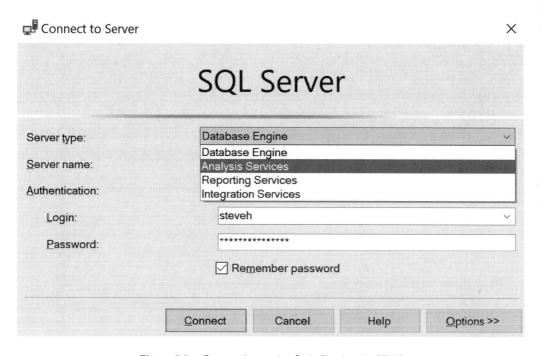

Figure 5.2 – Connecting to Analysis Services in SSMS

In this dialog, enter the name of the Analysis Services multidimensional instance you created. You should see the following in your **Object Explorer** (the screenshot shows various sections expanded to see the details of the deployed cube):

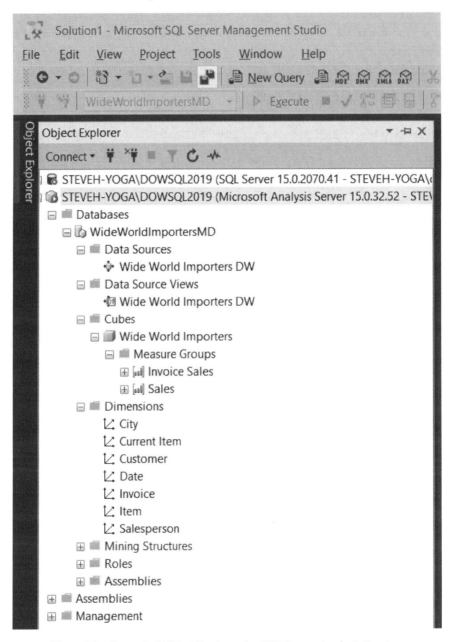

Figure 5.3 – Expanded Object Explorer for SQL Server Analysis Services

If you do not see a similar list of objects, refer to the previous chapter for building out your Analysis Services multidimensional model.

2. As shown in the following screenshot, you can click **New Query** or **MDX** to create a new MDX query window in SSMS:

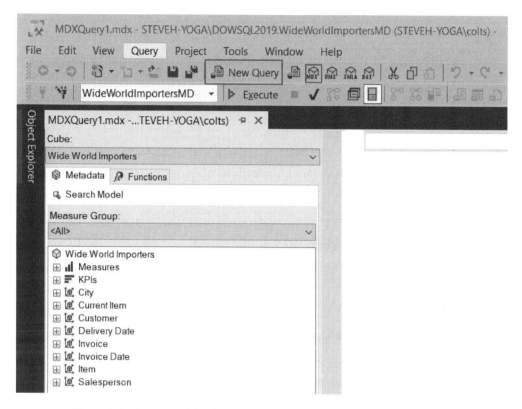

Figure 5.4 – Selecting either New Query or MDX to create a new MDX query

Once you have connected to the database, you should see the **Wide World Importers** cube in the **Metadata** tab displaying the structure and contents of your cube. (You may see **Invoicing** in the dropdown; if so, choose **Wide World Importers** from the list to continue.) The metadata information is very helpful when creating queries. You can drag and drop from the metadata window to the query panel to make queries. This helps with understanding how to shape the various data elements for the query.

3. Let's create a query that will show us the total sales for each **Bill To Customer**. We will build on this as we move forward. Start by typing SELECT into the query window.

4. Drag the **Bill To Customer** level from the **Customer** hierarchy onto the query window, as shown in the following screenshot:

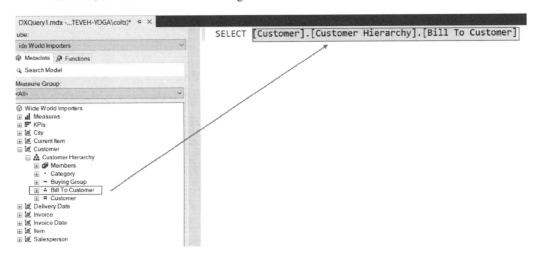

Figure 5.5 – Dragging Bill To Customer to the query window

5. Add the `.members` function to the level name. This will return the set of members.

6. Specify `On Columns` or `On 0` to specify you want to see this in the columns.

7. Next, add the `FROM` clause and drag or type the cube name `[Wide World Importers]` into the `FROM` clause.

8. Execute the query. It will display the default measure, which may vary for you as we did not explicitly set this value when we built the cube.

Your query should look like the following:

```
SELECT [Customer].[Customer Hierarchy].[Bill To
Customer].members on 0
FROM [Wide World Importers]
```

Your results should be similar to the following table:

N/A	Tailspin Toys (Head Office)	Wingtip Toys (Head Office)
3,283,017	2,847,550	2,820,061

Figure 5.6 – MDX query results

9. Add a WHERE clause or slicer for the fiscal year 2015. Expand the Invoice Date dimension. Then, expand the Invoice Date.Fiscal hierarchy and the Fiscal Year level. Drag FY2105 onto the query window after your WHERE clause. Your query should look like the following:

```
SELECT [Customer].[Customer Hierarchy].[Bill To
Customer].members on 0
FROM [Wide World Importers]
WHERE [Invoice Date].[Fiscal].[Fiscal Year].&[FY2015]
```

Execute the query and you should see smaller numbers in your results.

Now that you have successfully built your first query with MDX, we are going to walk through some variations that will be helpful for you to know as we continue to expand the cube and build more sophisticated queries. You can use principles from this section, such as drag and drop to simplify query building, in the next few sections.

Adding explicit measures to our query

In this example, we will modify the query to specify the measures we want to display and move our customers to the rows. Here is the final query:

```
SELECT { [Measures].[Profit],[Measures].[Total Excluding
Tax],[Measures].[Total Including Tax]} on columns
, [Customer].[Customer Hierarchy].[Bill To Customer].members on
rows
FROM [Wide World Importers]
WHERE [Invoice Date].[Fiscal].[Fiscal Year].&[FY2015]
```

You can see that we added three new measures as a set that we want to display on columns. We moved our existing customers to the rows. The rest of the query remained the same. You should now see results shaped like the following table:

	Profit	Total Excluding Tax	Total Including Tax
N/A	$10,279,633.40	$20,640,521.35	$23,736,602.00
Tailspin Toys (Head Office)	$8,254,259.50	$16,598,727.35	$19,088,538.64
Wingtip Toys (Head Office)	$8,281,417.95	$16,588,072.25	$19,076,285.13

Figure 5.7 – MDX query with filter results

Using NON EMPTY

As you recall, all queries include the intersection of all possible combinations. In a cube, many of those combinations can result in an empty value, or null. This is common in cubes and can cause some query results to be more than what we wanted. Let's look at the following query samples and their results. In this query, we want to see which customers had any Red items delivered in the calendar year 2015. In this query, we will introduce two new functions – crossjoin and children:

- crossjoin creates a Cartesian set that includes all the possible tuples between the Customers and Quantity measures. This allows us to specify the measure we are looking for and segment it by customer.

- children returns a set of next-level members or children in the hierarchy. In this case, we want to see the data by month for the year 2015. By requesting the children, we will get all the months.

By using these techniques, we can get all the results for who had Red items delivered. Here is the query:

```
SELECT CROSSJOIN([Customer].[Customer Hierarchy].[Customer].
members, [Measures].[Quantity]) on 0
, [Delivery Date].[Calendar].[Calendar Year].&[CY2015].children
on 1
FROM [Wide World Importers]
WHERE [Item].[Color].&[Red]
```

When you execute the query, you should see results like mine:

	Unknown	Tailspin Toys (Sylvanite, MT)	Tailspin Toys (Peeples Valley, AZ)	Tailspin Toys (Medicine Lodge, KS)	Tailspin Toys (Gasport, NY)	Tailspin Toys (Frankewing, TN)
	Quantity	Quantity	Quantity	Quantity	Quantity	Quantity
CY2015-Jan	288	(null)	(null)		5	(null)
CY2015-Feb	320	9	(null)	(null)		9
CY2015-Mar	276	(null)	(null)	(null)	(null)	(null)
CY2015-Apr	395	7	(null)	(null)		4
CY2015-May	290	(null)	(null)	(null)		5
CY2015-Jun	338	(null)		6	(null)	(null)
CY2015-Jul	331	(null)	(null)	(null)		4
CY2015-Aug	227	(null)	(null)	(null)	(null)	(null)
CY2015-Sep	340	(null)	(null)	(null)	(null)	(null)
CY2015-Oct	324	(null)	(null)	(null)	(null)	(null)
CY2015-Nov	286	(null)	(null)	(null)	(null)	(null)
CY2015-Dec	320	(null)		7	(null)	(null)

Figure 5.8 – MDX query with crossjoin results

What you will notice right away is that in many cases, there are no values within many of the cells. If you scroll more to the right, you will see stores where no reds have ever been purchased, such as `Frankewing, TN`. In our results, we want to hide those stores as they don't help. We can do that by adding `NON EMPTY` to the beginning of our `Customer` line. This will remove customers who have never had a red-colored item delivered. Here is the updated query. You can confirm the results in your execution:

```
SELECT NON EMPTY CROSSJOIN([Customer].[Customer Hierarchy].
[Customer].members, [Measures].[Quantity]) on 0
, [Delivery Date].[Calendar].[Calendar Year].&[CY2015].children
on 1
FROM [Wide World Importers]
WHERE [Item].[Color].&[Red]
```

After executing this query, you should be able to view only the customers who have had red-colored items delivered to them.

Adding calculated members to our query

We built the cube with many measures built into it, including `Quantity` and `Total Including Tax`. Both of those measures were designed to be summed. In the previous query, we used `Quantity` to determine how many red-colored items were delivered to our customers. Let's use that information to build out two measures we can use in our query – `[Measures].[Red Items]` and `[Measures].[% Red]`. Red items will be the sum of the quantity of items with the color red. We will use that measure to determine the percentage of red-colored items that were delivered.

When adding calculated members to a query, use the `WITH` clause. Each new member has a member definition in this format: `MEMBER name AS expression`. The order in which you create the members also matters.

> **Member clause note**
> Do not separate your MEMBER clauses with commas.

MDX orders its operations from top to bottom. If you build a new member that depends on a member created after that member, the query will fail. We have simplified the query to better illustrate this process. Here is the query with the new members and a table with the results:

```
WITH MEMBER [Measures].[Red Items] as SUM([Item].
[Color].&[Red],[Measures].[Quantity])

     MEMBER [Measures].[% Red] as [Measures].[Red Items] /
[Measures].[Quantity], FORMAT_STRING = 'Percent'


SELECT {[Measures].[Red Items],[Measures].[Quantity],
[Measures].[% Red]} on 0
, [Delivery Date].[Calendar].[Calendar Year].&[CY2015].children
on 1
FROM [Wide World Importers]
```

Execute the query and you should see the following results:

	Red Items	Quantity	% Red
CY2015-Jan	719	223,080	0.32%
CY2015-Feb	772	203,682	0.38%
CY2015-Mar	761	236,371	0.32%
CY2015-Apr	868	248,418	0.35%
CY2015-May	801	234,430	0.34%
CY2015-Jun	852	217,218	0.39%
CY2015-Jul	871	263,206	0.33%
CY2015-Aug	666	209,793	0.32%
CY2015-Sep	758	226,627	0.33%
CY2015-Oct	859	240,157	0.36%
CY2015-Nov	748	217,457	0.34%
CY2015-Dec	784	217,631	0.36%

Figure 5.9 – Results for MDX query with custom members

Let's add a WHERE clause that filters out any item with N/A as the color. This will be a better reflection of Red choices when a color can be selected. To do this, we will use the EXCEPT function to create a set for our WHERE clause. Here is the updated query and its results:

```
WITH MEMBER [Measures].[Red Items] as SUM([Item].
[Color].&[Red],[Measures].[Quantity])

    MEMBER [Measures].[% Red] as [Measures].[Red Items] /
[Measures].[Quantity], FORMAT_STRING = 'Percent'


SELECT {[Measures].[Red Items],[Measures].[Quantity],
[Measures].[% Red]} on 0
,[Delivery Date].[Calendar].[Calendar Year].&[CY2015].children
on 1
FROM [Wide World Importers]
WHERE (EXCEPT([Item].[Color].[Color].members,{[Item].
[Color].&[N/A]}))
```

The updated results are shown as follows:

	Red Items	Quantity	% Red
CY2015-Jan	719	82,328	0.87%
CY2015-Feb	772	75,654	1.02%
CY2015-Mar	761	85,148	0.89%
CY2015-Apr	868	88,581	0.98%
CY2015-May	801	87,252	0.92%
CY2015-Jun	852	79,005	1.08%
CY2015-Jul	871	96,888	0.90%
CY2015-Aug	666	73,973	0.90%
CY2015-Sep	758	85,550	0.89%
CY2015-Oct	859	84,165	1.02%
CY2015-Nov	748	74,566	1.00%
CY2015-Dec	784	81,367	0.96%

Figure 5.10 – MDX query results with N/A values removed

You can see how the `Red Items` column values did not change, but the `Quantity` values have been filtered by the slicer, which also impacted the `% Red` column. You will see that results in MDX are impacted by all filters, slicers, and calculations.

Throughout the remainder of the chapter, we will continue to introduce new functions, expressions, and concepts to expand your knowledge of MDX. However, this is by no means exhaustive and you will find a lot of information on the internet relating to MDX code. Because there have been few updates to multidimensional model support in SQL Server Analysis Services, older content is still relevant to solving problems with MDX. Now, we will add calculations to our cube, which will enhance our ability to query and our users' experience with the data.

Adding calculations and measures to your cube

We created some calculations while querying the cube. Now, let's make those a permanent part of the cube. In this section, we will switch from SSMS as our primary tool to Visual Studio and the SSAS project. We will continue to use SSMS for testing and experimentation, so you will need to have both tools open. One other thing, we have been using `Red` for a lot of our analysis. We will expand on that for our examples. In our use case here, we will assume that our business users are trying to determine what colors have the most impact on their business. Let's expand the color analysis for our cube.

Using the calculations section

Reopen your Visual Studio project if it is not open already. Once you have the project loaded, open the **Wide World Importers** cube design window. In the design window, select the **Calculations** tab. This will be our starting point for adding calculated measures and named sets built with MDX. Let's walk through the key parts of the **Calculations** tab as follows:

1. You will be able to create measures and named sets in the query pane. You will also be able to add comments here to make sure other designers understand what the calculations do.

2. The **CALCULATE** function should not be removed. As the comment notes, removing it will affect how the cube is aggregated and is not required for any work we are doing here.

3. The **Script Organizer** pane will list the calculation items created. It is also a quick reference for the order in which the scripts will be executed.

4. **Calculation Tools** has much of the same content we worked with in SSMS when creating our queries. Drag and drop is supported here as well.

The previous four steps are highlighted in the following screenshot:

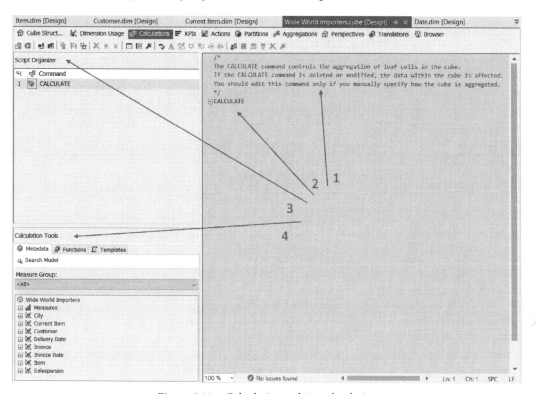

Figure 5.11 – Calculations tab in cube design

Now that you have a basic understanding of the **Calculations** tab, let's build out our color calculations.

Creating calculated measures

While you can type out the calculations directly in the **Calculations** tab, it is best to start by using the calculation creation form. Let's add our Red Items calculation to the cube using the form as follows:

1. You can open the form by right-clicking in the **Script Organizer** pane or by selecting **New Calculated Member** from the menu bar, as shown in the following screenshot:

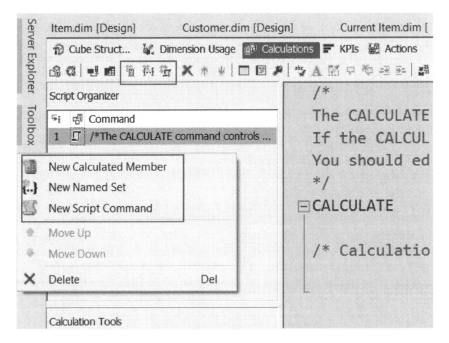

Figure 5.12 – Creating a new calculated member with the form

2. Select **New Calculated Member**, which opens the form shown here. We will walk through each value to create our Red Items calculated member:

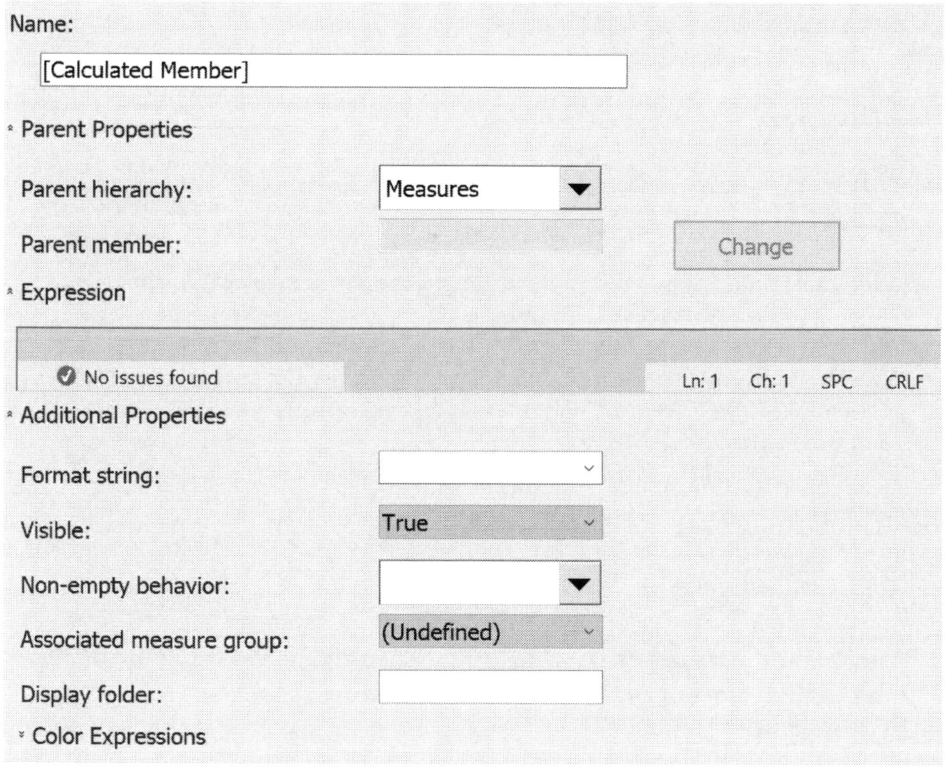

Name:

[Calculated Member]

᛭ Parent Properties

Parent hierarchy: Measures   ▼

Parent member: Change

᛭ Expression

> ✔ No issues found   Ln: 1   Ch: 1   SPC   CRLF

᛭ Additional Properties

Format string: ⌄

Visible: True   ⌄

Non-empty behavior: ▼

Associated measure group: (Undefined)   ⌄

Display folder:

᛭ Color Expressions

Figure 5.13 – New Calculated Member form

Let's discuss about some fields from the preceding screenshot:

- **Name**: The name will be [Red Items]. The square brackets are required in the form. It will not add them for you by default.

- **Parent hierarchy**: We are creating a calculated measure, so Measures is our **parent hierarchy**. You can create members that are part of other hierarchies or dimensions. You would select a different parent in that case.

- **Expression**: This is where the MDX calculation goes. Our calculation returns the quantity of red items:
  SUM([Item].[Color].&[Red],[Measures].[Quantity])

- **Format string**: This affects how the value is displayed in the end user tools. We would like to use the following format string: "#,##0;-#,##0". This option is not in the drop-down list. The closest is "#,##0.00;-#,##0.00", but we don't need decimal places. Your options are to type this string, including quotation marks, or choose the option with decimal places and remove them from the selection once you are done.

> **Format strings**
>
> Formatting the data for ease of understanding or standardization is common throughout cube design and MDX. Here are the basics to understanding format strings.
>
> **Strings**: Two options separated by a semicolon. The first value applies to all strings. The second value applies to nulls or empty strings. The value of this is that you can replace null with a value such as `No Data`.
>
> **Numbers**: Numbers have four options all separated by semicolons. The first value applies to positive numbers, the second applies to negative numbers, the third applies to zeros, and the fourth applies to null values. If you have one section, the format applies to all values. Typically, we use two options.
> **Dates**: Dates have a single section and a lot of options to support various types of display formats.
>
> There are also standard formats included, such as Short Date, which will format the date according to the system's short date format. If you want to dig into this more, Microsoft has a complete list of options online. Search for *MDX Format_ String* for more information.

- **Visible**: Some measures exist as supporting calculations. It is common to hide those by setting this property to `False`. In our case, we will leave this visible, which is the default, `True`.

- **Non-empty behavior**: Non-empty behavior instructs SSAS how to determine whether an empty value will be returned when a `NON EMPTY` query command is issued. You add measures to optimize this performance. In our case, we will select the `Quantity` measure, which means non-empty requests will use the `Quantity` measure to determine empty values instead of the calculation itself.

- **Associated measure group**: A cube can contain one or many measure groups. Our cube only has two measure groups, so we are not assigned the measure group. If you have several measure groups in your implementation, it will be helpful to users to associate the member with the best measure group.

- **Display folder**: This is an optional feature. We will use it to keep all our color calculations together. Enter `Color Analysis` as our display folder.

This is where the process feels a bit weird. You may have noticed that there was no save or close button on this form. This form has been writing the calculation to the script in the background. To see the work you have done, you need to change the view. The following screenshot shows you where the **Script View** and **Form View** buttons are on the toolbar:

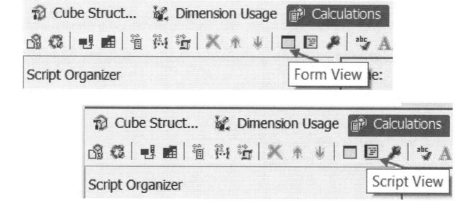

Figure 5.14 – Form View and Script View buttons in the Calculations tab

When you select **Script View**, you will see the entire script, including the work you were just doing. This view also hides the **Script Organizer** pane. When you are in **Form View**, you can go to each calculation or script to see whether there is a form for that specific calculation.

Go to **Script View** now. You will see the code that was generated for you. As you can see, each section is separated by semicolons. Your code should look like the following:

```
/*
The CALCULATE command controls the aggregation of leaf cells in
the cube.
If the CALCULATE command is deleted or modified, the data
within the cube is affected.
You should edit this command only if you manually specify how
the cube is aggregated.
*/
CALCULATE
;
CREATE MEMBER CURRENTCUBE.[Measures].[Red Items]
  AS SUM([Item].[Color].&[Red],[Measures].[Quantity]),
FORMAT_STRING = "#,##0;-#,##0",
NON_EMPTY_BEHAVIOR = { [Quantity] },
VISIBLE = 1 ,   DISPLAY_FOLDER = 'Color Analysis'  ;
```

As you can see, all the properties you set in the form are here. You can change the MDX here and it will be presented in the form with your changes.

Let's add a comment here. After the semicolon following `CALCULATE`, add the following code:

```
/* The next group of measures will be used for Color Analysis
*/
```

In our cube, we have eight identified colors. Use the **New Calculated Member** form to add calculated members for `Black`, `Blue`, `Gray`, `Light Brown`, `Steel Gray`, `White`, and `Yellow`. You should have eight measures in your calculations when you are done. You can also use the script view to cut and paste. Either option will result in the same work. However, the script view may result in errors if you are not careful.

The final step here is to go to **Form View** and move the `Red Items` calculated member below `Light Brown Items` as this will put them in alphabetical order. You drag the `Red Items` member to the location or use the arrow buttons located in the menu bar to manipulate its location.

Now is a good time to see our work in action. You can process our changes by clicking the **Process** button on the toolbar. Accept the default prompts. When the measure groups have completed processing, go back to SSMS and refresh your **Object Explorer** pane. You will now see a new folder in the `Measures` section called `Color Analysis`, which is where we are putting our calculations. Create a simple MDX query using one or more of your new measures. For example, let's create a query that shows the delivery of black and blue items each year:

```
SELECT {[Measures].[Black Items], [Measures].[Blue Items]} on 0
, [Delivery Date].[Calendar].[Calendar Year].members on 1
FROM [Wide World Importers]
```

As you can see, I no longer have to create the measures in each query; they are now a part of the cube structure itself.

Next, we need to add the percent of total measures to the cube. Using **Form View**, create the first measure using the following values:

- **Name**: [% Black Items]
- **Parent hierarchy**: Measures
- **Expression**: [Measures].[Black Items] / [Measures].[Quantity]
- **Format string**: "Percent"
- **Non-empty behavior**: Quantity
- **Display folder**: Color Analysis

Create the same calculation for each color as we did before. You will notice that we are using the calculated member we created previously in this calculation. The black percent member will fail when it is created before the black item count member. The dependency is sequential in the MDX script we are creating.

Creating named sets

Now that we have our calculated members created, we will look at creating a **named set**. A **named set** is a set created by MDX that we can reuse in our cube and related queries. When we created our calculations earlier, we added a slicer in the WHERE clause to eliminate items that did not have a color attribute as follows:

```
WHERE (EXCEPT([Item].[Color].[Color].members,{[Item].
[Color].&[N/A]}))
```

We can add this as a named set to use it in our calculations. Using **Form View**, select the [Yellow Items] calculated member from **Script Organizer**. Using the right-click menu or the toolbar, select **New Named Set**. This should open the **Named Set** form and place a new named set between your items' measures and % measures. In the form, there are fewer properties. For our new named set, complete the form with the following values:

- **Name**: [Items with Color]
- **Expression**: EXCEPT([Item].[Color].[Color].members, {[Item].
[Color].&[N/A]})
- **Type**: Dynamic
- **Display folder**: Color Analysis

You have created your first named set. We are using the Dynamic type for the named set. This means that the set will be re-evaluated based on the context established by the query. When the Static type is chosen, the set does not react to slicers in the WHERE clause or other influences. The set remains the same. Typically, Dynamic gives most users what they expect in cube querying. In certain cases, you may not want the set to recalculate each time for either performance (most common) or business reasons. Be sure to test both options in a variety of cases to validate that you are getting the response you desire.

Now that we have the new named set, we can use it in our % calculations. The business requirement is that the % of items of a specific color should only apply to items to which color can be a valid attribute. We should change the calculation expression to incorporate our named set as follows:

```
CREATE MEMBER CURRENTCUBE.[Measures].[% Black Items]
  AS [Measures].[Black Items] / SUM({[Items with
Color]},[Measures].[Quantity]),
FORMAT_STRING = "Percent",
NON_EMPTY_BEHAVIOR = { [Quantity] },
VISIBLE = 1 ,  DISPLAY_FOLDER = 'Color Analysis';
```

The denominator has been changed to use our new set with the Quantity measure. Now we have adjusted the calculation to meet the requirements of the business. Once you have applied those changes, process the cube. Next, we will build some KPIs to support our color analysis.

Adding KPIs to our cube

KPIs are used by businesses to evaluate performance over time. KPIs in multidimensional models in SSAS are server-based and can be used by various end user tools such as **Excel**. The advantage here is that a business KPI can be created and shared easily within an organization.

Understanding the basics of a KPI

A typical KPI is built on the following components:

- Goal or target
- Value or actual
- Status of the value compared to the goal
- Trend of the value to meeting the goal

These values can use indicators that typically work from a -1 to 1 value system. Here, -1 is measured as not meeting the goal, and 1 as meeting the goal. All these values are built with MDX, which is what we will dig into now.

Building your KPI

First, you need to open the **KPI** tab in the **Cube Design** window in your Visual Studio project. Once you have that open, create a new KPI by right-clicking in the **KPI Organizer** pane or selecting the **New KPI** option from the toolbar. This will open a form along the lines of what we used when creating calculated members, as shown in the following screenshot:

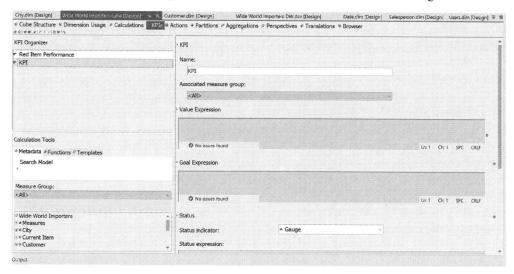

Figure 5.15 – New KPI form

Let's walk through creating a KPI for our cube, because a KPI is typically used to drive toward a goal. Continuing our theme of color analysis, our business wants to see the increase of the sale of red items by 10% **year over year** (**YOY**). Our KPI will be built with the following attributes:

- **Goal**: 10% red quantity growth YOY

- **Measure**: Red items

Our first step will be to add some more calculated members to support our KPIs. As part of the design and discovery process, it is common to use SSMS to work through the members you need and want to test with. You will find some *work in progress* code in GitHub that allows you to see some of the MDX queries used to explore the data for building the KPIs. Once the discovery is complete, the following supporting MDX calculated members need to be added to the cube. You can add these to the **Calculations** tab in the **Cube Design** window. I have added these members to a separate folder called KPI Support to keep us organized. Each measure works with [Measures]. [Quantity] and the [Invoice Date].[Fiscal] hierarchy, specifically with the [Fiscal Year] level. We will combine this measure with our various item colors to build out the KPIs. We can use them to create similar KPIs at a later time.

Here are the names and expressions for these calculations:

- `[Measures].[Current FY Quantity]`
  Purpose: Returns the total quantity for the current **fiscal year** (**FY**).
  Expression: `(ANCESTOR([Invoice Date].[Fiscal].currentmember, [Invoice Date].[Fiscal].[Fiscal Year]), [Measures].[Quantity])`

- `[Measures].[Previous FY Quantity]`
  Purpose: Returns the total quantity for the previous FY.
  Expression: `(ANCESTOR([Invoice Date].[Fiscal].currentmember, [Invoice Date].[Fiscal].[Fiscal Year]).prevmember, [Measures].[Quantity])`

- `[Measures].[Quantity YOY 10% Target]`
  Purpose: Calculates the current year target by multiplying the previous year quantity by 1.1.
  Expression: `[Measures].[Previous FY Quantity] * 1.1`

- `[Measures].[Quantity Status]`
  Purpose: Produces a value between -1 and 1 that can be used to signify the status of the KPI. If the current value is the previous FY value * 1.05 or less, the value will be -1. If it is greater than or equal to the target, the value will be 1. Between those amounts, the status will be set at 0.
  Expression: `CASE WHEN (ANCESTOR([Invoice Date].[Fiscal].currentmember, [Invoice Date].[Fiscal].[Fiscal Year]), [Measures].[Quantity]) < ((ANCESTOR([Invoice Date].[Fiscal].currentmember, [Invoice Date].[Fiscal].[Fiscal Year]).prevmember, [Measures].[Quantity]) * 1.05)`
  `THEN -1`
  `WHEN (ANCESTOR([Invoice Date].[Fiscal].currentmember, [Invoice Date].[Fiscal].[Fiscal Year]), [Measures].[Quantity]) > ((ANCESTOR([Invoice Date].[Fiscal].currentmember, [Invoice Date].[Fiscal].[Fiscal Year]).prevmember, [Measures].[Quantity]) * 1.1)`
  `THEN 1 ELSE 0 END`

Before we move on to creating the KPIs, there are several new expressions to add to your MDX vocabulary. ANCESTOR is a function that returns a member that is higher in the hierarchy. You can specify how many levels you want to go up or the specific level you want to go to. In our case, we want to be at the [Fiscal Year] level regardless of where we start.

Two member functions are used in these measures as well. currentmember refers to the member currently in context. It will be used as the reference point for the calculation. previousmember is used to go backward. nextmember also exists to move forward. In our case, if currentmember is FY2015, previousmember will return FY2014, and nextmember will return FY2016. These functions are used regularly to navigate between related members.

The final piece of code to note is the CASE statement. There are two common methods of handling this type of calculation – CASE and IIF. CASE is typically more efficient in processing, but IIF can work for simpler expressions. Both options evaluate an expression and return a result for a true and a false result. Learn both options so that you can have design options when creating MDX calculations.

Using our KPI form, here is the process we will go through to build this:

1. **Name**: Red Item performance

   Value Expression: In the value, we will use [Current FY Quantity] with [Item].[Color].&[Red]. This will give us the current year quantity, which is the value we will use as the *actual* value to compare with the goal. Here is the code: ([Measures].[Current FY Quantity], [Item].[Color].&[Red])

2. **Goal Expression**: The goal expression is the 10% target we created combined with the [Item].[Color].&[Red] level as well. Here is the code for the goal: ([Measures].[Quantity YOY 10% Target], [Item].[Color].&[Red])

3. **Status Expression**: The status expression uses the [Quantity Status] measure with the same [Item].[Color].&[Red] cross-reference. This will return -1, 0, or 1 depending on the criteria we set. Here is the code for the status: ([Measures].[Quantity Status], [Item].[Color].&[Red])

4. **Status Indicator**: Select the **Shapes** indicator type for our example. You should explore the built-in option to see how they react to your KPI.

This will complete our build. Be sure to process the cube when you have completed the KPI. If you want to explore more about using the KPIs, you can get more sophisticated using trends and other more advanced options. You can view the KPI indicators with **Excel**. We will dig into more about using **Excel** with your models in a later chapter, but this is really one of the best ways to confirm you have set up the indicators correctly. Here are the steps to connect Excel to your cube and view your KPIs:

1. Open **Excel** and connect to your **Analysis Services** server. The following screenshot describes where to find the connection you need to use:

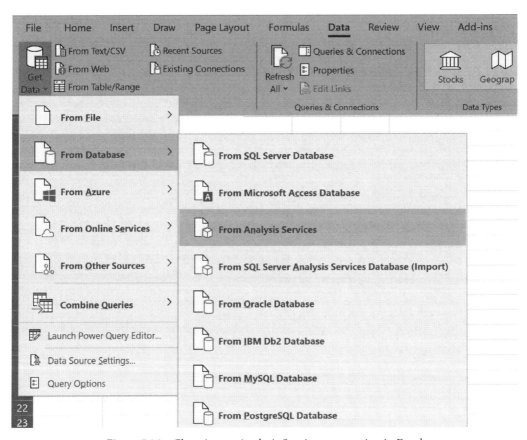

Figure 5.16 – Choosing an Analysis Services connection in Excel

2. Enter the name of your server and select the cube you have been working in. This will create an ODC connection for you to use in Excel.

3. For our purposes, we will choose to import the data to the current worksheet as a **PivotTable**, as shown here:

Figure 5.17 – Import dialog in Excel

4. In **PivotTable Fields**, search for **KPI** or scroll through the list until you find the KPI we created. Expand **Red Item Performance** and drag **Status** to the **Values** pane at the bottom.

5. Next, find **Invoice Date** in the field list. Expand the **Invoice Date.Fiscal** hierarchy and drag **Fiscal Year** to the **Rows** section. You should see something similar in your Excel workbook if your cube and the KPIs have no issues:

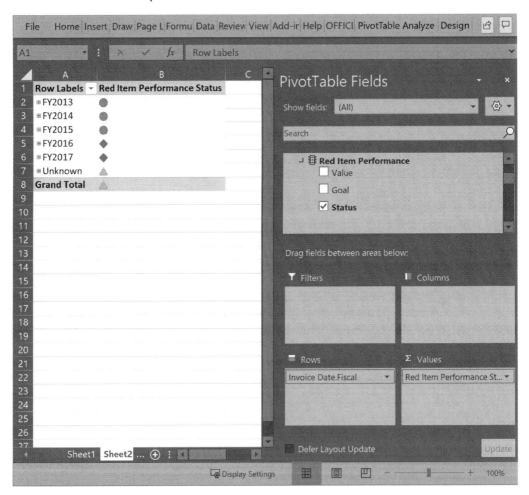

Figure 5.18 – KPIs displayed in Excel

Congratulations! You have added calculated members and KPIs to your cube. In the next section, we will explore some more MDX expressions so you can build more complex queries and calculations to meet your business needs.

Exploring more MDX expressions

Entire books have been written on MDX exclusively. MDX is a very powerful query and expression language. We have touched just a small part of what is possible. This section will present a few additional expressions and techniques for you to practice with. We will primarily be working in SSMS to illustrate both member creation and various query techniques. Any member created in SSMS can be moved to the cube, as we have demonstrated throughout this chapter.

Traversing hierarchies

Earlier in the chapter, we talked about how traversing the cube is like working with a family tree. Functions such as parent, children, ancestor, descendant, and even cousin exist in MDX. Here are some examples for you to use with our cube.

members

members returns all the members of a level or hierarchy depending on the context. We have used members in several queries already. Let's look at the City dimension for an easy example of using members. We can use members to determine which countries are included in our cube as follows:

```
select [City].[Geography].[Country].members on 0 from [Wide
World Importers]
```

As you can see, the members set function is a *dot* function. It will return all the members of the current level or hierarchy. In our case, we used a level, [Country], which resulted in only one result – United States. If you choose to remove [Country], the query will take a while to complete as it will return over 116,000 columns, which represent every value in the hierarchy.

parent

`parent` returns the member in the level above the current member. This function is a dot function that can be *stacked* and allows you to find grandparents as well. In this code example, we stack the `parent` function three-deep:

```
select { [Black Items] } on 0
, { [City] . [Geography] . [City] . & [114952]
  , [City] . [Geography] . [City] . & [114952] .parent
  , [City] . [Geography] . [City] . & [114952] .parent.parent
  , [City] . [Geography] . [City] . & [114952] .parent.parent.parent }   on
1
FROM [Wide World Importers];
```

The results are shown in the following table:

	Black Items
Tuscaloosa	736
Alabama	26,344
United States	1,101,101
North America	1,101,101

Figure 5.19 – Query results using the parent expression

As you can see here, we can ascend up the hierarchy using the `parent` function until we reach the top. Typically, we only use it up one level, but the functionality is there to use if needed.

children

We have discussed `parent`, and now we can delve into `children`. The `children` function is also a dot function. This function returns all the children in the next level down in the hierarchy. We can use the previously used example of Alabama. In this query, we want to see all the cities in Alabama. If we choose not to use the NON EMPTY keyword in the query, we will get all the cities regardless of whether they have data:

```
select [Black Items] on 0
, NON EMPTY [City] . [Geography] . & [Alabama] .children on 1
from [Wide World Importers];
```

descendants

descendants is one of the more complex hierarchy functions in MDX. It is very powerful with numerous variations. descendants returns data as sets of members. descendants uses a combination of current member position, targeted position, and the relationship between those two values to determine the set members.

Typically, you use the descendants function from a starting member. (There are other options, but they are more advanced and beyond the scope of this book.) You then specify the target level or number of levels from the current position. The number option is normally used with ragged hierarchies where the end is not uniform. We will focus our examples on the level version of the function.

The final option is very interesting. This option is the flag used to tell the function which set of data to return. There are eight different flags that can be implemented:

- SELF returns the values at the level specified. If it is at the level of the current member, it will return that member as well.

- AFTER returns the values below the level specified. It returns all the members after that level.

- BEFORE returns the values between the current member and the level specified. It will include the current member in the results, but no values from the level specified.

- BEFORE_AND_AFTER returns the values included in both the BEFORE and AFTER values, but not the specified values.

- SELF_AND_AFTER returns the level specified and below that level.

- SELF_AND_BEFORE returns the level specified and all members between the current member and that level, as well as the current member.

- SELF_BEFORE_AFTER returns all members from all levels below the current member and includes the current member as well.

- LEAVES returns leaf or lowest-level members between the current member and the specified levels. This option is very helpful when working with ragged hierarchies where the leaf levels often vary.

The following table illustrates how each flag affects what is returned when working with the descendants function:

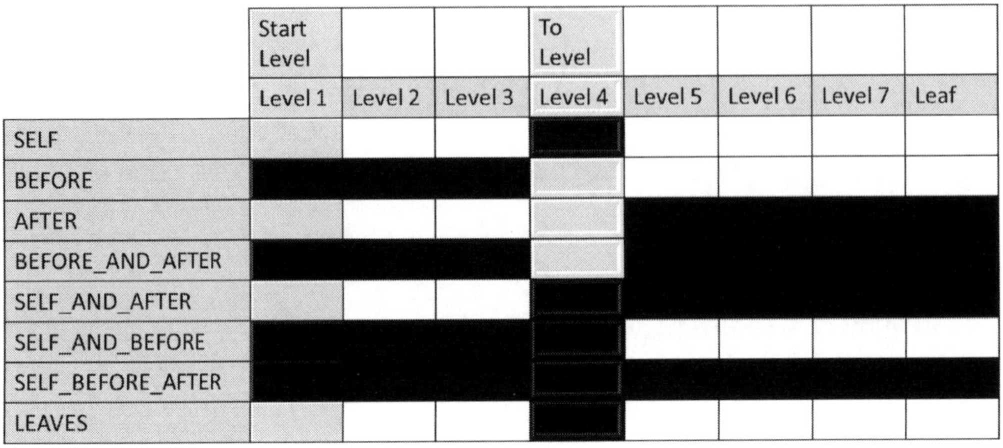

	Start Level			To Level				
	Level 1	Level 2	Level 3	Level 4	Level 5	Level 6	Level 7	Leaf
SELF				■				
BEFORE	■	■	■	▨				
AFTER				▨	■	■	■	■
BEFORE_AND_AFTER	■	■	■	▨	■	■	■	■
SELF_AND_AFTER				■	■	■	■	■
SELF_AND_BEFORE	■	■	■	■				
SELF_BEFORE_AFTER	■	■	■	■	■	■	■	■
LEAVES				■				

Figure 5.20 – Coverage by each descendant flag

Now that we understand the capabilities of descendants, let's walk through some examples using our cube. We will be using the Sales Region hierarchy in the City dimension. The starting point will be the Americas region. The target level will be the State level. Let's look at a few of the flag options with the same query.

The following queries illustrate the SELF, BEFORE, and AFTER flags in use. You will need to execute each query separately to generate the results shown later:

```
select {[Black Items]} on 0
, NON EMPTY descendants([City].[Sales Region].
[Region].&[Americas], [City].[Sales Region].[State Province],
SELF) on 1
FROM [Wide World Importers];
select {[Black Items]} on 0
, NON EMPTY descendants([City].[Sales Region].
[Region].&[Americas], [City].[Sales Region].[State Province],
BEFORE) on 1
FROM [Wide World Importers];
select {[Black Items]} on 0
, NON EMPTY descendants([City].[Sales Region].
[Region].&[Americas], [City].[Sales Region].[State Province],
AFTER)on 1
FROM [Wide World Importers];
```

SELF returns the `State` level values only. `BEFORE` returns three levels – `Region`, `Subregion`, and `Sales Territory`. `AFTER` returns the `city` level. The following table illustrates these results:

SELF	Black Items	BEFORE	Black Items	AFTER	Black Items
Puerto Rico (US Territory)	15,193	Americas	1,101,101	Aceitunas	44
Alaska	18,621	Northern America	1,101,101	Cataño	217
California	60,605	External	15,193	Corcovado	46
Hawaii	2,157	Far West	129,111	Indios	758
Nevada	7,986	Great Lakes	130,421	Isabela	267
Oregon	13,578	Mideast	162,179	Palmas del Mar	209
Washington	26,164	New England	52,019	Rafael Capó	169
Illinois	29,822	Plains	147,712	Rosa Sánchez	517
Indiana	20,724	Rocky Mountain	75,720	Aceitunas	1,647
Michigan	21,611	Southeast	238,934	Cataño	1,910
Ohio	37,250	Southwest	149,812	Corcovado	1,446

Figure 5.21 – MDX query results with descendant options

As you can see, you have a lot of ways to traverse down a hierarchy to return various sets that can be used in calculations.

FirstChild, FirstSibling, LastChild, LastSibling

These functions allow you to find the first or last child or sibling for a specific member. While this does not necessarily seem helpful for some dimensions, any specifically ordered dimension may find value using these functions. The child versions of the functions effectively return the first child in the children set. `sibling` functions operate in the same level. We don't have a lot of dimensions where the order is significant. For this example, we will use the `Date` dimension as it is the easiest to view the impact on:

```
select {[Black Items]} on 0
, NON EMPTY {[Invoice Date].[Calendar].[Calendar
Month].&[8]&[CY2015-Aug]
,[Invoice Date].[Calendar].[Calendar Month].&[8]&[CY2015-Aug].
firstchild
,[Invoice Date].[Calendar].[Calendar Month].&[8]&[CY2015-Aug].
lastchild
,[Invoice Date].[Calendar].[Calendar Month].&[8]&[CY2015-Aug].
firstsibling
,[Invoice Date].[Calendar].[Calendar Month].&[8]&[CY2015-Aug].
lastsibling} on 1
from [Wide World Importers];
```

Here are the results, including the members who are being referenced:

		Black Items
Current Member	CY2015-Aug	23,923
First Child	8/1/2015	140
Last Child	8/31/2015	640
First Sibling	CY2015-Jan	27,380
Last Sibling	CY2015-Dec	28,707

Figure 5.22 – MDX query results using child and sibling expressions

Sibling functions allow you to traverse the hierarchies in more interesting ways. This wraps up our discussion on hierarchy-focused MDX functions.

Exploring data with more MDX functions

In this section, we will explore some other commonly used functions that will help you build queries and calculations.

Crossjoin

We have used the `crossjoin` function once before in this chapter. Let's take a closer look at this function. The `crossjoin` function returns the cross product or Cartesian product between two sets. However, if both sets are in the same dimension, it will only return results that exist. The following queries and results illustrate these two methods of using `crossjoin`.

First, let's look at the more common usage, which is crossjoining two sets from different dimensions. If you want to eliminate empty values, use the NON EMPTY keyword in your query. In this query, we are going to create a crossjoin between December of the years we have and the states of Alabama and Georgia:

```
select [Black Items] on 0
, crossjoin({ [Invoice Date].[Calendar].[Calendar
Year].&[CY2013].lastchild,
    [Invoice Date].[Calendar].[Calendar Year].&[CY2014].
lastchild,
    [Invoice Date].[Calendar].[Calendar Year].&[CY2015].
lastchild,
    [Invoice Date].[Calendar].[Calendar Year].&[CY2016].
lastchild}
    ,
```

```
    {[City].[Sales Region].[State Province].&[Alabama],
      [City].[Sales Region].[State Province].&[Georgia]}) on 1
from [Wide World Importers];
```

Here are the results of the query using the `crossjoin` expression:

		Black Items
CY2013-Dec	Alabama	731
CY2013-Dec	Georgia	411
CY2014-Dec	Alabama	728
CY2014-Dec	Georgia	370
CY2015-Dec	Alabama	783
CY2015-Dec	Georgia	643
CY2016-Dec	Alabama	(null)
CY2016-Dec	Georgia	(null)

Figure 5.23 – MDX query results with the crossjoin expression

As you can see in the query results, we have effectively crossjoined the dates with the states in our sets. The next query illustrates the fact that crossjoining attribute hierarchies will only return those combinations with values. In this query, we are crossjoining items with the colors red and yellow with all possible sizes. As you can see, the results only represent existing combinations in the data:

```
select [Measures].[Quantity] on 0
, crossjoin({[Item].[Color].&[Yellow],[Item].[Color].&[Red]},
[Item].[Size].[Size].members) on 1
from [Wide World Importers];
```

Here are the results:

		Quantity
Yellow	1/12 scale	5,859
Yellow	1/50 scale	5,703
Red	1.5m	6,108
Red	1/12 scale	11,446
Red	1/50 scale	11,479

Figure 5.24 – MDX query results with crossjoin between color and size

As you can see in these results, not every size is returned. You need to keep this type of difference in mind to make sure you are getting the results you want from the function.

IIF and IsEmpty

IIf is used like the CASE statement we used to support our KPIs. This expression effectively tests a use case. If it results in true, then use the value in the second position; if it is not true, use the third value. Here is the structure: IIF(<condition>,<if true>,<if false>). IIF statements can be nested as well. You should use caution if you are nesting IIF statements to make sure your results are as expected.

IsEmpty is a function that determines whether a value is empty or null. It evaluates to TRUE or FALSE. We will use this in our IIF statement as part of the condition statement. In our next query, we will create a new member to evaluate whether the base measure is empty. If it is, the null value is replaced with the text No Sales:

```
with
member [Measures].[No Empty Quantity] as
IIF(ISEMPTY([Measures].[Quantity]),"No Sales", [Measures].
[Quantity])
select [Measures].[No Empty Quantity] on 0
, crossjoin({[Invoice Date].[Calendar].[Calendar
Year].&[CY2013].lastchild, [Invoice Date].[Calendar].[Calendar
Year].&[CY2014].lastchild, [Invoice Date].[Calendar].[Calendar
Year].&[CY2015].lastchild, [Invoice Date].[Calendar].[Calendar
Year].&[CY2016].lastchild}  ,
{[City].[Sales Region].[State Province].&[Alabama],   [City].
[Sales Region].[State Province].&[Georgia]}) on 1
from [Wide World Importers];
```

Here are the results with the null values replaced:

		No Empty Quantity
CY2013-Dec	Alabama	4198
CY2013-Dec	Georgia	2990
CY2014-Dec	Alabama	3507
CY2014-Dec	Georgia	2162
CY2015-Dec	Alabama	7186
CY2015-Dec	Georgia	4659
CY2016-Dec	Alabama	No Sales
CY2016-Dec	Georgia	No Sales

Figure 5.25 – MDX query with null values replaced

lag and lead

The last group of functions in this section is `lag` and `lead`. `lag` and `lead` move a number of positions before (`lag`) or after (`lead`) the current member. In our example here, we will use the `Date` dimension to illustrate this operation. We are building on some of the work we did with `lastchild`:

```
select [Black Items] on 0
,{ [Invoice Date].[Calendar].[Calendar Year].&[CY2013].
lastchild,
    [Invoice Date].[Calendar].[Calendar Year].&[CY2013].
lastchild.lag(1),
    [Invoice Date].[Calendar].[Calendar Year].&[CY2013].
lastchild.lag(6),
    [Invoice Date].[Calendar].[Calendar Year].&[CY2013].
lastchild.lead(1),
    [Invoice Date].[Calendar].[Calendar Year].&[CY2013].
lastchild.lead(6)} on 1
from [Wide World Importers];
```

These are the results:

		Black Items
Starting Month	CY2013-Dec	24,200
Month - 1	CY2013-Nov	20,988
Month - 6	CY2013-Jun	24,656
Month + 1	CY2014-Jan	25,534
Month + 6	CY2014-Jun	30,042

Figure 5.26 – MDX query results with lag and lead expressions

As you can see in the results, the `lag` and `lead` functions support some interesting results. While we used dates in our example, you can use these functions with sequential values, such as order or invoice numbers.

Creating more calculations with aggregation and math functions

We have been focused on a lot of functions to support various ways of traversing or grouping members to apply calculations. However, we have kept the calculations fairly straightforward. In this section, we will work with some common aggregation or math functions.

Sum

SUM is one of the most basic functions. It effectively sums values in a set. We have used this fairly extensively in this chapter. One key understanding is that any set can be used to define the context for the values to be summed:

```
MEMBER [Measures].[Red Items] as SUM([Item].
[Color].&[Red], [Measures].[Quantity])
```

This is our example from earlier in the chapter. This works by summing all the items that have a color attribute of red. You can swap out that section for any valid set using a variety of functions. This example illustrates a more complex example:

```
WITH MEMBER [Measures].[No Territories] as
SUM(
  EXCEPT(
    descendants([City].[Sales Region].[Region].&[Americas],
                [City].[Sales Region].[State Province], SELF)
  , {[City].[Sales Region].[State Province].&[Puerto Rico (US
Territory)],[City].[Sales Region].[State Province].&[Virgin
Islands (US Territory)]})
      , [Measures].[Quantity])
select {[Measures].[Quantity],[Measures].[No Territories]} on 0
from [Wide World Importers];
```

This query returns two values built on Quantity. The No Territories measure eliminates two US territories from the calculation. As you can see, multiple set operations occur in the calculation of the sum.

Count

COUNT can be a dot function or a normal function. It effectively operates the same way in both cases as it returns a count of members in the referenced set. One key difference when using COUNT() is that you have an option to include or exclude empty values – INCLUDEEMPTY or EXCLUDEEMPTY:

```
with member [Measures].[State Province Count] as [City].[Sales
Region].[State Province].count

    member [Measures].[No Territories Count] as

        COUNT(EXCEPT(descendants([City].[Sales Region].
[Region].&[Americas],[City].[Sales Region].[State Province],
SELF), {[City].[Sales Region].[State Province].&[Puerto Rico
(US Territory)],[City].[Sales Region].[State Province].&[Virgin
Islands (US Territory)]}) ,INCLUDEEMPTY)

select {[Measures].[State Province Count],[Measures].[No
Territories Count]} on 0

from [Wide World Importers]
```

This query returns the count of all the members in the State Province level of the Sales Region hierarchy in the State Province Count measure. No Territories Count looks at the descendants of the Americas region and then eliminates the territories. The counts are off by one additional value as the N/A member is not a part of the Americas region.

Avg, Median, and Divide

Avg and Median both use the same format as Sum – Function(set, [calculation]). Both functions ignore null or empty values in the calculations. This is very important to understand. Let's look at the two ways to handle averages as an example. Typically, we calculate an average as the sum of the values divided by the count of the members. For example, you might calculate average sales as the total of sales divided by the count of sales. However, if one of those sales is null, the math is different.

Let's take five sales with discounts of $100, $20, $30, $55, and null. What is the result you want? If the fifth sale is valid as a transaction even though the discount does not exist or is null, the math would be $205/5 = $41 average discount amount. If you were to use the Avg function in MDX, the math would be $205/4 = $51.25. Both results are valid, but you need to understand that this will affect your results. Be sure that you know which is correct to meet your business needs.

Before we show the sample code, one other function becomes relevant. `Divide` handles division operations better than using /. `Divide` handles divide-by-zero issues by returning a null or empty value when executed. You can add the third parameter to replace a divide-by-zero error with an alternative value. In our example here, we do not set the third parameter:

```
with
member NEProfit as SUM([City].[Sales Region].[Sales
Territory].&[New England].children, [Measures].[Profit])
member NETerritoryCount as COUNT([City].[Sales Region].[Sales
Territory].&[New England].children)
member NEAvgProfit as AVG([City].[Sales Region].[Sales
Territory].&[New England].children, [Measures].[Profit])
member NEMedianProfit as MEDIAN([City].[Sales Region].[Sales
Territory].&[New England].children, [Measures].[Profit])
member NEAvgProfitCalc as DIVIDE([Measures].
[NEProfit],[Measures].[NETerritoryCount])
select { [Measures].[NEProfit]
    , [Measures].[NETerritoryCount]
    , [Measures].[NEAvgProfit]
    , [Measures].[NEAvgProfitCalc]
    , [Measures].[NEMedianProfit] } on 0
from [Wide World Importers];
```

Here is the result using these various math functions:

NEProfit	NETerritoryCount	NEAvgProfit	NEAvgProfitCalc	NEMedianProfit
$3,813,022.75	6	$762,604.55	$635,503.79	631784.65

Figure 5.27 – MDX query results using math functions

You can expand the math functions with additional tuples or sets to make more refined calculations.

TopCount and BottomCount

TopCount and BottomCount can be used for top 10 or bottom 10 measurement types. They are easy to use. Here is the sample code for using these functions:

```
select [Measures].[Quantity] on 0
, topcount([Items with Color], 5) on 1
from [Wide World Importers];
select [Measures].[Quantity] on 0
, bottomcount([Items with Color], 5) on 1
from [Wide World Importers];
```

You will also find TopPercent and BottomPercent functions that can be used the same way. The count is handled as a percent for those functions.

Working with time

The following functions are two of the building blocks for working with time calculations in MDX.

ParallelPeriod

ParallelPeriod returns the measures you are querying from a previous period. For example, if you want to see the same value for June 2015 in the previous year, you can use ParallelPeriod to get that result. You would specify the level you want to use as the parallel period, which, in our example, is year. Then select how many periods you want to look back at. The default is one. Then you specify the member you want to start from. In our MDX query, we are going to use a technique that will return this value over a set using the currentmember function as well. We are going to look at the sales quantity for 2016 and look back to 2015 as the previous year:

```
with
member [Measures].[PY Quantity]
as ([Measures].[Quantity],parallelperiod([Invoice Date].
[Calendar].[Calendar Year], 1, [Invoice Date].[Calendar].
currentmember))
    , FORMAT_STRING = '0,000'
select {[Measures].[Quantity], [Measures].[PY Quantity]} on 0
, [Invoice Date].[Calendar].&[CY2016].children on 1
from [Wide World Importers]
```

When you run the query in SSMS, you will get the following results:

	Quantity	PY Quantity
CY2016-Jan	250,297	217,931
CY2016-Feb	216,618	203,070
CY2016-Mar	252,408	236,872
CY2016-Apr	251,945	253,471
CY2016-May	270,036	223,741
CY2016-Jun	(null)	223,838
CY2016-Jul	(null)	266,768
CY2016-Aug	(null)	204,532
CY2016-Sep	(null)	231,852
CY2016-Oct	(null)	233,207
CY2016-Nov	(null)	220,911
CY2016-Dec	(null)	224,073

Figure 5.28 – MDX query results with ParallelPeriod expression

As you can see, we don't have current data for some of the data, but previous year data does exist. This type of calculation is common in cubes.

PeriodsToDate and Aggregate

This topic will cover the generic PeriodsToDate function, and we will look at some of the other to date functions, such as MTD, QTD, and YTD. PeriodsToDate is the basis for the other functions. The other function we will cover in this section is Aggregate. The Aggregate function creates a member that is the aggregated value over a set. You can apply various aggregation functions and numeric expressions to this member and the aggregation will be applied. You can also specify numeric expression to the function if you want to limit the result to that value. In our use case, we will use the Aggregate function with the PeriodsToDate function to aggregate values over the time period we are working with:

```
with
member [Delivery Date].[Calendar].[First7Months2015] as
        Aggregate(
            PeriodsToDate(
                [Delivery Date].[Calendar].[Calendar Year]
                , [Delivery Date].[Calendar].[Calendar
Month].&[8]&[CY2015-Aug]))
member [Delivery Date].[Calendar].[Aug2015YTD] as
        Aggregate(
```

```
                   YTD([Delivery Date].[Calendar].[Calendar
Month].&[8]&[CY2015-Aug]))
select {([Delivery Date].[Calendar].
[First7Months2015],[Measures].[Quantity])
           ,([Delivery Date].[Calendar].
[Aug2015YTD],[Measures].[Quantity])}on 0
    , [Items with Color] on 1
from [Wide World Importers]
```

You will notice in the results you get that the values are the same. Both calculations are effectively YTD through August 2015:

	First7Months2015 Quantity	Aug2015YTD Quantity
All	1,836,198	1,836,198
Black	228,247	228,247
Blue	126,328	126,328
Gray	67,828	67,828
Light Brown	58,872	58,872
Red	6,310	6,310
Steel Gray	(null)	(null)
White	178,900	178,900
Yellow	2,344	2,344

Figure 5.29 – MDX query results using the aggregate function

This concludes the MDX function walkthrough for this book. We have tried to give you sufficient examples and information to let you build out your cube. However, this is only a subset of the MDX functions available to you. While MDX tends to be difficult to master, it is still very powerful and flexible as an analytics language.

Summary

This concludes the section on multidimensional models in SQL Server 2019 Analysis Services. The goal has been to get you working with the tools and provide support for your next steps working with cubes. While this is by no means exhaustive, you should have a good understanding of dimensional design, multidimensional models, and MDX. These skills will allow you to create analytic solutions for the business and your users on multidimensional models. The lessons learned with MDX will support more complex calculations and queries that are commonly needed to properly report on business metrics.

The next few chapters will build out a similar model using tabular model techniques with DAX. Multidimensional models are mature and complex. You will likely discover that tabular models are easier to use but have some limitations for which multidimensional models are better suited. In the next chapter, we will dig into tabular models!

Section 3: Building and Deploying Tabular Models

In this section, we will be creating and deploying multiple tabular models using Visual Studio, SQL Server Management Studio, and Power Pivot in Excel. We will create a similar model to the multidimensional model, as well as models unique to tabular format.

This section comprises the following chapters:

- *Chapter 6, Preparing Your Data for Tabular Models*
- *Chapter 7, Building a Tabular Model in SSAS 2019*
- *Chapter 8, Adding Measures and Calculations with DAX*

6
Preparing Your Data for Tabular Models

Tabular models are the newer analytics model structure implemented in SQL Server. The underlying analysis engine is columnar, not multidimensional, which means there are some different considerations for data preparation. The **VertiPaq** analysis engine was originally introduced in Excel and now supports Power BI datasets and Analysis Services tabular models. The technology behind VertiPaq uses a number of column-based algorithms to improve storage and performance. This technology allows Analysis Services to compress and structure the data for optimized performance. One other key design change is that tabular models match various relational data structures and are not reliant on a dimensional model for success.

In this chapter, we will look at the range of options, from minor preparation to star schema-based approaches. We will walk through prototyping tabular models with Excel Power Pivot capabilities. Because tabular models can be implemented without a lot of data prep at times, we will conclude the chapter by looking at some of the techniques needed to clean up projects that may have started out poorly. This chapter contains the information you need to build sustainable tabular models to drive business solutions for your organization.

In this chapter, we're going to cover the following main topics:

- Prepping data for tabular models
- Data optimization considerations
- Prototyping your model in Excel with Power Pivot

Technical requirements

In this chapter, we will be using the **WideWorldImporters** and **WideWorldImportersDW** databases from *Chapter 1, Analysis Services in SQL Server 2019*. You should connect to the database with **SQL Server Management Studio** (**SSMS**).

We will be using Excel to build the Power Pivot model prototype. For our examples, we will be using the Excel version that comes with Office 365 ProPlus. The other latest versions of Excel should allow you to participate in the hands-on examples as well.

Prepping data for tabular models

With multidimensional models, a star schema is required in the underlying data source. However, with tabular models, a star schema is not required. This means that data preparation is not as clear as it is with multidimensional models. In this section, we will explore some key considerations that are involved when preparing data for tabular models.

Contrasting self-service and managed deployments

Tabular model designs have their origins in self-service technologies such as **Power BI** and **Excel**. Why does this matter? Because well-designed dimensional models still perform better and are easier to develop solutions for. Self-service models often focus only on the immediate business need and not on lasting performance or growth. When the number of consumers of an analytics model is one or just a few, the impact is minimal. However, when scaling the models beyond a limited set of users, performance and usability become key considerations in design.

SQL Server Analysis Services tabular models are created in Visual Studio and managed at the server level. They are not self-service by nature. Technology development teams are responsible for maintaining, supporting, and enhancing these models. Those teams are also required to follow specific rules and processes to maintain the quality and functionality of the models.

A normal process in the industry is that when self-service models are difficult for the business to manage, they call on their internal technology teams to take them over. The problem with this scenario is that **service-level agreements (SLAs)**, compliance requirements, and the overall need for security get in the way of business expectations. While this is not the focus of this book, you need to consider how to qualify tabular models as a different management process from self-service models.

Let's wrap this section up with a few contrasting points on the differences between self-service and managed deployments in the context of tabular model implementations in a business:

- Analysis Services tabular models support larger models than self-service tools. They are built on a server and can scale to the size of the memory in the server, which often exceeds the capabilities of the self-service environments.

- Self-service tools allow quicker changes due to the lack of controls and processes used when working with tabular models. This can be both good and bad. Self-service models can adapt quickly but are susceptible to bad data and processes that can lead to bad decisions being made. Tabular models take more time but are built around controls and processes to help achieve better data quality.

- Analysis Services tabular models are created with Visual Studio, a developer tool. Power BI and Excel are end user tools, which makes them easier to use and more approachable for designers of all levels. One key difference here is that Visual Studio projects have good source control and standard deployment options with versions that can be easily implemented by developers. This allows clear change tracking, which is not as easy to accomplish with self-service tools.

As you can see, the contrasts really come down to industry and corporate controls that have been traditionally managed by IT teams and model sizes. When these requirements become important, tabular models are required to support the business.

The impact of Power BI

Microsoft's Power BI product continues to change and fill gaps in enterprise implementations. Microsoft continues to invest in Power BI Premium, which has wider support for datasets and other additional capabilities. Power BI still has limitations in source control and other typical IT processes. Until the gap is closed, Analysis Services tabular models will continue to fill those needs for businesses with larger datasets and specific management controls for data and design.

Using a star schema data warehouse

The work that is required to create and maintain a star schema or dimensional data warehouse built on Kimball practices was described in detail in *Chapter 3, Preparing Your Data for Dimensional Models*. The principals behind a dimensional model make any analytics solution work well. A dimensional model is organized to support reporting and analysis with a focus on conformed dimensions and established measures.

A tabular model based on a dimensional data warehouse is one of the simplest implementations to do. In our case, we can use the star schemas we created in *Chapter 3, Preparing Your Data for Dimensional Models*, as shown in *Figure 6.1*. We created views to support two measure groups in the multidimensional model:

1. **Sales**: This has the detail-level sales for **Wide World Importers**. This star schema includes item-level sales:

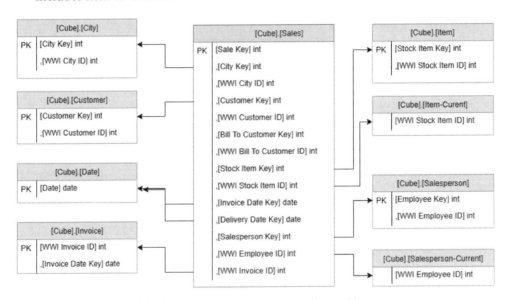

Figure 6.1 – Sales star schema views for Wide World Importers

2. **Invoice Sales**: This measure view has the data aggregated to the invoice. This pattern is very helpful in tabular models as it allows them to optimize for aggregations:

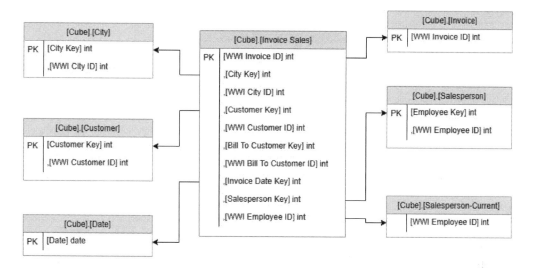

Figure 6.2 – Invoice sales star schema views for Wide World Importers

This is a case where the work is completed in the data warehouse and no additional preparations are required to support using this same schema with a tabular model. We will also look at some options that will support role-playing dimension design.

> **Role-playing dimensions in tabular models**
>
> Unlike multidimensional models, role-playing dimensions are not natively supported in the tabular model. In our case, we have role-playing relationships created with the **Date** dimension. The invoice and delivery dates are mapped to the same dimension.

Using non-star schema databases

When a tabular model is created on a database that has not been modeled with a star schema, you have a couple of options. The first option is obvious. Use the existing data structure as is and pull the data directly into the model. Using the tabular model features, you can rename columns to make them more user friendly. You can also add measures and columns to build out the model.

The other consideration is shaping the data before landing it in the model. This can be done using the **Power Query** feature in tabular model design. For example, Power Query can remove unused columns and add columns during the load process, as shown in the following screenshot:

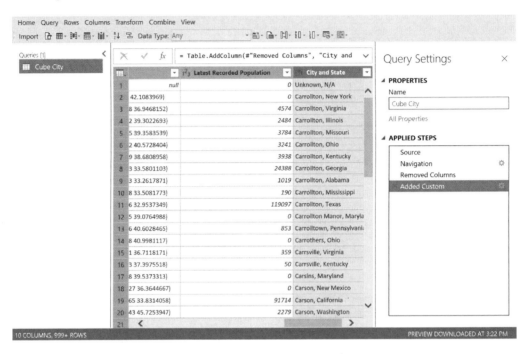

Figure 6.3 – Power Query example

Power Query can be used to filter data, add and remove columns, and format data for use in the tabular model. This allows us to bypass loading star schema databases in simpler operations. The key consideration here is that the data will be transformed during the refresh process and the operations may not be as efficient as we see in modern **extraction, transformation, and load** (ETL) tools such as **SQL Server Integration Services (SSIS)**.

Using nontraditional sources

One of the key characteristics in a data warehouse is that the source of the data for the analytics and reporting systems is one single source. Report and dashboard designers know that the data they are looking for is organized and managed by the data warehouse team and should be able to be trusted. However, today's analytics needs do not always make it to the data warehouse. Marketing teams are a great example of a group whose needs change constantly. They use tools such as Google Analytics, Facebook, and even YouTube to collect data and build reports. Often, these systems are not included in the data warehouse, and adding them is complicated.

Power Query allows model designers to add these data sources to tabular models and shape the data to allow it to be mashed up with a data warehouse or other traditional data sources. While this may not be the best long-term solution, it allows the data warehouse and analytics teams to create solutions quickly to support the business. If the business team is using Power Query in Power BI to collect this data initially, that work can be used to provide guidance and code to add to the larger tabular model projects.

The other common use case for data outside of the data warehouse is as general-purpose data managed by a third party. We often see weather, traffic, and census data sourced from third parties, including governments. The cost of pulling that data into a warehouse via traditional means typically results in a low return on investment. With the Power Query capability in SQL Server 2019 Analysis Services, businesses can add that data with minimal impact. More importantly, the third party will be responsible for quality and freshness, not the business teams.

Data optimization considerations

Another consideration when preparing your data for tabular models is the data refresh options available. Typically, data is imported into your tabular model similar to the process we used with multidimensional models. Imported data is loaded into memory and optimized by the VertiPaq engine. This involves a high level of compression, including columnar data storage techniques. The functions of compression and memory combine to create an optimized model with performance. Here are some key considerations when using data refresh:

- **Refresh frequency**: The data is only as fresh as the last import. If the data source has been updated recently, the data may be out of sync. This is less of an issue when you are loading data from a data warehouse. The data warehouse is typically loaded in batches as well. If you match your refreshes to the batch loads, your data will be consistent with the data warehouse. If you have chosen to use the transactional database for the source, that database is written frequently too. Thus, your data will only be as fresh as the latest import.

- **Refresh time**: Because the refresh process is importing the data into the model, you must consider the time for doing that operation. If you have used Power Query to shape a significant amount of your data, that will add to the refresh time because all data will need to be reshaped each time. You can partition the data to reduce the processing time in tabular models.

- **Query performance**: The import option has the best query performance. The data that is loaded into memory has been optimized for queries. Your users will notice the performance improvement in most cases. Typically, imported tabular models perform better than multidimensional models and DirectQuery tabular models.

The other data refresh option in tabular models is **DirectQuery**. DirectQuery does not import data into SQL Server Analysis Services. It uses the data source's engine to execute the queries. In our example, a DirectQuery model built on the data warehouse would send SQL statements to the data warehouse to fulfill user requests. The user experience will look like the import method, but the data is returned directly from the data warehouse, and not from memory in Analysis Services. Here are some key considerations when working with DirectQuery:

- **Real-time connection**: The data being served to users via DirectQuery is "real time" from the data source. Changes in the source will immediately be reflected in the user experience. DirectQuery makes it possible to have operational dashboards in tabular models. The other consideration here is that the data is dependent on the performance of the underlying source, and the network connectivity between the tabular model and the data source.

- **One data source**: DirectQuery has limited data source support. The first limitation is that a tabular model using DirectQuery can only use one data source. You cannot mash up data in DirectQuery. Secondly, DirectQuery only supports a limited set of relational sources at this time, including SQL Server, Azure SQL Database, Oracle, and Teradata.

- **Not limited by memory**: DirectQuery tabular models are not limited in size compared to the memory in Analysis Services. Because the data is returned from the data source data system, all the data is available for analysis. However, there is a limit on the number of rows returned – one million – although this can be adjusted if required.

As you can see, tabular models have flexibility in their storage and query capabilities. We recommend that you always start with the import mode and only use DirectQuery when you have a specific use case that requires it.

Now that we have looked at the tabular model refresh options, let's look at using Excel to create a tabular model.

Prototyping your model in Excel with Power Pivot

One of the cool things about using tabular models is that you can prototype your model using Excel. In this section, we will walk through creating a `PowerPivot` model to demonstrate building a prototype that we will upload to SQL Server Analysis Services in *Chapter 7, Building a Tabular Model in SSAS 2019*. We will work with the `Invoice Sales` star schema illustrated in *Figure 6.2* earlier in this chapter. Let's get started:

1. Open **Excel** and create a new workbook. **Power Pivot** is built in, so no additional installs or extensions are required.

2. Next, we need to open the **Power Pivot** window. Go to the **Data** tab in **Excel** and click the **Go to the Power Pivot Window** button on the ribbon as shown in the following screenshot:

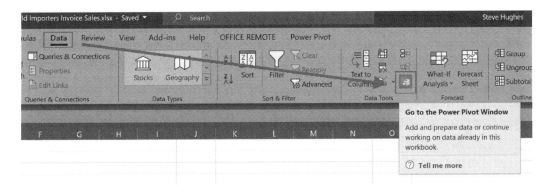

Figure 6.4 – Opening Power Pivot in Excel

If you have never opened **Power Pivot** before, you will be prompted to enable the **Data Analysis** features. You should now see a new window open with a ribbon as shown in the following screenshot:

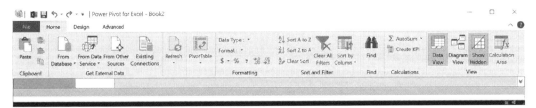

Figure 6.5 – Power Pivot window

3. Connect to the `WideWorldImportersDW` database by choosing **From Database** and selecting **From SQL Server**. This will open the **Table Import Wizard**, as shown in the following screenshot:

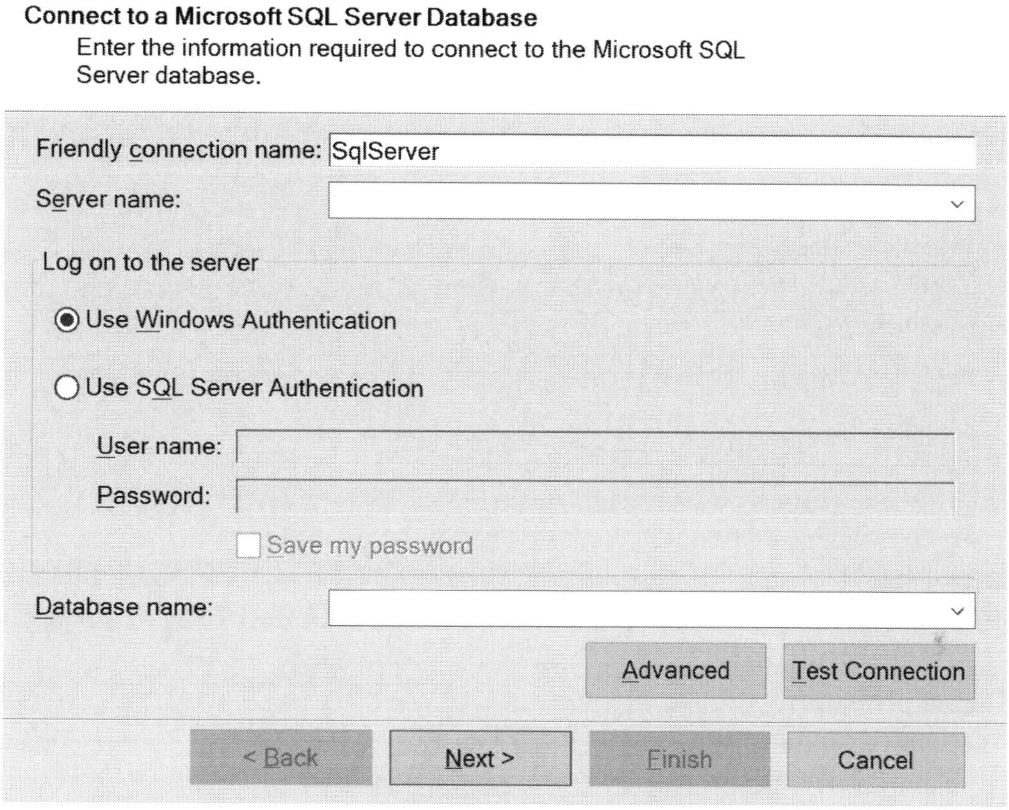

Connect to a Microsoft SQL Server Database

Enter the information required to connect to the Microsoft SQL Server database.

Friendly connection name:	SqlServer
Server name:	

Log on to the server

⦿ Use Windows Authentication

○ Use SQL Server Authentication

User name:	
Password:	

☐ Save my password

Database name:	

[Advanced] [Test Connection]

[< Back] [Next >] [Finish] [Cancel]

Figure 6.6 – Table Import Wizard in Power Pivot

4. Fill in the connection information for your `WideWorldImportersDW` server and database and click **Next >**.

5. In the next screen, choose **Select from a list of tables and views to choose the data to import** and click **Next >**.

6. Select the following views from the **Cube** schema in the **Select Tables and Views** dialog: **City**, **Customer**, **Date**, **Invoice**, **Invoice Sales**, and **Salesperson**. You can leave the **Friendly Name** column. You should note that this dialog will try to create friendly names by recognizing syntax such as case and underscores. When you have selected those views, click **Finish** to load the data into Power Pivot as shown in the following screenshot:

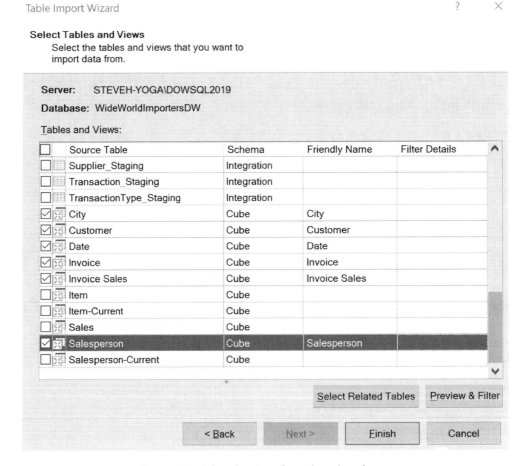

Figure 6.7 – Select the views from the cube schema

Be wary of the amount of data in your sources

This process will try to load all the data from the selected tables into Power Pivot, which will consume memory on the device you are using. You should always use caution when using this feature or your device may run out of memory if the dataset you select is too large.

7. When the process is completed, you should see a dialog with the row counts for the views that were imported. You can close the window if it looks similar to mine, as shown in the following screenshot:

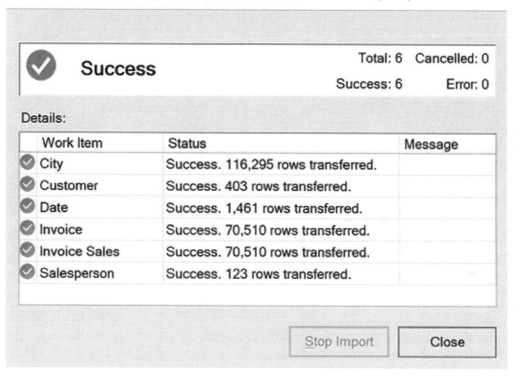

Figure 6.8 – Pivot table successfully loaded

8. Review the imported data. You should see six tabs, one for each view we created. Before we move to the next step, let's get a short tour of Power Pivot using the following screenshot as reference. In the center of the screen is the data that has been imported into Power Pivot. To the right of the data you can see the option to add another column, which we will do shortly. Below the data is the **Calculation Area**, which is used to create measures:

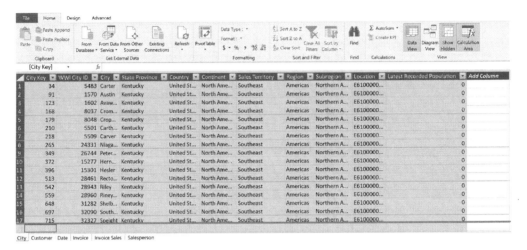

Figure 6.9 – Power Pivot data view

9. We also need to create relationships, as there were no foreign keys. You can create relationships using the **Create Relationships** button on the **Design** tab. However, it can be helpful to use **Diagram View** to create and view the relationships visually. Click **Diagram View** in the ribbon to change the view.

10. To create relationships, drag each dimension key onto the **Invoice Sales** fact table to the matching key. For example, drag the **Date** field from the **Date** table to **Invoice Date Key** in the **Invoice Sales** table. We rearranged the tables to look like a star schema. The following screenshot shows the rest of the relationships laid out:

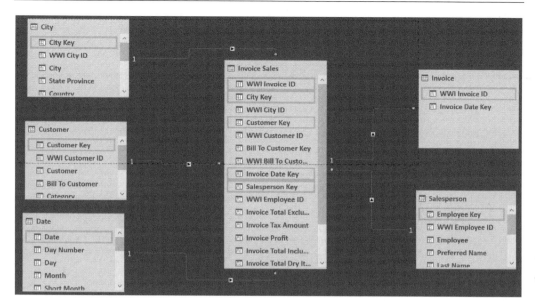

Figure 6.10 – Power Pivot relationships

The following table describes the relationships in detail:

Invoice Sales Field	Related Table	Related Field
WWI Invoice ID	Invoice	WWI Invoice ID
City Key	City	City Key
Customer Key	Customer	Customer Key
Invoice Date Key	Date	Date
Salesperson Key	Salesperson	Employee Key

Figure 6.11 – Power Pivot relationships defined

11. To add a couple of calculations to support our model, let's go back to the **Data View**. Now, click on the **Invoice Sales** tab. We will be adding two measures. The first will sum **Invoice Total Including Tax** and the other will calculate the average of **Invoice Total Including Tax**.

12. To create the sum, click any cell in the calculation area. We typically choose a cell near the column we are working with. Type in the following formula: `Invoice Total:=sum('Invoice Sales'[Invoice Total Including Tax])`.

13. Add another calculation below `Invoice Total`. It will be `Invoice Average`. Use the following code for this: `Invoice Average:=AVERAGE('Invoice Sales'[Invoice Total Including Tax])`.

14. Go ahead and set the format for both measures to currency ($ on the ribbon).

15. Go to the **City** tab. Let's add a calculated column with `City` and `State Province`. Click on **Add Column** and then add this to the formula: `=City[City] & ",  " & City[State Province]`. Rename the column `City and State`.

16. Let's give our model a test run. On the ribbon, click **PivotTable**. This will create a PivotTable in **Excel**, connected to our model. In the new PivotTable, add our new measures from the `Invoice Sales` section to the `Values` section. Then add our new column, `City and State`, to Rows. Your PivotTable should look similar to the following screenshot:

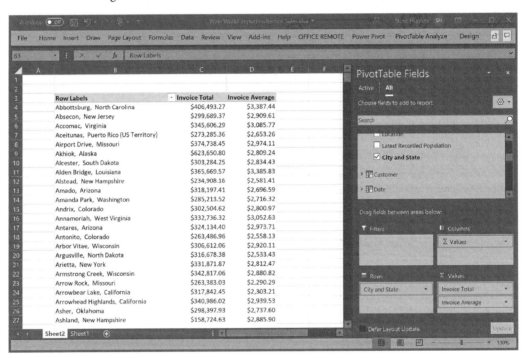

Figure 6.12 – PivotTable using our Power Pivot model

We will use the model in *Chapter 7, Building a Tabular Model in SSAS 2019*, to illustrate how to deploy this to Analysis Services. Using Power Pivot with Excel allows developers to build models locally and work with a rapid development and test cycle. When the model meets the needs of the business, they can easily promote the model to Analysis Services in most cases.

> **What about using Power BI to pivot?**
>
> Power BI can serve a similar purpose. It allows developers to rapidly build solutions and prototype in a similar and often easier way than Power Pivot in Excel. However, there is no automated way to promote the Power BI dataset to SQL Server Analysis Services right now. Power BI also has a more significant focus on the visualizations, whereas Power Pivot is focused on model creation.

Before we wrap up the chapter, save your Excel workbook with Power Pivot so we can use it for our later exercises in the coming chapters.

Summary

As you can see, data preparation is not as important for tabular models. In short, tabular models can be built quickly on less-than-great data structures. However, if you want to build models for a longer duration, it is best to build out a tried and true dimensional model. Once you have determined the foundation to build on, you can use that information to determine how you want to work with data – either via refresh or DirectQuery.

We also covered how to use Excel and Power Pivot to design and prototype an analytic model that can be imported into Analysis Services. Using Power Pivot is a great way to learn how to work with tabular model design, using Power Query to load and manipulate the data.

In the next chapter, we will build tabular models from the ground up in Visual Studio. We will also use the Power Pivot model we created in this chapter to create a new tabular model. Let's create some tabular models!

7
Building a Tabular Model in SSAS 2019

In the previous chapter, we looked at the various ways in which data can be prepped and used with tabular models. This chapter focuses on using that data to build out tabular models that we can use for analysis. When you have completed the work in this chapter, you will be able to build tabular models from various types of data sources.

In this chapter, we will build out four tabular models to demonstrate building from the **data warehouse** and also from the **transactional database source**. We will also create a **DirectQuery** version of the data warehouse model. We will wrap up model creation by importing the **Power Pivot** model we created in the previous chapter.

Apart from this, we will create a solution that supports multiple models or projects. Like with the multidimensional model build, we will pull in the data, create tables, set relationships, and add some custom columns and hierarchies. This will result in the completion of basic tabular models that will be enhanced with **Data Analysis Expression** (**DAX**) in the following chapter.

In this chapter, we're going to cover the following main topics:

- Creating the solution and first tabular model

- Creating a tabular model with DirectQuery

- Creating a tabular model on transactional data

- Importing a Power Pivot model into Analysis Services

- Deploying and processing your completed models

Technical requirements

In this chapter, we will be using the `WideWorldImportersDW` and `WideWorldImporters` databases from *Chapter 1, Analysis Services in SQL Server 2019*. You should connect to the database with **SQL Server Management Studio (SSMS)**. You will be using views created in *Chapter 3, Preparing Your Data for Multidimensional Models*. If you are starting with this chapter, you will need to apply the views from *Chapter 3, Preparing Your Data for Multidimensional Models*, to the `WideWorldImportersDW` database before we start.

This chapter will also require the use of **Visual Studio 2019 Community Edition** to create the **Analysis Service project**. We will also be importing the Power Pivot model we created in *Chapter 6, Preparing Your Data for Tabular Models*, so have that to hand as well.

Creating the solution and first tabular model

We will be creating four tabular models in this chapter. The first and second models will be built on the data warehouse and the third one will be built on the transactional database. We will then wrap up with the imported model. Each of these will be created as projects in a single Visual Studio solution. This will allow us to manage the shared settings effectively. Let's get started:

1. Open **Visual Studio** and create a new project. Choose the **Analysis Services Tabular Project** as shown in the following screenshot. If you don't see it in your list, search for `Tabular` to find the correct template:

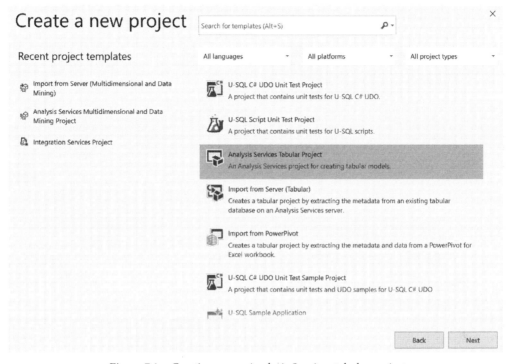

Figure 7.1 – Creating a new Analysis Services tabular project

2. Configure your new project. Give the project and the solution a name. We are naming our first project `WideWorldImportersTAB` as this will be the primary model we will work with in the following chapters:

Figure 7.2 – Configuring your Analysis Services tabular project

3. When you click **Create**, you will be presented with a dialog to choose which SSAS server you will use for your workspace. Tabular projects can create an integrated workspace. This feature allows you to work with tabular model projects without having access to a specific SSAS instance. In our case, we will select a workspace server. We have already set up an Analysis Services instance with a tabular model, so it makes sense for us to use it. If you are working on a company model and you don't have access to a specific server, then the integrated workspace will allow you to design and create the model.

Choosing the integrated workspace or a workspace server

Workspace databases are required when working with tabular models in Visual Studio. These databases are used to contain the data imported during the design process. Microsoft recommends using the **Integrated workspace** option. The primary reason is that there can be a lag when working with a remote workspace server. If you have the **SQL Server Analysis Services (SSAS)** instance running on the same device as Visual Studio, then both options are viable. If you are unable to do this, use the integrated workspace option. The only potential impact will be permissions to the database servers. You may need to choose a different impersonation method to load data.

4. Because we are working with SSAS 2019, set **Compatibility level** as **SQL Server 2019 / Azure Analysis Services (1500)**. This is the latest version of Analysis Services tabular models. The project will support different levels, allowing you to target the appropriate server instance. The following screenshot shows the settings we used. Click **OK** when you complete this step:

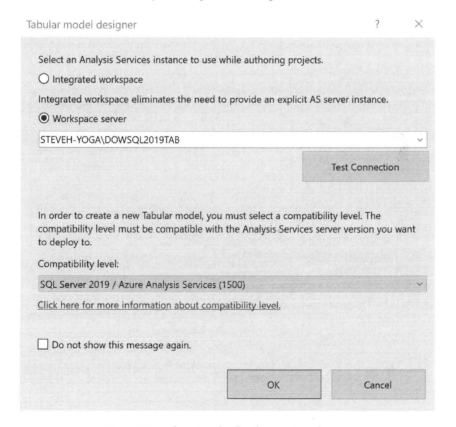

Figure 7.3 – Choosing the development workspace

What is a compatibility level anyway?

When Analysis Services tabular models are updated with SQL Server or **Azure Analysis Services**, some features are not always compatible with the version you have worked in. The compatibility level allows Microsoft to release new features and functionality without impacting your currently delivered projects. The design and management tools such as SSMS and Visual Studio work with multiple compatibility levels. Not only do the tools work with compatibility levels, but the server engines on premises and in the cloud do as well. This allows you to gain shared benefits when you upgrade while minimizing risk to your currently deployed models. This is truly an awesome pattern Microsoft has made available. It was necessary for them in Azure as it minimizes the support and version issues that have been common in software. While compatibility models will eventually be deprecated, their implementation has enabled us to take advantage of improvements and use a measured approach to upgrade our models. Compatibility levels are not *automatically* upgraded, which means you need to manage the transition. In the end, this is something to be aware of when working in new or older versions.

5. Now that you have the settings in place, click on **Complete the creation of the project**. You will now have a new solution with one tabular model project, as shown here:

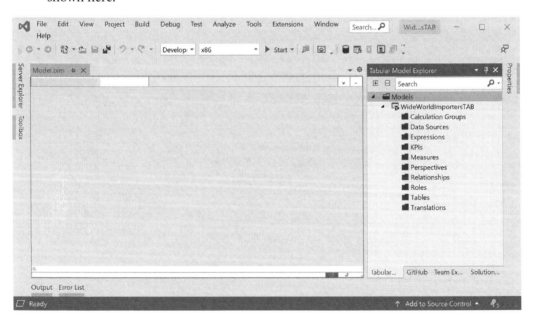

Figure 7.4 – New tabular model project

Importing data into your model

Our next step is to create the data source. For this project, we will be using the Cube schema we created in *Chapter 3*, *Preparing Your Data for Multidimensional Models*. This will allow us to create a tabular model based on the same star schema as our multidimensional model:

1. Right-click on the Data Sources folder and select **Import from Data Source…** This will open the **Get Data** dialog, as shown here:

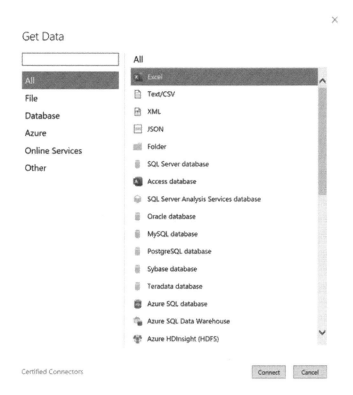

Figure 7.5 – Get Data dialog

2. Select **Database** to filter the available connector list and then select **SQL Server Database**. Then, click on **Connect**.

3. In the **SQL Server database** connection dialog, enter the name of the server that you created for WideWorldImportersDW. While it is optional, go ahead and enter the database name as well, WideWorldImportersDW. Then, click **OK**.

4. The next window prompts us for our credentials to access the SQL Server database.

In *Chapter 4, Building a Multidimensional Cube in SSAS 2019*, we added the multidimensional service account to the SQL Server database. We will now add the tabular service account to the SQL Server database so we can use the **Impersonate Service Account** option as **Windows | Impersonation Mode**.

> **Tip**
> If you are using the integrated workspace, you may want to create a SQL Server login instead of using the service account.

We will need to add the service account to the db_datareader role in WideWorldImportersDW. To quickly implement the solution I used, run the following scripts in SSMS connected to your **SQL Server Data Engine** instance:

1. First, you will need to open your services console or **SQL Server Configuration Manger** to get your service account name. In my case, the account name is NT Service\MSOLAP$DOWSQL2019TAB. Here are the scripts to add this user to your data warehouse:

```sql
USE [Master]

CREATE LOGIN [NT Service\MSOLAP$DOWSQL2019TAB] FROM
WINDOWS WITH DEFAULT_DATABASE=[master], DEFAULT_
LANGUAGE=[us_english]

GO

-- Execute the following after running the statement
above

USE [WideWorldImportersDW]

GO

CREATE USER [SSASTABSys] FOR LOGIN [NT SERVICE\
MSOLAP$DOWSQL2019TAB]

GO

USE [WideWorldImportersDW]

GO

ALTER ROLE [db_datareader] ADD MEMBER [SSASTABSys]

GO
```

If you experience issues while executing the script, try executing each statement individually.

2. Once you have the user in place, choose **Impersonate Service Account** and click **Connect**. You may see an encryption warning. For our purposes, click **OK** to continue.

   The next task is to select the tables or views that will be used in our model. As we noted before, we will be using the **Cube schema**, which is made up of views.

3. In the **Navigator** dialog, select the list of Cube schema objects except `Cube.Salesperson-Current`. You can preview the content of each table when you select it. This allows you to visually confirm that the tables or views you are selecting are correct or have the expected data. Once you have selected all the Cube views, your **Navigator** dialog should look like the following screenshot:

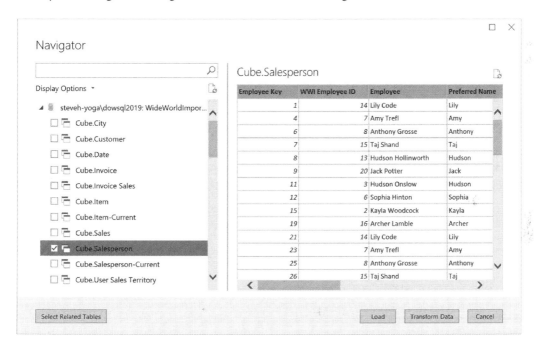

Figure 7.6 – Navigator dialog with Cube schema

> **Select Related Tables**
>
> The **Select Related Tables** button can be helpful when views are not used. This button uses the foreign key relationships in the underlying database to add tables related to the selected table. In our database, picking a **Fact** table and clicking this button would result in the related dimension tables being selected. However, if you follow the practice of using views as an interface layer (which we recommend), then relationships are not present to be used, which is our case here.

We have two options to continue, **Transform Data** or **Load**. **Transform Data** will open the **Power Query** dialog and allow us to make some changes to the data we are loading. **Load** simply loads the data as is. Load is most effective when you are doing some discovery on the data and experimenting.

We recommend that you choose **Transform Data** to complete a couple of tasks that are helpful right away. First, the table names that get pulled through from the source include the schema name. We would want to remove that as it is not useful to our users. Second, this is a great opportunity to remove columns that will not be used in the model. In our case, we will be using most, if not all, of the columns from our tables. In later model builds, this will become more relevant.

4. Now, click **Transform Data** to open **Power Query**.

    Now that we have the **Power Query Editor** open, let's change the names of our tables. In the editor, our tables are listed on the left in the **Queries** pane. You can change the name by right-clicking the query and selecting **Rename**, or you can select the table and change the name in the **Properties** panel on the right, as highlighted in the following screenshot:

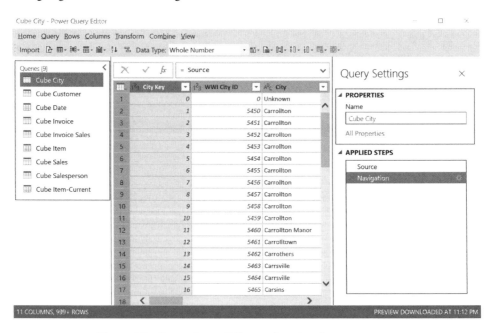

Figure 7.7 – Power Query Editor – changing the query name

5. Remove `Cube` from all the query or table names. Once you have completed that, click **Import** in the upper-left corner. This will import the data to our model using the workspace and we can continue making modifications to the model in Visual Studio.

Once you have imported the data, take a minute to check out the data in Visual Studio. This experience is like working with the data in Power Pivot in Excel.

Before moving to the next step, open **SQL Server Management Studio** and connect to the tabular model instance you selected for your workspace. You will see a tabular model there with a GUID as part of the name. This is your workspace database. You can see the tables and you can browse the database with the same browser used with multidimensional models:

Figure 7.8 – Browsing the workspace model in SSMS

6. Now that the data has been imported, we need to add the relationships to the model. To do this, you need to switch to the **Diagram** view. There are two small buttons in the lower-right corner of the model designer that changes the view. Refer to the following screenshot to see where they are as they are not easily identifiable. If you are using a high-resolution monitor, they almost disappear:

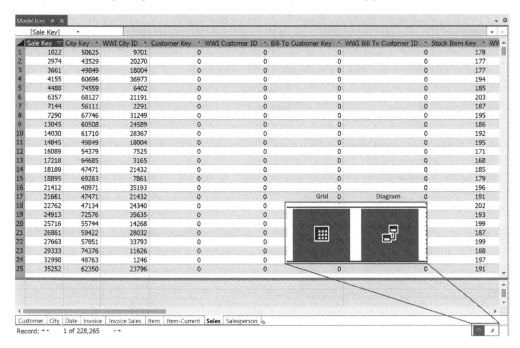

Figure 7.9 – Grid and Diagram view buttons

7. Select the **Diagram** view shown in the preceding screenshot and the screen will switch to the following view:

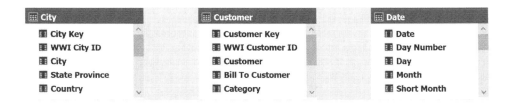

Figure 7.10 – Diagram view before relationships have been created

In this view, we can create the relationships by dragging the keys from the dimensions to their matching foreign key in the fact tables. The following table shows the mapping for our model:

Dimension (From)		Fact (To)	
Table	Column	Table	Column
Customer	Customer Key	Invoice Sales	Customer Key
Customer	Customer Key	Sales	Customer Key
City	City Key	Invoice Sales	City Key
City	City Key	Sales	City Key
Date	Date	Invoice Sales	Invoice Date Key
Date	Date	Sales	Invoice Date Key
Date	Date	Sales	Delivery Date Key
Item	Stock Item Key	Sales	Stock Item Key
Item-Current	WWI Stock Item ID	Sales	WWI Stock Item ID
Invoice	WWI Invoice ID	Invoice Sales	WWI Invoice ID
Salesperson	Employee Key	Sales	Salesperson Key
Salesperson	Employee Key	Invoice Sales	Salesperson Key

Figure 7.11 – Relationship mapping table

After you have created these relationships, your diagram view should look something like the following screenshot:

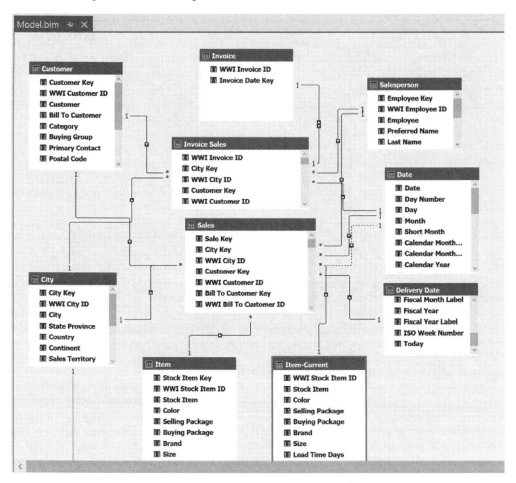

Figure 7.12 – Diagram view with relationships

Now is a good time to break down relationships in tabular models. These relationships operate differently to the multidimensional model we created earlier. If you double-click any relationship line, this will bring up the following **Edit Relationship** dialog:

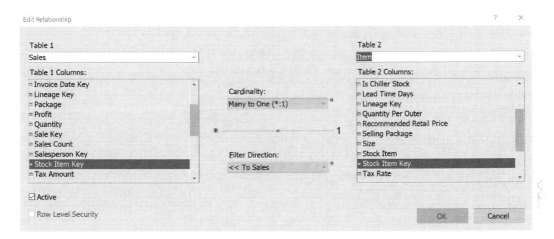

Figure 7.13 – Edit Relationship dialog

Let's now dig into tabular model relationships:

- **Tables and Columns**: These dropdowns list the tables you can build relationships between. The column lists specify the columns involved in the relationships. Tabular models only support single-column relationships. Composite or multiple-column relationships are not supported.

- **Cardinality**: This option specifies whether the relationship is **Many to One** ($*:1$), **One to Many** ($1:*$), **One to One** ($1:1$), or **Many to Many** ($*:*$). If you import tables, these relationships will be established. When we create the relationships, Visual Studio evaluates and applies the relationship cardinality that fits based on the data. You can use this dialog to fix any relationship issues that are discovered.

> **Many to many relationships, new in SQL Server 2019**
>
> Currently, many to many relationships are only supported in SSAS 2019, Azure Analysis Services, and Power BI after the July 2019 release. Your model must be set to the 1500 compatibility level to use this functionality. If you have a business need to support this functionality, you should choose to use Analysis Services to create your tabular model. Earlier compatibility levels had no support or relationship workarounds to support many to many relationships. In some cases, the effective functionality may be achieved by bi-directional cross filtering or DAX functions. Neither of these solutions are optimal.

- **Filter Direction**: One of the cool things about working in tabular models is the built-in cross filtering. The relationships define the filtering direction to help manage the user experience. Cross filtering is the process where selecting a value in a live connected solution automatically filters the contents. For example, in the relationship we are showing, if you pick Item A, then the `Sales` table would be filtered to show only matching sales. Any sale without Item A would no longer be visible.

  When using star schemas, the filter direction usually affects the fact tables in the design (the many side of the one-to-many relationship). We have one relationship between `Invoice` and `Invoice Sales` that is 1:1 and that is both directions. If you want users to experience dimensions being filtered by fact table selections, you can change the filter direction to `<< To Both Tables >>`.

- **Active**: Tabular models only allow one active relationship between tables. In our model, we have a role-playing dimension with `Date`. It is currently related to both the delivery date and invoice dates in our model. We will use the relationship with `Invoice Date Key` as the `Active` relationship. This makes it the default relationship when interacting with the `Date` dimension.

  The dashed line in the model signifies that the other relationship is inactive. This relationship exists but requires DAX to be used. The alternative approach is to add a copy of the table to the model to support an active relationship. This also requires additional memory to support this. For this model, let's leave the relationship with the delivery date as inactive.

The last property is **Row Level Security**. We will discuss this in more detail in the following chapter on security. Now, let's move ahead and mark the date table.

Marking the date table

In the next step, we will mark the date table. Tabular models use **Data Analysis Expressions (DAX)** for adding calculations to the model. DAX has time intelligence functions such as ENDOFMONTH, NEXTDAY, and TOTALMTD. These functions require a date table to be *tagged* in your model.

In our model, we have created a Date dimension that meets the requirements. To mark the Date table, follow these steps:

1. Right-click on the Date table.

2. Select **Date**.

3. Then, select **Mark As Date Table**, as shown in the following screenshot:

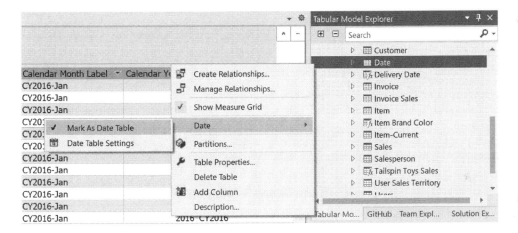

Figure 7.14 – Mark As Date Table

This will open a dialog prompting you to select the field in the table that is a unique identifier and is a date data type. In our model, the Date field will be automatically selected as it meets the criteria.

4. Click **OK** to complete the process.

Two other criteria must be met to qualify as a **Date Table** besides data type and unique identifier. The dates in the date table must be sequential and without gaps. Don't use fields from tables that are not sequential, such as fact tables. The other requirement is that the date field must be at the day granularity. If using a field that is a Datetime data type, it cannot contain partial days or time. Our model already has relationships based on this column. We can now support time intelligence functions in our model. In the next section, we will add hierarchies to the model.

Adding hierarchies to the model

As with our multidimensional model, hierarchies improve the user experience by making the relationships between fields in the table clear. Unlike multidimensional models, hierarchies don't impact performance or optimize aggregations. Their purpose is to improve the user experience. Let's match the hierarchies created in the multidimensional model.

Let's create the `Geography` hierarchy in the `City` table:

1. First, change to the **Diagram** view.

2. Locate the `City` table in your model diagram.

    This hierarchy will be `Continent | Country | State Province | City`. When you create a hierarchy in your project, it will always use the first column or field as the top level. You can rearrange the order later if needed.

3. Select **Continent** in the `City` table.

4. You can now right-click and select **Create Hierarchy** from the shortcut menu, which will add `Continent` to your new hierarchy. You can also use the **Create Hierarchy** button in the table header to create a blank hierarchy. If you use the shortcut menu option, you will see a generic hierarchy (**Hierarchy1**) created at the bottom of the `City` table in the diagram. It will have the `Continent` field as the first level in the hierarchy, as shown in the following screenshot:

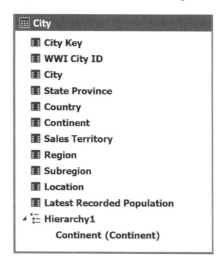

Figure 7.15 – New hierarchy in the City table

You will notice right away that the field name is repeated. You can rename the levels if it will improve the user experience. In our current model build, we will leave the field names intact. We have done the work in the underlying views to support a good user experience.

You can add levels by dragging the field in the table to the position you need in the hierarchy. You can use the **Maximize** button in the upper-right corner of the table to open the table in a view that is easier to work with each specific table.

5. Drag **Country**, **State Province**, and **City** into your new hierarchy in that order.

6. Double-click the hierarchy name or right-click and select **Rename** to give your new hierarchy a name. In this case, we are calling this hierarchy Geography.

Once you have completed these steps, your City table should look like the following screenshot, with your new Geography hierarchy in place:

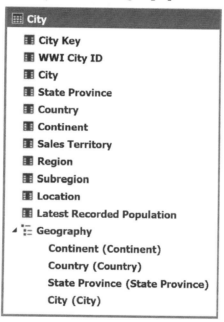

Figure 7.16 – Completed Geography hierarchy in the City table

Follow the preceding process to add the remaining hierarchies to the dimension tables in our model. We will rename the label fields for the `Date` hierarchies by removing `Label` from the field names. This is the only field name change we will make. Use the following table to guide you through the changes you need to make:

Table	Hierarchy	Fields
City	Geography	Continent Country State Province City
City	Sales Region	Region Subregion Sales Territory State Province City
Customer	Customer Hierarchy	Category Buying Group Bill To Customer Customer
Date	Calendar	Calendar Year (Calendar Year Label) Calendar Month (Calendar Month Label) Date
Date	Fiscal	Fiscal Year (Fiscal Year Label) Fiscal Month (Fiscal Month Label) Date
Item	Item Brand	Brand Stock Item
Item-Current	Current Item Brand	Brand Stock Item

Figure 7.17 – Hierarchy definitions

You will also be able to view the hierarchies in the **Tabular Model Explorer** pane in Visual Studio, as shown in the following screenshot. However, the only management operations available currently are the ability to delete the hierarchy or rearrange the levels. You must use the **Diagram** view of the model to add additional hierarchies, change fields in your existing hierarchies, or rename levels:

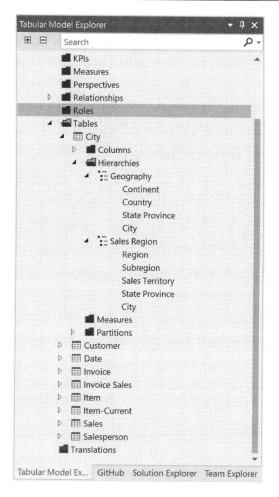

Figure 7.18 – Tabular Model Explorer – City table hierarchies

In the next section, we will add measures to our model.

Adding some measures to our model

Now, let's expand our model by adding some basic measures. We will add many more measures in the next chapter. Let's add the `Total Sales Amount`, `Invoice Line Count`, and `Invoices` measures to the `Sales` table:

1. In Visual Studio, open the **Grid** view for the model and select the `Sales` table from the tabs at the bottom.

2. Next, select the `Total Including Tax` column. This should highlight the entire column. With that column selected, use the sum symbol on the toolbar to add a new calculated measure. Use the following screenshot to help locate the button on the toolbar:

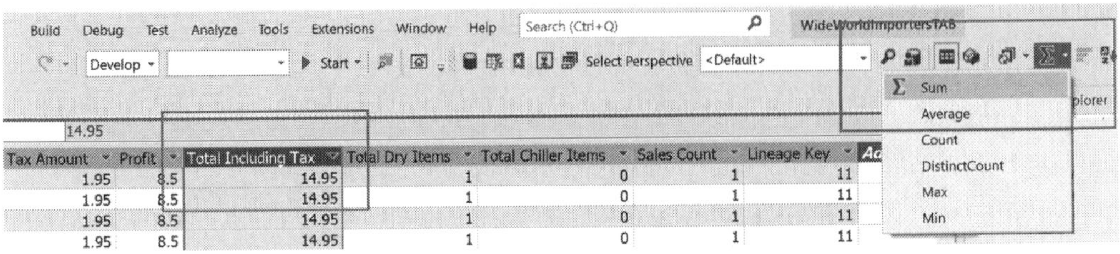

Figure 7.19 – Adding a new calculated measure to your model

After clicking the button, you will find a new measure in the measure panel at the bottom of the grid and below the `Total Including Tax` column, as shown here:

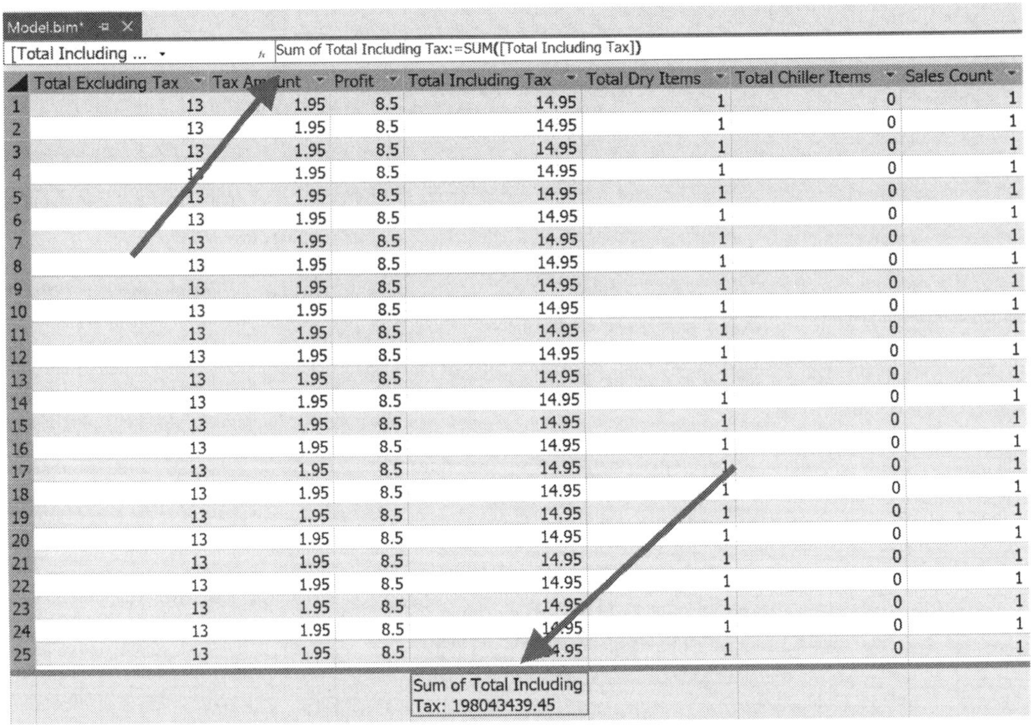

Figure 7.20 – Results of creating a new measure with the Sum button

3. Let's fix this new calculation. We should rename it `Total Sales` and set the format to **Currency**. We can rename this by changing the name in the formula bar. Currently, the formula is, `Sum of Total Including Tax:=SUM([Total Including Tax])`. By changing it to `Total Sales Amount:=SUM([Total Including Tax])`, we have renamed the calculation. You will see the change in the calculation grid as well.

4. Next, let's add the currency format. You can do that by changing the **Format** property in the **Properties** window, as shown in the following screenshot:

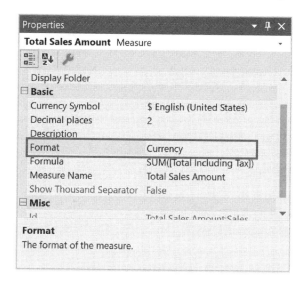

Figure 7.21 – Changing Format in the Properties window

You can also adjust **Currency Symbol** and **Decimal places** here.

> **Formatting measures and columns in tabular models**
>
> You can format all measures and columns in tabular models using the same pattern. You need to go to the properties of each measure and column and choose the formatting style you want to use. The format strings are the same here as in the multidimensional models. We encourage you to take the time to set the formats for all columns in your models. This greatly improves the user experience.

5. Let's add the invoice line count. Highlight the `Sales Count` column and click the **sum** button. Rename the measure `Invoice Line Count`. Change the format for this measure to **Custom** and use the following format string: `0,0`. This will add commas to the number.

6. Finally, we will add the `Invoices` measure. Highlight the `WWI Invoice ID` column. In this case, we will use the drop-down menu from the sum button and select **DistinctCount**. This will give us the number of invoices represented here. Use the same formatting as used in the `Invoice Line Count` measure.

DistinctCount in tabular versus multidimensional

The use of the **DistinctCount** aggregation has great value in data analytics solutions. However, multidimensional models require these calculations to be performed in separate measure groups due to negative performance impact on existing measure groups. With the release of **VertiPaq**, Microsoft added better support for distinct count measures. If you require distinct count measures in your models, tabular models are a better choice versus multidimensional models.

Managing partitions in tabular models

Partitions in tabular models allow you to reduce the processing or refresh burden in your model. Partitioning your tables involves choosing ways to separate your data into smaller chunks. Every table has a default, single partition. If your model can be partitioned so that less data has to be refreshed at a time, you can shorten your data refresh windows. Let's now add some partitions to the `Sales` table. Select the `Sales` table, and then click the **Partitions** button from the toolbar, as shown in the following screenshot:

Figure 7.22 – The Partitions button on the toolbar

This will open the **Partition Manager** dialog. Here, you can see the current partition definition, as shown here. By default, the table has a single partition called `Partition`. The definition of that partition is in M or Power Query, as shown in the **Query Expression** textbox:

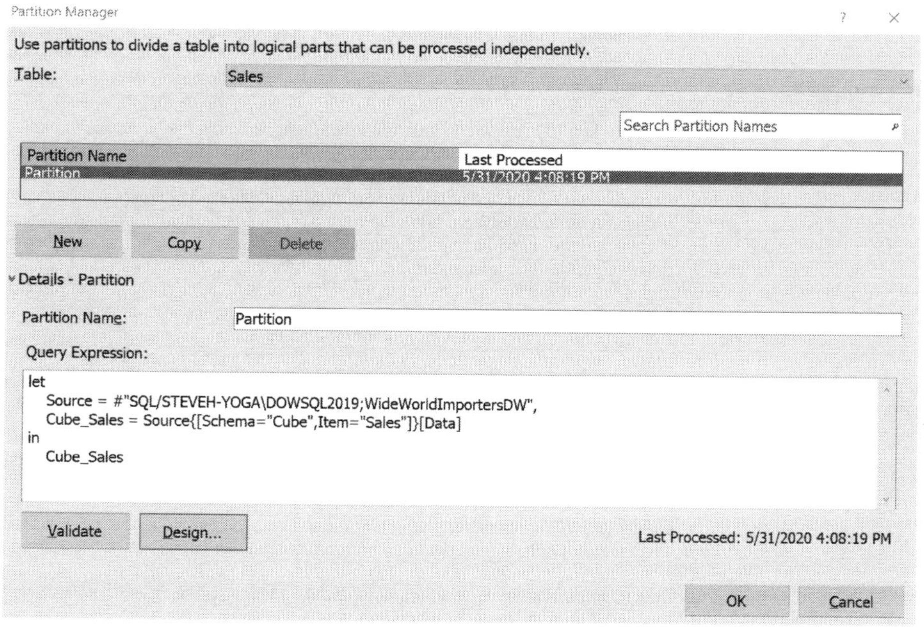

Figure 7.23 – Partition Manager with one partition

We are going to create two partitions, `History` and `Current`. The `History` partition will include data up to 1/1/2015. The `Current` partition will cover from 1/1/2015 to the present date. The first step is to change the existing partition to only include the information before 1/1/2015. Let's do this as follows:

1. Click the **Design** button. This will open **Power Query Editor** for the partition.

2. Now, scroll over to the `Invoice Date Key` column and click the arrow on the right side of the column to open the column menu.

3. Then, select **Date Filters** and choose **Before**:

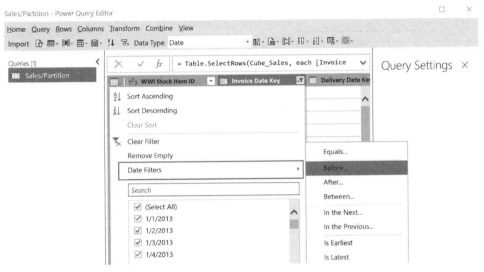

Figure 7.24 – Date filters for the partition

This will open a dialog that allows you to select the date you want the partition to cover up to.

4. Enter 1/1/2015 as the date and click **OK**.

5. To save this, click the **Home** button and choose **Close & Update**. This will reset the partition to the date range you selected and load the data in the range specified.

    The resulting query for your partition should look like the following:

```
let
    Source = #"<<server>>;WideWorldImportersDW",
    Cube_Sales = Source{[Schema="Cube",Item="Sales"]}
[Data],
    #"Filtered Rows" = Table.SelectRows(Cube_Sales, each
[Invoice Date Key] < #date(2015, 1, 1))
in
    #"Filtered Rows"
```

6. To create the next partition, copy the partition. Go to **Power Query Editor** for this partition by clicking the **Design** button again. Now, let's update the query.

7. In the **Query Settings** pane on the right, you will see **Applied Steps**.

8. Click the gear beside the **Filter Rows** step. This will reopen the date filter dialog.

9. Change the filter option to **is after or equal to**. This will cover the dates for the Current partition:

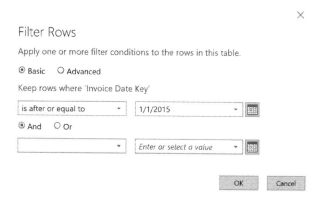

Figure 7.25 – Filter Rows dialog for partitions

10. Click **OK** to set the new filter and then **Close & Update** the partition.

11. The final step is to rename the partitions History Partition and Current Partition. Click **OK** when you are done. You can see the partitions you created in **Tabular Model Explorer**, as shown here:

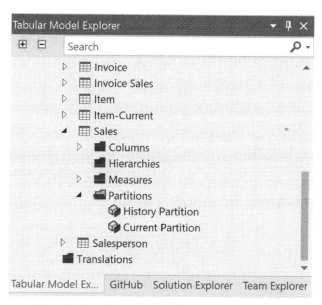

Figure 7.26 – Partitions in Tabular Model Explorer

Congratulations! You have created a tabular model that is similar in design to the multidimensional model you created previously. This model is an in-memory model that fully refreshes the data in the model using a star schema data warehouse as its underlying data source. Next, we will look at the other design models you can use with tabular models.

Creating a tabular model with DirectQuery

Now that we have created our first model, which was built on a data refresh or data load model, we will create a tabular model with DirectQuery in this section. By way of a brief reminder, a DirectQuery model does not store the data in Analysis Services; it sends native queries to the data source to return the data that was requested. We will be creating a new project and model that will be designed from the ground up for DirectQuery.

> **Copy issues with models and converting to DirectQuery**
>
> While the documentation notes that you can simply change the mode to DirectQuery and fix any errors, this did not occur with our model. After removing partitions, we continued to receive odd errors, so we are going to create the model from scratch in this exercise. If you are interested in trying to do this, you should use a copy of your original model. Create a new tabular model project and replace the code (view the code from **Solution Explorer** on the `Model.bim` file). This will give you a safe baseline to start with. You will need to remove the partitions we created on the `Sales` table to get past the first round of errors.

Creating a new tabular model project

We will be creating a new project in our existing solution. Let's get started:

1. From **Solution Explorer**, right-click the solution name, `WideWorldImportersTAB`, choose **Add**, and then click **New Project** from the menu.

2. In the **Add a new project** dialog, choose **Analysis Services Tabular Project**, and then click **Next**.

3. Name your project `WideWorldImportersDQ` and click **Create**. You can select the workspace server to complete the process.

Converting the new model to DirectQuery

These steps will change from in-memory to direct query, which sends queries to SQL Server to be executed:

1. First, confirm you are working in the correct project in **Solution Explorer**. If you followed the naming conventions I used, you should be in the WideWorldImportersDQ project, as shown here:

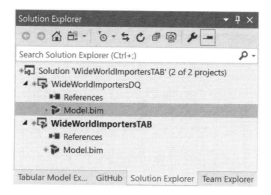

Figure 7.27 – Solution Explorer – Tabular solution

2. Select Model.bim as shown in the previous screenshot and view the properties for that file.

3. Locate the **DirectQuery Mode** property and set the value to **On**:

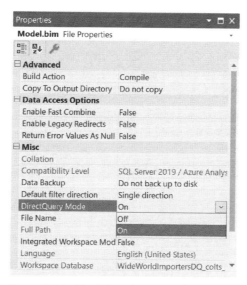

Figure 7.28 – The DirectQuery Mode property

4. To create a new data source, right-click **Data Sources** in **Tabular Model Explorer** and choose **New Data Source**. The first thing to notice in the **Get Data** dialog is that there are fewer data sources to choose from. That list contains currently supported data sources for DirectQuery and is not limited to Microsoft data sources. Oracle and Teradata are also supported:

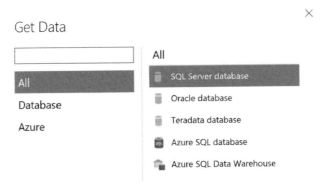

Figure 7.29 – DirectQuery Get Data options

5. Now, choose **SQL Server database** and click **Connect**. Complete the connection information process to connect to `WideWorldImportersDW`. Once done, be aware that this is the only connection you can have in a DirectQuery tabular model. This is one of the limitations using a DirectQuery tabular model.

6. Next, we will connect tables to our model. Right-click on the data source you created and select **Import new tables**.

7. In the **Navigator** dialog, select **Fact.Sale**. Then, click the **Select Related Tables** button. This should add the dimension tables related to **Fact.Sale**. For our purposes, this will be a good option to demonstrate DirectQuery. Select **Load** when this is done. Ironically, we are neither importing nor loading data in this scenario. You will see from the **Data Processing** dialog shown next that no data is actually loaded into the model:

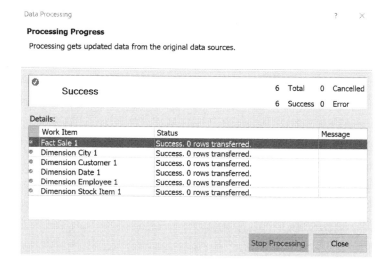

Figure 7.30 – Processing Progress for DirectQuery

You will notice that the grids are empty in Visual Studio. We will resolve that in the next section by adding sample partitions. If, during this process, you are unable to click on other tabs, you may need to save your progress and restart Visual Studio before moving to the next section.

Adding sample partitions to the DirectQuery model

When working with DirectQuery, you only see the metadata for the model. In order to design with data, which is the normal process when working with tabular models, you need to create sample partitions that bring some data into memory so it can be worked with at design time. These partitions are only used during the design process.

Let's create sample partitions. We will start with the `Fact Sale` table:

1. Click on the **Fact Sale** tab and then click the **Partitions** button in the toolbar to open **Partition Manager**.

   The default partition is designated as the **DirectQuery** partition. When deployed, this is the only partition that will be visible to users. Unlike the previous work we did with partitions, you will see a new button called **Set as a Sample**.

2. Select the existing **DirectQuery** partition and click **Copy**. This new partition is designated as the sample.

3. Next, click the **Design** button when the copied partition is selected.

4. In the **Power Query Editor** window, select **Invoice Date Key** and filter the dates for the year **2015** as shown. This will limit the sample we will work with during design time to **Invoice Date** in 2015. This is very important if you are using DirectQuery with very large tables. This will limit the sample of rows so you can test the design in Excel without issues:

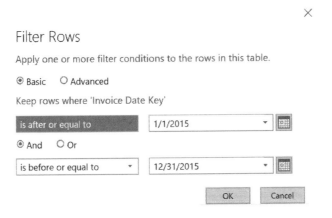

Figure 7.31 – Filter Rows for sample partition

Even after creating the sample partition, the data does not display in the grid. This is because development with DirectQuery models is still difficult and limited at this time.

You can create sample partitions for the dimensions as well at this point. I chose not to filter the dimensions so we could be assured that the data works as expected. This is a simple process of making a copy of the partition and then processing the partitions.

Enhancing your DirectQuery model

While you have limited ability to enhance DirectQuery tabular models, Analysis Services serves as a semantic layer for your relational data. So, what can you do?

- **Renaming objects**: You can rename columns and tables to improve the customer experience.

- **Adding Measures**: You can add measures using the same technique we used with the in-memory models. Select the column to add the measure to and then click the **Sum** button on the toolbar.

- **Adding Columns**: You can add calculated columns to the tables as well.

Previewing the data with Excel

In order to preview the data in the model, your best option is to use the **Analyze in Excel** option. Look for the Excel icon in the middle of the toolbar. This will open the **Analyze in Excel** dialog. At the bottom of the dialog, you have the option to choose **Sample data view** or **Full data view**. **Sample data view** will use the smaller in-memory dataset. **Full data view** will work with the full dataset. Sample data will allow you to work with the data more efficiently, which is valuable when testing the updates:

Figure 7.32 – Analyze in Excel with DirectQuery models

DirectQuery models allow you to query larger datasets that may not fit in memory. These models also support *real-time* changes to the underlying data source. They are not the preferred solution in tabular models, but they are definitely a good option when required. We will now move forward and create a tabular model on transactional data.

Creating a tabular model on transactional data

We are now going to create a model based on *unprepared* data. There are cases where building on the transactional system may be your best option due to business or other technical reasons. This allows you to build an analytics solution without necessarily building out a data warehouse. This process will use **Power Query** extensively to build out the solution.

We will start the process by adding another SSAS tabular project to our solution. Let's name this one `WideWorldImportersPQ` for Power Query. Let's get started on our new model:

1. Add a new data source to the model. This time, we will be connecting to the transactional database we restored, `WideWorldImporters`.

2. Next, we will import the tables. Right-click the data source and select **Import New Tables**. Here is the list of tables to select in the navigator: `Application.TransactionTypes`, `Sales.CustomerCategories`, `Sales.Customers`, and `Sales.CustomerTransactions`.

3.   Once you have the tables selected, click **Transform Data**. This will open **Power Query Editor** so that we can modify the tables.

We are going to create a simple model so we will be removing columns, changing some names, and making other adjustments to prepare the data for the model. The next steps will walk through this process for each table's clean-up. This process is very similar to transforming data with ETL tools but is typically referred to as **shaping the data** with this toolset.

Let's start with the `Sales Customers` query. We will only be keeping the `CustomerID`, `CustomerName`, and `CustomerCategoryID` columns:

1. You can easily do this by selecting the three columns we want to keep.

2. Then, right-click on one of the columns and choose **Remove Other Columns**. The following screenshot shows the highlighted column and the menu option:

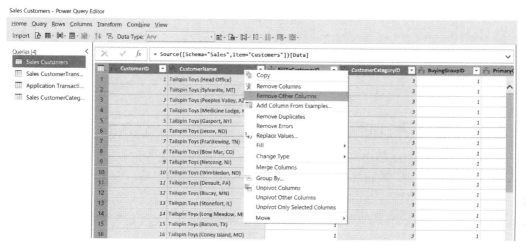

Figure 7.33 – Removing columns in Power Query

3. Once that is complete, rename the query Customers and add a space to CustomerName so that it becomes Customer Name.

4. We will keep only two fields from Application TransactionTypes – TransactionTypeID and TransactionTypeName. Rename the query Transaction Types and the name column Transaction Type.

5. Only two fields will be retained for the Sales CustomerCategories query – CustomerCategoryName and CustomerCategoryID. Rename the query Customer Categories and the name column Customer Category.

6. The last query, Sales CustomerTransactions, will have a few more columns – CustomerTransactionID, CustomerID, TransactionTypeID, InvoiceID, TransactionDate, and TransactionAmount. Rename the query Customer Transactions. Add spaces to the TransactionDate and TransactionAmount column names.

> **Update permissions in the database to process**
>
> Depending on how you are authenticating to the `WideWorldImporters` database, you may either get an error on permissions or only get the data partially loaded. The `WideWorldImporters` table, `Sales.Customers`, has special permissions associated with it. The simplest way to bypass this for our purposes is to give the user you are connecting with `sysadmin` permissions in the server. *This is not a best practice.* When working with business databases, your DBA team should know the correct permission set required to access your data.

7. When you are done with the changes to the queries, click on **Close & Apply** or **Close & Update** from the **Home** menu. The option changes depending on whether this is a new query or a query you are changing. This will load the grid with the data we shaped for this model.

While this was not an exhaustive review of the Power Query capabilities in designing tabular models, this gives you the opportunity to see that the data does not have to be pristine in order to be consumed by a tabular model. We encourage you to explore these capabilities to better understand the various ways in which you can shape data with Power Query. Let's now import a Power Pivot model into Analysis Services.

Importing a Power Pivot model into Analysis Services

In the previous chapter, we created a Power Pivot model in Excel. In this section, we will import that model into Analysis Services.

Once again, we will be adding another Analysis Services tabular project to our solution. In this case, the steps include importing the Power Pivot model. Let's get started:

1. Open **Solution Explorer** in Visual Studio. Right-click the solution and select **Add | New Project**.

2. In the **Add a new project** dialog, search for `tabular`. You should see an option called **Import from PowerPivot**. Select that option and click **Next**.

3. Give the new project a name like `WideWorldImportersPowerPivot` and click **Create**. You should use the same settings for your workspace server and click **OK**.

4. You will then be presented with an **Open** dialog. Browse to the Excel workbook you created previously and click **Open**. When the process completes, you should see your model with the data loaded.

That's all it takes to import the model from Power Pivot in Excel. You should now have four tabular model projects that have been created in various ways. The next section wraps up the chapter by deploying these models to SSAS.

Deploying and processing your completed models

As we wrap things up by deploying and processing your models, you need to be aware that these will increase the memory pressure on your development solution. We recommend that you remove all but the first model when we are done to save on resources. That model will be used in the following chapters as well.

To deploy your projects, right-click the project and choose **Deploy**. This will load the data model on Analysis Services. Keep in mind that the workspace versions of the databases will be on the server if you have Visual Studio open and are working in a model. Start with the `WideWorldImportersTAB` and `WideWorldImportersPQ` projects.

When you deploy the `WideWorldImportersPowerPivot` project, you will get a message about upgrading the model to the latest compatibility level, as shown in the following screenshot:

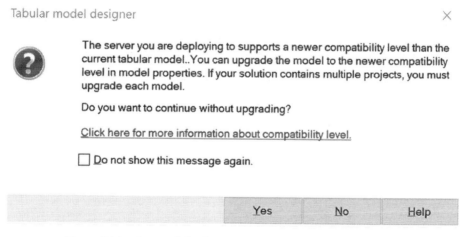

Figure 7.34 – Compatibility level warning for the Power Pivot model

In this case, we will select **No**. Let's update our model prior to processing:

1. Click on the `Model.bim` file in **Solution Explorer** and go to the **Properties** model.

2. In the **Compatibility Level** property, you should see **SQL Server 2014 / SQL Server 2012 SP1 (1103)** as the current level. Change that to **SQL Server 2019 / Azure Analysis Services (1500)**.

3. You will get a warning saying that the change is irreversible. Click **Yes** and continue.

Now that you have updated the model, deploy it to Analysis Services.

> **Instability in Visual Studio 2019 – restarts required**
>
> Throughout this chapter, you may experience odd errors, including errors that say the model is already open after you make a property change like the compatibility level. Close Visual Studio and reopen the solution. If you are new to working with data tools in Visual Studio, especially the business intelligence tools, you will find this frustrating. While not the best working situation, restarting the IDE seems to clear up most of these issues during the development cycle.

The last project we will be deploying is the DirectQuery project. Right-click and deploy it to Analysis Services now. Because this is a DirectQuery model, you will notice that only the metadata was loaded to the server.

Once you have deployed all the models, close Visual Studio and open SSMS. Connect to your tabular model and you should see all the new tabular models deployed without the GUIDs. If you still see a GUID-based model, either Visual Studio is still running with a model in design mode or you set your workspace up to retain the workspace models.

That wraps up the various ways in which you can create a tabular model.

Summary

In this chapter, you have learned to create tabular models from various source configurations, such as star schemas and transactional databases. You have created a DirectQuery model that uses the underlying data store to process the requests, and you imported your Power Pivot model into Analysis Services as well. The skills you have learned here will support your ability to deliver tabular models that meet business needs regardless of the data sources. You will also be able to explain the value of improving the data sources to create more robust analytic models.

Don't forget to remove the Power Query and Power Pivot models to keep your memory management on your development server in check. You can remove the other two databases as well because we will be using workspace databases for the next chapter. However, you will need to redeploy `WideWorldImportersDQ` and `WideWorldImportersTAB` for later chapters.

The next chapter focuses on using DAX, or Data Analysis Expressions, to expand your model even more. We will look at more complex measures and columns. We will also deploy some KPIs and calculated tables. Let's go expand those models!

8
Adding Measures and Calculations with DAX

Now that you have created your tabular models, we will look at expanding the models further using **Data Analytic Expressions**, or **DAX**. Like MDX for multidimensional models, DAX is designed for use with Microsoft's **VertiPaq** engine. While MDX is modeled after SQL (SELECT…FROM…WHERE), DAX was designed for use by business and data analysts already familiar with Excel functions. In some ways, it is a *happy medium* between **Multidimensional Expressions** (**MDX**) and Excel functions. We can use DAX to create columns, measures, and query the database.

In this chapter, you will learn all there is to know about DAX, which will help you to enhance your existing models to meet the business requirements. Without the calculations you create with DAX, the user experience with the models will not be as good as it could be. DAX calculations allow your users to have business-ready calculations at their fingertips. Without these calculations in the models, users would need to add them in their tools. Not only is this not user friendly, but it often leads to calculation variances between the reports different users create.

In this chapter, we're going to cover the following main topics:

- Understanding the basics of DAX
- Adding columns and measures to the tabular model
- Creating measures with the `CALCULATE` function
- Working with time intelligence and DAX
- Creating calculated tables
- Creating calculation groups (new in SQL Server 2019)
- Creating KPIs
- Querying your model with SQL Server Management Studio and DAX

Technical requirements

In this chapter, we will be using the first tabular model we created in *Chapter 6, Preparing Your Data for Tabular Models*, **WideWorldImportersTAB**, to exercise DAX. We will be working with our Visual Studio project as well. Lastly, you will need to have Excel ready for testing and SSMS for querying.

Understanding the basics of DAX

One of the key differences in DAX is that it is used to build expressions and formulas, not traditional style queries. SQL works with tabular sets of data and MDX works with multidimensional sets. DAX was designed more like Excel functions. This works well when creating calculated measures and calculated columns. So, unlike MDX and SQL, there is no **SELECT … FROM … WHERE** structure. There are a few other concepts we need to review before we start creating calculations.

When working with DAX, you need to consider the context the function applies to. When creating calculated columns, the context is the row. You can use anything in the row to help build the column with DAX. Other functions apply to the table or just the column. When creating DAX calculations, you need to check the context to make sure you are using the function correctly.

Table names and field names use special syntax. Table names are typically enclosed in single quotes, `'Table Name'`, and columns are enclosed in brackets, `[Column Name]`. When working with tables, you may see some calculations that do not use single quotes. They are not required when there are no spaces or special characters in the name of the table. For example, `Item` and `'Item'` are both valid table names in our model. IntelliSense demonstrates the standard practices when used.

Finally, whenever working with DAX, you always start with an equals sign. This is true in both measures and calculated columns. You can add the name of the measure before the equals sign. The base syntax for measures is `[Measure Name]:=<Measure Calculation>`. When creating a calculated column, the formula bar does not contain the name; it is simply `=<Column Calculation>`.

Adding columns and measures to the tabular model

We can add value and usability to our model by adding measures and columns. In the previous chapter, we created `Invoices`, `Invoice Line Count`, and `Total Sales Amount` on the `Sales` table. We created these using the **Autosum** button on the toolbar. This is the simplest way to add basic measures to your tables. **Sum**, **Average**, **Count**, **DistinctCount**, **Min**, and **Max** are available using this button. As we did previously, simply select the column you want to create the measure for and use the **Autosum** menu to create the measure. Rename the measure as desired, add some formatting, and you are good to go.

We will look at other options in this chapter to manually create measures and calculated columns. Like Excel, we can use the formula bar to create and manage our measures. The following screenshot shows the formula bar and the formula buttons (highlighted):

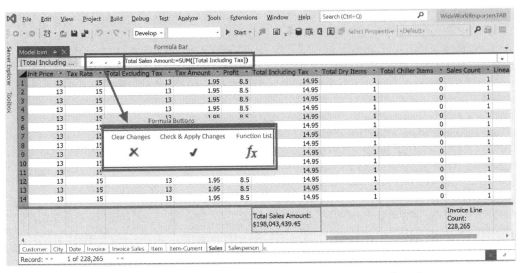

Figure 8.1 – DAX Formula Bar and Formula Buttons in Visual Studio

Both calculated columns and measures use the formula bar to display the calculation and the name of the calculation.

> **Note**
>
> Visual Studio has issues with some high-resolution monitors that cause some of the buttons to be very small as it does not scale. This is particularly an issue with data tools and, depending on your monitor resolutions, some buttons and text will appear as they do in the preceding screenshot. We will show the details where we can, so that you can identify the buttons and text used throughout the book.

As you can see in the preceding screenshot, there are three buttons on the formula bar to help you create calculations. The red **X** is used to cancel the changes you made. The green check mark will check and apply the changes. Keep in mind that you are actively adding these to a tabular model in your workspace. When applied, it will create and deploy the calculation to the workspace. Canceling changes becomes necessary when troubleshooting issues with your calculation that cause it to not deploy correctly.

The third button on the formula bar is **fx**, which is a function list. This allows you to add a function to your formula. It also shows you the syntax and basic description of the function. In the following screenshot, we opened the **Insert Function** dialog and have highlighted **AVERAGEA**. This function creates an average of the numeric values in the column while ignoring the non-numeric values:

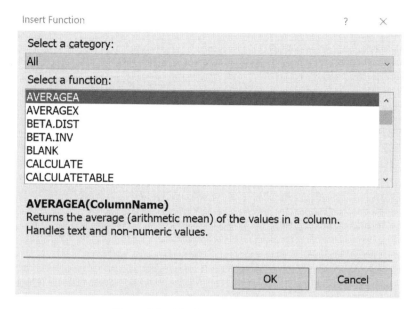

Figure 8.2 – The Insert Function dialog

As you can see in the screenshot, there are many functions available to you. This is a good way to explore them. The dialog also has a **Select a category** dropdown. This will filter the functions to one of the following areas:

- **Date & Time**: These functions are typically referred to as **time intelligence** functions. Some are basic, which capture the date part, but others require the Date table to support functions such as NEXTYEAR.

- **Math & Trig**: Just like the category implies, these are math functions such as SQRT (returns the square root of a number) and MOD (returns the remainder in a division calculation).

- **Statistical**: This is one of the most frequently used categories as it supports counts, averages, and standard deviation.

- **Text**: You can use the functions here to concatenate, trim, and search string values.

- **Logical**: Logical functions include IF, AND, and NOT, which allow you to add decision logic to your calculations.

- **Filter**: This list includes various types of functions that limit the set of values included in calculations. Some of these filters have explicit functionality to work with selected values or to even remove other filters from the calculation.

- **Information**: Most of the functions you will use in this category are IS functions; for example, checking to see whether a value is a number (ISNUMBER) or whether the field is empty (ISEMPTY). They are often used with the Filter functions to properly apply calculations.

- **Parent/Child**: These are PATH functions that work with a list of IDs. The functions here are used to traverse hierarchies.

> **Implicit calculations**
>
> Like Excel, tabular models have the concept of implicit calculations. If you have a value in a column that is numeric, by default, a sum calculation for that column is created. You do not need to add the calculation. However, to make sure you get your expected result, we recommend that you build calculations that meet those needs. This will allow you to apply any business corrections or any other adjustments needed at a later time. Also, some tools will treat value columns as attribute columns. Calculated measures clearly define the value role.

Before we create our calculations, there are two other buttons to call out on the formula bar. The formula buttons we have been looking at are on the left side of the formula bar. On the right side of the formula bar are two buttons. The first button looks like a down arrow. You can use this button to expand the formula section so you can see longer DAX expressions. The button furthest to the right will open a basic **DAX Editor**. This allows for more screen space when creating complicated or long DAX expressions, as shown here:

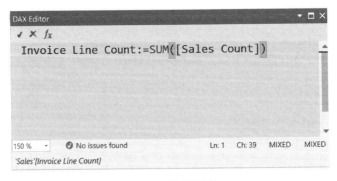

Figure 8.3 – DAX Editor

Now that we are familiar with adding columns and measures to the table, let's learn how to create item calculations.

Creating item calculations

In *Chapter 5, Adding Measures and Calculations with MDX*, we created calculations based on item colors. In this section, we will go through a similar process, creating calculated columns and measures to support item counts by color. Through the next steps, we will create a column to determine how many red items are on each line and then create some calculations based on that information. In the next section, we will do a similar process, but use the CALCULATE function to create the values:

1. In your Visual Studio project, go to the Sales table in the model.

2. Scroll over to the right and you will see a blank column at the end with the words **Add Column**. Click the column header.

3. In the function bar, start by giving the column a name. We will call this column Red Items. Let's start the function with the following code: Red Items:=.

4. In order to identify which items are red, we need to refer to the Item table. DAX has a function to look up values in related tables called RELATED. This will return the related value from the table, which, in our case, is items whose color is red. We will use the RELATED('Item'[Color]) code to find the related item color. This function works well when creating calculated columns that refer to columns from other tables. However, if the relationship does not exist, this will return an error.

5. In the end, we want to populate our column with Quantity from the line we are on whenever the item's color is red. Here is the full formula to return the desired result:

```
Red Items:=IF(RELATED('Item'[Color])="Red",
   Sales[Quantity], 0)
```

We now have a column that contains the quantity of red items for each row. The value 0 is used when the row does not have red items. Keep in mind that this formula uses the row as its context to determine the relationship and return the quantity.

6. Now that we have the Red Items column, we can create a measure that returns the sum. Click in the measures area below the column. Go to the formula bar and use the following code to create the Total Red Items measure:

```
Total Red Items:= SUM(Sales[Red Items)
```

7. While you have the measure highlighted, let's fix the format. In the measure properties, set the format to **Custom** and use the following code for the format string: 0,0. Now we are done with the basics of adding red items.

In DAX, you will notice that many functions, such as SUM and AVERAGE, have suffixes such as A and X or a combination thereof. The base functions work as expected; the calculation is based on the column or field specified. Let's start with SUMX to see the difference. SUMX evaluates the table and returns the sum of the values based on the expression you create for the table. When we created the sum for red items, we created a column and then summed those values. In this case, we will use a single function for the measure; no column is required:

1. Select a field in the measure grid on the Sales table.

2. In the formula bar, enter the following calculation: Total Blue Items:=SUMX('Sales',IF(RELATED('Item'[Color])="Blue", Sales[Quantity],0)). You can see in the formula that we moved the same calculation we used for the Red Items column into the measure itself. This eliminates the need for the additional column.

3. Finally, set the format for this measure to 0,0 using the **Custom** format option in the measure properties.

> **Note**
>
> You may decide that you need the column as well as the calculation. Keep in mind that columns are calculated and stored in memory to improve performance. Measures are calculated *on the fly* when requested. You may find that your performance varies depending on how you create the calculation. Furthermore, you may want those values in columns if you have other calculations you would like to use them with.

Let's wrap up this section by creating the rest of the color measures for the remaining item colors (black, gray, light brown, steel gray, white, and yellow) using the SUMX function format. Remember to set the formatting to keep the measures consistent when you add those measures now.

In the next section, we will look at the variations of the COUNT and AVERAGE measures.

The COUNT and AVERAGE measures

The COUNT and AVERAGE measures have variations that can be used to understand the various ways in which DAX does calculations. We have already looked at the SUMX function and how it uses the table as the base for the calculation. The syntax and functionality are the same for COUNTX and AVERAGEX. They both will perform the calculation over the table based on the expression you provide.

In the next steps, we are going to create additional metrics based on Invoice Profit in the Invoice Sales table:

1. First, we need to switch to the Invoice Sales table. Find the Invoice Profit column and select a field in the measure grid.

2. The first measure we will create is Average Invoice Profit. For this measure, we will use the AVERAGE function. This will give us the average or mathematic mean for all the invoices. Here is the formula for this measure:

   ```
   Average Invoice Profit:=AVERAGE('Invoice Sales'[Invoice
       Profit])
   ```

3. The next measure will be to demonstrate AVERAGEX. We will look for the average profit for sales made in Indiana. Once again, we will use the RELATED function to find the matching State Province instance from the City table. This will filter the invoices and give us an average profit for Indiana sales.

   Here is the formula for the Indiana profits:

   ```
   Average Indiana Profit:=AVERAGEX('Invoice
       Sales',IF(RELATED(City[State Province])="Indiana",'Invoice
       Sales'[Invoice Profit],""))
   ```

4. Now, to demonstrate the COUNTA measure, we are going to copy the Invoice Profit column and set some of the values to NULL. COUNTA counts non-empty cells, whereas COUNT will count only those cells containing values.

5. In **Tabular Model Explorer**, right-click the Invoice Sales table and select **Table Properties**.

6. In the **Edit Table Properties** dialog, click the **Design** button. This will open the **Power Query Editor** for the table.

7. Find the **Invoice Profit** column. Right-click the column header and select **Duplicate Column**. This will create a copy of the column in the table called **Invoice Profit – Copy**.

8. Right-click the header again and choose **Replace Values**. In this dialog, use 40.00 for **Value To Find**. Use null as the **Replace With** value (null is case-sensitive. You may get an error if you use any capital letters. The error you will see is that text is not permitted). Your dialog should look like the one in the following screenshot:

Replace Values

Replace one value with another in the selected columns.

Value To Find

40.00

Replace With

null

OK	Cancel

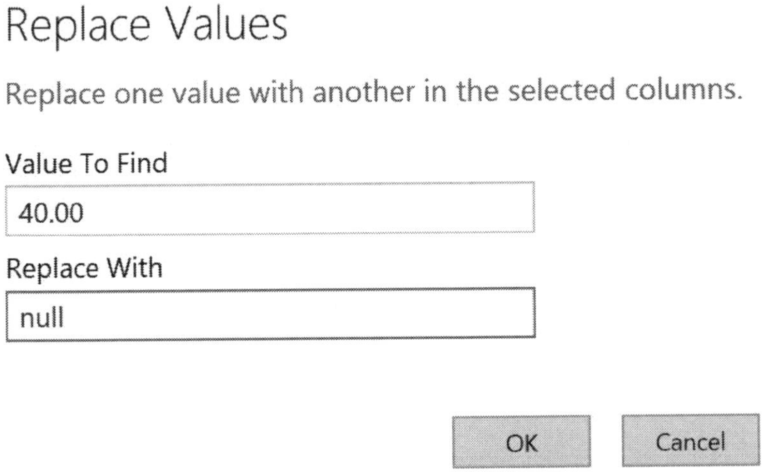

Figure 8.4 – The Replace Values dialog in Power Query

9. Click **OK** to complete the process.

10. To verify that the change has been applied properly, you can click the down arrow on the column header and filter for **(null)**, as shown in the following screenshot. This will show the values you changed:

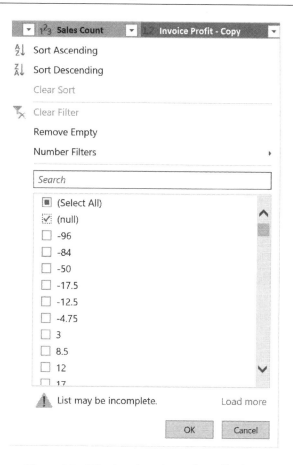

Figure 8.5 – Filtering the column for null values

11. Once you have finished reviewing the change, be sure to remove the filter step from the **Applied Steps** section by clicking the delete button, as shown in the following screenshot. Then you are ready to move to the next step:

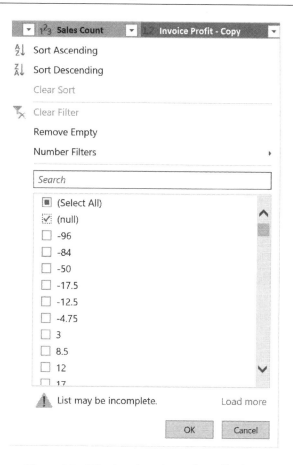

Figure 8.6 – Removing the filter

12. Go to **Home** and choose **Close & Update**. Then, click **OK** to close the **Table Properties** window.

13. Back on the `Invoice Sales` table, you will see the **Invoice Profit – Copy** field you added at the end of the table. If there are no values in the column, process the table using the **Process Table** button on the toolbar shown here:

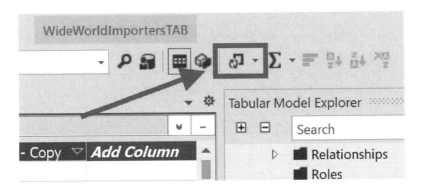

Figure 8.7 – The Process Table button

14. Now that we have the **Invoice Profit – Copy** field, create a COUNT calculation – `Count Inv Profits:=COUNT('Invoice Sales'[Invoice Profit - Copy])`. This returns the count of non-empty values in the column.

15. Create the COUNTA measure: `CountA Inv Profits:=COUNTA('Invoice Sales'[Invoice Profit - Copy])`. This also returns the count of non-empty values in the column. Effectively they have the same value, but we are not discovering how many invoices do not have a profit or loss recorded.

These measures have helped us see profits. The next measures will help us identify missing profits using DAX.

Identifying missing profits

We will now add another column that will help us identify invoices missing profits:

1. Click on **Add Column** in your `Invoice Sales` table.

2. In the formula bar, we are going to use the ISBLANK function to identify those columns' missing values. Use this formula to create the column: `=ISBLANK('Invoice Sales'[Invoice Profit - Copy])`.

3. Name the column `Missing Profit`. The `Missing Profit` column contains TRUE and FALSE as values.

4. First, let's add the standard COUNT function to this column. Use the following calculation: `Total Profit Count:=COUNT('Invoice Sales'[Missing Profit])`. When you apply the change, your cell will report an error. If you read the tooltip for the error, you will see that COUNT does not work with **BOOLEAN** data type columns.

5. Update the formula by using the COUNTA function as follows: `Total Profit Count:=COUNTA('Invoice Sales'[Missing Profit])`. This will now return the full number of rows with a value in it. The COUNTA function can be used effectively for various column types.

6. The final step is to answer the question, "How many invoices are missing profit calculations?". We can use two measures to answer this question. Click an empty space in **Measures Grid** to create your new measure. This answer can now be done with simple math: `Total Profit Count - Count Inv Profits`. Here is the complete formula: `Invoices Missing Profits:=[Total Profit Count]-[Count Inv Profits]`.

The steps so far in this section have been used to exercise various aspects of using DAX with tabular models. As you were working through this section, you likely realized that the editor for building measures and columns with the tabular model is not very elegant. While working with the editor, IntelliSense can even get in the way. The more you work with the tool, the easier it will be.

Before we move to the next section, all the measures we have created respond to filters, slicers, and cross-filtering in visualization tools. For example, if your visualization tool has a date slicer, we can find the number of red items sold during that range just by using our measure. It will filter the measure by the date selected. We will explore some ways to ignore filters and build more complex calculations using the CALCUATE function in the next section.

Creating measures with the CALCULATE function

In the previous section, we created measures that gave us counts for each of the colors for our items. We will be using the CALCUATE function to create formulas that return the percentage of a color versus the total of colored items in the model. To do this, we will need to eliminate those items whose color is N/A. We will use the CALCULATE function to do this.

The CALCULATE function allows us to add filters to the calculation we are trying to work with. CALCULATE does not allow the use of a measure in its expression. It also returns a single value. The filters for this function need to return a table, so the work we did with our item filter in the count calculations will need to be handled as a table filter. The other important note here is that the CALCULATE function's filters override other filters that may be applied by external operations in visualization tools. The calculation will be performed over the tables as specified in the filter.

Let's get started with creating our percentage calculations:

1. Open the Sales table in your model in Visual Studio.

2. Select a cell in the measure grid. We will be creating similar measures for each of the colors. Here is the measure we will be adding for red items:

    ```
    % of Red Items:=[Total Red Items] /
    CALCULATE(SUM(Sales[Quantity]),FILTER('Sales'
    ,RELATED('Item'[Color])<>"N/A"))
    ```

    Let's break this down so you can understand the parts better. The numerator is the measure we created previously – Total Red Items. While a column is required for this calculation, the rest of the measures require the use of the following syntax as we see with blue items (this is the preferred approach):

    ```
    Total Blue
    Items:=SUMX('Sales',IF(RELATED('Item'[Color])="Blue",
    Sales[Quantity],0))
    ```

3. Next, let's look at the FILTER function we used. This is similar to the IF functionality in our color count measures. The FILTER function creates a table based on the criteria specified. We are eliminating any Sales line where Item has a color of N/A. This means that our measures will be calculating the percentage of red items for all items that have color.

    In the CALCULATE function, we are calculating the sum of Quantity over the table returned by the filter. This gives the sum of all the colored items sold in the Sales table. This completes the denominator.

    We use a standard division operation to create the percentage.

4. Finally, change the formatting to **Percentage** in **Measure Properties**. It will automatically use two decimal places.

5. Wrap this up by creating the percentages for the remaining colors: blue, black, gray, steel gray, light brown, yellow, and white.

Now, we mentioned before that designing measures is difficult, including the fact that IntelliSense will get in the way. Let's now review some helpful tips to save you from frustration here:

1. First, copy the original `% of Red Items` calculation from the formula bar.

2. Next, click into the next cell in the measure grid and paste the formula into the bar.

3. Normally, I would try to double-click `Red` and replace it with `Blue` to finish this off. However, this does not work as expected all the time, or even most of the time. Instead, for the name of the measure, place your cursor at the beginning or end of the word. Then, delete the word using backspace or delete and type in the new value.

4. For the calculation itself, we need to change the value from `[Total Red Items]` to `[Total Blue Items]`.

IntelliSense can complicate editing

At times, it is difficult in Visual Studio to highlight the words in the formula bar. You can delete the expression and start typing. IntelliSense will want to help, so, you let it. However, you may get partial results in Visual Studio such as `[Total Blue Items]Items]`, which is obviously incorrect. Now you need to eliminate the extra characters. The other option is to delete the entire formula and type it in. Then, click at the end of the formula (do not use *Tab* or *Enter*). Then, click *Enter* and it will work. Hopefully, this will help you use the formula bar more efficiently when creating measures.

Let's now look at how we can perform key calculations using the `ALL` function.

Using the ALL function with CALCULATE

Before we move on, there is another key calculation that can be performed using the `CALCULATE` function. We often need to create calculations that are in reference to the grand total and we don't want external filters to change how the denominator for those calculations is performed. In this case, we can use the `CALCULATE` function with the `ALL` function to guarantee the results.

Let's use this capability to calculate the percentage of total invoices. The purpose of the calculation is to have a flexible numerator that honors context filtering, whereas the denominator will be static and count all of the invoices and ignore the filters:

1. Change to the `Invoice Sales` table in your model.

2. Select a cell in the measure grid below the **WWI Invoice ID** column.

Where should you put measures in the measure grid?

Throughout the creation of measures in this chapter, we have been adding measures under columns that are used. However, this is not required. We are doing this to make finding the measures a bit easier. The reality is that it does not matter where you put the measure in the grid. By now, you must have noticed that all measures contain full references to tables. The grid is simply a way to see the results of a calculation quickly. All measures are considered to be part of the tabular model as a whole and not bound to a table or column. So, if you have a pattern that you would prefer to use, go for it. We will continue to keep calculations on tables that *make sense* and near primary columns being used.

---

3. Let's now review the formula we will use to create the calculation:

```
% of All Invoices:=COUNT(Invoice[WWI Invoice ID]) /
CALCULATE(COUNT(Invoice[WWI Invoice ID]),ALL('Invoice
Sales'))
```

You can see that we use the standard COUNT function to count the invoices.

4. Next, we use the CALCULATE and ALL functions to override other filters to create the denominator. When applied, this will be 100%.

5. Change the format to **Percentage**. You should see the result as 100% in the measure grid.

6. There is no way in Visual Studio to validate that the percentage worked as expected. Let's use the **Analyze in Excel** feature to test this measure. Click the **Excel** icon in the toolbar. This will open an Excel workbook with a PivotTable connected to your tabular model.

7. Add % of All Invoices to the **Values** panel. This will add the value to the PivotTable with the value 100.00% in the only cell.

8. Next, use the Search function in the **PivotTables Fields** panel and search for Buying Group. Select the **Buying Group** option in the **More Fields** section of the Customer table. This will add **Buying Group** to the rows. You can see that the % of All Invoices works as designed as shown in the following screenshot:

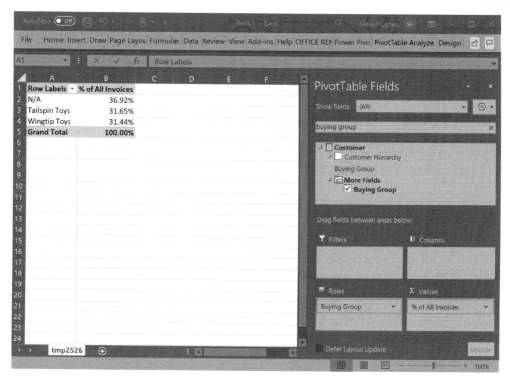

Figure 8.8 – Analyzing new calculations in Excel

9. Close **Excel** when you are done exploring. You can use this feature to validate formulas as needed.

We are now ready to look at some time intelligence functions.

Checking your work with Excel

Use the **Analyze in Excel** feature available in Visual Studio to check your work often. This is a great way to make sure the calculation responds to filtering, slicing and dicing, and visualization as expected. This feature creates a connection to your workspace model and runs queries there. This is a quick way to work with the model you are currently designing.

Working with time intelligence and DAX

The time intelligence functionality is an important part of any analytics solution. Tabular models are no exception. DAX has several functions that support time intelligence. In order for these functions to work, a table in the model must be marked as **Date Table**. In *Chapter 7, Building a Tabular Model in SSAS 2019*, we marked our date table as the date table for this purpose. The requirements for the date table are called out in that chapter as well.

Time intelligence functions in DAX allow you to perform calculations with your data over supported time periods. This includes year, quarter, month, and day. Some of the functions are common, including the `to date` functions such as `YTD`, `QTD`, and `MTD`. Others have specific use cases, such as the `BALANCE` functions, which can be used to calculate a value at the end of a period such as a month, `CLOSINGBALANCEMONTH`.

We are going to create a few calculations using the `Invoice Sales` table. We will be checking our calculations using **Analyze with Excel**. The data we are working with is not in the current time period, so we will not be able to rely on the calculations in the measure grid. We are going to create a set of annual calculations. Here is what we will be creating in the next set of steps:

- Invoice sales YTD
- Invoice sales next year
- Invoice sales previous year

Creating the YTD measure

Let's get started by creating the `YTD` measure:

1. Open your model in Visual Studio and navigate to the `Invoice Sales` table in the model.

2. We will be using the **Invoice Total Including Tax** field for these calculations. You can select a cell in the measure grid to start creating these formulas. Let's keep these calculations in the same area for ease of use.

3. The first calculation we are going to create is `Invoice Sales YTD`. We will be using the `TOTALYTD` function. This function takes the following four parameters:

    a) `expression`: The `expression` is the calculation, which is `SUM('Invoice Sales'[Invoice Total Including Tax])` in our case.

    b) `dates`: Next is the `dates` parameter. We need to reference a date column or a date table that has a single date column. We will be using `'Date'[Date]` from our model as the date column.

    c) `filter` and `year_end_date`: These two parameters are optional. You can filter the data being evaluated and specify a specific year end date if needed. We will not be using either of these options.

    The full formula we are using is as follows:

    ```
    Invoice Sales YTD:=TOTALYTD(SUM('Invoice Sales'[Invoice
    Total Including Tax]),'Date'[Date]).
    ```

4. Let's check our work in Excel. Click the **Analyze in Excel** button. In the PivotTable, add the `Invoice Sales YTD` measure to the **Values** area and then add `Calendar Year` from the `Date` table to the **Rows** area. You can see that each year shows the YTD value for that year. You should see results similar to the worksheet shown here:

Row Labels ▾	Invoice Sales YTD
2013	$52,563,272.64
2014	$57,418,916.89
2015	$62,090,220.81
2016	$25,971,029.11
Grand Total	$25,971,029.11

Figure 8.9 – YTD results in Excel

Close Excel and then move on to the next two calculations.

Creating a calculation for next year's sales

Now we are going to create the calculation for next year's sales. While this sounds predictive, it is useful when looking at changes for the following year when evaluating values:

1. Click on a new cell in the measure grid. The NEXTYEAR function returns a table of dates that match the criteria. In order to use this function, we will use the CALCULATE function as well. Here is the code to create the next year's sales calculation:

   ```
   Invoice Sales Next Year:=CALCULATE(SUM('Invoice
   Sales'[Invoice Total Including Tax]),
    NEXTYEAR('Date'[Date]))
   ```

   You will see that the calculation in the measure grid returns (blank) as the result. This is because no values exist in the next year.

2. Before we check next year's values, let's create the previous year's sales measure as well. The PREVIOUSYEAR function has the same syntax and returns a list of dates like the NEXTYEAR function:

   ```
   Invoice Sales Previous Year:=CALCULATE(SUM('Invoice
   Sales'[Invoice Total Including Tax]),
    PREVIOUSYEAR('Date'[Date]))
   ```

   This calculation also shows (blank) in the measure grid results. Let's get back into Excel.

3. Click **Analyze in Excel** to open Excel again.

4. Add both of our new measures to the **Values** area. They still show no results.

5. Add Calendar Year to the **Rows** area. To make the comparison clearer, you can also add the Invoice Sales YTD measure to the **Values** area. Your results should look similar to the following screenshot. The results have been formatted as currency in Excel to make reading the results easier:

Row Labels	Invoice Sales YTD	Invoice Sales Next Year	Invoice Sales Previous Year
2013	$52,563,272.64	$57,418,916.89	
2014	$57,418,916.89	$62,090,220.81	$52,563,272.64
2015	$62,090,220.81	$25,971,029.11	$57,418,916.89
2016	$25,971,029.11		$62,090,220.81
Grand Total	$25,971,029.11		

Figure 8.10 – Excel results for the next year and previous year functions

6. Close Excel when you are done creating and checking the time intelligence functions.

Now that we have worked with time intelligence functions, let's move on to creating calculated tables.

Creating calculated tables

Calculated tables in tabular models are built using DAX and purely calculations. Calculated tables allow you to create role-playing dimensions, filtered row sets, summary tables, or even composite tables (made from columns of more than one table). We will demonstrate the use cases in this section.

Creating a delivery date table to support role playing

In our model, we have used two dates – **Invoice Date** and **Delivery Date** – in the `Sales` table. We have been using **Invoice Date** as our primary date in the model. This means that in order to refer to **Delivery Date** in calculations, you need to use the `USERELATIONSHIP` function. Both **Invoice Date** and **Delivery Date** are related to our `Date` table. However, only the relationship with **Invoice Date** is active.

You can visually identify inactive relationships in the **Diagram** view. In the following screenshot, you can see the two relationships. The inactive relationship is signified by the dotted line. Solid lines are active relationships:

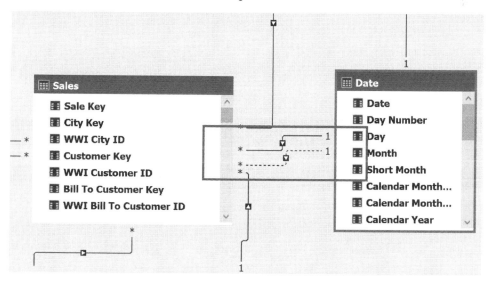

Figure 8.11 – Date relationships in the Diagram view

Using USERELATIONSHIP

If you have an inactive relationship that you want to use, the syntax is fairly straightforward. You should have an inactive relationship in place to use this function. (Do not use USERELATIONSHIP with active relationships.) In our model, you can create a calculation to show quantities by delivery date. You can use the following calculation to accomplish this: `Total Items by Delivery Date:=CALCULATE(SUM(Sales[Quantity]), USERELATIONSHIP(Sales[Delivery Date Key],'Date'[Date]))`.

You will need to use Excel to see the results in action.

Let's get started with our `Delivery Date` table:

1. In **Tabular Model Explorer**, right-click the `Tables` folder and select **New Calculated Table**. You need to be in the **Grid** view to do this.

2. To create our calculated copy, simply add the following formula: `='Date'`. This should result in the new table being loaded with the same data as the `Date` table.

3. Rename the table `Delivery Date` in the **Properties** window and you are done. You have created your first calculated table.

4. Let's wrap this up by adding the relationship. Go to the **Diagram** view and add the relationship between the `Delivery Date` table and the `Sales` table by using the `Date` field from the `Delivery Date` table and `Delivery Date Key` from the `Sales` table. Now you have an active relationship to use for more expanded analysis according to the date of delivery:

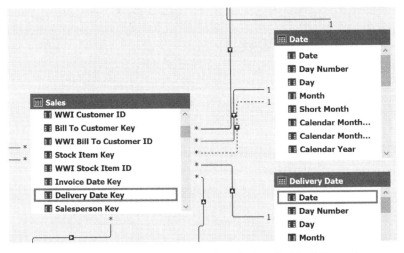

Figure 8.12 – New relationship with the calculated table delivery date

We have just created a calculated table that can be used to support a role-playing dimension. Now, we will use a filtered row set to create a calculated table.

Creating a filtered row set calculated table

In this example, we will create a calculated table that is filtered. We will use the `Invoice Sales` table as our base table. We will be filtering the `Invoice Sales` table for sales only made by the Tailspin Toys buying group:

1. Right-click the `Tables` folder in **Tabular Model Explorer** and click **New Calculated Table**.

2. In this case, we will use the `FILTER` function to reduce the rows to those from Tailspin Toys. Here is the formula we used:

```
=FILTER('Invoice Sales',RELATED(Customer[Buying Group])="Tailspin Toys")
```

3. Rename the table `Tailspin Toys Sales`.

> **Delayed refresh in calculated data**
>
> In some cases, the newly created data will not show right away in the calculated tables. You know it is working if there are no errors and you get a record count in the lower-right corner while the table is selected. We can force the data to refresh in the designer by closing and reopening Visual Studio if you want to see the data to confirm the table is working as expected.

In our case, we have just created the table. To effectively use the table moving forward, you should add relationships to support the work you want to do. Calculated tables function the same as imported tables, but they do not retain relationships when created. You will need to add them.

Creating a summary calculated table

We will create a summary calculated table that will show all the numbers of items we have by color and brand:

1. Right-click the `Tables` folder in **Tabular Model Explorer** and click **Create Calculated Table**.

2. For this table, we will be using the `SUMMARIZECOLUMNS` function. This will allow us to reduce rows and create the summary we are looking for. Logically, this is like creating an aggregated SQL statement with `GROUP BY` clauses. We will be creating the table with three columns: `Color`, `Brand`, and the count of items in that selection. Here is the formula for this table:

```
=SUMMARIZECOLUMNS('Item'[Brand],'Item'[Color],"Item Brand
Color Breakdown", COUNT('Item'[Stock Item Key]))
```

3. Rename the table `Item Brand Color`. Your results should look like the following screenshot:

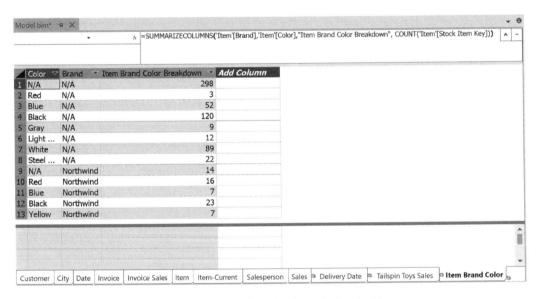

Figure 8.13 – Item Brand Color calculated table

As you can see, if you want to create some pre-aggregated or summarized tables to make the data easier to use for your end users, that capability is built into tabular models with DAX. Next, we will create a calculated table that brings more columns from other tables.

Creating a composite calculated table

We are going to use a new DAX function, GENERATE, to build out our composite table. The GENERATE function returns a Cartesian product from two tables that have matching rows between them. We are going to expand on our previous table and bring in the sales numbers from the Sales table with the help of another SUMMARIZE function:

1. Right-click the Tables folder in **Tabular Model Explorer** and click **New Calculated Table**.

2. Here is the code to build our table:

```
=GENERATE(SUMMARIZE('Customer',Customer[Buying
Group]),    SUMMARIZE('Item', 'Item'[Brand],'Item'[Color]
,"Item Brand Color Breakdown", SUMX(RELATEDTABLE(Sales),
Sales[Quantity]))
)
```

We will break it down for ease of understanding:

a) The first summarized table returns the list of buying groups. SUMMARIZE generates a table based on groups by logic.

b) The next summarized table joins **Item** and **Sales** to create a summarized set of quantities sold by color and brand. GENERATE brings these together in a Cartesian product and you should get results similar to the following screenshot:

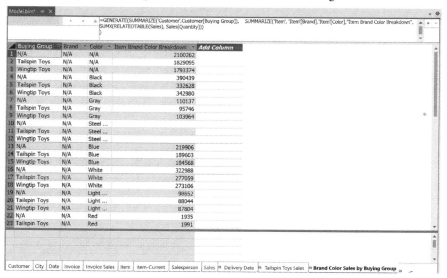

Figure 8.14 – Composite table results

3. Now, rename the table to Brand Color Sales by Buying Group.

You have now walked through building multiple calculated tables to serve different purposes. We only added the relationship to the `Delivery Date` table. If you want to add relationships to other tables, make sure to include a column that can be used to build a relationship between the target tables.

Creating calculation groups

Calculation groups are new to tabular models. You can only use this functionality if your model is set to **Compatibility Level = 1500**. Now, why is this important? As tabular models become more prevalent, we see more and more calculations being added to models. Many times, users grab a common set of calculations in various settings. For example, we created YTD, next year, and previous year measures for **Invoice Sales**.

If you want to do the same calculations for **Invoice Profit**, you will need to create new measures to support this. With calculation groups, you can create a group of metrics that work with various measures. We could use a calculation group to create the time intelligence calculations that can be shared across measures.

Getting ready to create calculation groups

Before we create our calculation group, we need to make sure our measures and model are ready. First, this functionality only works with explicit measures. Explicit measures are measures that are created in the model and not built implicitly in the visualization tools. (For example, Power BI generates implicit measures for numeric columns, and this is not supported.) In order to make sure this is handled correctly, it is necessary to set `discourageImplicitMeasures` to `TRUE` for the model. Let's set that now.

First, you will not find `discourageImplicitMeasures` as a property of the model. As per Microsoft documentation, it is exposed in the **Tabular Object Model** (**TOM**). What the documentation does not tell you (at least easily) is how to check or modify this value. This property appears to be set to `true` by default if you are using a 1500 level model, which we are. However, if you upgraded or changed the level at some point, this value may not be set correctly. Let's look at the setting to confirm or change it in our model:

1. In **Solution Explorer**, find the `WideWorldImportersTAB` project and its `Model.bim` file.

2. Right-click the file and then choose **View Code**. If you have the file open in design view, you will be asked to close the file before opening it to view the code.

3. You can now see the TOM that is built in JSON. I have copied the first few lines of the JSON to highlight the property. If your model's `discourageImplicitMeasures` property is set to `false`, change it to `true` now. (JSON is case-sensitive. Make sure you use lowercase for the property.) Remember, this property will not be in models whose `compatibilityLevel` value is less than 1500:

```
{
    "name": "SemanticModel",
    "compatibilityLevel": 1500,
    "model": {
        "culture": "en-US",
        "discourageImplicitMeasures": true,
```

    If you do not see this property, you can add the property to your file and save the changes.

4. You can now change the view back to designer view from **Solution Explorer**. We are now ready to create a calculation group. If you have not already closed the code view of the file, you will be prompted to close it before continuing.

Now that we have the requirements out of the way, let's create a new calculation group.

Creating your calculation group

Keeping with our year theme from the previous section, we are going to create a calculation group with YTD, previous year, and next year as the calculations:

1. Find the `Calculation Groups` folder in **Tabular Model Explorer**.

2. Right-click the folder and choose **New calculation group**.

3. Select the calculation group in **Tabular Model Explorer**. It will likely be named something like `CalculationGroup 1`.

4. In the **Properties** window, change the name to `Annual Calcs`.

5. Next, set **Precedence** to 25. Precedence determines that a processing order for more than one group is created. We don't want to leave it as 0 as other groups you create in the future may need to be calculated first.

6. Next, expand the `Columns` folder under `Annual Calcs`. Let's rename the calculation column `Annual Metric`.

7. We will now add the first metric, YTD. Expand the `Calculation Items` folder and select the default item in the folder.

8. Rename the default item `YTD`.

9. Next, click the ellipses button in the `Expression` property to open the DAX Editor.

   Enter the following code into the editor:

   ```
   CALCULATE(SELECTEDMEASURE(),DATESYTD('Date'[Date]))
   ```

   This formula uses the `SELECTEDMEASURE` function. This function and others with `SELECTEDMEASURE` in the name were created specifically for calculation groups. These functions work with the measure that is selected to be used with the calculation group. We will demonstrate this functionality once we have our other metrics in the group. Be sure to apply your formula changes before moving to the next step.

   > **Change to how DAX is formatted**
   >
   > This is the only instance where we use DAX without using an equals sign. Using an equals sign only raises an error, but the calculation group will not work correctly if you use an equals sign.

10. Right-click on the `Calculation Items` folder to add a new calculation item. We are planning to create two new items, so repeat this process while you are here. This will give you two items with default names.

11. Rename one of the items `Previous Year` and the other `Next Year`.

12. The `Previous Year` expression is
    `CALCULATE(SELECTEDMEASURE(),PREVIOUSYEAR('Date'[Date]))`.

13. The `Next Year` expression is
    `CALCULATE(SELECTEDMEASURE(),NEXTYEAR('Date'[Date]))`.

14. Apply the DAX formulas to save your updates.

15. We want to have the metrics in a specific order. You will be unable to change the `Ordinal` property without a field to support sorting. Right-click on the `Columns` folder and add a column.

16. Change the column name to `Sort Order`. You can now set the `Ordinal` value for each of the items you created. I ordered them 1-3 in the following order: YTD, `Next Year`, `Previous Year`.

In the following section, we will look at the issues that may occur when setting the sort order and how to work around these issues.

Issues with setting the sort order

In some cases, developers have experienced issues setting the ordinal. When the column is changed, it tries to save the value, but fails with an error message that says the value in not valid. The workaround for this problem is to open **Solution Explorer** and choose to view the code on the `model.bim` file. Search for `calculationGroup` and add the following line after the expression statement: `"ordinal" : 1`. You can update all the calculation items in the code. Save your changes and open the designer.

You will see that the changes are applied to your calculation items. There appears to be some issue with the early implementation of this functionality. This workaround will allow you to use the latest functionality in spite of some issues with the designer.

For reference, here is an example of a complete `calculationItems` with the ordinal added:

```
"calculationItems": [
    {
        "name": "YTD",
        "expression":
 "CALCULATE(SELECTEDMEASURE(),DATESYTD('Date'[Date]))",
        "ordinal" : 1
    },
```

Let's now test the calculation group in Excel.

Testing your calculation group in Excel

The `Annual Calcs` calculation group is now complete. You should be able to test this with the **Analyze in Excel** function. Add some measures to your **Values** areas (for example, `Red Items`, `Blue Items`). Add `Annual Calcs` to **Rows** and you will see the `YTD` item. Add `Calendar Year` from the `Date` table to the **Columns** area and you can see all the items. You should see something similar to the following screenshot:

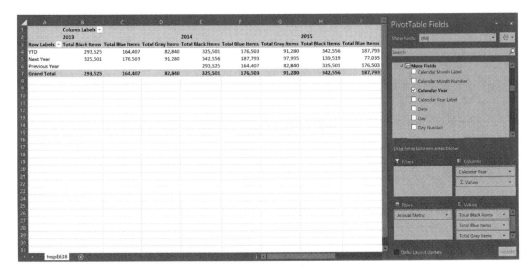

Figure 8.15 – Analyzing the calculation group in Excel

Now that we have seen how to create different calculated tables, let's create **Key Performance Indicators** (**KPIs**) that help in evaluating performance.

Creating KPIs

KPIs are used by businesses to evaluate performance over time. Businesses use KPIs in dashboards to show progress toward specific goals or targets. KPIs use a combination of symbols and numbers to represent current states and trends. KPIs in tabular models in SSAS are server-based and can be used by various end user tools such as Excel and Power BI. The advantage here is that a business KPI can be created and shared easily within an organization. This allows multiple users to include KPIs in their reporting with ease and consistency.

Understanding the components in a tabular model KPI

In tabular models, KPIs are more simplistic than the KPIs in multidimensional models. They are also much easier to create. KPIs are created directly from the measures. When creating a KPI, you need to understand the five components that make up the KPI:

- **Base value**: The base value is the measure you select when creating the KPI. It is what you are measuring against the target.

- **Target value**: The target value can be either an absolute value or a different measure. In either case, the value needs to be scalar to work with your KPI.

- **Target pattern**: There are four patterns available in the KPI designer. The colors red (bad), yellow (mid), and green (good) are used for the patterns. The first is the standard pattern where high is good and low is bad. The second pattern reverses the order. The other two patterns are based on whether closer to the target is better or worse. You can see the patterns in the following KPI dialog screenshot.

- **Target threshold**: The threshold uses percentages to illustrate proximity to the target. You can move the indicators to change how the target pattern returns good or bad indicators.

- **Icon style**: These are the icons you want to use to visualize the base value relationship to the target based on the threshold marks:

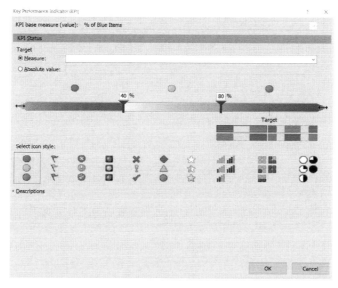

Figure 8.16 – Key Performance Indicator dialog

Now that we have a good understanding of the components that make up a KPI, let's build it.

Building your KPI

We will create a KPI to show whether we are meeting our goal of selling 30% blue items for all items we sell with a color. We will base this on our `% of Blue Items` measure in the `Sales` table:

1.   Locate the `% of Blue Items` measure in the `Sales` table.

2.   Right-click the measure and select **Create KPI** from the menu. This will open the KPI dialog.

3.   We are going to use 0.3 (30%) as our target. Switch the **Target** to **Absolute Value** and set the value to `0.3`.

4.   The threshold value is updated to match our target of `0.3`. Set the yellow mark to `0.15` and the green mark to `0.25`.

5.   You can choose a different icon style, but we will use the default colored dots also known as the **stoplight**.

6.   Click **OK**. You can now see an icon with the measure, so you know a KPI has been created, as shown here. The following screenshot illustrates this:

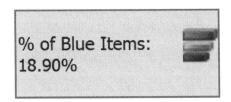

Figure 8.17 – Measuring with KPIs

You can now check this out using Excel once again. You can drag **KPI Status** to the **Values** section. Then, add the **Sales Region** hierarchy to rows. You can drill in and see how each region and levels below the region are performing. You should see something like our results shown here:

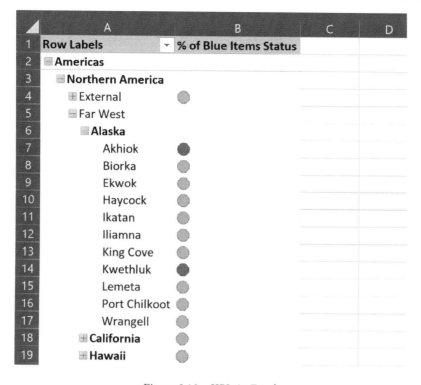

Figure 8.18 – KPIs in Excel

As you can see, adding simple KPIs to your model is easy. You can add targets with other measures you have created as well.

Querying your model with SQL Server Management Studio and DAX

To wrap up the chapter, we are going to create a query in SSMS using DAX. First, DAX is not a query language, so the syntax is not as easy to understand at first for SQL users. The first difference is that you must start every query with EVALUATE. The EVALUATE function is used to analyze a table and return the values in the same way as a SELECT statement does with relational databases. To use EVALUATE, your outermost function must resolve to a table. Let's work through an example of this process:

1. Open **SQL Server Management Studio** and connect to your tabular model instance. You should see your workspace database there.

2. Right-click your workspace database and select **New Query** followed by **DAX**.

3. Add the EVAULATE statement.

4. In the first query, let's get the `Item` table using `EVALUATE('Item')`. Execute the query to return the contents of the `Item` table. You will notice that no measures are included in the results. Calculated columns will be returned, but measures are not scoped to a table.

5. For our next query, let's use the `GENERATE` function we used previously:

```
EVALUATE (
    GENERATE (
        SUMMARIZE('Customer',Customer[Buying Group]),
        SUMMARIZE('Item',
            'Item'[Brand],
            'Item'[Color],
            "Item Brand Color Breakdown",
            SUMX(RELATEDTABLE(Sales),
            Sales[Quantity]))
    ))
```

We have used this same query before. Now you can see how you can test the results prior to adding it as a calculated table.

6. We can also order the results in our DAX query by adding the `ORDER BY` clause after our table definition. Let's order the results according to the buying group. Here is the updated code with the results sorted by buying group:

```
EVALUATE (
    GENERATE (
        SUMMARIZE('Customer',Customer[Buying Group]),
        SUMMARIZE('Item',
            'Item'[Brand],
            'Item'[Color],
            "Item Brand Color Breakdown",
            SUMX(RELATEDTABLE(Sales),
            Sales[Quantity]))
    ))
ORDER BY Customer[Buying Group]
```

7. Let's eliminate the N/A group. We can add the START AT clause to let SSMS know where we want to start the results at. This only works with the ORDER BY clause:

```
EVALUATE (
    GENERATE (
        SUMMARIZE('Customer',Customer[Buying Group]),
        SUMMARIZE('Item', 'Item'[Brand],'Item'[Color],
            "Item Brand Color Breakdown",
            SUMX(RELATEDTABLE(Sales),
            Sales[Quantity]))
    ))
ORDER BY Customer[Buying Group]
START AT "Tailspin Toys"
```

8. The DEFINE keyword can be used to add measures or other values for use in your query. In this query, we shake it up a bit and create a query that uses dates and colors with a custom sales measure:

```
DEFINE
MEASURE 'Sales'[Sales Total] = SUM('Sales'[Total
Excluding Tax])
EVALUATE (
    SUMMARIZECOLUMNS (
        'Date'[Calendar Year]
        , 'Item'[Color]
        , "Total Sales"
        , CALCULATE([Sales Total])
        ))
```

You can see that there are many creative ways to create queries in DAX. It does take some time to get used to, but you can work with DAX to test queries and check your tabular model with SSMS.

Summary

That wraps up our chapter on DAX. So much more can be done with DAX. We encourage you to explore the functions and try new things with your data. In this chapter, you added measures, calculated columns, calculated tables, calculation groups, and KPIs to your tabular model. We concluded the chapter by using SSMS to query the data.

You can use your DAX skills here to continue to expand and improve your tabular models. These improvements will help your users have a more complete experience with your models. You can also use DAX query techniques to review the data in your models and continue to improve data quality and validate results.

The next chapter is our first chapter focused on visualizations. We begin our visualization journey with Excel. We have been using Excel quite a bit in this chapter to check our work. In the next chapter, we dig deeper and create some dashboards and learn a number of Excel functions that help us make Excel look great while delivering the data.

Section 4: Exposing Insights while Visualizing Data from Your Models

This section will cover using Power BI and Excel to visualize the data from your model. The ability to visualize data effectively will help business users gain insights to support decision making with the data you have modeled.

This section comprises the following chapters:

- *Chapter 9, Exploring and Visualizing Your Data with Excel*
- *Chapter 10, Creating Interactive Reports and Enhancing Your Models in Power BI*

9
Exploring and Visualizing Your Data with Excel

We have now created multidimensional and tabular models in the previous chapters. The data is ready, so let's visualize it. We will start our data visualization in Excel. Microsoft Excel has been the most prolific analytics tool on the market for years. While that is not its primary focus, its utility, simplicity, and reach far exceed those of its nearest competitor.

In this chapter, we will connect our models to Excel, build out some reports and dashboards, and explore the differences between these models in Excel. We will wrap up the chapter with some advanced visualization techniques that are unique to Excel when working with analytical models built in SQL Server. We will be creating two Excel workbooks, one for each model. This will allow us to compare how the models interact with Excel.

When you are finished with this chapter, you should be comfortable with connecting both multidimensional and tabular models to Excel and building basic reports with their data. You will also learn some advanced techniques that will help with the creation of dashboards and unique visualizations in Excel.

In this chapter, we're going to cover the following main topics:

- Connecting Excel to your models

- Building visualizations with your models

- Building and enhancing an Excel dashboard

- Advanced design with CUBE functions

- Sharing your Excel dashboards with others

Technical requirements

In this section, you will need to deploy and have running the multidimensional model (**WideWorldImportersMD**) that you created in *Chapter 3*, *Preparing Your Data for Multidimensional Models*, *Chapter 4*, *Building a Multidimensional Cube in SSAS 2019*, and *Chapter 5*, *Adding Measures and Calculations with MDX*. You will also need the tabular model we expanded in *Chapter 6*, *Preparing Your Data for Tabular Models*, deployed and running (**WideWorldImportersTAB**). We will not be working with the workspace version of your tabular models. You will also need Microsoft Excel to work through the hands-on work in this chapter. All of the examples in this chapter will be using the latest version of Excel in Office 365 ProPlus at the time of writing (the *May 2020* release). Because Excel is updated continually via a subscription model, some examples may look different for you.

Connecting Excel to your models

Let's get started with Excel by creating two workbooks that will allow us to work through the design process with both model types. Our workbooks are called WideWorldImporters-MD.xlsx and WideWorldImporters-TAB.xlsx. This matches the naming convention we have used throughout this book. Now that we have our workbooks created, let's get connected to our models.

Connecting to the multidimensional model

Multidimensional models (or cubes) and Excel have been working together for a very long time. One of the great things about multidimensional models is the high level of interactivity and capabilities that Excel seamlessly supports. This functionality propelled cubes to the forefront of ad hoc analysis in businesses throughout the world. Let's begin:

1. Open your multidimensional workbook, `WideWorldImporters-MD.xlsx`.

2. On the **Data** tab, select **Get Data | From Database | From Analysis Services**. These steps are illustrated in the following screenshot:

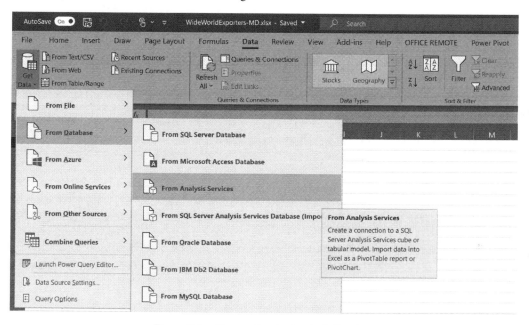

Figure 9.1 – Connecting to Analysis Services

3. In the **Data Connection Wizard**, enter your SSAS Server name and click **Next**. You need to use the SSAS instance for your multidimensional model. Be sure to choose the correct server.

4. In the next dialog, the **Data Connection Wizard**, you should see the **Wide World Importers** cube and the **Invoicing** perspective as shown in the following screenshot:

Select Database and Table

Select the Database and Table/Cube which contains the data you want.

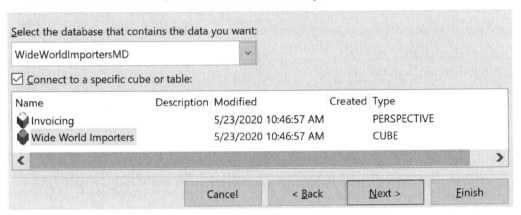

Figure 9.2 – Select the cube to connect to

You may recall in *Chapter 3, Preparing Your Data for Multidimensional Models,* we created a perspective that was a subset of our cube. This is a scenario where perspectives can support a better user experience in Excel. It is very common for cubes to be large and overflowing with objects. Perspectives allow you, as the designer, to organize logical groups of objects for your users so they can work easily with the analytics you have prepared for them.

5. Now, choose **Wide World Importers** and click **Next**.

6. The next dialog will save the connection file to the default location on your PC. If you plan to distribute this workbook to other users, you can use this file to share the connection with the workbook. We will leave it in the default location at this time. We will give this connection a better, more friendly name: `Wide World Importers MD`. This will make it easy to identify when using that connection with a different workbook later.

7. Now click **Finish**.

8. This will open the **Import Data** dialog shown in the following screenshot. We now have some different options to choose for how we want to bring the data from our cube into our database initially:

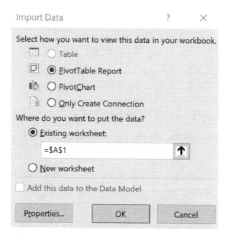

Figure 9.3 – Import Data options in Excel

As you can see in the preceding screenshot, we have a number of options to work with. Some options are not available when working with direct connections to SSAS, such as viewing the data in a **Table** and the choice to **Add this data to the Data Model**.

> **Note**
>
> The data model is the underlying Power Pivot model in Excel. We cannot use that with direct connections to Analysis Services models. This makes sense as they are effectively the same structure. Analysis Services models, both tabular and multidimensional, should be considered ready for use and do not require additional mashup or manipulation in Power Pivot.

Out of the four options in the following list, the first two are the key options to consider after creating your connection:

i) The first is how you want to view the data. The default is to create a **PivotTable report**. This is the most common pattern to start working with the data. This effectively allows Excel users to interact with the data from the cube in an ad hoc manner.

ii) The second option will create the PivotTable and a matching **PivotChart**. While interesting, you will typically find that it is easier to work with the **PivotTable** and then add the PivotChart later.

iii) The third option here is to **Only Create Connection**. If you use Excel to create a lot of reports or dashboards, you will likely use this option more frequently, as you can use the connection to create multiple visualizations in Excel where and how you want to.

iv) The other option is to choose where you want to create the PivotTable or PivotChart. The default will be the cell selected when you choose **Get Data** from the menu. If you don't select a cell, you will typically see the **A1** cell selected on the first sheet of the workbook. You can change this location by selecting a different cell in the workbook. If you have chosen to create a connection only, you will not be able to choose the location because no object is being created.

9. Now, for our first connection, we will leave the default settings as they are and click **OK**. This will create the PivotTable in the upper-left corner and connect to the cube. Your workbook should look like the following screenshot and you are ready to start querying and visualizing data from your cube in Excel:

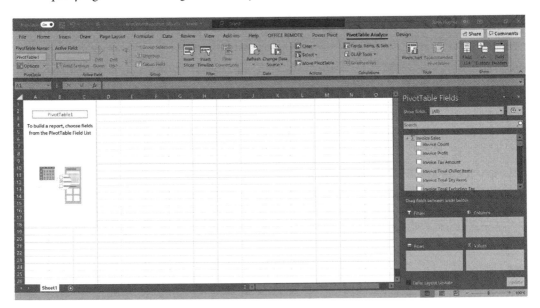

Figure 9.4 – PivotTable with Analysis Services model

Let's now connect Excel to our tabular model.

Connecting to the tabular model

The process to connect to the tabular model is nearly identical to connecting Excel to the multidimensional model. We will call out the steps here and refer to the preceding screenshots where relevant:

1. Open the workbook you created to connect to your tabular model. Ours is called `WideWorldImporters-TAB.xlsx`.

2. On the **Data** tab, select **Get Data** | **From Database** | **From Analysis Services**.

3. In the **Data Connection Wizard**, enter the SSAS Server name for your tabular model and click **Next**. Be sure to choose the correct server.

4. In the next dialog in the **Data Connection Wizard**, you should see the **Model** cube. Tabular models are all called **Model** by default. You will also notice that the dialog refers to the model as a **Cube**. Be sure to check your database name in the dropdown as shown in the following screenshot. If you still have Visual Studio open with your model, you will see the name of your database with the **Globally Unique Identifier** (**GUID**), which means it is a workspace model, and will get a different name, and it will close when the project is closed:

Select Database and Table

Select the Database and Table/Cube which contains the data you want.

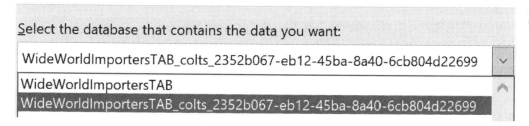

Figure 9.5 – Deployed and workspace tabular model databases

5. Choose **WideWorldImportersTAB** and click **Next**.

6. The next dialog will save the connection file to the default location on your PC. If you deploy this broadly, you can use this file to help distribute your workbook. We will leave it in the default location at this time. We will give this connection a better, more friendly name: `Wide World Importers TAB`. This will make it easy to identify when using that connection with a different workbook later. Now click **Finish**.

7. This will open the **Import Data** dialog. As we did in the previous section, let's leave the defaults and click **OK**. The workbook will have a **PivotTable** and the **PivotTable Fields** area open. You now have a successful connection to your tabular model in Excel.

You should now have two workbooks connected to your Analysis Services models. As you can see, Excel shares the connection method between the two models. This typically keeps the learning curve low if you are transitioning between the model types. Let's start exploring the visualization options in Excel.

Building visualizations with your models

For the remainder of this chapter, we will be creating the visualizations and queries primarily using our multidimensional model. We can do this because Excel interacts with both models in a similar way. Where differences appear, they will be called out to make you aware. Let's get started.

Understanding the PivotTable Fields panel

Before we get into the details of designing visualizations in Excel, let's break down the **PivotTable Fields** panel in Excel. How data is presented from each model type does vary here and we will look at those differences.

The **PivotTable Fields** panel in Excel is made up of two main sections, first, the **Fields section**, and second, the areas they are put into in the PivotTable, called **Areas to Place Fields**, as shown in the following screenshot:

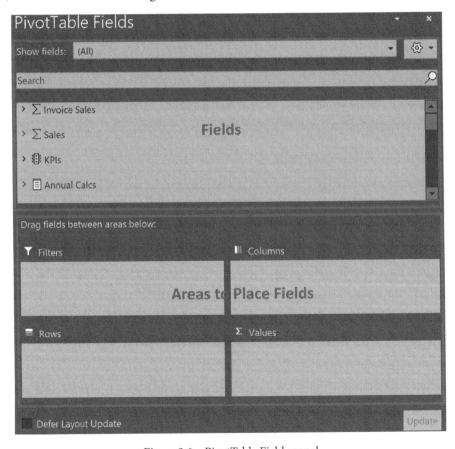

Figure 9.6 – PivotTable Fields panel

Let's understand the features of the **PivotTable Fields** panel:

- The **Show fields** dropdown filters the field list to the group as defined in the model. In multidimensional models, the fields are organized by measure group. We have two measure groups in this scenario – **Sales** and **Invoice Sales**. Tabular models are based on tables. In tabular models, this shows all the tables and calculation groups. Keep in mind that this only filters the list of available fields to choose from, it does not filter data or results. It is simply a mechanism to reduce the field list for ease of use.

- The area labeled **Fields** shows the available fields you can choose from. The fields are grouped either by the *source*, such as tables and measure groups, or *data type*, such as KPIs.

- The area labeled **Areas to Place Fields** specifies where the fields should be placed in the PivotTable. The **Values** area typically takes numeric values, which commonly have a *sigma* or sum symbol by them. Text or attribute fields make up **Rows** and **Columns**. These are most commonly marked by a table symbol in **Fields**. The **Filter** area will create a drop-down filter option for your PivotTable and also uses text or attribute fields.

When we created our multidimensional model, we placed the measures on colors that we created into a folder called `Color Analysis`. You will find these measures in the **Values** group in the **PowerPivot Fields** panel. This group contains a folder called `Color Analysis`. You can see how these folders help organize calculations for ease of use for users.

> **Implicit calculations are turned off**
>
> In our tabular model, we have turned off implicit calculations. Only the measures we create in the model can be added to the **Values** section. In older versions of tabular models, this is not the default. If that feature is turned off, you can drag numeric fields from the tables that aren't in measures and Excel will create an implicit calculation.

When you add fields to the area, the assumption is that we are adding row and column headers in the PivotTable like a matrix visualization. The values to be calculated, dropped into the **Values** section, are effectively sliced by the row and column combination. The last section is the **Filter** section, which applies to the PivotTable we are working in.

Now that you have a basic understanding of the **PivotTable Fields** panel, let's create some visuals.

Creating a PivotTable

The activity of creating a PivotTable is the same using either model. For the following steps, we will be using the multidimensional model in our `WideWorldImporters-MD` workbook. When we originally created the connection, a simple PivotTable was created in the workbook. We will use this as our starting point. The next steps will create a PivotTable visualization with the color analysis we did in both models. The steps are as follows:

1. In the field list, find the `Color Analysis` folder in **Values**. Select **% Black Items** and **% Blue Items** from the list of fields. You should now see these measures in the **Values** area in the bottom-right corner of the **PivotTable Fields** panel. You will also see these fields in the Excel worksheet as column headers with the values below them. As you can see in the worksheet, the formatting from the server is pulled through to the worksheet. If you click in the field with the percentage value in it, you can also see that the formatting in the cell is applied to a highly precise value.

2. Now that we have our first set of values in place, let's add some rows. Find **City** and select **Sales Region**. This will add the **Sales Region** hierarchy to the rows. You can see that one value, **Americas**, has a cross next to it. If you click the cross, you will see the next level in the hierarchy, which is **Northern America**. Expand that to see a list of regions under **Northern America**.

    There are two more levels in the hierarchy, **State Province** and **City**. This is the concept of drilling down. The creation of hierarchies in either type of model is intended to give users an easy-to-use, well-defined drill-down path. As you can see, the calculations represent the percentages of blue or black items in the context of the row or region level.

3. Let's add employees to the columns. This will give us the percentage of sales by employee and item colors that have been selected:

    i) Find **Salesperson** and **Employee** in the field list.

    ii) Drag **Employee** to the **Columns** area and drop it above the **Values** item in the same area. If you drop it below **Values**, you can drag it above **Values** or you can click the down arrow to move it in the direction you need.

    If you selected the **Employee** field in the field list, it may have dropped **Employee** into the **Rows** areas. You can drag it over to **Values** or select **Move to Column Labels** to move it to the **Columns** area.

4. To wrap up our first **PivotTable**, drag the **Invoice Date.Calendar** hierarchy into the **Filters** area.

5. Using the drop-down functionality in the filter in the grid, select **CY2016** to filter the data for calendar year 2016. When you have completed this, your PivotTable should look similar to the following screenshot. Take some time to try variations of rows, columns, and filters as you explore your model with Excel:

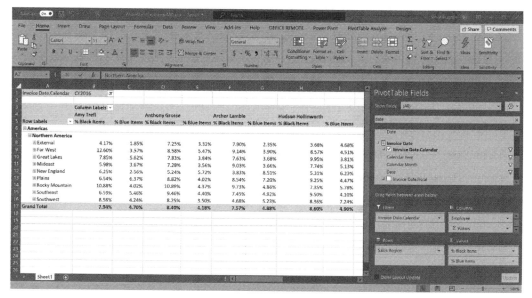

Figure 9.7 – Our first PivotTable created in Excel

Visible and hidden fields in our models

During the creation of our models, we have various ways to hide fields from the tools that are interacting with the model. In multidimensional models, it is common to add fields to a hierarchy and then not show the base fields. This optimizes performance and cube size. We can also explicitly hide fields in the model design as well. We have similar options in the tabular model. We can choose to hide fields from the users explicitly.

You will notice in our tabular model that all fields remain visible, whereas we hid some fields in our multidimensional model. The **City** dimension highlights this difference well. In our multidimensional model, we created two hierarchies that contained all the fields. These fields are not visible outside of the hierarchy, whereas, in our tabular model, the same hierarchies exist but a **More Fields** list is available as well. This list contains all the fields. This has different design options and needs to be planned for your model creation.

There is little performance impact, if any, from including all the fields in tabular models. In multidimensional models, hierarchies support better aggregated performance based on storage and you need to be more intentional about what you expose in your model.

As we wrap up this section on PivotTables, you must understand that the value of creating models is that users can plug into and view data as they wish. You can repeat this experience in the tabular model workbook. The primary differences are the numbers (we have additional filters on the tabular model calculations) and the fact that the `Date` table is used to get the **Calendar** hierarchy. In the tabular model, we do not start with role-playing dimensions. Next, we will add a PivotChart to our workbook.

Adding a PivotChart

We will now add a PivotChart to our workbook. Add a sheet to your workbook to get us started, then proceed with the following steps:

1. We already have a connection to our model so we can reuse that connection. Go to the **Data** tab and select **Existing Connections**.

2. In the **Existing Connections** dialog, choose **Connections** and select the connection for your multidimensional model, **Wide World Importers MD**. Click **Open**.

3. This will open the **Import Data** dialog. Choose **PivotChart** and click **OK**.

4. You should now have a blank PivotChart in the middle of your spreadsheet with the **PivotTable Fields** pane. Let's start by adding in the `% Black Items` and `% Blue Items` values. Select those to add them to the **Values** area. You should see the default column chart created with those.

5. Drag the **Invoice Date.Calendar** hierarchy into the **Axis (Categories)** area. This will update the bar chart to show the percentages by year. We now have a nice start to a chart visualization. Your chart should be similar to the following chart:

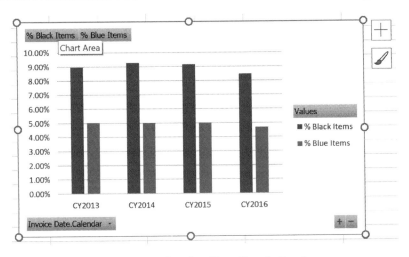

Figure 9.8 – Our first PivotChart in Excel

There are a few parts of the **PivotChart** you need to understand before moving forward:

i) You can see that the fields we have added to the chart are also represented as field buttons. They allow you to modify the chart in various ways. If you right-click on the buttons, you can change the order, move them to a different area, or remove them altogether.

ii) You can change the hierarchy level as well. Click the down arrow to the right of the **Invoice Date.Calendar** button. This will expand the hierarchy selector, which allows you to adjust the level or filter levels out if you prefer. You can drill up or down with the plus (+) and minus (-) buttons in the lower right of the chart. This is not very readable in our scenario, but the option is there if you choose to use it.

iii) The plus symbol at the top, outside of the chart area, allows you to choose the chart elements you want to see in the chart. Let's add a Chart Title with the name `Black & Blue Analysis`. The paintbrush below the plus (+) button allows you to change the color scheme and style of the chart. We will not change ours at this time, but you should still look at the options.

6. With the chart selected, click the **Design** tab in the Excel ribbon.

7. Click the **Change Chart Type** button to see the types of charts we can use to visualize our data. We are going to change our chart to a line chart.

8. Select the **Line** option in the **Change Chart Type** dialog. Choose **Line with Markers** from the selections at the top of the dialog and click **OK**. The chart should now look like the following screenshot:

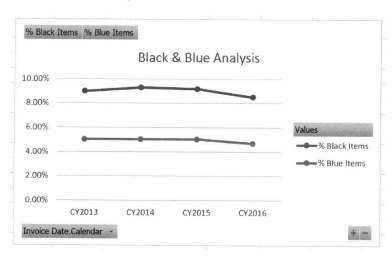

Figure 9.9 – Line chart with a title

You now have a nice line chart that shows the variance in the percentages of blue versus black items sales by calendar year. We will use this chart in the next section as well.

Adding slicers

Slicers in Excel are buttons that allow you to filter the contents of your workbook in a highly visual and touch-friendly way. Slicers have been in Excel for quite a while. In this section, we are going to add an **Employee** slicer to the **Black & Blue Analysis** chart. The last step in the section will show how to apply this slicer to the PivotTable we created. This works because both items share a connection. Let's begin:

1. With the chart selected, navigate to the **PivotChart Analyze** tab on Excel's ribbon. Click **Insert Slicer**.

2. This opens the **Insert Slicers** dialog. It shows you all the fields you can use to filter the chart. Slicers do not support hierarchies, but levels in hierarchies can be selected. If you choose a hierarchy or the top-level item, all of the fields will get separate slicers. Find the `Salesperson` table and choose the **Employee** item to create our slicer. Click **OK**.

3. This will drop the **Employee** slicer in the middle of your sheet, usually not where you want it. You can move the slicer around to where you want it. We will place the slicer to the right of the chart.

4. Click on the dot on the bottom of the slicer and expand the slicer until the scrollbar disappears and you can see all of the salespeople. When you have the slicer in place and expand your sheet, it should look as follows:

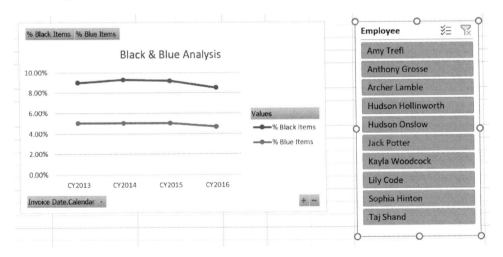

Figure 9.10 – Slicers added to the PivotChart

At the top of the slicer, there are two buttons next to the title. The first toggles the multiselect option. The second clears any filter applied. The slicer is single-select by default.

5. Choose a **salesperson** to filter the data. The chart will now show the sliced or filtered data. The unselected salespeople are now white or unhighlighted. If a slicer has options with no data, those buttons are typically gray and cannot be selected.

6. In the final step, we will show you how to apply the slicer's filtering to the PivotTable we created initially. Select the **Employee** slicer. Then select the **Slicer** tab on the ribbon. Next, click **Report Connections**:

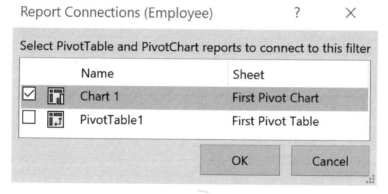

Figure 9.11 – Report Connections dialog for the Employee slicer

7. In the **Report Connections** dialog shown in the preceding screenshot, you can see the reports that share a connection with the slicer. They do not need to be on the same sheet to be affected. Select **PivotTable1** and click **OK**.

8. Now, look at the values on the PivotTable in your first sheet. Go back and change the slicer and see how the values have changed.

9. Before we move to the next section, go back to the slicer and deselect this connection. You can also try using the multiselect functionality and clearing the filter to familiarize yourself with those features.

Slicers can be used with any field or fields that interact with the data in your Excel PivotTables and charts. While dates can be filtered with slicers, we will demonstrate a timeline with the PivotTable. One last point on slicers: you can create the same slicer with tabular models. The process is identical to the preceding steps.

Adding timelines

Timelines are special filter controls that support date fields. They have the ability to build out the date hierarchies natively. This means that the data types of the field need to be of the date data type (for example, Date or DateTime).

Date tables in our models

This control requires that the table or dimension be designated as the date or time table. In the multidimensional model we created, the `Date` dimension was designated as a `Time` type in the dimension's properties. In our tabular model, the `Date` table was *marked as the date table*. These property settings are picked up by the control. When working with the multidimensional model, you will see two options for the timeline control, `Invoice Date` and `Delivery Date`. Both of these are built on the same `Date` dimension as role-playing dimensions. This functionality is not supported the same way in tabular models. Even though we created a calculated table that supports the delivery date, only one table can be marked as the date table so only one option is available from the tabular model.

Let's look at the steps to add timelines:

1. Open the worksheet in Excel where you created your first PivotTable.

2. Click on the PivotTable. Remove the **Invoice Date.Calendar** filter from the PivotTable. Click the down arrow on the field name in the **Filters** area in the **PivotTable Fields** pane. Select **Remove Field** to remove that filter.

3. On the ribbon, go to the **PivotTable Analyze** tab and click **Insert Timeline**.

4. In the **Insert Timelines** dialog, choose **Invoice Date** and click **OK**.

5. Like the slicer, the timeline control is dropped into the middle of your sheet. Let's move it to the right of the PivotTable. Your sheet should look as follows:

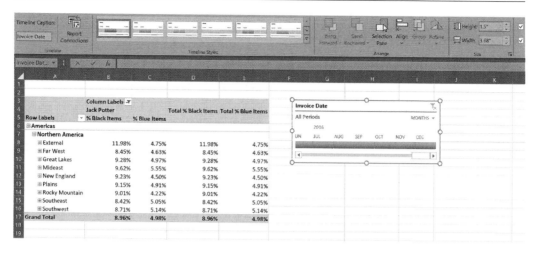

Figure 9.12 – PivotTable with a timeline

The timeline control has some cool features we want to highlight here. Let's start with the dropdown that shows **MONTHS** right now. If you select the down arrow you will see **YEARS, QUARTERS, MONTHS,** and **DAYS** as options. This changes the granularity of the highlighted bar in the visual. You can select one or more months in the bar that is shown in the middle. When you make a selection, the **All Periods** label in the upper left will display what is selected, such as **Feb 2016**.

The scroll bar at the bottom of the visual lets you scroll through the available options. Be aware that the dates shown in the visualization cover the date range supported in your date table. For example, if you select **Aug 2016**, the PivotTable will no longer contain data as our dataset does not contain data past the middle of 2016.

6. Change the dropdown to **YEARS**. Select **2015**.

7. Change the dropdown to **MONTHS**. You will see that the months are filtered for **2015** as well. Select **JAN**.

8. On either side of the bar for **JAN**, you can drag to expand the selection. Try this now by expanding the selection to include **FEB** and **MAR**.

You can use the same steps to connect this filter to the PivotChart we created that we used when connecting the slicer. Review the preceding steps if you want to experiment with connecting this to the PivotChart as well. You can remove the filter by clicking the button with the filter and the red **X** on it.

Also, like the slicer control, the timeline control can be added using the same process with your tabular model. We are going to put this all together in the next section.

Building and enhancing an Excel dashboard

The focus of this section is to turn our work into a full dashboard for our users. We will explore some more advanced techniques to make our dashboards more user friendly and interactive. We will continue to focus on the multidimensional model and highlight the differences that occur with tabular models.

We are going to combine everything we have created so far into a single sheet and make various enhancements along the way. Let's get started.

Moving the PivotTable and the filter

Let's move the PivotTable and the filter:

1. Our first step is to move the PivotTable. Select the PivotTable and navigate to the **PivotTable Analyze** tab on the ribbon. Then select **Move PivotTable** in the **Actions** section on the tab.

2. In the **Move PivotTable** dialog, we will be keeping the PivotTable on the existing worksheet. Set **Location** to **B13** by selecting that cell in the sheet. Click **OK** when you have updated the location.

3. Next, move the **Invoice Date** filter to a location in the upper-left corner of the worksheet.

Updating the Employee slicer

Let's now move the **Employee** slicer:

1. We will move the **Employee** slicer next. You can simply select the slicer, then cut and paste it to the first sheet. Paste it next to the timeline filter. It will overlap the PivotTable a bit, but we will fix that in the next step.

2. Resize the slicer by making its height the same as the timeline. Next, double the width of the slicer. The top of your worksheet will look something like the following screenshot once you have resized the slicer:

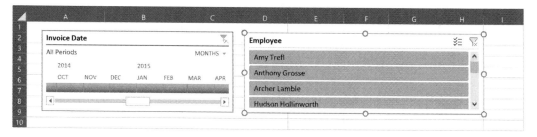

Figure 9.13 – Timeline and slicer resized and repositioned

3. With the slicer selected, navigate to the **Slicer** tab on the ribbon. Select **Slicer Settings** on the menu. This opens the **Slicer Settings** dialog shown here:

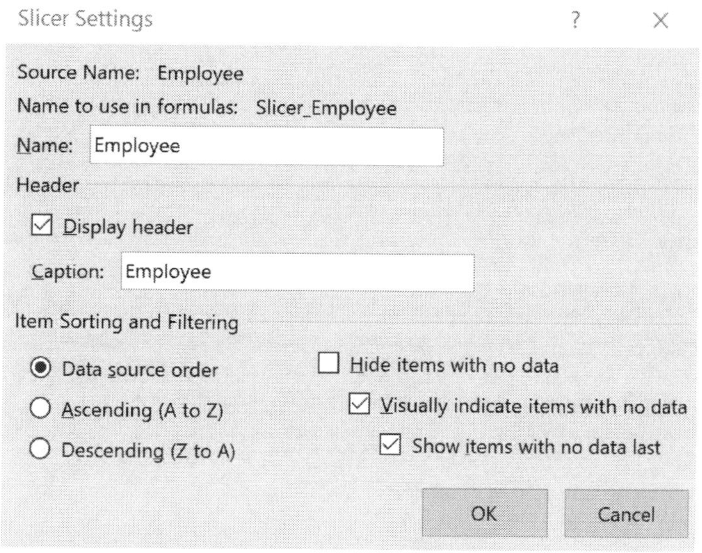

Figure 9.14 – Slicer Settings

We are going to make a number of changes in this dialog over the next few steps. **Name** is the name of the field we pulled from the model. For our purposes, we can keep the name.

4. We will keep the **Display header** option on. However, we will change the name to Salesperson, which is a better description for the slicer.

5. The next section in the dialog is **Item Sorting and Filtering**. Because we are working with names, we can change the sort order to **Ascending (A to Z)** to make sure it sorts as we want. If the data you are using in the slicer is not sorted correctly in the server, this is the opportunity to sort the values in a more user-friendly fashion.

The filtering section has three options:

i) By default, **Visually indicate items with no data** and **Show items with no data last** are selected. Items with no data are grayed out and moved to the bottom of the list with these settings. You can keep the slicer data in order by deselecting the last option. This will still gray out options with no data but not move them to the bottom.

ii) If you select the top option, the other two options cannot be selected. The first option, **Hide items with no data**, will completely remove slicer items from view if no data exists. You will need to determine the best option for your users based on the content to filter. We will leave this setting on its default. Click **OK** to close the dialog and save our setting changes.

6. We would still like to show all the options in our slicer. We can do this by changing the column count. In the **Slicer** tab, change the **Columns** value from 1 to 3. You may need to adjust the size of the slicer in order to remove the vertical scroll bar.

7. The last step for the slicer is to add the PivotTable back into the **Report Connections** dialog. Select **Report Connections** and add the PivotTable to the connections. Your worksheet should look like the following screenshot:

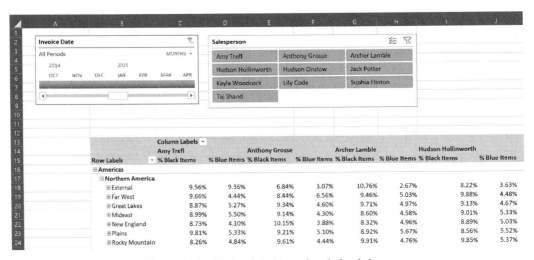

Figure 9.15 – Updated dashboard with fixed slicer

This wraps up the slicer settings. Let's continue modifying our Excel dashboard.

Adjusting the other PivotTable

We will now adjust the PivotTable:

1. We now need to move the PivotChart from the other tab to the first sheet. Cut and paste the PivotChart next to our slicer.

2. This takes up more space than we have at the top of the sheet. You can add rows above the PivotTable, which will push it down further on the sheet. The other option is to use the **Move PivotTable** option used in *Step 2* of the *Moving the PivotTable and the filter* section. Add enough rows for the PivotChart to fit cleanly above the PivotTable. Your sheet should now look like the following screenshot:

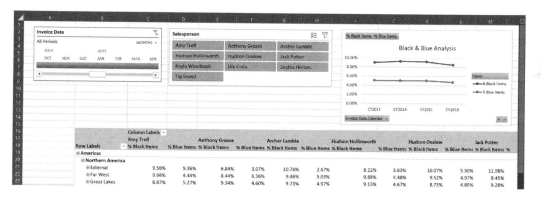

Figure 9.16 – Updated dashboard with PivotChart added

3. Select the PivotChart and go to the **PivotChart Analyze** tab on the Excel ribbon. There are two buttons on the far right of the menu:

   i) The first button, **Field List**, will show or hide the **PivotTable Fields** pane. You can use this option if you are not planning to add any additional data to the PivotChart.

   ii) The second button is the **Field Buttons** drop-down list. The field buttons are the gray areas in the preceding screenshot. The list contains the area for each set of field buttons. We don't have a reason to leave any field buttons on our chart. Choose **Hide All** to remove or hide the buttons on the chart.

4. When we have copied the chart to the new tab, we may have broken the connections to the slicer. We also need to add a connection to the timeline. Select the PivotChart. Go to the **PivotChart Analyze** tab on the ribbon. Click **Filter Connections** to open the **Filter Connections** dialog.

5. Select both filters if they have not already been selected. This will apply the **Employee** slicer and **Invoice Date** timeline selections to the PivotChart. Click **OK** to apply the changes and close the dialog.

6. In the PivotTable, you may have noticed that **Column Labels** and **Row Labels** are showing. You can hide those labels using a similar set of buttons to those we used when cleaning up the PivotChart:

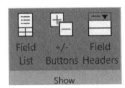

Figure 9.17 – Showing the options for PivotTables

7. Click **Field Headers** to remove those labels. **Field List** will hide the **PivotTable Fields** pane while working with the PivotTable.

8. The **+/- Buttons** option will remove the ability to drill up or down in the PivotTable. We will use this option to fix the rows in the PivotTable to show the **Northern America** regions only.

9. While we were changing the size of the cells in the PivotTable, the slicer may have moved around. In order to prevent that from happening as we continue to work on the dashboard design, we need to fix the position of the slicer. Right-click on the slicer and select **Size and Properties** from the shortcut menu. This opens the **Format Slicer** pane in Excel.

10. In **Format Slicer**, expand the **Properties** section and choose **Don't move or size with cells**. Once you have made the change you can close the **Format Slicer** pane.

Cleaning up our dashboard design

Let's clean up the dashboard:

1. Let's clean up some other items as we wrap up this phase of our design. First, let's hide the gridlines. On the **View** tab on the ribbon in Excel, you can choose to hide the gridlines.

2. We can also hide the headings here. But before we hide those, reduce the size of column **A** to move the PivotTable closer to the left side of the sheet. The goal is to leave a small margin there.

3. Once you have it adjusted to your liking, you can hide **Headings** from the **View** tab. This will clean up the dashboard for a better user experience when it is deployed.

4. Our PivotChart moved when we adjusted the size of column **A**. Select the chart and navigate to the **Format** tab. Select **Format Selection** on the menu to open the **Format Chart Area** pane in Excel.

5. You need to open the **Size** and **Properties** sections in the **Format Chart Area** pane. This is the third button on the pane, as shown here:

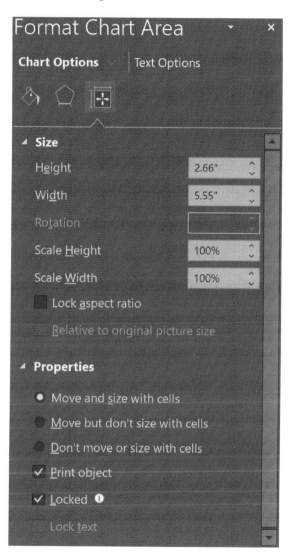

Figure 9.18 – Format Chart Area – Size and Properties pane

6. In the **Properties** section, choose **Don't move or size with cells** to lock the PivotChart in place on the dashboard. Then close the **Format Chart Area** pane.

Once all these steps are completed, your sheet should look similar to the following screenshot:

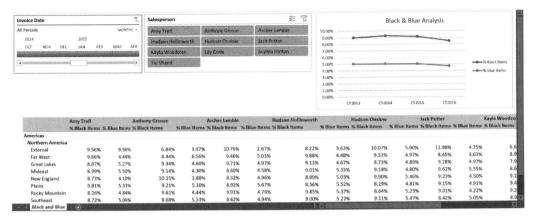

Figure 9.19 – Our black and blue dashboard after formatting

So now what? We have cleaned up our dashboard with slicers, timelines, PivotCharts, and PivotTables. The same steps can be used for the tabular models. We will now look at one other advanced design feature, which will allow us to add some nice visuals to fill in the space between the filters and the PivotTable.

Advanced design with CUBE functions

This section covers the CUBE functions available in Excel. This functionality allows you to operate on data from Analysis Services without using PivotTables or PivotCharts. These techniques are advanced and require basic **Multidimensional Expression** (**MDX**) skills. However, we will walk you through the simplest way to learn and use these functions initially.

We will use these functions to create the following three single-value visualizations on our dashboard:

- Total black items sold in the selected period
- Total blue items sold in the selected period
- Black and blue items sales amount in the selected period

In the next sections, we will walk through the steps to add these measures and apply the timeline filter to them.

Adding PivotTables to a new sheet

Let's begin by adding PivotTables:

1. In our multidimensional workbook, add a new sheet.

2. Add another PivotTable to this sheet (**Data | Existing Connections | Wide World Importers MD**).

3. In this PivotTable, select **Blue Items** and **Black Items** from the `Color Analysis` folder.

4. Add another PivotTable from the same connection.

5. Add **Total Excluding Tax** from the **Sales** values to the **Values** area of the new PivotTable.

6. Add **Color** from the `Item` table to the **Filters** area.

7. Expand the filter and click the **Select Multiple Items** option at the bottom. Then select **Black** and **Blue** from the options. The filter will now show (**Multiple Items**) as the selection.

Converting the PivotTable to formulas

We will now convert PivotTables to formulas:

1. Select a value from the first PivotTable. On the **PivotTable Analyze** tab in the ribbon, expand the **OLAP Tools** menu and select **Convert to Formulas**. You should see the PivotTable formatting disappear for these values.

2. Select the cell that has `Black Items` in it. In the formula bar you will see the following function:

```
=CUBEMEMBER("Wide World Importers MD","[Measures].[Black
Items]")
```

CUBEMEMBER is one of a set of functions that can use the connection to refer to a value in the cube using MDX syntax. In this case, the formula returns the name of the member, which is `Black Items`. The field below this uses a different formula:

```
=CUBEVALUE("Wide World Importers MD",B$1)
```

It is using CUBEMEMBER to determine the value to display in the cell. In our use case, we need to merge these into a single formula.

3. In a new cell, use the following formula to return the count of Black Items:

```
=CUBEVALUE("Wide World Importers MD","[Measures].[Black
Items]")
```

4. Now we need to add the timeline slicer to this formula. We will use the name of the timeline filter to return the filter member to use in our formula:

```
=CUBEVALUE("Wide World Importers MD","[Measures].[Black
Items]",Timeline_Invoice_Date)
```

If we wanted to add the **Employee** slicer, we would add the name to the formula as well. The formula is building an MDX calculation based on the intersection of the members we have chosen. By not including the **Employee** slicer, these values will have the values for the filtered period regardless of the salespeople who may be selected. This adds flexibility to the design.

5. Now, create another formula for Blue Items:

```
=CUBEVALUE("Wide World Importers MD","[Measures].[Blue
Items]",Timeline_Invoice_Date)
```

6. Now we can add these values to the dashboard, copy each formula, and add it to a cell on the dashboard below the filters and above the PivotTable. Your dashboard should look like the following screenshot:

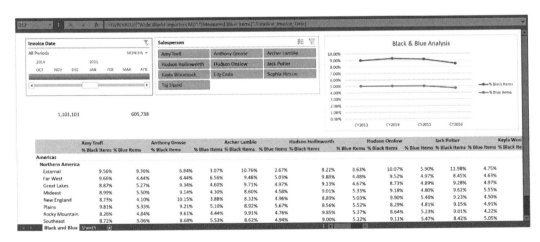

Figure 9.20 – Black and blue dashboard with raw item counts

7. Now let's create the formula for the sales amount. Return to the new sheet we created. Select the PivotTable with the filters. Once again, go to the **PivotTable Analyze** tab on the ribbon and select **Convert to Formulas** in the **OLAP Tools** menu.

   This time we get a **Convert to Formulas** warning message. This warning message prevents users from unintentionally converting their PivotTables. This operation is irreversible, so Excel is confirming the change.

   We have the option here to convert the report filters as well. There are times you may want to keep the filters in place. For example, if we wanted to continue to filter values in our formulas using the filter as is, then we would leave this box unselected. However, in our case, we want to get all the parts of the PivotTable converted to formulas so we can build a filtered value for our dashboard. Select the **Convert Report Filters** option and click **Convert** to complete the process.

8. Now that we have the various parts converted, select the field with (Multiple Items) in it that uses a new CUBESET function to create a set that is used to filter the measure:

```
=CUBESET("Wide World Importers MD","{[Item].
[Color].&[Blue],[Item].[Color].&[Black]}","(Multiple
Items)")
```

   The set is named Multiple Items and is used in the CUBEVALUE function by referring to the cell in the function options (B4 in our workbook) as follows:

```
=CUBEVALUE("Wide World Importers MD",$B$4,$A$6,Timeline_
Invoice_Date)
```

   By using what we have discovered here, we can complete the custom CUBEVALUE formula for our dashboard:

```
=CUBEVALUE("Wide World Importers MD", CUBESET("Wide
World Importers MD", "{[Item].[Color].&[Blue],[Item].
[Color].&[Black]}"), "[Measures].[Total Excluding
Tax]",Timeline_Invoice_Date)
```

9. As you can see, we embedded the CUBESET function into the CUBEVALUE formula to get the result we wanted. This formula can now be copied onto our dashboard the same way we did for the others.

Formatting the new fields

Now that we have our new metrics copied into fields, we can format them (it is helpful to turn **Gridlines** and **Headings** back on during this process. Be sure to hide them when you are done formatting these values):

1. Select four cells using the cell with the value as the upper-left cell, then choose **Merge and Center** from the **Home** tab on the ribbon. This will create a larger block to display the number.

2. From the same tab, click the **Middle Align** button to center the values in the middle of the merged cells vertically.

3. Increase the font size for those cells to 14 or to a size you like.

4. Merge and center the two cells above the newly configured cells. We will use this as our header. Add text to these merged cells to be the labels – `Black Items`, `Blue Items`, and `Black & Blue Sales`.

5. Format the sales cell as **Currency** as we did not format the **Total Excluding Tax** measure in the tabular model.

6. Highlight the six cells you created at this point and add borders and shading to suit your desired look for the dashboard. When you are done, your dashboard should look similar to ours, as follows:

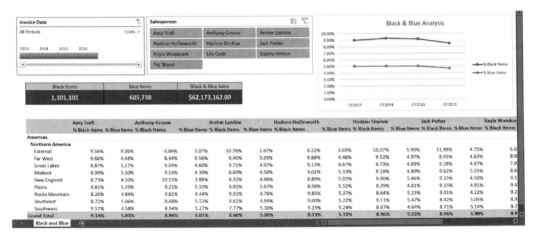

Figure 9.21 – Completed black and blue dashboard

This completes the basic dashboard for Excel. You can create the same dashboard using the tabular model data as well. The functionality is the same. Using the **OLAP Tools** functionality effectively sends MDX to the tabular model as well. As a result, you will see that the naming conventions used with the tabular model are the same as those used with the multidimensional model.

For example, the **Measures** dimension is used in the tabular model formulas, but that actual dimension is not in the tabular model. This is handled by the communication protocols and drivers between Excel and SSAS.

In the next section, we will explore some options that can be used to share your completed dashboard.

Sharing your Excel dashboards with others

Now that you have this awesome dashboard created, how can you share it? It is easy to share it by sending it to others via email, but you always risk them making changes to the data or design. If you want to share this with users while limiting their ability to edit, there are several good options such as OneDrive, SharePoint, and even Power BI workspaces. The next sections help you prepare for deploying your workbook to be shared.

Checking your capabilities

In order to share using one of the key services such as Power BI or SharePoint Online, you need to have access to these services and the services need to have access to the location of your model. Both services require Microsoft 365 subscriptions to use. The SharePoint solution will be similar to an on-premises deployment if you have that available.

Checking your credentials

When deploying to an online service, you need to make sure that the credentials you will be running under have access to the database. In all of our examples here, we have been running entirely locally. When you move to an online service, your credentials need to have access to your local server in order to refresh the data. You will be able to push the Excel sheet to SharePoint or OneDrive, but any data refresh will require **Active Directory** in order to complete the authentication process.

Deploying your workbook

You can deploy your workbook to OneDrive (personal or corporate), SharePoint, or Power BI. However, in order to properly share your Excel workbook with a live connection to Analysis Services, Analysis Services must be on the Active Directory or Azure Active Directory domain for the easiest and most optimal deployment.

If you have created your dashboard in an Active Directory-supported environment, you should be able to refresh the data as required. If you are working in a disconnected development environment, this may not be possible. While you can deploy the workbook, none of the interactive functionality will work because the query is not using the correct credentials.

Use the following steps to deploy your dashboard to OneDrive:

1. Open the **OneDrive** location you want to upload the file to.

2. Use the **Upload** button and choose your file to deploy your Excel dashboard to **OneDrive** as shown here:

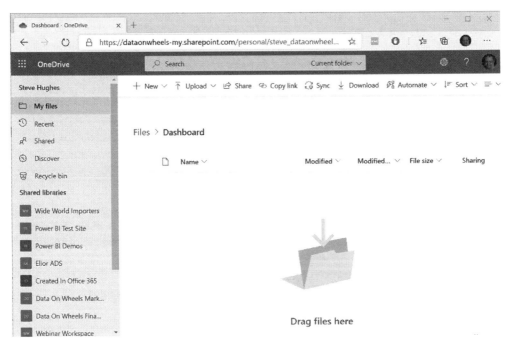

Figure 9.22 – OneDrive upload location

3. Open your **Dashboard** in **OneDrive**. This will be the online experience for your dashboard.

4. Now that you have your dashboard deployed, you can use the **Share** button as shown here to share it with others:

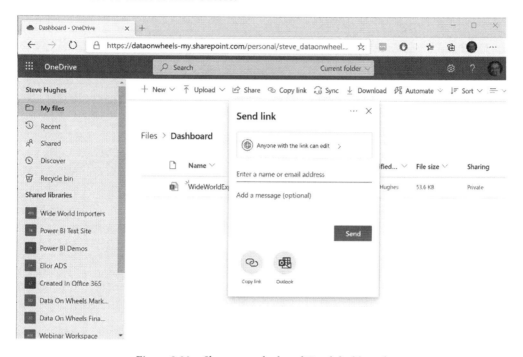

Figure 9.23 – Share your deployed Excel dashboard

This is just one approach you can use to share your dashboard with others. As you may have noticed in the link, this is the equivalent of sharing your dashboard on SharePoint.

Summary

In this chapter, you saw the various types of interaction you can have with multidimensional and tabular models when working with Excel. You created PivotTables and charts and supported these with timeline and slicer filters. These skills you learned will help you to visualize your data using Excel and both multidimensional and tabular models. You are also now able to enhance your Excel workbook visualizations to make them more appealing to your users and focus on the data to support your business scenario.

In the next chapter, we will use Power BI Desktop to live-connect to our models and create a similar dashboard. When the goal is to visualize the data in your models for users, Power BI has more visual capabilities than Excel.

10
Creating Interactive Reports and Enhancing Your Models in Power BI

In *Chapter 9, Exploring and Visualizing Your Data with Excel*, we connected our models to Microsoft Excel. In this chapter, we will connect our models to **Power BI**, build out some reports and dashboards, and enhance the models in Power BI. You will be able to use these techniques to create compelling visualizations for your users. The goal with Power BI is to clearly visualize data to help users make informed decisions quickly while at the same time interact with the data to dive into the details.

We will wrap up the chapter by demonstrating how to add measures to the live connection Power BI dashboard and how to deploy your desktop files to share in the Power BI service online. We will be creating two Power BI Desktop files, one for each model. This will allow us to compare how the models interact with Power BI.

In this chapter, we're going to cover the following main topics:

- Creating Power BI visualizations using live connections
- Understanding live connections and import for Power BI with SSAS models
- Adding measures to Power BI when using tabular models and live connections
- Deploying your Power BI report to a Power BI workspace

Technical requirements

In this section, you will need to have your multidimensional model that was created in *Chapter 3*, *Preparing Your Data for Multidimensional Models*; *Chapter 4*, *Building a Multidimensional Cube in SSAS 2019*, and *Chapter 5*, *Adding Measures and Calculations with MDX*, deployed and running (**WideWorldImportersMD**). You will also need the tabular model we expanded in *Chapter 6*, *Preparing Your Data for Tabular Models*, deployed and running (**WideWorldImportersTAB**).

We will not be working with the workspace version of your tabular models. You will also need the Power BI Desktop client to work through the hands-on work in this chapter. All of the examples in this chapter will use the June 2020 release version of Power BI Desktop. Because Power BI Desktop is updated monthly, some examples may look different for you. If you do not have Power BI Desktop installed yet, you can go to the Microsoft Store and search for Power BI Desktop to get the latest free version downloaded locally.

Creating Power BI visualizations using live connections

Let's start creating our Power BI visualizations using the recommended connection method – **live connections**. We will review more details about this connection type versus the import method in the next section.

To get started, we will need to create Power BI Desktop files to support each model type:

1. Open and save two Power BI Desktop files – `WideWorldImporters-MD.pbix` and `WideWorldImporters-TAB.pbix`.

2. When you open a new Power BI Desktop file, you will see a splash screen with some information on it. Go ahead and close that window. Both desktops should look similar to the following screenshot when you are ready:

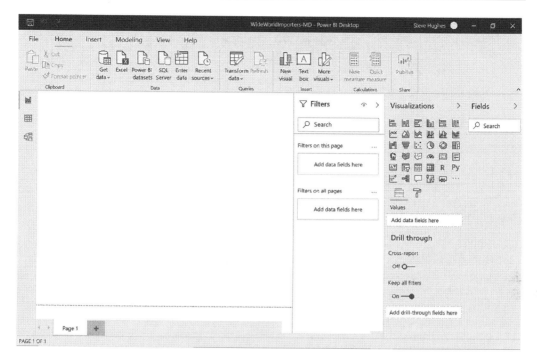

Figure 10.1 – New Power BI Desktop Window

Remember, your Power BI Desktop surface may be different than the one we have shown in the preceding screenshot. In most cases, the core functionality we will be exploring in this chapter should be possible in future versions. But if you see significant differences, you should review the changes since our version was released by checking out the Power BI blog at https://powerbi.microsoft.com/en-us/blog/.

Before we launch into our work, let's do a quick tour of the desktop:

- Across the top, you will see the ribbon that is common across many Microsoft products.

- On the left below the ribbon, you can see three buttons. They change the design view that you see. Their functionalities are listed here:

a) The default is the report design surface.

b) The table button opens the data view which is like the view, we see when working with tabular models in Visual Studio.

c) The third button is used to show the relationships. Remember that you can use Power BI to model design work as we did with tabular models.

- On the right side are three panels that open by default in the report design view. From left to right, they are **Filters**, **Visualizations**, and **Fields**:

  a) The **Filters** panel allows you to apply filters to various parts of the report, including the visual you are working with, the page you are on, or the entire report.

  b) The **Visualizations** panel is where you select and modify any visualization you want to work with. The options in this panel vary greatly depending on the visualization you are working with.

  c) Finally, the **Fields** panel displays the tables, fields, and measures we can add to our report.

Let's now learn how to connect to data sources in Power BI.

Connecting to data sources in Power BI

Power BI supports three types of connections when working with data sources. They are as follows:

- The first and most common type is **import**. The import method connects to a data source and imports the data into memory. This is typically the best performing and has the most design capabilities within Power BI.

- **DirectQuery** is the second option. DirectQuery can be used with a limited set of data sources. It does not import the data, but instead sends queries back to the source, allowing the source system to execute the query. This is mostly used with large data warehouses where import is impractical. DirectQuery is not supported for SSAS.

- Finally, there is a special connection type for Analysis Services and Power BI data models – **live connect**. Live connect is only an option for Analysis Services and Power BI models. It works like DirectQuery but is optimized for analytic models. We will be using live connect to create our reports in this section.

Live connecting to the multidimensional model

Now that you have a basic understanding of connections, let's connect our Power BI desktop to our multidimensional model:

1. Click the down arrow on the **Get data** button on the ribbon and select **Analysis Services**:

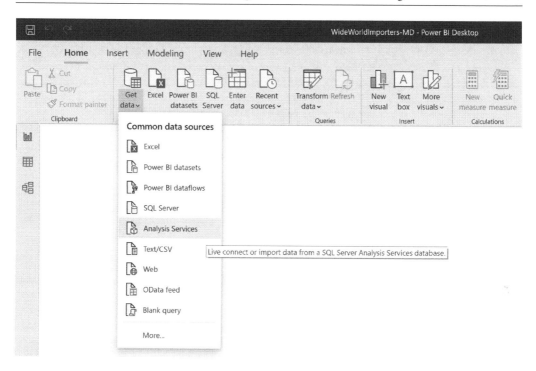

Figure 10.2 – Get data from Analysis Services

2. In the **SQL Server Analysis Services database** dialog, you will need to add the **Server** name for your multidimensional model. Since we know the database name we are targeting, add that as well. Make sure that the **Connect live** option is selected. Then click **OK**:

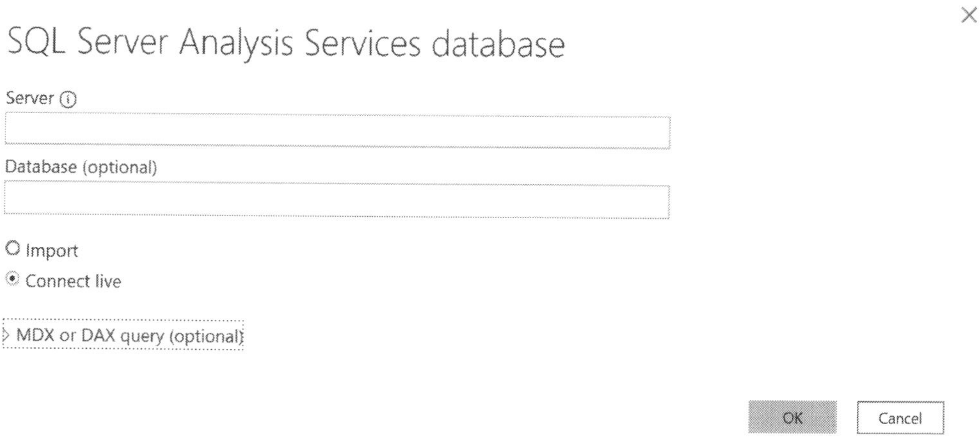

Figure 10.3 – SQL Server Analysis Services database connection information

3. The next dialog is the **Navigator** dialog. Here, you can see our database with the cubes and perspectives listed out. In our model, we have one cube – **Wide World Importers** – and one perspective – **Invoicing**. We will be using the **Wide World Importers** cube for our dashboard.

4. When you click on **Wide World Importers**, the **Navigator** dialog lists the dimensions and measures that will be brought into the designer. (You may also notice that the **Navigator** dialog calls our cube a *perspective* as well. The **Navigator** dialog does not distinguish between cubes and perspectives.) Once you have selected **Wide World Importers**, click **OK**.

The **Navigator** dialog with the multidimensional model looks as shown in the following screenshot:

Figure 10.4 – Navigator dialog with the multidimensional model

We are now connected to the multidimensional model. Your desktop should now look like the following screenshot:

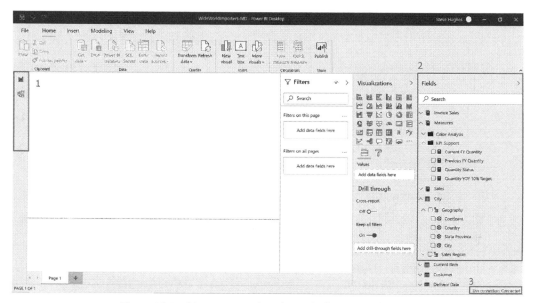

Figure 10.5 – Live connected to the multidimensional model

You should notice a couple of changes:

- On the left, the data view is not available. Because the data is not imported, the data is not readily available for viewing. As of June 2020, the relationship or model window is available in preview. At the time of writing, the relationships from the cube are not represented in this view. You should expect improvements to this view from Microsoft in the future.

- The other key change is that the **Fields** panel is populated with the dimensions and measures from our model. You can expand the various tables and groupings to see the fields and values we will be using in our report design.

- The last thing you should notice is also highlighted in the preceding screenshot. In the lower-right corner, you will see the following: **Live connection: Connected**. This lets you know the type of connection you are using in the current design environment.

Live connecting to the tabular model

The following steps will walk you through the process of adding a tabular model live connection to Power BI:

1. Open your other desktop file, `WideWorldImporters-TAB.pbix`.

2. Click the down arrow on the **Get data** button on the ribbon and select **Analysis Services** (Refer to *Figure 10.2*).

3. In the **SQL Server Analysis Services database** dialog, you will need to add the **Server** name for your tabular model. Since we know the database name we are targeting, add that as well. Make sure that the **Connect live** option is selected. Then click **OK** (Refer to *Figure 10.3*).

You will not get a **Navigator** dialog unless you do not enter the database name, which is different from our experience with Excel. Once the connection is made, the **Fields** list is populated, and we can see the **Live connection: Connected** information in the lower-right corner. You should notice that the **Fields** list shows all the tables from our tabular model as tables whereas the multidimensional model differentiated between measure groups and dimensions. The other key difference is that the preview for the model view shows the relationships in our tabular model, which were missing from our multidimensional view.

Now that we have connected to both models, let's start by creating a dashboard (or Power BI report) as we did with Excel in the previous chapter. We will be replicating the following screenshot in both model types as much as we are able. Then we will add some additional visuals that highlight the use of Power BI with our models:

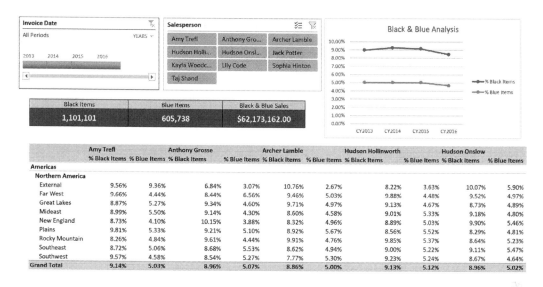

Figure 10.6 – Excel dashboard from Chapter 9

Let's get started with our multidimensional report.

Building our Power BI report with multidimensional data

Open your Power BI desktop file that is connected to your multidimensional model. For some additional space on the design surface, we collapsed the **Filters** panel by clicking the > at the top of the panel. The steps in the following section will help us to create the visuals and filters to reproduce a similar dashboard in Power BI using multidimensional data. As done previously, the data will be focused on our black and blue items. Let's start by adding the core visuals to the dashboard.

Creating the base dashboard in Power BI

Let's begin by creating the base dashboard in Power BI:

1. Let's start by creating a table with salespeople, regions, and percentages (%) of items sold. In the **Fields** panel, expand **Measures**, then **Color Analysis**. You should see the following expanded in your **Fields** panel:

Figure 10.7 – Color Analysis measures in the Fields panel

2. Select **% Black Items** and **% Blue Items**. This will add those measures to the default visual on the design surface. In our case, this created a column chart. You will see in the **Fields** panel that our choices have been marked, as shown in the following screenshot. This helps you know which fields are used in your report:

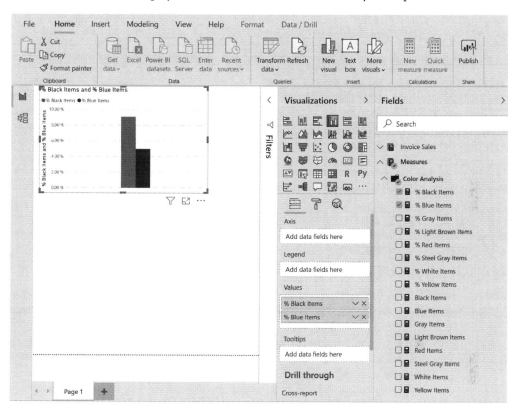

Figure 10.8 – Added the % measures to Power BI Desktop

3. While the **column chart** is the default visual, we will be using a **matrix visual**. This is easy to change – with the visual highlighted, locate the matrix visual in the **Visualizations** panel and click it. This will change the visual to look like the following:

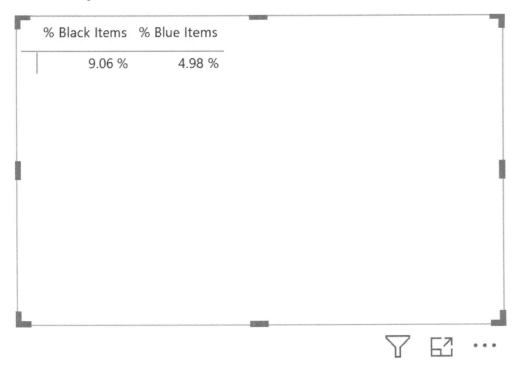

Figure 10.9 – Column chart changed to matrix visual

4. Now let's add our additional fields. Locate the **City** table and select the **Sales Region** hierarchy. This should add the **Sales Region** hierarchy to the **Rows** section of your matrix.

5. Next, find the **Salesperson** table and choose **Employee**. This should add the salesperson's name to the columns in your matrix. The **Employee** field will be in the **Columns** section of your matrix's properties. Your Power BI Desktop matrix visual should look like the following:

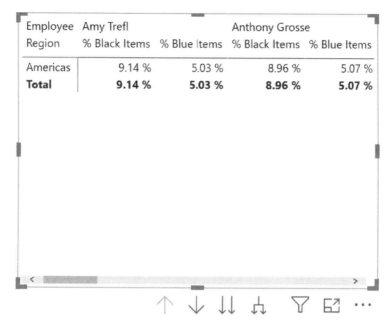

| Employee | Amy Trefl | | Anthony Grosse | |
Region	% Black Items	% Blue Items	% Black Items	% Blue Items
Americas	9.14 %	5.03 %	8.96 %	5.07 %
Total	**9.14 %**	**5.03 %**	**8.96 %**	**5.07 %**

Figure 10.10 – Added fields to the matrix visual

6. Drag the matrix control to the bottom of your page and expand it so it fills the bottom of the page.

7. The final step is to drill down the hierarchy to display similar information to what we see in the **pivot table** in Excel. The following screenshot shows the resulting table and the button used to drill down:

Expand all down one level in the hierarchy

| Hudson Hollinworth | | Hudson Onslow | | Jack Potter | |
% Black Items	% Blue Items	% Black Items	% Blue Items	% Black Items	% Blue Items
9.13 %	**5.12 %**	**8.96 %**	**5.02 %**	**8.96 %**	**4.98 %**
9.13 %	5.12 %	8.96 %	5.02 %	8.96 %	4.98 %
8.22 %	3.63 %	10.07 %	5.90 %	11.98 %	4.75 %
9.85 %	5.37 %	8.64 %	5.23 %	9.01 %	4.22 %
8.89 %	5.03 %	9.90 %	5.46 %	9.23 %	4.50 %
9.88 %	4.48 %	9.52 %	4.97 %	8.45 %	4.63 %
9.13 %	4.67 %	8.73 %	4.89 %	9.28 %	4.97 %
8.56 %	5.52 %	8.29 %	4.81 %	9.15 %	4.91 %
9.01 %	5.33 %	9.18 %	4.80 %	9.62 %	5.55 %

Figure 10.11 – Matrix with Sales Region drilled down to the Region level

The next part of the process is to add a line chart.

Adding a line chart

The steps to add a line chart are as follows:

1. Click on a blank space on the design surface.

2. Then go to **Color Analysis** and select **% Blue Items** and **% Black Items**. Like before, this will add a column chart to the report.

3. With the chart highlighted, select the **Line Chart** option in **Visualizations**. This will change the chart to the line chart with two dots on it as follows:

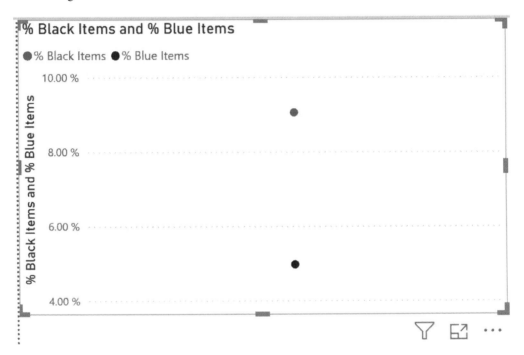

Figure 10.12 – Change from the default chart to a line chart

4. Now, let's add the calendar years to the axis. Go to **Invoice Date | Calendar** hierarchy and select **Calendar Year**. The chart will now look like this:

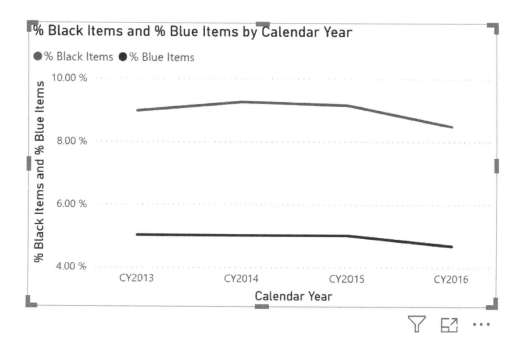

Figure 10.13 – Adding years to the line chart

5. The chart has all the years and **Unknown**. In order to remove **Unknown** from the visual, we need to expand the **Filters** pane.

6. In the **Filters on this visual** section, expand **Calendar Year**.

7. Change the **Filter type** to **Advanced filtering**.

8. Choose **is not** from **Show items** and enter the Unknown value.

9. Click **Apply filter** to remove the Unknown value from just this visual. The following screenshot shows the **Filters** pane when the setting is applied:

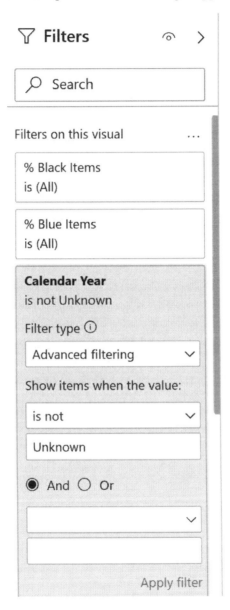

Figure 10.14 – Filtering Unknown from Calendar Year

10. Let's add markers to the line chart. With the line chart still highlighted, click on the paint roller, and expand **Shapes**. Click **Show Marker** to add markers to the chart.

11. In the same area, expand the **Title** section and change the title to **Black & Blue Analysis**. Wrap up this visual by changing the size to fit in the upper-right corner of the report. Now on to the next visual. At this point, your report should look like the following screenshot:

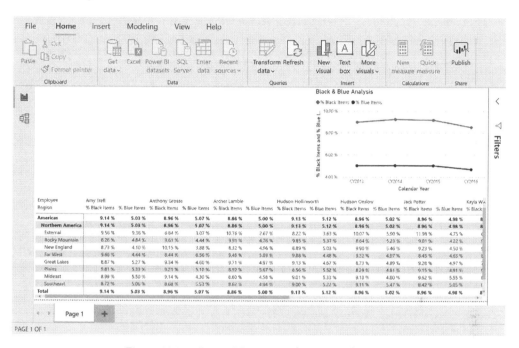

Figure 10.15 – Power BI report with two visualizations

Now let's add the counts and amounts for black and blue items as cards in the report.

Adding cards to our visuals

In Power BI, we will be using the card visualization for each metric – **Blue Items**, **Black Items**, and **Black & Blue Sales** as follows:

1. On the **Fields** panel, find the **Sales** measure group and select the **Quantity** measure. This will add the **Quantity** value as the default chart.

2. Change the chart type to **Card** in **Visualizations**.

3. In the **Filters** panel, add the **Color** field from the **Item** dimension to the **Filters** on this visual. Select **Black** from the list of options. The quantity will now be filtered for black items only.

4. Click on the paintbrush to open the properties for the card. Find **Title** and turn it on. Add `Black Items` as the title.

5. Change **Alignment** to centered and the font size to **30**. Change **Background color** to a light blue.

6. Lastly, change **Display units** to **None** in the **Data label** area of the properties. This will display the actual value on the card.

7. Finish this visual off by resizing the card so we can fit three of these side by side. Your report should look like the following screenshot at this point:

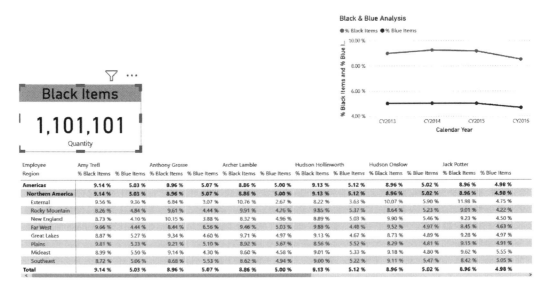

| Employee | Amy Trefl | | Anthony Grosse | | Archer Lamble | | Hudson Hollinworth | | Hudson Onslow | | Jack Potter | |
Region	% Black Items	% Blue Items	% Black Items	% Blue Items	% Black Items	% Blue Items	% Black Items	% Blue Items	% Black Items	% Blue Items	% Black Items	% Blue Items
Americas	**9.14 %**	**5.03 %**	**8.96 %**	**5.07 %**	**8.86 %**	**5.00 %**	**9.13 %**	**5.12 %**	**8.96 %**	**5.02 %**	**8.96 %**	**4.98 %**
Northern America	**9.14 %**	**5.03 %**	**8.96 %**	**5.07 %**	**8.86 %**	**5.00 %**	**9.13 %**	**5.12 %**	**8.96 %**	**5.02 %**	**8.96 %**	**4.98 %**
External	9.56 %	9.36 %	6.84 %	3.07 %	10.76 %	2.67 %	8.22 %	3.63 %	10.07 %	5.90 %	11.98 %	4.75 %
Rocky Mountain	8.26 %	4.84 %	9.61 %	4.44 %	9.91 %	4.76 %	9.85 %	5.37 %	8.64 %	5.23 %	9.01 %	4.22 %
New England	8.73 %	4.10 %	10.15 %	3.88 %	8.32 %	4.96 %	8.89 %	5.03 %	9.90 %	5.46 %	9.23 %	4.50 %
Far West	9.66 %	4.44 %	8.44 %	6.56 %	9.46 %	5.03 %	9.88 %	4.48 %	9.52 %	4.97 %	8.45 %	4.63 %
Great Lakes	8.87 %	5.27 %	9.34 %	4.60 %	9.71 %	4.97 %	9.13 %	4.67 %	8.73 %	4.89 %	9.28 %	4.97 %
Plains	9.81 %	5.33 %	9.21 %	5.10 %	8.92 %	5.67 %	8.56 %	5.52 %	8.29 %	4.81 %	9.15 %	4.91 %
Mideast	8.99 %	5.50 %	9.14 %	4.30 %	8.60 %	4.58 %	9.01 %	5.33 %	9.18 %	4.80 %	9.62 %	5.55 %
Southeast	8.72 %	5.06 %	8.68 %	5.53 %	8.62 %	4.94 %	9.00 %	5.22 %	9.11 %	5.47 %	8.42 %	5.05 %
Total	**9.14 %**	**5.03 %**	**8.96 %**	**5.07 %**	**8.86 %**	**5.00 %**	**9.13 %**	**5.12 %**	**8.96 %**	**5.02 %**	**8.96 %**	**4.98 %**

Figure 10.16 – Multidimensional report with the card added

8. We need two more of those cards. We will copy and paste two more next to the existing card. We will change the properties of these new cards to show the number of blue items and the total amount sold for both black and blue items.

9. Let's update the middle card to the blue item quantity. In the **Filters** pane, change **Color** from **Black** to **Blue**. Then update the title to `Blue Items`.

10. Now, for the last card, the card on the right, we will update this to support the number of sales for black and blue items. Click on that card. Now add **Blue** to the filter. This will give us the aggregate of both items. Change the field to **Total Including Tax**. Update the card's title to `Black & Blue Sales`:

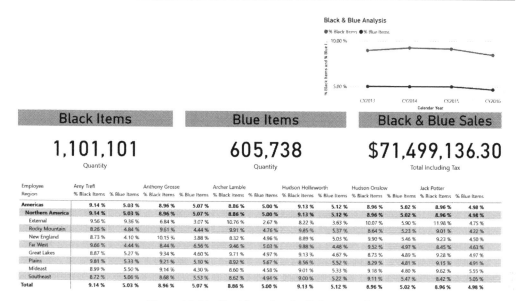

Employee Region	Amy Trefl		Anthony Grosse		Archer Lamble		Hudson Hollinworth		Hudson Onslow		Jack Potter	
	% Black Items	% Blue Items	% Black Items	% Blue Items	% Black Items	% Blue Items	% Black Items	% Blue Items	% Black Items	% Blue Items	% Black Items	% Blue Items
Americas	9.14 %	5.03 %	8.96 %	5.07 %	8.86 %	5.00 %	9.13 %	5.12 %	8.96 %	5.02 %	8.96 %	4.98 %
Northern America	9.14 %	5.03 %	8.96 %	5.07 %	8.86 %	5.00 %	9.13 %	5.12 %	8.96 %	5.02 %	8.96 %	4.98 %
External	9.56 %	9.36 %	6.84 %	3.07 %	10.76 %	2.67 %	8.22 %	3.63 %	10.07 %	5.90 %	11.98 %	4.75 %
Rocky Mountain	8.26 %	4.84 %	9.61 %	4.44 %	9.91 %	4.76 %	9.85 %	5.37 %	8.64 %	5.23 %	9.01 %	4.22 %
New England	8.73 %	4.10 %	10.15 %	3.88 %	8.32 %	4.96 %	8.89 %	5.03 %	9.90 %	5.46 %	9.23 %	4.50 %
Far West	9.66 %	4.44 %	8.44 %	6.56 %	9.46 %	5.03 %	9.88 %	4.48 %	9.52 %	4.97 %	8.45 %	4.63 %
Great Lakes	8.87 %	5.27 %	9.34 %	4.60 %	9.71 %	4.97 %	9.13 %	4.67 %	8.73 %	4.89 %	9.28 %	4.97 %
Plains	9.81 %	5.33 %	9.21 %	5.10 %	8.92 %	5.67 %	8.56 %	5.52 %	8.29 %	4.81 %	9.15 %	4.91 %
Mideast	8.99 %	5.50 %	9.14 %	4.30 %	8.60 %	4.58 %	9.01 %	5.33 %	9.18 %	4.80 %	9.62 %	5.55 %
Southeast	8.72 %	5.06 %	8.68 %	5.53 %	8.62 %	4.94 %	9.00 %	5.22 %	9.11 %	5.47 %	8.42 %	5.05 %
Total	9.14 %	5.03 %	8.96 %	5.07 %	8.86 %	5.00 %	9.13 %	5.12 %	8.96 %	5.02 %	8.96 %	4.98 %

Figure 10.17 – Dashboard with all data visuals

Now that we have the core visuals in place, we want to add the two slicers to the dashboard – `Invoice Date` and `Salesperson`.

Adding slicers to our visuals

Slicers let us add interactive filtering. We will be adding `date` and `salesperson` slicers in the following steps:

1. Add a slicer visual to your report. Once you have it there, add the **Date** field to the slicer. You may get an error saying hierarchy slicers don't work unless you are using SQL Analysis Services 2019 or newer, as shown in the following screenshot:

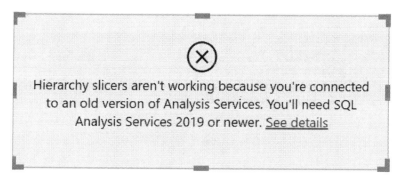

Figure 10.18 – Hierarchy slicer error with a multidimensional model

As I am sure you are aware, we are using SQL Analysis Services 2019. This error message is misleading. The actual issue we are dealing with is that the hierarchy slicers are not supported with multidimensional models. As you work through additional design with multidimensional models, you should be aware that some functionality is not available for use with multidimensional models. Now, let's move forward and fix this slicer to work with our multidimensional data.

We have two options to fix our slicer:

i) The first option is to determine that we only want a year filter.

ii) The second option is to allow all levels of filtering.

The next few steps will create both types of filters. So you can see the difference, we will remove the year filter and instead use the relative date filter.

2. Make a copy of the slicer with the error. Now, click on the slicer. In the **Visualizations** panel, you can see the hierarchy in the **Field** section as shown here:

Figure 10.19 – Hierarchy fields in the slicer control

As you can see, all the fields in the **Calendar** hierarchy are present. Because the hierarchy is not supported in the slicer, you need to specify which field you want to use in the slicer.

3. Click the **X** to remove **Calendar Month** and **Date** from the first slicer. This will make the slicer a year slicer for your data. Your slicer will have the **Calendar Year** options, which can be selected.

4. On the second slicer, remove **Calendar Month** and **Calendar Year**. This will show the individual dates in the slicer. You should have both slicers on your report now, which should look like the slicers shown in the following screenshot:

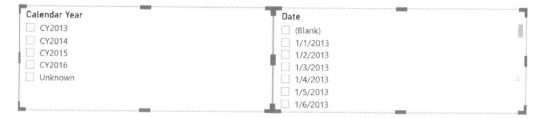

Figure 10.20 – Two date slicers using different levels in the hierarchy

5. In the year slicer, you can choose between the **List** view or **Dropdown** view. The **List** view is the default. Dropdowns can be used to conserve space. They still allow multiple selections and have **All** as the top level.

6. To change the view, you need to select the down arrow in the upper-right corner of the visual. Be aware that the down arrow is only visible when you hover over that corner. Choose **Dropdown** for the year slicer:

Figure 10.21 – Slicer view menu

7. We are going to change the view in the **Date** slicer as well. However, remember that the **Date** field is a date data type. This adds additional options for the view – **Between**, **Before**, **After**, and **Relative Date**. Choose **Between**:

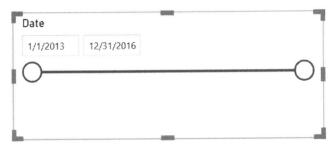

Figure 10.22 – Date slicer using the Between view

8. Now, remove the **Year** slicer and make sure the **Date** slicer is near the left edge of the report. Your report should look similar to the following screenshot at this point:

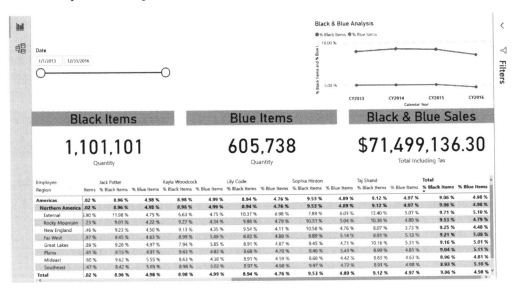

| Employee | Jack Potter | | | Kayla Woodcock | | Lily Code | | Sophia Hinton | | Taj Shand | | Total | |
Region	Items	% Black Items	% Blue Items	% Black Items	% Blue Items	% Black Items	% Blue Items	% Black Items	% Blue Items	% Black Items	% Blue Items	% Black Items	% Blue Items
Americas	.02 %	8.96 %	4.98 %	8.98 %	4.99 %	8.94 %	4.76 %	9.53 %	4.89 %	9.12 %	4.97 %	9.06 %	4.98 %
Northern America	.02 %	8.96 %	4.98 %	8.98 %	4.99 %	8.94 %	4.76 %	9.53 %	4.89 %	9.12 %	4.97 %	9.06 %	4.98 %
External	5.90 %	11.98 %	4.75 %	6.63 %	4.75 %	10.37 %	6.98 %	7.89 %	6.03 %	13.40 %	5.07 %	9.71 %	5.10 %
Rocky Mountain	.23 %	9.01 %	4.22 %	9.27 %	4.34 %	9.98 %	4.79 %	10.31 %	5.04 %	10.38 %	4.80 %	9.53 %	4.79 %
New England	.46 %	9.23 %	4.50 %	9.13 %	4.35 %	9.54 %	4.11 %	10.58 %	4.76 %	8.07 %	3.73 %	9.21 %	5.08 %
Far West	.97 %	8.45 %	4.63 %	8.99 %	5.49 %	8.82 %	4.88 %	9.89 %	5.14 %	8.91 %	5.13 %	9.21 %	5.08 %
Great Lakes	.89 %	9.28 %	4.97 %	7.94 %	5.85 %	8.91 %	4.87 %	9.45 %	4.71 %	10.16 %	5.31 %	9.16 %	5.01 %
Plains	.81 %	9.15 %	4.91 %	9.43 %	4.82 %	8.68 %	4.70 %	8.46 %	5.43 %	8.99 %	4.81 %	9.04 %	5.11 %
Mideast	.80 %	9.62 %	5.55 %	8.63 %	4.38 %	8.91 %	4.59 %	8.68 %	4.42 %	8.83 %	4.63 %	8.96 %	4.81 %
Southeast	.47 %	8.42 %	5.05 %	8.98 %	5.02 %	8.97 %	4.98 %	9.97 %	4.72 %	8.91 %	4.98 %	8.93 %	5.10 %
Total	.02 %	8.96 %	4.98 %	8.98 %	4.99 %	8.94 %	4.76 %	9.53 %	4.89 %	9.12 %	4.97 %	9.06 %	4.98 %

Figure 10.23 – Multidimensional report with the Date slicer

9. Now we can wrap up our dashboard by adding the salesperson filter. In Excel, we used slicer buttons to create this filter. However, a direct equivalent does not exist in Power BI. Drop a slicer control in place and add the **Employee** field to the slicer.

That wraps up our multidimensional report. Let's switch to using the tabular model for our live connection.

Building our Power BI report with tabular data

Now that we have our multidimensional Power BI report complete, let's create the report based on our tabular model. Open your Power BI Desktop file that is connected to your tabular model. For some additional space on the design surface, we collapsed the **Filters** panel by clicking the > at the top of the panel.

The following steps will create the visuals and filters to create the same dashboard in Power BI using tabular data. Once again, the data will be focused on our black and blue items:

Let's start by creating the matrix with salespeople, regions, and percentage (%) of items sold:

1. In the **Fields** panel, expand **Sales**. The first difference you will notice is that **% of Blue Items** is a **key performance indicator** (**KPI**).

2. Select **% of Black Items**.

3. Then expand the **% of Blue Items** KPI and select **Value**. This will create the default column chart with **% of Black Items** and **% of Blue Items**. The **Fields** panel should look like the following screenshot:

Figure 10.24 – Tabular measures in the Fields panel

4. While the column chart is the default visual, we will be using a matrix visual. This is easy to change – with the visual highlighted, locate the matrix visual in the **Visualizations** panel and click it. This will change the visual to look like the following:

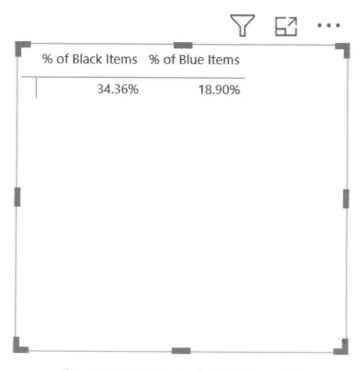

Figure 10.25 – Matrix visual with tabular model

5. Now let's add our additional fields. Locate the **City** table and select the **Sales Region** hierarchy. This should add the **Sales Region** hierarchy to the **Rows** section of your matrix. Unlike when we added this with the multidimensional data, the matrix recognized the hierarchy and added the + symbol to allow interactive drilling as shown here:

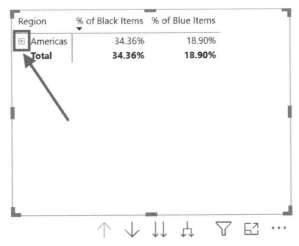

Figure 10.26 – Matrix control using tabular data with + highlighted

6. Next, find the **Salesperson** table and choose **Employee**. This should add the salesperson's name to the columns in your matrix. The **Employee** field will be in the **Columns** section of your matrix's properties.

7. Drag the matrix control to the bottom of your page and expand it so it fills the bottom of the page.

8. The final step is to drill down the hierarchy to display similar information to what we see in the pivot table in Excel. You can use the plus (+) symbol shown in the previous screenshot to expand the first two levels of the hierarchy easily. You can use the same expand button that we used with the multidimensional report as well.

As we did in the *Building our Power BI report with multidimensional data* section, we will also add a line chart for our tabular model data.

Adding a line chart for the tabular model data

The steps to add a line chart are as follows:

1. Click on a blank space on the design surface. Then go to **Sales** and select **% Blue Items** > **Value** and **% Black Items**. As before, this will add a column chart to the report.

2. With the chart highlighted, select the **Line Chart** option in **Visualizations**. This will change the chart to a line chart with two dots on it.

3. Now, let's add the calendar years to the axis. Go to the `Date` table and select **Calendar Year Label**. Remember that in our tabular model, **Date** is *marked as the date table*.

4. Let's add markers to the line chart. With the line chart still highlighted, click on the paint roller, and expand **Shapes**. Click **Show Marker** to add markers to the chart.

5. In the same area, expand the **Title** section and change the title to `Black & Blue Analysis`.

6. Next, go back to the **Fields** area for the visual properties.

7. Click the down arrow by **Calendar Year Label**, choose **Rename**, and rename the field to `Calendar Year`, removing `Label` from the name. This will update the axis title on our line chart. You can see the menu that includes the **Rename** option for the field shown in the following screenshot:

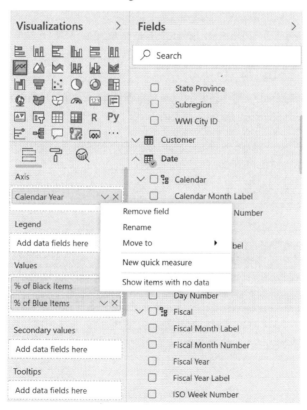

Figure 10.27 – Rename axis in Power BI

8. Wrap up this visual by changing the size to fit in the upper-right corner of the report. Now on to the next visual. At this point, your report should look like the following screenshot:

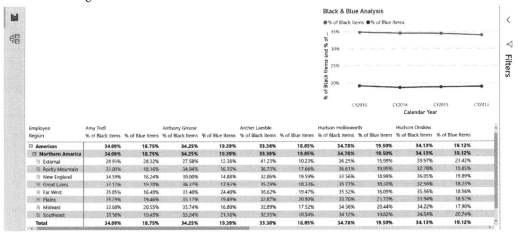

Figure 10.28 – Tabular model Power BI report with two visualizations

Now let's add the counts and amount for black and blue items as cards in the report.

Adding cards to tabular data

As done previously, we will be using the card visualization for each metric – **Blue Items**, **Black Items**, and **Black & Blue Sales** as follows:

1. On the **Fields** panel, find the **Sales** table and select the **Total Black Items** field. This will add the **Total Black Items** value as the default chart.

> **Implicit measures are turned off**
>
> When we built our tabular model, we turned off implicit measures by setting **DiscourageImplicitMeasures** to TRUE. By making this change, we are unable to use **Quantity** as a measure. If you want to use **Quantity** as a measure in Power BI, you will need to create a **Total Quantity** measure or similar in the tabular model and redeploy the model. Multidimensional models always explicitly call out measures in the design process, which is why we were able to use **Quantity** in the multidimensional report. Implicit measures are frequently used in Power BI report design, so this may cause confusion with some report designers using live connected models.

2. Change the chart type to **Card** in **Visualizations**.

3. Click on the paintbrush to open the properties for the card. Find **Title** and turn it on. Add `Black Items` as the title.

4. Change **Alignment** to centered and the font size to `30`.

5. Turn off **Category label**.

6. Change **Background color** to a light blue.

7. Lastly, change **Display units** to **None** in the **Data label** area of the properties. This will display the actual value on the card.

8. Finish this visual off by resizing the card so we can fit three of them side by side. Your report should look like the following figure at this point:

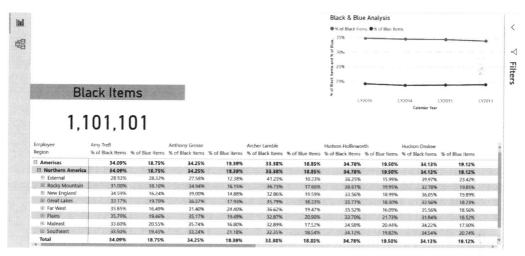

Figure 10.29 – Tabular report with the card added

9. We need two more of those cards. We will copy and paste two more next to the existing card. We will change the properties of these new cards to show the number of blue items and the total amount sold for both black and blue items.

10. Let's update the middle card to the blue item quantity. In the filter, change the field to **Total Blue Items**. Then update the title to `Blue Items`.

11. Now, for the last card, the card on the right, we will update this to support the number of sales for black and blue items. Change the field to `Total Sales Amount`. Update the card's title to `Black & Blue Sales`.

12. To complete this step, we need to add a filter to the card as well. Expand the **Filters** panel and locate **Filters on this visual**. From the **Fields** panel, locate **Item Brand Color** and drag the **Color** field into the **Add data fields here** area. Select **Black** and **Blue** from the list. That completes the work on this card.

We will now add slicers to our report.

Adding slicers to the tabular data visuals

Follow the steps outlined to add slicers:

1. Add a slicer visual to your report. Once you have it there, add the **Calendar** hierarchy from the **Date** table to the slicer. Unlike the issues we saw with the multidimensional report, the **Calendar** hierarchy works in the slicer. The new hierarchy slicer allows you to expand down the hierarchy to choose the date filter you want to apply.

2. Finally, add another slicer for **Salespeople**. Add another slicer to the report.

3. Add the **Employee** field to the slicer.

4. Rename the **Field** to `Salesperson` by clicking the down arrow by the field and choosing **Rename**. Both of your reports should look similar. Here is our finished tabular model report:

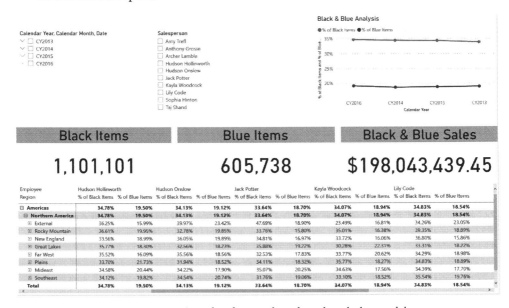

Figure 10.30 – Completed report based on the tabular model

This concludes the design of the basic Power BI report based on the tabular model. Let's now have a rundown on live connections and import for Power BI.

Understanding live connections and import for Power BI with SSAS models

The reports we created in the previous section connect live to the multidimensional and tabular models in Analysis Services. When using this capability, queries are sent to Analysis Services and the results are returned. While some caching is done to improve performance, the overall solution is dependent on the performance of Analysis Services and the network connectivity with Power BI.

The alternative approach is to import the data, which results in the data being loaded into memory in Power BI. This is most valuable when you need to mash up data between multiple data sources. However, if you are working with SSAS to import a lot of data, you will find there are often performance issues when importing that much data. You will likely be required to create MDX or DAX queries to make sure the data can be mashed up as expected. Refreshing performance with multidimensional models has proven to be a poor solution in many situations.

We recommend that you move to the underlying data source to create Power BI solutions if you need to import a lot of data from SSAS. For example, in our solution, we have a well-formed dimensional model in SQL Server. Rather than trying to import all the data from the multidimensional database, it would make more sense to import the data from a relational database using the star schema views.

Given the choice between import or live connections, you should use live connections. Typically, we see more developers start with Power BI and move to tabular models when they need additional scale. Only use import when you need a smaller subset of the data to be mashed up with other data.

Power BI has an additional capability to enhance the model when using tabular models. We will discuss that next.

Adding measures to Power BI when using tabular models and live connections

As we saw earlier, with the lack of support for the hierarchy slicer, new measures can only be added to tabular models when using a live connection. This functionality is not supported with multidimensional models. In this section, we will add a measure to our tabular model report. This allows us to expand on the model without changing the underlying model. Let's begin:

1.   Open your tabular model Power BI report.

2.   Add a new page to the report so we have a clean design canvas to work with. Select the **Sales** table as we will be adding a **Total Quantity** measure there.

3.   There are two standard ways to create new measures in your report. On the **Home** ribbon, you can see the **Calculations** section, which has two buttons – **New measure** and **Quick measure**. We will start by creating a simple new measure. First, click **New measure**:

Figure 10.31 – Create calculated measures buttons

When you click the **New measure** button, Power BI Desktop takes you to the following window. This window simplifies measure creation by allowing you to set **Name**, the datatype, and **Home table** at the top. The ribbon in this view has formatting available as well:

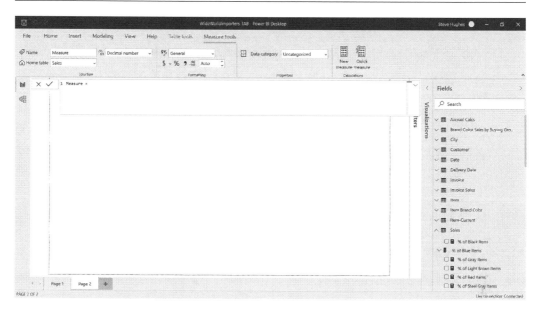

Figure 10.32 – The new measure window in Power BI Desktop

> **Mind your measures**
>
> Power BI has this annoying feature related to the location of measures. It puts the measure in the table you have selected in the **Fields** panel. If you just click the **New measure** button and have not explicitly selected the table you want to see the new measure created in, it will drop the new measure in the first table in your list. In our model, this is the **Annual Calcs** table. In *step 2* of our process here, you should have selected the **Sales** table. This is the reason why. If you forget to do this, the **New measure** view in Power BI desktop has the ability to change the **Home table**.

Now that we are here, we will begin creating our new measure.

Creating a new measure

The steps to create a new measure are as follows:

1. Change the name of our measure to `Total Quantity` by replacing the word `Measure` in the formula bar or by changing the **Name** field in the ribbon.

2. Next, confirm that **Home table** is set for **Sales**.

3. Since **Quantity** is not a decimal number, change the data type to **Whole number**.

4. In the formula bar, we will be creating a simple sum measure with the **Quantity** field. Here is the formula: `SUM('Sales'[Quantity])`.

5. Set the formatting to **Whole number** as well.

6. Find the new measure and add it to your report by selecting it. You will get the default column chart.

7. Add **Sales Territory** from the **City** table and you can see how **Total Quantity** is broken down by territory.

8. Now let's use the **Quick measure** option. Click **Quick measure** on the ribbon to add another measure.

A quick word on Quick measures in Power BI

Quick measures are preconfigured DAX calculations to help Power BI report designers easily create more complex calculations. There are time intelligence, category, filter, and even text-based calculations included. These calculations are created by Microsoft and its partners to support better Power BI development. This is an area in which to expect changes on a regular basis in Power BI.

---

9. Unlike **New measure**, **Quick measure** opens up a new dialog called **Quick Measures**. You select the calculation and add fields from the model to complete the creation of the measure. For our report, let's add the **Average per category** calculation. Select that calculation from the list.

10. Add **Total Sales Amount** from the **Sales** table to the **Base value** field. You can either scroll through the list on the right or use **Search** to find the value more quickly.

11. From the **Item** table, add **Size** to the **Category** field. Your dialog should look like the following screenshot:

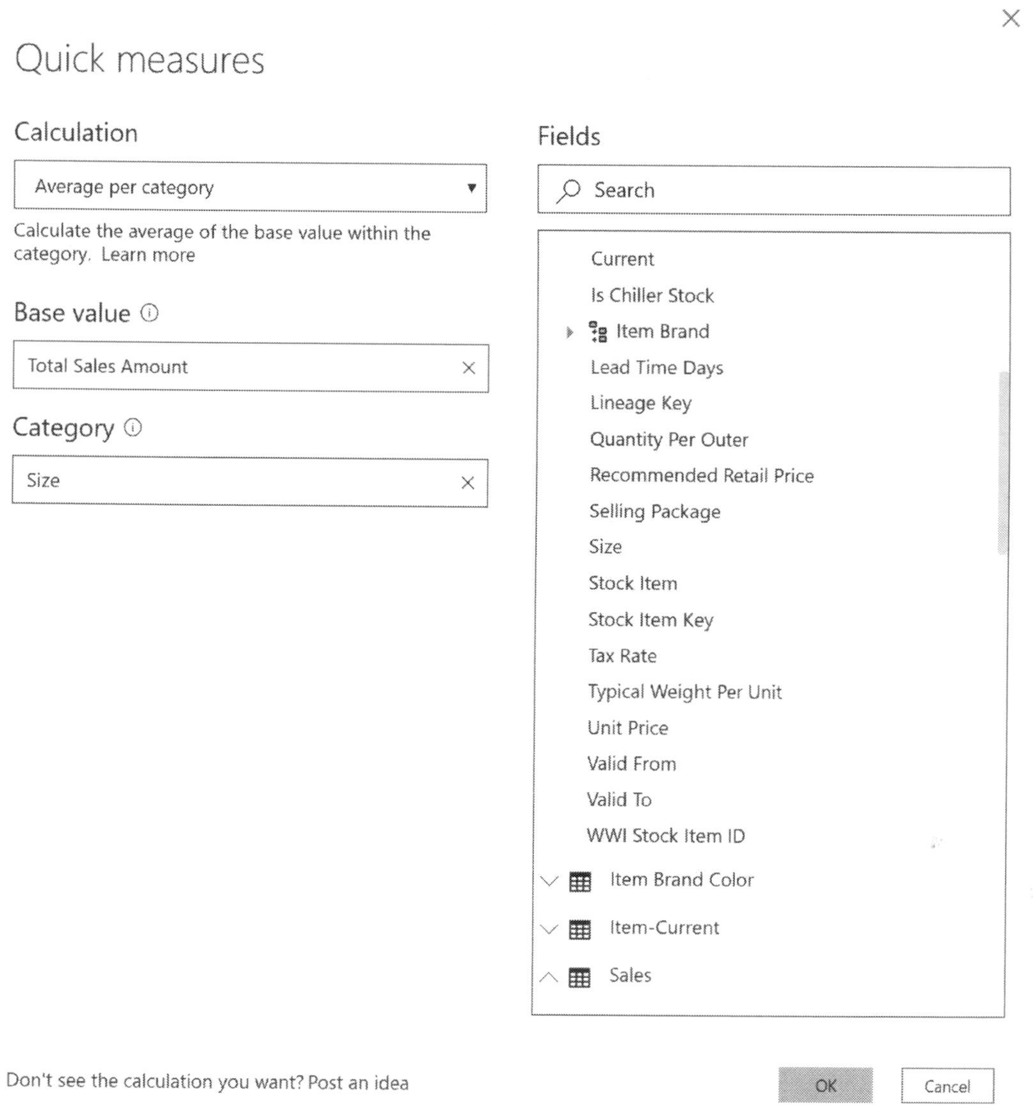

Quick measures

Calculation

Average per category ▼

Calculate the average of the base value within the category. Learn more

Base value ⓘ

Total Sales Amount   ×

Category ⓘ

Size   ×

Fields

🔍 Search

Current

Is Chiller Stock

▸ 🔡 Item Brand

Lead Time Days

Lineage Key

Quantity Per Outer

Recommended Retail Price

Selling Package

Size

Stock Item

Stock Item Key

Tax Rate

Typical Weight Per Unit

Unit Price

Valid From

Valid To

WWI Stock Item ID

∨ ▦ Item Brand Color

∨ ▦ Item-Current

∧ ▦ Sales

Don't see the calculation you want? Post an idea

OK   Cancel

Figure 10.33 – Quick measures dialog

12. Click **OK**. This will open the measure dialog with the new measure created. It generates the following DAX:

```
Total Sales Amount average per Size = AVERAGEX(
KEEPFILTERS(VALUES('Item'[Size])),CALCULATE([Total Sales
Amount]))
```

You can add this measure to your report and explore how it interacts with your data. If the calculation is close to what you want to do, you can modify it. Quick measures generate the measure for you and are a great way to learn more complex DAX syntax. They are also a great way to create a starter measure you can modify as needed.

As you can see, you can add measures to enhance your report based on tabular models. You can also use Power BI to prototype new measures you may want to add back into your tabular model for others to use. Working with DAX in Power BI is much easier than using Visual Studio.

In our next section, we will explore how to deploy our Power BI reports to the service.

Deploying your Power BI report to a Power BI workspace

A Power BI report can be deployed to the Power BI service online or to **Power BI Report Server**, which runs in **SQL Server Reporting Services** (**SSRS**). In this section, we will look at deploying the report to the service, which is the most common and recommended approach.

> **Power BI Report Server**
>
> Power BI Report Server is the on-premises deployment option for Power BI reports. However, it requires specific licensing with SSRS or Power BI Premium. This option allows customers who still have concerns about the cloud an option to deploy locally. Be aware that a different Power BI Desktop application is required because Power BI Report Server does not keep pace with its online peer. Some of the functionality we have demonstrated in this chapter may not be compatible depending on your current version of Report Server. We will not be discussing this option due to these restrictions.

We have been working in Power BI Desktop, which is the free tool available to everyone. If you want to share the work you have done, the best option is to deploy to the Power BI service. In order to deploy to Power BI online, you will need a Power BI Pro license. If your organization runs Microsoft 365, you may have a license and personal workspace available. If not, check out Power BI's website for the latest free trial options to explore this functionality.

Adding a gateway and deploying our tabular report

In order to access on-premises data sources, you will need to add a gateway to your development server. This gateway allows Power BI to successfully request data from the data sources. The gateway fully manages the connectivity and responds to requests from Power BI. This is important as Power BI does not require direct connectivity to your on-premises environment to work with the data.

You can download the gateway and find more details about the gateway at this location: `https://powerbi.microsoft.com/en-us/gateway/`. There are two gateway options – **personal mode** and **standard mode**. Live connections with **SQL Server Analysis Services** (**SSAS**) are only supported in the standard mode.

The next steps download the gateway in Standard mode. Depending on security, network, and other restrictions in your environment, you may not be able to continue:

1. Download the gateway in the standard mode.

2. Install the gateway on your development server. Keep in mind that we are using this to demonstrate deployment. You should not consider this a production deployment recommendation for the gateway.

3. Register the gateway using the same account you have Power BI associated with. When this process is complete, you should see a confirmation dialog showing that Power BI is ready to go, as shown in the following screenshot:

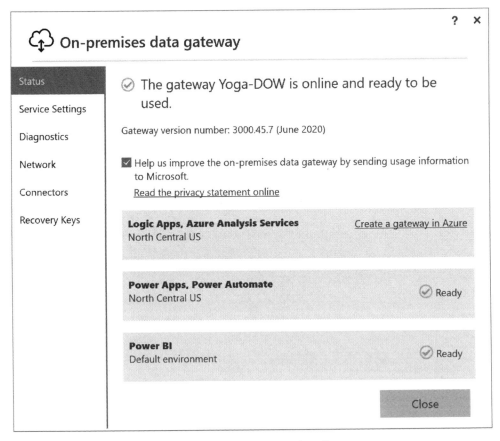

Figure 10.34 – Power BI gateway install success

4. Now browse to `https://app.powerbi.com/groups/me/gateways` to view the gateway online.

5. In the browser, you should see a link to **Add data sources to use this gateway**. Click that link and complete the information for the connection to your tabular model. You will need a local user on the server to map to this gateway. That user needs to have access to your SSAS instance as well:

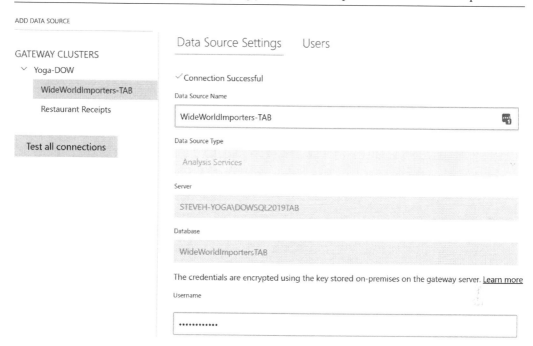

Figure 10.35 – Data Source Settings in the Power BI gateway

6. If you have your gateway configured with a data connection, the next step is to deploy your Power BI Desktop file to Power BI. Click the **Publish** button on the ribbon to continue.

   If you have not logged into your Power BI environment yet, you will be prompted to do so.

7. In the **Publish to Power BI** dialog, choose **My workspace**, and click **Select**. You will now see the **Publishing to Power BI** dialog, which will show the progress of the deployment. Click the **Open 'WideWorldImporters-TAB.pbix' in Power BI** link to open the published report in the Power BI service.

8. If all the connectivity is working correctly, you should have the interactive dashboard available on your Power BI site. If you are not connected to Active Directory (common with development environments), you may not be able to connect to the data even though all the settings and connectivity appear to be in order.

This is the best way to share your dashboards within your organization. Troubleshooting gateway issues is beyond the scope of this book.

Summary

In this chapter, you have used Power BI to visualize data from both Analysis Services models. By creating similar dashboards with both model types, you should have seen the differences when creating the dashboards. You will also have learned that connecting live and deploying to the Power BI service are the preferred options to take advantage of the best of Analysis Services and Power BI.

We also walked through expanding the measures in our Power BI models and then the deployment options available for Power BI. Microsoft continues to make changes to Power BI and tabular models in Analysis Services so those are the preferred technologies in most cases.

In the next chapter, we will dive deeper into security options available to both types of models. We will look at specific Analysis Services security features including implementing row-level security.

Section 5: Security, Administration, and Managing Your Models

There are more advanced topics that are required to understand as you deploy your solution to users. In this section, we will explore practices and tools for securing and maintaining your models once they are deployed.

This section comprises the following chapters:

- *Chapter 11, Securing Your SSAS Model*
- *Chapter 12, Common Administration and Maintenance Tasks*

11

Securing Your SSAS Models

Now that we have created our models and built reports and dashboards, we will wrap up the book with chapters on security and maintenance. This chapter focuses on securing the server and the data in your models. We will review the capabilities that **SQL Server Analysis Services** (**SSAS**) brings and the unique features available to each type of model. A significant part of this chapter will describe what you can do to implement different or enhanced security. Some of the topics in this chapter will not have hands-on exercises because of the complexity or enterprise nature of security implementations.

In this chapter, we're going to cover the following main topics:

- Reviewing security settings for SSAS

- Setting up user roles in servers and databases

- Implementing data security in multidimensional models

- Implementing data security in tabular models

Technical requirements

In this section, you will need to have your multidimensional model that was created in *Chapter 3, Preparing Your Data for Multidimensional Models, Chapter 4, Building a Multidimensional Cube in SSAS 2019*, and *Chapter 5, Adding Measures and Calculations with MDX*, deployed and running (**WideWorldImportersMD**). You will also need the tabular model we expanded in *Chapter 6, Preparing Your Data for Tabular Models*, deployed and running (**WideWorldImportersTAB**). We will not be working with the workspace version of your tabular models.

You will also need **SQL Server Management Studio** (**SSMS**) and **Microsoft Excel** to work through the hands-on work in this chapter. To work through all of the examples in this chapter, you will require the latest version of Excel in **Office 365 ProPlus**. At the time of writing this chapter, all examples were carried out in Excel in the Office 365 ProPlus May 2020 release. Because Excel is updated continually via a subscription, some examples may look different for you. You will need SSMS to review and make modifications to some security settings and to validate security implementations in some cases.

You will also need the SQL Server relational database we created in *Chapter 3, Preparing Your Data for Multidimensional Models*, for some of the security modifications. We will need to add tables to the database and incorporate those tables into our Visual Studio solutions to support some of the more advanced security techniques.

Reviewing security settings for SSAS

SSAS builds on a rich history of security built into the platform with a focus on keeping vital business data secure. In this section, we will review the core security properties and their impact on your environment.

Opening the security settings for the server

While the core engine that runs each mode (multidimensional and tabular) is different, much of the management is shared. This means the properties can be found in the same location and modified in the same way. You will see that some types of properties only apply to one of the modes. However, for security settings, they are the same. But first, let's open our security settings so that we can review the impact:

1. Open SSMS and connect to both instances of SSAS.

2. Right-click on the name of the instance and select **Properties**, as shown in the following screenshot:

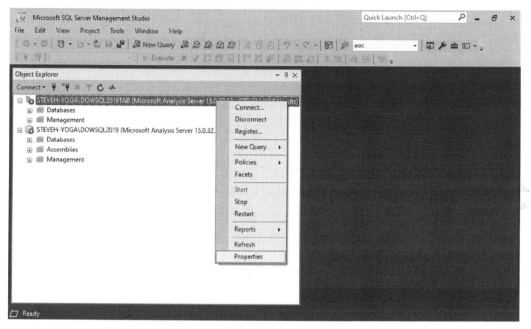

Figure 11.1 – Server properties in the shortcut menu

This will open the **Analysis Services Properties** dialog to the **Information** page. While your first instinct would be to open the **Security** page, that is not what we are reviewing in this section.

3. Click on the **General** page.

4. Select **Show Advanced (All Properties)**.

5. Scroll down until you see the four properties listed in the **Security** section. *Steps 3, 4, and 5* have been highlighted in the following screenshot:

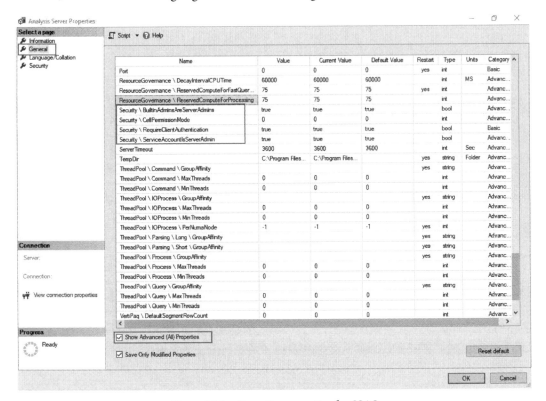

Figure 11.2 – Security properties for SSAS

Before we leave this section, let's review how to modify these properties on the **General** page:

- The first column is the **Name** column. This column organizes the properties into groups and subgroups. In our current case, we are looking at the properties that are part of the **Security** group. There are a number of other properties and groups, some of which we will cover in *Chapter 12, Common Administration and Maintenance Tasks*, which covers maintenance and operations.

- Next, you will see three value columns: **Value**, **Current Value**, and **Default Value**:

    a) Use the **Value** column to make a change to the property.

    b) **Current Value** is the value currently in use with this instance.

    c) **Default Value** is a reference to what the default is, so you can determine whether you should go to the default or not.

- The **Restart** column informs you if a restart is required to apply the change. Some changes show immediately when changed and will be reflected in **Current Value** after the value is changed. However, if a restart is required, the property may not yet be applied. This column makes you aware of the impacted properties.

- The **Type** and **Units** columns describe the type of data expected in the property:

  a) The **Type** column lets you know the data type required for the property, such as `int` or `bool`.

  b) The **Units** column lets you know what you should expect to see or put in the column. For example, **Sec** is used for those properties whose value is expressed in seconds; **Folder** is used to inform you that the property expects a folder location; and **MS** is used for milliseconds.

- The **Category** column is used to separate **Basic** from **Advanced** properties. When you click the **Show Advanced (All) Properties** box, the advanced properties are made visible.

> **WARNING: Changing server properties can negatively impact your model**
>
> Be aware that changing these properties is similar to making registry changes in Windows. You should test the impact of these changes prior to making any changes in a production environment. Be especially cautious when working with properties that require a restart as you will need to plan a maintenance window to minimize the impact on your users when making these changes.

In the next section, we will start digging into some specific security properties in detail.

Allowing anonymous access to your model

When you first open the **Analysis Services Properties** window, you only see the basic option, **Security \ RequireClientAuthentication**, which was pointed out in the previous section. This property is set to **true** by default.

Disabling this property or setting it to **false** is the first step in enabling anonymous access to your SSAS instance. Analysis Services is secured with Active Directory by default. This is required because the data in most models is considered sensitive or important to the business. If you have data that you want to make publicly available and not require an Active Directory account to access it, you start by setting this to **false**. The full process requires the following steps to complete:

1. Open **Analysis Services Properties** to the server you want to enable anonymous access for.

2. Update the **Security \ RequireClientAuthentication** property to **false**.

3. Edit connection strings that are used to access this server. Add the `Impersonation Level = Anonymous` parameter.

4. Create a new role in the SSAS database that you want to allow anonymous access to and apply permissions to the role you want to use (we explore creating and managing roles later in this chapter).

5. Add **Anonymous Logon** as a member of your newly created role.

> **WARNING**
>
> This allows unauthenticated access to your server and database. We recommend only using this for specific datasets you would consider public.

This will effectively allow any client or user to access the data in this database based on the role permissions allowed. We recommend that you do not use this except in special cases. The default does not allow anonymous access and typically requires some level of named access to view your models.

Understanding advanced security properties

This section covers the advanced security properties in SSAS and their impact on your models. The first two properties are related to how administrator and service accounts are treated within Analysis Services:

- **Security \ BuiltInAdminsAreServerAdmins**: This property determines whether local administrators for the server or machine are Analysis Server admins. This is set to **true** by default. You may need to change this if your company has specific security requirements related to system admins and access to data.

- **Security \ ServiceAccountsServiceAdmin**: This property specifies whether the service account that Analysis Services is running under is an administrator account. This property is set to **true** by default as well. This is typically not an issue as the service account is provided by the security management organization. However, as with built-in admins, if you need to change this to meet internal security policies, the capability is here.

- The third option visible in the advanced view is **Security \ CellPermissionsMode**. We recommend leaving this with the default value of **0**. There is no current documentation on this property, so no updates are necessary or recommended.

While most of the security settings we adjust are in the properties window, some can only be changed in the underlying msmdsrv.ini file. We will discuss these settings next.

Setting security properties in msmdsrv.ini

Some properties are only available in SSAS's configuration file – msmdsrv.ini. In other cases, if your changes are not saved in the properties window, you can make the changes in this file as well. To set the security properties, let's first find and open the file.

Finding and opening the file

This file exists for all your installed instances of SSAS regardless of the mode. If you installed SQL Server with the default install locations, you will find the msmdsrv.ini file in the following folder: C:\Program Files\Microsoft SQL Server\MSAS15.<<instance name>>\OLAP\Config. Replace <<instance name>> with the name of your instance – for example, DOWSQL2019.

> WARNING
> Changing this file directly could adversely affect your SSAS instance. Use caution when making changes.

You can open this file with any text editor. For our demonstration purposes, I have created a copy to prevent issues from working directly with this file in my environment.

Other properties related to security

In the `ConfigurationSettings` section, you will find a security section. It has some additional settings for securing your server, as shown here:

```
<Security>
  <DataProtection>
      <RequiredProtectionLevel>1</RequiredProtectionLevel>
  </DataProtection>
  <AdministrativeDataProtection>
      <RequiredProtectionLevel>1</RequiredProtectionLevel>
  </AdministrativeDataProtection>
  <RequireClientAuthentication>1</RequireClientAuthentication>
  <SecurityPackageList/>
  <DisableClientImpersonation>0</DisableClientImpersonation>
    <BuiltinAdminsAreServerAdmins>1</
BuiltinAdminsAreServerAdmins>
  <ServiceAccountIsServerAdmin>1</ServiceAccountIsServerAdmin>
  <ErrorMessageMode>2</ErrorMessageMode>
  <CellPermissionMode>0</CellPermissionMode>
  <HighTrustTokenSignerCert/>
  <NormalTrustTokenSignerCert/>
  <ServerSchannelTokenSignerCert/>
</Security>
```

You can see the properties we worked with previously. The only property we will call out here is `DataProtection \ RequiredProtectionLevel`. This is an important setting as it defines the data encryption level for all client requests. The default level is 1, which requires encryption. Encryption of data can cause some performance impacts. If your environment needs better performance and the network infrastructure is secured sufficiently, you can potentially use one of the other options. Here are the options for data protection in Analysis Services:

- 0: No encryption, cleartext allowed

- 1: Encryption required, no cleartext (default)

- 2: Cleartext is allowed but only with signatures, less secure than encryption

That wraps up the settings we will cover in this chapter for Analysis Services security. We will now start looking at roles, permissions, and database security for your models.

Setting up user roles in servers and databases

In this section, we will cover the various roles that exist in the databases and servers. Custom roles are also possible. These can limit the data that is seen by users, allowing you to build a more complete solution, reducing overall maintenance. Let's now see how to add members to the server administrator roles.

Adding members to the server administrator role

The server administrator role in SSAS has *unlimited access* to the server, databases, objects, and all data in the instance. Because of this unlimited access to objects and data, it is very important to understand who has that access. When we were installing the servers in *Chapter 1, Analysis Services in SQL Server 2019*, we added the current user to this role. This allowed us to have unfettered access and functionality while working through the tasks in this book. However, in a production configuration, you need to be clear who has access. In our case, we have at least three groups or individuals who were added during the install process:

- **Local administrators**: This group has access by default. If you want to remove them from this group, change **Security \ BuiltInAdminsAreServerAdmins** to **false** to remove their access. This group is not listed on the **Security** page in the **Analysis Services Properties** dialog. Remember that you need at least one other named administrator before removing this group.

- **Service account**: This account is granted access by default as well. If you want to remove this account from the server administrators, you will need to change **Security \ ServiceAccountsServiceAdmin** to **false**. Be aware that the service account can be used to grant access to various clients. Removing access will effectively remove access from those customers as well.

- **You**: If you added your current user account during the installation, you should see the user listed on the **Security** page of the **Analysis Services Property** window. This user can be removed from the properties dialog. For now, we will leave this user in place *by design*.

Now that you can see what users exist in the role, let's add another user to the administrator role. These instructions work with both instance modes, multidimensional and tabular:

1. Open the **Analysis Server Properties** window by right-clicking on the server name and selecting **Properties**.

2. Go to the **Security** page.

3. Click **Add…** to add another user. This opens the standard **Select Users or Groups** Windows dialog. This dialog allows you to search the local computer, domains, or other supported security locations to allow access to valid users. If you click the **Advanced…** button, you can use a more sophisticated search option.

4. Select the user or group to add to this role, then click **OK**. You should see the new user added. Depending on the type of account added, you may see the name in a different format than you were expecting. For example, `joe@somewhere.com` may be added as `Joe` because this dialog does not support email-style usernames.

Remember that any groups or users added here have unlimited access to the data as well as the objects in the server. Any other security applied to the user will be ignored because Analysis Services uses optimistic security.

One last thing before we add roles to the models or databases – there are no other server-level security options for Analysis Services. All other security and roles are applied from the database to the data.

Adding a read-only role to the multidimensional model

For this section, you will be working with your multidimensional model. We will be adding a role to the database that will allow read access to all our data. This is a typical operation in databases. This role can be assigned to users or groups to provide access:

1. Open your Visual Studio multidimensional project.

2. Right-click on the `Roles` folder and select **New Role…**.

3. This will open the **Roles** design view, as shown in the following screenshot. Be aware that the dialog has options specific to multidimensional models. Multidimensional models have a much richer security experience than tabular models:

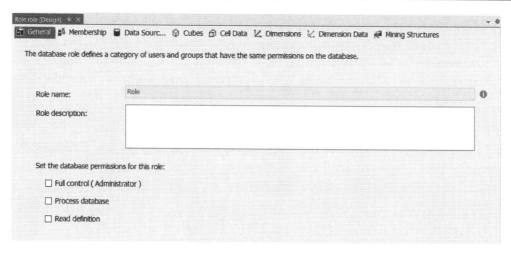

Figure 11.3 – Multidimensional model – create role

Before we create the role, there are three permissions shown that we will not be using in this case – **Full control (Administrator)**, **Process database**, and **Read definition**:

i) **Full control** is the equivalent of the server administrator role but scoped to the database.

ii) **Process database** is specifically for system roles that can be used to refresh or process the database. It allows users or groups in this role to refresh the data from the sources.

iii) Finally, **Read definition** allows users and groups to see the objects and structures in the database but not the data. This permission allows a user to connect SSMS to the database and see the objects. When used with the **Process database** permissions, a user can browse the Analysis Services database in SSMS and process the desired object without visibility of the data. We don't need those permissions for the read-only role we are creating.

4. Change the name of the role to `Read Only`. This can be done by right-clicking on the **Role.role** name in **Solution Explorer** and choosing **Rename**.

5. Select the **Cubes** tab.

6. Select **Read** from the drop-down list in the **Access** column for our single cube – **Wide World Importers**.

7. If you have users or groups in your environment to add, select the **Membership** page and add them there. You do not need to add members to create the role, which is important for supporting sophisticated security structures that are required by many organizations. Once deployed, members can be added to the production environment.

8. Once you are done, save your changes.

With multidimensional databases, you can have multiple cubes. If you want a global read-only role, you will select **Read** access for all the cubes on the list. We only have one cube currently. We will now add the read-only role to the tabular model.

Adding a read-only role to the tabular model

For this section, you will be working with your tabular model. As in the previous section, we will be adding a read-only role to the database:

1. Open the Visual Studio tabular model solution.

2. Open the database to which you will be adding the role. In our example, this is `WideWorldImportersTAB`.

3. Right-click on the `Roles` folder and select **Roles** to open **Role Manager**, as shown in the following screenshot:

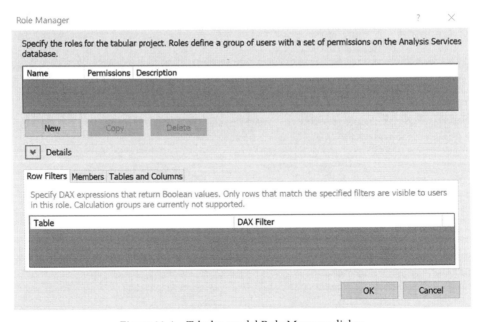

Figure 11.4 – Tabular model Role Manager dialog

4. Click on the **New** button to begin creating the new role.

5. Change the name of the role to `Read Only`.

6. Select the **Read** option from the **Permissions** drop-down list. Unlike the various options available to multidimensional models, this allows query access to the data in the entire tabular model. We will create roles that use row filters in a later section, but those filters are applied to users with the **Read** permission selected.

7. If you have users or groups in your environment to add, select the **Members** tab and add them there. You do not need to add members to create the role, which is important to support more sophisticated security structures required by many organizations. Once deployed, members can be added to the production environment.

8. Once you are done with these changes, select **OK** to save your changes and add the role.

Before we move on to the next section, there are two permissions shown that we will not be using in this chapter but you should be aware of their use – **Administrator** and **Process**:

- **Administrator** is the equivalent of the server administrator role but scoped to the database.

- **Process** is specifically for system roles that can be used to refresh or process the database. It allows users or groups in this role to refresh the data from the sources.

> **SSMS and Visual Studio access restricted**
>
> The roles we have created do not allow a user to access the data via design tools such as SSMS and Visual Studio. For multidimensional models, you must provide **Read definition** access to allow users to view the definition in SSMS's Object Explorer if the user is not in an administrator role. For tabular models, you need to have **Administrator privileges** or be in the server administrator role.

Let's now implement data security in multidimensional models.

Implementing data security in multidimensional models

Now that we have created a read-only role, let's go a little deeper with security. The read-only role was secured at the cube level. As we mentioned before, users who are part of this role have read access to all the content in the cube. In this section, we will work with dimensional- and cell-level security. We will start with dimension hierarchy-level security, and then demonstrate how to add dynamic security to support more complex scenarios. We will wrap this section up by showing how to secure data at the cell level.

> **Adding a local or test user for security testing**
>
> Before we start creating the role, you will need to have a local user you can test with. Because adding a user is unique to your environment, we cannot add the specifics here for every situation. If you are using Windows 10 for your development environment and you are disconnected from a domain, you can use the following link to add a local user that can be used: `https://support.microsoft.com/en-us/help/4026923/windows-10-create-a-local-user-or-administrator-account`. If you are attached to a domain and are able to request a test user account for these purposes, we recommend that. For other systems, you will need to look up what is required.

Adding customer roles with dimension hierarchy security

We currently have two customers in our cube – **Tailspin Toys** and **Wingtip Toys**. In our design, these are part of the **Customer** dimension and are at the `Bill To Customer` level in **Customer Hierarchy**. We will create two roles to secure our data based on these customers. Let's get started:

1. Open your Visual Studio multidimensional solution.

2. Right-click on the **Roles** folder and select **New Role**.

3. Let's start with Tailspin Toys. Name the role `Tailspin Toys Group`.

4. Select the **Cubes** tab.

5. Choose **Read** from the **Access** options for the **Wide World Importers** cube. This will guarantee that users who are only members of the **Tailspin Toys Group** role will be able to view the data in the cube. Permissions are accumulative, which means each role that a user is a member of adds to their permissions.

6. Select the **Dimension Data** tab.

7. Choose the **Customer** dimension in the top drop-down list. Your dialog should look like the one in the following screenshot:

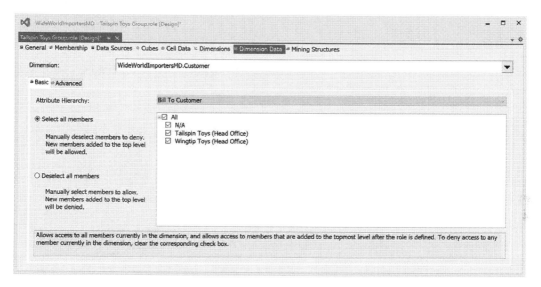

Figure 11.5 – Creating a dimension hierarchy role in Dimension Data

Before we move on to the next steps, we need to understand our options when creating this role.

First, you will see that the **Bill To Customer** attribute hierarchy is already selected (if it is not selected for you, select it from the list of hierarchies). For this role, we will use the basic options. We have two choices: **Select all members** and **Deselect all members**.

By default, **Select all members** is selected. If we use this option, we choose to explicitly deny access to a hierarchy member. The effective result is that new members will be visible to this role. This option is most effective if you have a specific level that needs to be hidden from most users. If the users who would access the hidden level are all administrators with full control, an additional group would not be necessary.

When you select **Deselect all members**, the members in the list on the right become deselected. In this case, explicit access will be granted for users in this role. This would be the option used when managing access to the specific set of data. When new members in the hierarchy are added, they will not be visible to users in this role. We will be setting up roles with this type of access.

8. Choose **Deselect all members**.

9. In the attribute list, select **Tailspin Toys (Head Office)**. Your **Create Role** dialog should look as in the screenshot here:

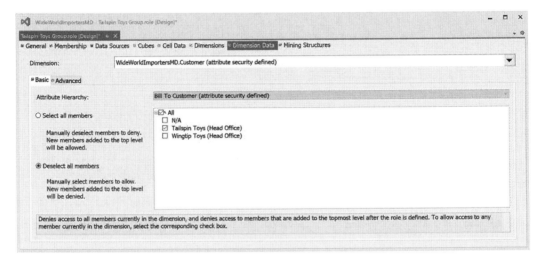

Figure 11.6 – Tailspin Toys Group role attributes selected

10. Save your changes to apply the role to your project.

Now that we have created our role, how do we verify that it works? We can use SSMS to verify whether our role works as expected. Here are the steps:

1. In Visual Studio, deploy and process the cube to apply your changes to the database.

2. In SSMS, expand the `Cubes` folder in the `WideWorldImportersMD` database.

3. Right-click the **Wide World Importers** cube and select **Browse**. This will open the built-in cube browser in Management Studio.

4. In the **Metadata** panel on the left side of the screen, expand **Measures** and the `Sales` folder. Drag **Quantity** onto the open panel on the right. Click the link (**Click to execute query**) to update the view.

5. Next, in the **Metadata** panel, expand the **Customer** dimension and **Customer Hierarchy**.

6. Drag **Bill To Customer** into the results area and execute the query. You should now see three rows with the customers and quantities visible, as shown here:

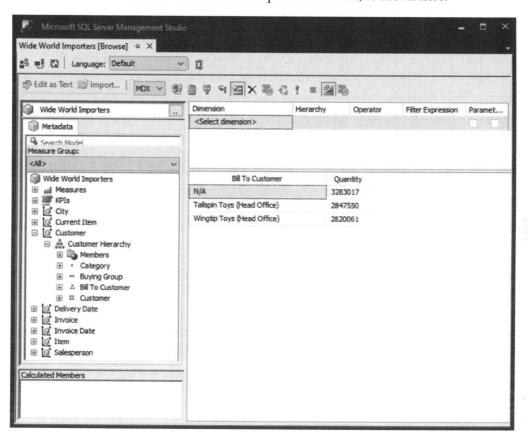

Figure 11.7 – Cube browser with Bill To Customer and Quantity

7. Click the **Change User** button, as shown in the following screenshot:

Figure 11.8 – Change user in the Cube browser

8. This will open the **Security Context** dialog for the browser. **Current User** is selected when the dialog first opens. If you had a user you wanted to test, you could select them here. We will be testing the use of the role we created. Select **Roles** and choose **Tailspin Toys Group**, as shown here:

Figure 11.9 – Choose Tailspin Toys Group in the role security context

9. Click **OK** for both dialogs to change the context. This will clear the results window.

10. Drag `Quantity` and `Bill To Customer` back into the results pane and execute the query. You can see that the query is now filtered for the role and only Tailspin Toys data is being displayed. You can clear the grid by right-clicking the results pane and choosing **Clear Grid**.

Now that we have the Tailspin Toys Group role created, we need to create a role for Wingtip Toys. In this exercise, we will use the advanced options to create the role so that you can see how complex security options can be applied to the cube:

1. Back in Visual Studio, right-click the `Roles` folder to add a new role.

2. Name the new role `Wingtip Toys Group`.

3. In the **Cube** tab, add **Read** access to the **Wide World Importers** cube:

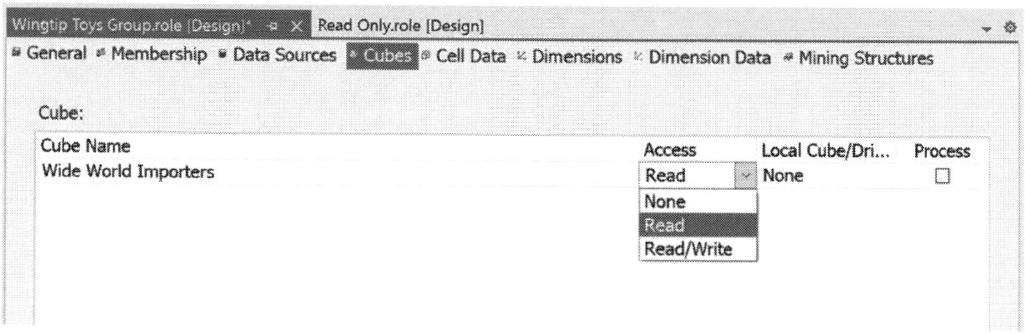

Figure 11.10 – Allowing read access to the cube

4. Now, select the **Dimension Data** tab and choose the **Advanced** tab.

5. Choose the **Customer** dimension and the **Bill To Customer** attribute.

6. Like before, we will be allowing access to Wingtip Toys. Click the **Edit MDX** button for **Allowed member set**. This will open an **Expression Builder** dialog to help create the **Multidimensional Expressions (MDX)** used for the role.

7. In **Expression Builder**, expand the **Customer** dimension and **Customer Hierarchy**.

8. Expand the `Bill To Customer` level in the hierarchy and drag the `Wingtip Toys (Head Office)` member to the `Expression` area. This will add the following text to the expression area: `[Customer].[Customer Hierarchy].[Bill To Customer].&[Wingtip Toys (Head Office)]`.

9. Click **Check** to verify that the expression is valid for this use. If it passes the check, click **OK** to add it to **Allowed member set**.

10. The code from **Expression Builder** has been added to **Allowed member set**. While the code passed the MDX syntax check, it is not valid for setting dimension security. The reason is that the expression includes the `Customer` hierarchy in the name. You should secure data on the base attribute hierarchy. When you review the list of attributes, custom hierarchies are not included in the list. You will need to update the code and remove the `Customer Hierarchy` reference. The expression needs to be updated to the following code, which also includes the curly braces to define the set, which would be considered a best practice:

```
{[Customer].[Bill To Customer].&[Wingtip Toys (Head
Office)]}
```

The **Role Properties** dialog should look like the one in the following screenshot when you have completed the changes:

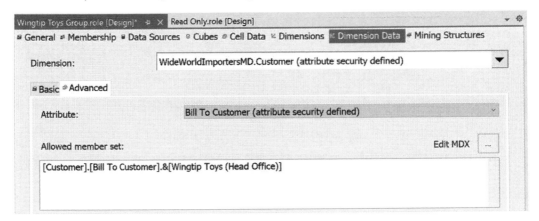

Figure 11.11 – Wingtip Toys group role MDX set

11. Save your changes, then process the cube.

You can test this role using the same steps we used for testing the Tailspin Toys Group role in the cube browser in SSMS after the changes have been deployed and processed. You can see how you can use MDX to handle more complex security scenarios with dimensional security. Next, we will be adding dynamic security to our cube.

Before moving on to dynamic dimension security, we have added these roles using Visual Studio. However, you can create the same roles using SSMS. All the dialogs will look the same for that process. If you choose to add your roles in SSMS, you will need to plan to redeploy them if you need to redeploy the solution. Visual Studio will overwrite roles created in SSMS only.

Adding sales group security with dynamic dimension security

We have added security to filter for the two customers in the previous section. We will now be using the dynamic dimension security concepts to add security for salespeople. While our example is a small set of users, when there are a lot of possible security combinations or there is a change in the organization, dynamic security is a better option. For example, if you have hundreds of sales territories that can be reassigned to salespeople each year, managing dimension security and roles can become tedious.

Dynamic dimension security gives you the ability to handle the complexity and movement of users within your organization. It applies security to dimensions based on an allowed list of users. This section walks through the process of creating dynamic security in your multidimensional model.

Dynamic dimension security takes several steps to implement. For this exercise, you will be working with the relational database and the Visual Studio solution. We will be adding support for users and security mapping. Let's get started.

Adding a new dimension and measure group to support dynamic security

Let's begin:

1. We need to add tables to the relational database. Open SSMS and connect to the relational database, `WideWorldImportersDW`.

2. The first table we will add is `Dimension.Users`. This table will hold the user information that we will use with dynamic dimension security. Here is the script we will use for this table:

```
create table Dimension.Users (
        [User Key] int identity(1,1) not null
    , [User Login] varchar(100) not null
    , [User Email] varchar(200) null
    , constraint PK_Dimension_User primary key clustered
([User Key]))
```

3. The next table is used to map users to the sales territories. When we add it to the cube, it will be a measure group. Therefore, this will be part of the `Fact` schema – `Fact.UserSalesTerritory`:

```
create table Fact.UserSalesTerritory (
        [User Key] int,
        [Sales Territory] nvarchar(50),
        [Is Allowed] bit  )
```

4. Next, we need to add values to use in our solution. We will add two users and map them to different territories. If you want to test this with visualization tools, you will need to create local users.

> **Local or test users**
>
> The creation of local or test users will vary depending on your environment and the steps to do so are beyond the scope of this chapter. If you need additional guidance, we recommend getting guidance for your particular solution. For example, we are using local users created in Windows 10 in our examples. You may not be able to create local users or you may be running a server environment. Refer to the most recent environment documentation to create test users.

The following is the code to insert the users and map them to the sales territories. This code uses sample users. Replace them with the local users you have created. Be mindful of the domain and username you are using as they may be different from the ones used in the example:

```
insert Dimension.Users ([User Login],[User Email])
select 'local\joe','joe@local.com'
union select 'local\sue','sue@local.com';


insert Fact.UserSalesTerritory ([Sales Territory],[User
Key],[Is Allowed])
select 'Great Lakes', [User Key], 1 from Dimension.Users
where [User Login] like 'local\joe'
union select 'Plains', [User Key], 1 from Dimension.Users
where [User Login] like 'local\sue';
```

5. We need to add views for our cube. The `Cube.Users` view is easy. Here is the code for that view:

```
create view Cube.Users as (select [User Key], [User
Login], [User Email] from Dimension.Users);
```

6. In order to properly build the relationship in the cube to support dynamic security, we need to add mappings at the key level. However, that can be tedious even in our dataset. We have over 100,000 cities in the base dimension. We will use the view to map the `City` level. This allows us to build clean relationships in the cube and support changes to the dimension in our security structure. Here is the code for that view:

```
create view Cube.[User Sales Territory] as
(select distinct ust.[User Key] , ust.[Sales Territory]
    , ust.[Is Allowed], dc.[City Key]
from Fact.UserSalesTerritory ust inner join Dimension.
City dc on ust.[Sales Territory] = dc.[Sales Territory])
```

7. Now that we have the data in the database, we need to create the supporting SSAS objects. Open WideWorldImportersMD.sln.

8. Add the two new views to **Data Source View**. If you need a refresher on how to do this, review the instructions in *Chapter 4, Building a Multidimensional Cube in SSAS 2019.*

9. Create a relationship between the two views on the **User Key** field.

10. Create a relationship between the User Sales Territory table and the City table on the **City Key** field. Your data source view should have the following diagram in it:

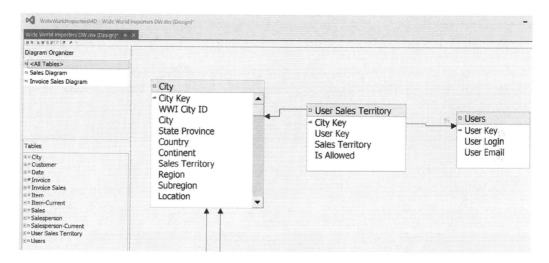

Figure 11.12 – Data Source View with new security tables

11. Add the **Users** dimension to the project based on the Users table. **User Key** will be the key value and the **User Login** field can be used for the name.

12. Now, we will add our new fact table as a new measure group in our cube. Open the cube designer and add the fact table as a new measure group and the **Users** dimension as a new cube dimension (refer to *Chapter 4, Building a Multidimensional Cube in SSAS 2019*, for detailed instructions if you need further guidance to add these objects to the cube).

A new measure has been added to the User Sales Territory measure group as part of this process – **User Sales Territory Count**. This is a simple row count measure that we will use in the creation of the role, as shown in the following screenshot:

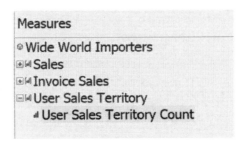

Figure 11.13 – New User Sales Territory Count measure

13. Deploy the changes to the server and process the cube. Don't close Visual Studio yet; we will come back to that tool to wrap up this section.

Adding dynamic security role

The next step is to add a dynamic security role. Here are the steps:

1. In Visual Studio, right-click the Roles folder in the WideWorldImportersMD database to open a new **Role** design window.

2. Name the role Dynamic Sales Territory.

3. On the **Cubes** tab, allow **Read** access for the **Wide World Importers** cube.

4. On the **Dimension Data** tab, choose the City dimension and click the **Advanced** tab.

5. In **Allowed member set**, add the following code:

```
NONEMPTY([City].[City].members,
(StrToMember("[Users].[User Key].["+UserName() + "]"),
[Measures].[User Sales Territory Count]))
```

This code uses the UserName() function to return the user for the query. It will return the currently logged-in user. The set evaluates all city members where there is a valid count associated with the user and returns those city members that the current user is allowed to see.

6. Finally, we need to add our test users to **Membership** in the role. Because these users are not members of any other role, they will not have access until they are added here.

7. Save your project and deploy the changes to the cube. Be sure to fully process the cube to make sure all changes have been applied.

Testing your new dynamic role

Now that the role has been created, let's test the role. For this test, we will use Excel:

1. Open a new Excel workbook.

2. Click the **Get Data** button and choose **From Database** and then **From Analysis Services**.

3. In the **Data Connection Wizard**, change the **Log on credentials** option to **Use the following User Name and Password**.

4. Enter the local user you created for the **Plains** sales region, enter your server name, and click **Next**.

5. Choose the **Wide World Importers** cube and click **Finish**.

6. Select **Pivot Table Report** to add to your worksheet and click **OK**.

7. From **PivotTable Fields**, add `Quantity` from the `Sales` measure group to the **Values** section.

8. Next, add the **Sales Region** hierarchy from the **City** dimension to the **Rows** section.

9. In the pivot table, expand the levels in the **Sales Region** hierarchy. What you will notice is that you can still see all the regions. We are using the user who is limited to the **Plains** sales region. Why do they see all the roll-up data? Because we are secured at the lowest level, `City`, the roll-up data is still visible to users who have restrictions on the data. In some cases, this works well.

For example, if you only want to hide the detailed data, this is great. But if you want to hide the roll-up data and even the members of the dimension, you have to set one other property in the role – **Visual Totals**. **Visual Totals** limits visibility in the client tools to data that they are able to see. Here is how Excel displays the data currently:

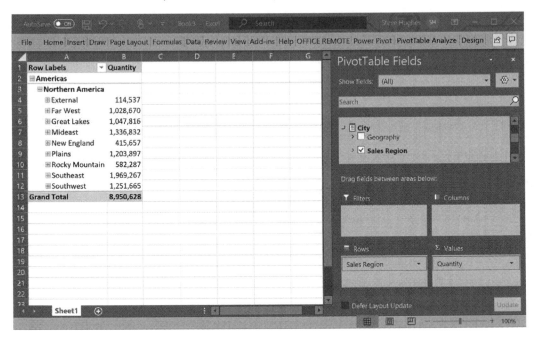

Figure 11.14 – Excel with Visual Totals disabled in the Dynamic Sales Territory role

If you drill down into some of the levels, you will see that the City level is only visible for the **Plains** territory, which is to be expected. Let's turn on **Visual Totals** and retest with Excel.

Using Visual Totals

The following are the steps to turn on **Visual Totals**:

1. In Visual Studio, open the **Dynamic Sales Territory** role.

2. Go to the **Dimension Data** page and click the **Advanced** tab.

3. At the bottom of the window, you will see **Enable Visual Totals**. Click the checkbox to enable visual totals and save your changes.

4. Deploy and process the cube to apply the changes to the deployed database.

5. Go back to your Excel workbook and refresh the data. You should now see that the data is limited to the `Plains` sales territory. All of the roll-up data, including level totals and grand totals, only includes aggregations from the data that the user has permissions to view. Your Excel workbook should look as in the following screenshot:

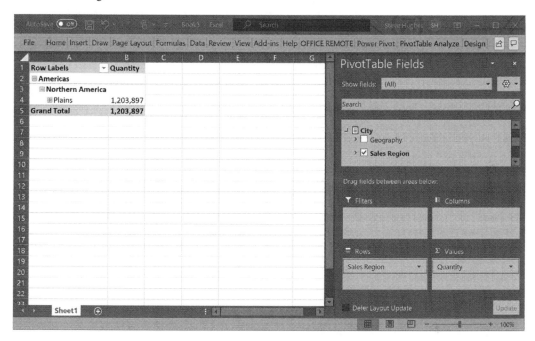

Figure 11.15 – Excel workbook with Visual Totals enabled

This wraps up the work with dimension security in multidimensional models. Before we leave this section, we want to call out one other clean up task. In Visual Studio, you should hide the measure group and dimension used for security. You can do this by changing the `Visible` property to `False`. You can hide the `User Sales Territory Count` measure in the `User Sales Territory` measure group and the **Users** dimension in the **Dimension Usage** tab of the cube designer. Users do not need to have access to that data as it clutters the user experience. Now that we have basic and dynamic security, let's look at cell-level security next.

Adding inventory group security with cell-level security

We have implemented a few variations of data security that are focused on dimensions. In most cases, this level of data security is sufficient for most businesses. However, Analysis Service multidimensional models support cell-level security as well. This will allow you to add additional restrictions to data at the cell level. Be aware that users will see replacement values when querying data that returns results they are not able to see (for example, #N/A). They will know that the data exists and that it is restricted or not available to them.

In our example, we are going to limit access to our new role to the `Quantity` measure in sales. We will call our new role `Inventory Group`. Let's get started:

1. Open your Visual Studio multidimensional project.

2. Right-click on the `Roles` folder and select **New Role**.

3. Name the new role `Inventory Group`.

4. On the **Membership** page, add the user you want to test this role with. Do not use the same users you used with dynamic security previously. If you need to reuse user accounts, remove them from previous roles to prevent issues with security testing.

5. Next, give the role **Read** access to the **Wide World Importers** cube on the **Cubes** tab.

6. On the **Cell Data** page, select **Enable read permissions**.

7. Unlike **Dimension Data** security, the MDX here is more specific. It will allow the role to see a specific set of cells. **Dimension Data** used a set, whereas here, we will be focused on a measure based on the context of the query. In our role, we will be allowing this role to view the `Quantity` measure in the `Sales` measure group. Here is the code you will add to the **Allow reading of cube content** box in the window:

```
Measures.CurrentMember IS [Measures].[Quantity]
```

8. Save the changes to the role.

9. Deploy and fully process your cube to apply the changes to the database.

10. Check your work with Excel, as described in the previous section. Be sure to use the account you used for this role. The following screenshot illustrates the applied cell-level security:

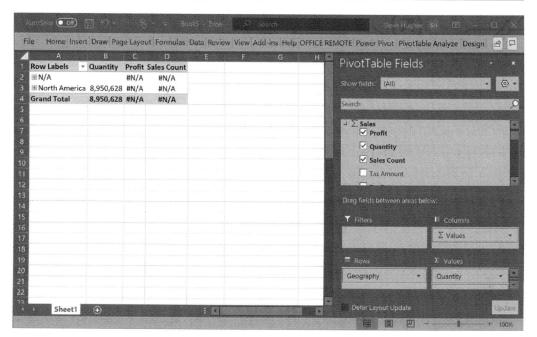

Figure 11.16 – Cell-level security demonstrated in Excel

> **Important note**
>
> If the user account was used for one of the previous roles, you may get different results. Remember that permissions in Analysis Services are accumulative.

Cell-level security is a powerful option in SSAS multidimensional models. However, it comes with a performance impact. If you have a large cube, you may see serious performance issues with this security model. It may be more valuable to create a separate cube in the database to isolate the data as you need. It will also be a cleaner user experience if you have a lot of users interacting with the data. The measures will not be available in that case.

This concludes the section on multidimensional data security. As you can see, multidimensional models have extensive flexibility in their security options. There are two key takeaways as we wrap up this section. First, unless the user is in an administrator role, they will not be able to access the model without explicitly being added to a role with permissions. Second, role permissions are accumulative. Users get the sum of all the roles, so plan your security with this in mind. Now, let's look at tabular model data security.

Implementing data security in tabular models

Just to recap, we have covered the administrator roles for Analysis Services, which give full access to the model, and we have created a **Read Only** role for the tabular model. In tabular models, dimensional and cell-level security are not available. When we created the **Read Only** role, we set the database level permission as **Read** in the **Role Manager**.

In the following sections, we will create two additional roles – `Tailspin Toys Group` and `Dynamic Sales`. The first will use the **Row Filters** option to limit a user's access to the data based on the filter. The second role will be dynamic and will leverage some of the work we did to support the multidimensional dynamic dimension security.

Creating a role to limit access to a customer

Now, we are going to limit what users can see by creating a new role that will limit the data to Tailspin Toys. To do this, we will use row filters. Let's get started:

1. Open `WideWorldImportersTAB.sln` in Visual Studio.

2. Choose the **WideWorldImportersTAB** project in **Solution Explorer**.

3. In **Tabular Model Explorer**, right-click the `Roles` folder and click **Roles…**. This will open the **Roles Manager** dialog, as shown in the following figure:

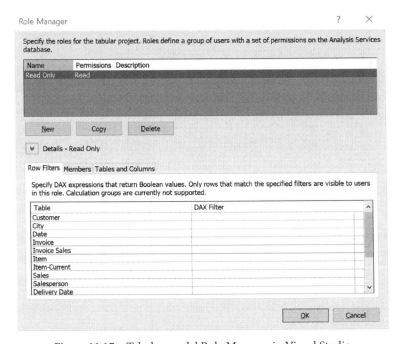

Figure 11.17 – Tabular model Role Manager in Visual Studio

4. Click **New** to create a new role.

5. Name the new role `Tailspin Toys Group` and give the role read permissions to the database by selecting the **Read** option in the **Permissions** column.

6. Add one of the users you created in the multidimensional exercise to the **Members** tab. If you did not create a user during the previous exercise, you will need to create a local user to test the role.

7. Go to the **Row Filters** tab. You should see the list of tables with a **DAX Filter** option. We will be applying a DAX filter to the `Customer` table. The filter must return a Boolean value (true or false). The security will be applied to all queries through the relationships in the model.

8. Click on the `Customer` table and add the following code to the **DAX Filter – Customer** box at the bottom of the page:

```
=Customer[Bill To Customer]="Tailspin Toys (Head Office)"
```

9. Click **OK** to save the role.

10. Process the model in order to deploy the changes to the server.

Testing the new role in Excel

Now that we have deployed the changes to the server, let's test the new role in Excel, as follows:

1. Open a new Excel workbook to test your new role.

2. Choose **Get Data**, then **From Database** and **From Analysis Services**.

3. Add the name of your tabular model Analysis Server and change the credentials to the user you added to the role you created. Click **Next** and finish creating your connection.

4. Create the PivotTable with the defaults.

5. Add **Customer Hierarchy** from the `Customer` table to the **Rows** section in **PivotTable Fields**.

6. Add **Total Sales Amount** from the `Sales` table to the **Values** section in **PivotTable Fields**.

7.   Expand **Customer Hierarchy** in the pivot table. You will see that only **Tailspin Toys** is visible in the results, as shown in the following screenshot:

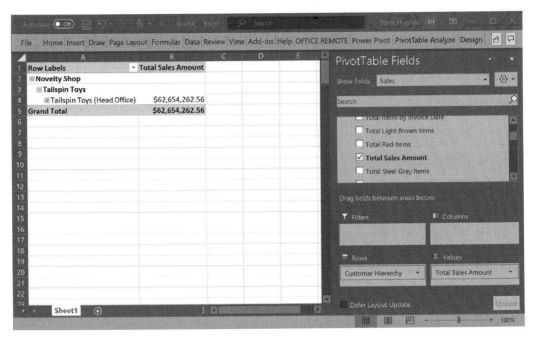

Figure 11.18 – Excel showing Tailspin Toys Group role access

This type of security can be used to manage access to tabular data easily. You can add filters to multiple tables to further refine the access of the data to your users. This is the recommended approach to applying security to your tabular models. Next, we will look at implementing dynamic security for sales territories.

Adding dynamic security for sales territories to the tabular model

Dynamic dimension security takes several steps to implement. For this exercise, you will be working with the relational database and the Visual Studio solution. We will be adding support for users and security mapping.

Using the existing relational tables

Before we dig into this section too deeply, if you have not created the relational tables to support dynamic security in multidimensional models, please review that material earlier in the chapter to set up the tables in the *Adding sales group security with dynamic dimension security* section. The same tables and views will be used to apply dynamic security to our tabular model. We will be using the `Dimension.Users` and `Fact.UserSalesTerritory` tables and the `Cube.Users` and `Cube.User Sales Territory` views.

Let's get started:

1. Open `WideWorldImportersTAB.sln` in Visual Studio.

2. Choose the **WideWorldImportersTAB** project in **Solution Explorer**.

3. Switch to **Tabular Model Explorer** and expand the **Data Sources** folder.

4. Right-click on your data source and choose **Import New Tables**.

5. Select the **Cube.Users** and **Cube.User Sales Territory** views from the list and click **Load** to add the tables to your model.

6. Rename `Cube Users` to `Users` and `Cube.User Sales Territory` to `User Sales Territory`. You can also set the `Hidden` property for both tables to `True` because users do not need access to these tables for analysis.

7. In the diagram view, add the relationships between **Users** and **User Sales Territory** on **User Key**.

8. Add a relationship between the User Sales Territory table and the City table on **City Key**. This effectively creates a many-to-many relationship between **Users** and **City** through the User Sales Territory table. The relationship should look as in the following screenshot:

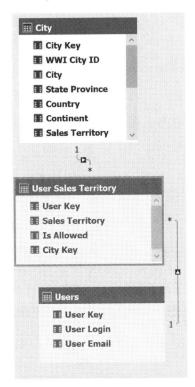

Figure 11.19 – Relationships that support security

9. Return to **Solution Explorer** and deploy the **WideWorldImportersTAB** database.

10. In **Tabular Model Explorer**, right-click the Roles folder and click **Roles…**. This will open the **Roles Manager** dialog.

11. Click **New** to add a new role.

12. Name your new role Dynamic Sales and select the **Read** database permission.

13. Add the users you created for this exercise to the **Members** tab.

14. The security we will be applying is to the two tables with values in them – `Sales` and `Invoice Sales`. Locate the `Sales` table on **Row Filters** and add the following code to the **DAX Filter** area by the table:

```
= Sales[City Key] = LOOKUPVALUE('User Sales
Territory'[City Key],'User Sales Territory'[City Key],
Sales[City Key], 'Users'[User Login], USERNAME())
```

15. Next, locate the `Invoice Sales` table and add the following code to the filter for that table:

```
= 'Invoice Sales'[City Key] = LOOKUPVALUE('User Sales
Territory'[City Key],'User Sales Territory'[City
Key], 'Invoice Sales'[City Key], 'Users'[User Login],
USERNAME())
```

16. Click **OK** to save the role. Deploy the database to publish the changes.

17. Use Excel to test the security setting by connecting to your model with one of the security logins you created.

The code in the DAX filters uses the LOOKUPVALUE function to return the matching key value for the current context of the query. In our example, we have the dynamic security anchored on `City Key`. The function returns the matching city key from the `User Sales Territory` table using filters for the current user (`USERNAME()`) and the city key from the `Sales` or `Invoice Sales` table, respectively. If no match is found, an empty or NULL value is returned, which prevents the data from being displayed.

When working with dynamic security in tabular models, you should be aware that there is no efficient way to validate that the solution is working as intended. Understanding the structure of the query and how the filter works is very important for implementing this correctly. You should assume that some trial and error will be required to verify that the security is working as expected.

Summary

In this chapter, we covered the server, database, and data-level security options for both types of Analysis Services models. Multidimensional models have a much richer and more sophisticated set of options. You can use both the design of the database and the security options to build a robust security solution. Tabular models have fewer options and must be included in the overall design of the solution. In this chapter, you learned how to manage the security setting at the server level and create roles in both types of models. Data is the lifeblood of business, and these skills will help you protect this greatest of assets.

In the next chapter, we will be looking at maintenance and operational tasks for SSAS.

12

Common Administration and Maintenance Tasks

Now that we have our models created and secured, we will wrap up the book with some maintenance and administration tasks that are common to database and Analysis Services solutions. We have some key topic areas to start the chapter, covering larger topics such as backups and scaling. The chapter wraps up with a section on several smaller topics to support your models as you move forward.

The tasks described in this chapter are key to making your **SQL Server Analysis Services (SSAS)** models production ready. Whether you need to plan for business continuity, expanding data needs, or better performance, the techniques you will learn in this chapter will provide the basic skills you need in order to manage production deployments.

In this chapter, we're going to cover the following main topics:

- Understanding the languages

- Backing up and restoring SSAS databases

- Processing or refreshing the data in your models

- Scaling your models

- Discovering how your models are performing

We will wrap the chapter up with a section containing tips and tricks to use with SQL Server Analysis Services.

Technical requirements

For this chapter, we will be using **SQL Server Management Studio** (**SSMS**) and **Visual Studio** to perform the various operations in the chapter with the databases we created in previous chapters. We will also be using **SQL Server Performance Monitor** for some of the tuning and monitoring exercises.

Understanding the languages

When working with Analysis Services, you will frequently be using code that is not MDX or DAX. **XML for Analysis**, or **XMLA**, has been around since the early days of Analysis Services and is used for many maintenance operations for both modes – multidimensional and tabular. As the name clearly states, this is an XML-based language. Multidimensional models are actually defined using XMLA as well.

If you right-click an object in SSMS and choose the script option, it will generate a `Create` script in XMLA. For example, scripting the `City` dimension as a `Create` script generates the following XMLA (only the first few lines are displayed for brevity):

```xml
<Create xmlns="http://schemas.microsoft.com/
analysisservices/2003/engine">
    <ParentObject>
        <DatabaseID>WideWorldImportersMD</DatabaseID>
    </ParentObject>
    <ObjectDefinition>
        <Dimension xmlns:xsd="http://www.w3.org/2001/XMLSchema"
xmlns:xsi="http://www.w3.org/2001/XMLSchema-instance"
xmlns:ddl2="http://schemas.microsoft.com/analysisservices/2003/
engine/2" xmlns:ddl2_2="http://schemas.microsoft.com/
```

```
analysisservices/2003/engine/2/2" xmlns:ddl100_100="http://
schemas.microsoft.com/analysisservices/2008/
engine/100/100" xmlns:ddl200="http://schemas.microsoft.com/
analysisservices/2010/engine/200" xmlns:ddl200_200="http://
schemas.microsoft.com/analysisservices/2010/
engine/200/200" xmlns:ddl300="http://schemas.microsoft.com/
analysisservices/2011/engine/300" xmlns:ddl300_300="http://
schemas.microsoft.com/analysisservices/2011/
engine/300/300" xmlns:ddl400="http://schemas.microsoft.com/
analysisservices/2012/engine/400" xmlns:ddl400_400="http://
schemas.microsoft.com/analysisservices/2012/
engine/400/400" xmlns:ddl500="http://schemas.microsoft.com/
analysisservices/2013/engine/500" xmlns:ddl500_500="http://
schemas.microsoft.com/analysisservices/2013/engine/500/500">
        <ID>City</ID>
        <Name>City</Name>
```

The code for this dimension is much longer than shown here. It includes the SQL used to load the data, estimated row counts, data types, and much more. Measure groups include aggregations and partitions, both of which can be scripted individually. When working with multidimensional models, XMLA can help you perform maintenance operations as well as help you dig into potential design issues when it is not easy to work on a project in Visual Studio.

In SSAS 2019, tabular models move away from XMLA in most operations and use **Tabular Model Scripting Language** (**TMSL**). TMSL is JSON formatted. Like XMLA for multidimensional models, TMSL is the underlying code used for storing and manipulating the object model. Using the same aforementioned example, if you generate a create script in SSMS for the City table in your tabular model, this will generate the following TMSL (limited to the first few rows for brevity):

```
{
  "create": {
    "parentObject": {
      "database": "WideWorldImportersTAB"
    },
    "table": {
      "name": "City",
      "columns": [
        {
          "name": "City Key",
```

```
            "dataType": "int64",
            "sourceColumn": "City Key"
        },
```

Similar to XMLA in multidimensional models, TMSL in tabular models contains data types, hierarchies, and partitions. One important distinction is that the tabular model stores all tables in the same fashion and structure, whereas multidimensional models have distinct storage options for dimensions, measure groups, aggregations, and so on. Because TMSL uses JSON, the syntax is streamlined, resulting in smaller, more manageable file sizes.

> **TMSL and XMLA with Tabular**
>
> XMLA still works with tabular models. The preferred approach is to use TMSL; however, TMSL is built on XMLA protocols. If you manage both types of models, you may find it beneficial to focus on XMLA, so you can manage with one language rather than two.

Now that you have been introduced to the languages, let's dig into the first maintenance topic – backing up and restoring your models.

Backing up and restoring SSAS databases

We are often asked about backing up SSAS databases as part of normal operations. Before we get into the *how*, we should understand *when* and *why*. Typically, both multidimensional and tabular model types are for analysis only. The underlying data is the source and that source retains all the data to refresh our models. If your models are small, you can reload them entirely from the source, which is usually a data warehouse or an operational data store.

> **Databases and models**
>
> A point of clarification here: the term *model* is interchangeable with database in this section. While models refer to the design method, *database* is a more generic term that covers both multidimensional and tabular models. Effectively, both models are stored as databases. When working with administrative tasks, such as backing up and restoring, the syntax uses database terminology, which is like relational database terms and functions making administration simpler.

In the case of small models, backups are not really necessary. If a model becomes corrupted or unusable, you can redeploy the database and refresh it. Small models load very efficiently. It is when these databases take more time to reload that you should begin to use backup and restore the operations. The other way to protect your systems and data is to use synchronization, which also supports scaling out. We will be discussing scaling out using synchronization in detail in a later section in this chapter.

Backing up your databases

You can back up your databases using two primary methods – graphically with SSMS or scripting with XMLA or TMSL. Using Management Studio is an easy way to create a backup file or generate the script for usage in scheduling tools.

The following steps are used to create a backup of your multidimensional database. The same instructions will work for your tabular model databases. The only difference is where the backups will be located. Let's get started:

1. Open **SQL Server Management Studio** and connect to your multidimensional Analysis Services instance.

2. Right-click on the `WideWorldImportersMD` database and choose **Back Up...** This will open the **Backup Database** dialog, as shown here:

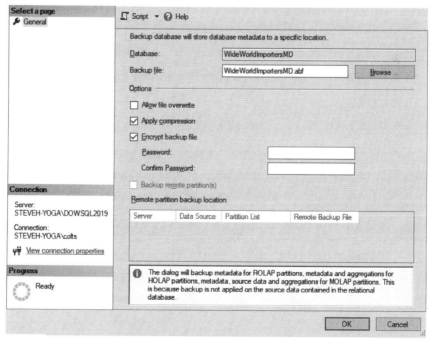

Figure 12.1 – Backup Database window for multidimensional databases

3. You can update the name of the file and the location of the backup here. Be sure to use the .abf file extension for the filename. The folder list is limited to the locations from server settings. You can see the information in the **Save File As** dialog shown here:

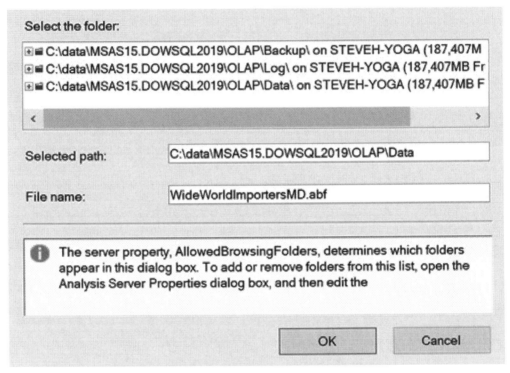

Figure 12.2 – Save File As dialog for Analysis Services backups

In order to add options for the storage location, you will need to be a server administrator and modify the **AllowedBrowsingFolders** setting in **Server Properties** to add or change the location. This is an Advanced property, so you will need to show Advanced properties to change the AllowedBrowsingFolders values. Once there, you can change the list. The following is an example of the default settings from our install:

```
C:\data\MSAS15.DOWSQL2019\OLAP\Backup\|C:\data\MSAS15.
DOWSQL2019\OLAP\Log\|C:\data\MSAS15.DOWSQL2019\OLAP\Data\
```

This list is pipe (|) delimited. This property only affects folders that are visible when using a dialog box to open, create, or manage files in Analysis Services.

There is one other server property to be aware of when backing up Analysis Services databases – `BackupDir`. The `BackupDir` property contains a single directory path that is the default backup location for SSAS databases when the location is not explicitly called out in the backup dialog or scripts. If you choose to change the default location of the backup file, you must allow the SSAS service account permissions to read and write to that location.

4. Next, we need to determine what additional settings we want to use. **Allow file overwrite** allows us to overwrite an existing backup file with the same name. This is OFF by default to prevent accidental overwrite. In our scenario, we will leave this as the default.

5. **Apply compression** is checked by default. This will keep the overall file size smaller. We recommend that you leave this value checked.

6. **Encrypt Backup File** is also on by default. This is important to use. Often, large amounts of confidential business data are stored in your models. This option protects that data from being easily opened and viewed. Unlike relational databases, SSAS models are text-based and can be opened and viewed by standard editors. While not easy or convenient, this is a data security risk you should avoid. Password protecting your backups with encryption is a simple step to deter unwanted access to the content of the files.

7. The final option relates to multidimensional models only. Because multidimensional models can support remote partitions, you have the option to back those up here as well. This is an advanced design that we have not covered in this book. As a result, this option is not enabled. This option will not be visible for tabular model backups.

8. Click **OK** to create the backup.

If you run through this process again, instead of clicking **OK**, use the **Script** button at the top of the dialog box to generate the script. When you click the button, it will ask you if you want to add the password to the script. If you choose to add the password, be aware that the password will be included in the script in plain text. You may choose to leave the password in place if you plan to schedule the process. In that case, include a generic password you can use as placeholder in the script to be replaced during execution with a parameter.

XMLA backup script with a password is as follows:

```
<Backup xmlns="http://schemas.microsoft.com/
analysisservices/2003/engine">
  <Object>
```

```
        <DatabaseID>WideWorldImportersMD</DatabaseID>
    </Object>
    <File>WideWorldImportersMD.abf</File>
    <Password>steve</Password>
</Backup>
```

XMLA backup script without a password is as follows:

```
<Backup xmlns="http://schemas.microsoft.com/
analysisservices/2003/engine">
    <Object>
        <DatabaseID>WideWorldImportersMD</DatabaseID>
    </Object>
    <File>WideWorldImportersMD.abf</File>
</Backup>
```

TMSL backup script with a password is as follows:

```
{
    "backup": {
        "database": "WideWorldImportersTAB",
        "file": "WideWorldImportersTAB.abf",
        "password": "steve",
        "allowOverwrite": false,
        "applyCompression": true
    }
}
```

As you can see in these scripts, none of them have the folder path, which means they will be stored in the default folder specified by the BackupDir property. XMLA does not explicitly call out the default properties; it assumes the defaults are used. If you change the default, it adds the property to XMLA. TMSL has all the properties shown unless a password is not used. In that case, the password property is not visible.

Change the filename in the XMLA script (for example, add 01 to the name), and execute it in SSMS. This will return the following XMLA result, signifying that you have successfully backed up your database:

```
<return xmlns="urn:schemas-microsoft-com:xml-analysis">
    <root xmlns="urn:schemas-microsoft-com:xml-analysis:empty" />
</return>
```

If you execute the script again, you will receive an error in the **Messages** tab letting you know that the file exists already. Now, perform the same process with the tabular model backup code in TMSL. As we called out in the beginning section on languages, TMSL is built on the XMLA protocols. Successfully executing TMSL returns the same result as the XMLA execution. Furthermore, SSMS does not have an option to execute TMSL. You use the XMLA query window to execute TMSL. This applies to all TMSL operations as we work through other maintenance and operational tasks in this chapter.

Restoring your databases

Now that we have the backups created, let's restore a database. For this exercise, we will once again be using the multidimensional database as the example. The same process will work when restoring tabular models, but remember that if you restore multiple tabular models, your memory consumption will increase substantially. Be cautious when restoring tabular models.

1. Open **SQL Server Management Studio** and connect to the Analysis Services multidimensional instance.

2. Right-click the databases folder and choose **Restore**. This will open the **Restore Database** window shown here:

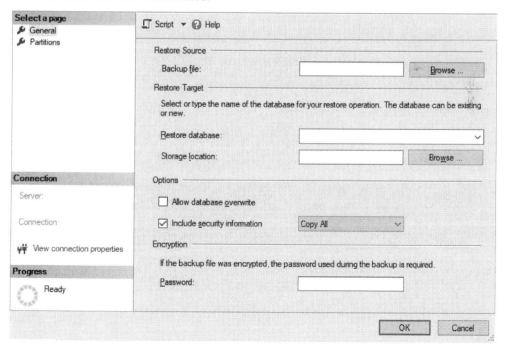

Figure 12.3 – Restore Database dialog

The **Restore** operation is divided into three sections: **Restore Source**, **Restore Target**, and **Encryption**. We will work through each of these settings in the next steps.

3. When you click **Browse** to choose your **Restore Source**, it displays the folders you have specified in the **AllowedBrowsingFolder** server setting. Because we chose to back up our databases to the default location, choose the `Backup` folder. Currently no files are visible. Expand the folder to view the backup files in that folder and choose a file to restore, then click **OK** to close the **Locate Database** Files window..

4. Now that we have the source file selected, we need to make decisions about **Restore Target**. Only one database exists in our backup; select `WideWorldImportersMD`. Rename that database `WideWorldImportersMD01`.

5. Next, choose the location for the data to be restored to. In this case, we will select the `Data` folder from our list.

6. In the **Options** section, choose to allow the database to be overwritten. We are choosing to leave the default and create a new database to make sure we do not impact any of our existing work.

7. The **Include security information** option is related to keeping the roles that have been created. You can choose to restore with no roles by deselecting the **Include** option. When **Include** is selected, a drop-down menu is displayed where you have the option to either copy everything (**Copy All**) or to copy only the roles without members (**Skip Members**). The default is to leave all roles and members intact. For our purposes, let's turn this option off.

8. The final step is to add the encryption password you created for this backup.

9. Before clicking **OK** to complete the process, script this restore process to a new window so you can see the XMLA that is used in the `Restore` process. The code should look similar to the following:

```
<Restore xmlns="http://schemas.microsoft.com/
analysisservices/2003/engine">
<File>C:\data\MSAS15.DOWSQL2019\OLAP\Backup\
WideWorldImportersMD01.abf</File>
    <DatabaseName>WideWorldImportersMD01</DatabaseName>
    <Security>IgnoreSecurity</Security>
    <Password>steve</Password>
```

```
<DbStorageLocation xmlns="http://schemas.microsoft.com/
analysisservices/2008/engine/100/100">C:\data\MSAS15.
DOWSQL2019\OLAP\Data\</DbStorageLocation>
</Restore>
```

10. You can run the script or click **OK** in the dialog to complete the restore operation. If it is successful, you will see the same XMLA result script that you saw during the backup execution when running the script. Refresh **Object Explorer** in SSMS to see your new database.

You can browse the database immediately. The backup operation restored the database, including the data ready to go. When you are done exploring the data, you can delete that database to save resources and space.

All the same options apply for tabular models in the restore operation. A file location is required to hold the database when the server is shut down. While tabular models do not use disk storage while they are in operation, they do have to store the data and structure on disk when the server is not running.

When working with scheduling or ETL tools, you will find that Microsoft tools such as SQL Server Agent and SSIS support the execution of XMLA scripts. Because SSAS is a mature product, other scheduling tools often support XMLA, which is why it is still used to manage tabular model instances. Next, we will look at the methods to refresh data in your models.

Processing or refreshing the data in your models

In both models, you reload or refresh the data in your models using *processing*. Processing your cube, dimension, table, or database will refresh the data in the defined object. In this section, we will be separating the processing options for multidimensional and tabular models. Remember that multidimensional models focus on reloading data to disk, whereas tabular models focus on loading data to memory.

Processing multidimensional models and their components

Most storage objects in a multidimensional database can be processed from the top-level object or database to aggregations within a measure group. Up to this point, we have been processing the database by right-clicking the database and choosing **Process**. Now we will look at other options for processing data and why you may choose certain options.

Let's review the processing options available to us. The following chart shows which objects can be processed with the type of processing supported for each object:

Process Type	Database	Cube	Measure Group	Partition	Dimension
Default	X	X	X	X	X
Full	X	X	X	X	X
Data		X	X	X	X
Index		X	X	X	X
Clear		X	X	X	X
Add			X	X	X
Update					X

Figure 12.4 – Processing types and multidimensional object cross reference

Each of the next sections break out the processing options and how they affect the data in your multidimensional model object.

Process Default

As the name indicates, this is the *default* processing option when you choose to process a multidimensional object. Analysis Services analyzes the cube to determine the best or the most needed processing type.

Process Full

This option dumps all the data and reloads it. While we were building our cube, we used this option frequently. This option is required when changes are made to the structure of a cube, such as during development and testing. This option applies to all objects and is the best way to repair or optimize a multidimensional object that may be having issues, in particular, performance or data issues. Fully processing the database or targeted object will clean up most cube issues.

Process Data and Process Index

Process Data drops and reloads only the data. It does not rebuild aggregations or indexes. This option is used to reload partition data.

Process Index rebuilds the indexes and aggregations for the partitions and similar measure data. These two options are often used together to refresh partition data and make sure indexes and aggregations are rebuilt to improve query performance.

Using these options together allows you to refresh the partitions and aggregated data without fully reloading the cube, measure group, or partition.

Process Clear

Process Clear is straightforward. It removes all data from the processed object and does not reload it.

Process Add

Process Add is used to add new fact data to measure groups and partitions. It limits processing to affected partitions.

When used with dimensions, it updates the dimension with new members and updates the attribute properties as needed. Be aware, when used with dimensions, you must use XMLA. For some reason, Microsoft chose to make this an XMLA-only option, so this option is not available in the wizards.

Process Update

Process Update updates dimension attributes based on reading the data for the dimension.

Data mining processing options

Two processing options affect data mining structures in multidimensional models – **Process Structure** and **Process Clear Structure**. Process structure prepares cube data for model processing, including fully processing the cube, but does not process the models. Process clear structure removes the training data from the mining models. We do not cover data mining with Analysis Services in this book. Typically, data mining models are now created with specialized tools. While the functionality still exists in SSAS, it is used infrequently.

Other processing options

Besides the processing types noted in the previous section, there are additional options that can be used to customize or optimize cube processing. The following window has two tabs: **Processing options** and **Dimension key errors**:

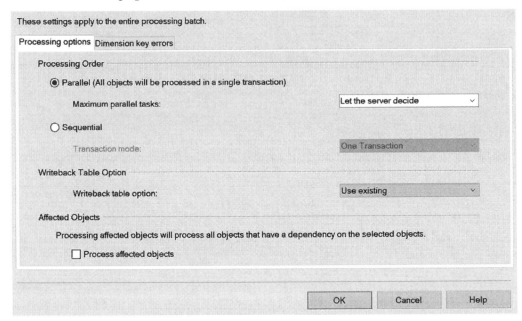

These settings apply to the entire processing batch.

Processing options | Dimension key errors

Processing Order

◉ Parallel (All objects will be processed in a single transaction)

Maximum parallel tasks: Let the server decide ⌄

○ Sequential

Transaction mode: One Transaction ⌄

Writeback Table Option

Writeback table option: Use existing ⌄

Affected Objects

Processing affected objects will process all objects that have a dependency on the selected objects.

☐ Process affected objects

OK   Cancel   Help

Figure 12.5 – Changing the processing options

As you can see, in the **Processing options** tab, you have three areas you can change: **Processing Order**, **Writeback Table Option**, and **Affected Objects**. We have not implemented writeback functionality in our exercises as this setting impacts how the tables used to support writeback functionality are handled. Let's go through **Processing Order** and **Affected Objects** in detail:

Processing Order has two key options: **Parallel** and **Sequential**.

Parallel processing allows Analysis Services to maximize the use of the CPU capacity on the server and load data in parallel streams. You have the option here to manage the number of parallel processes you want to run. This can be adjusted to optimize resources available to the server. All the data will be committed in the same transaction when using parallel processing.

When using **Sequential** processing, each object being processed is handled as an independent object. Now, **Sequential** has two **Transaction modes** to choose from: **One Transaction** and **Separate Transactions**. The two modes are explained here:

- If you choose **One Transaction**, the entire set of objects being processed must be complete and processed as one. While this is happening, the objects are not available for querying until all of them are complete.

- When using **Separate Transactions**, the objects are committed independently and become available for querying when each object is complete. The default setting here is a good place to start – **Parallel**, with the option **Let the server decide**.

The last setting on this tab is **Affected Objects**. One point that needs to be clarified immediately with regard to this setting is that it refers to *affected* objects, not *dependent* objects. If an object has an explicit dependency on another object, that object will be processed. Affected objects include aggregations that may refer to a dimension. Processing the dimension will not automatically trigger the aggregations for a partition to be rebuilt by reprocessing the partition. However, if this property is set to `True`, the partition would be processed even though the dependency is not there. Use this setting carefully as it could unintentionally cause more objects to be processed than you planned for.

The other tab has an exhaustive list to support various types of error handling for dimension key processing errors. When processing dimensions, errors such as duplicate keys, missing keys, null keys, and similar can occur. Analysis Services uses several default settings to handle these. Most result in a warning or a message. Use the options in this section to customize your error handling to meet the business requirements in your environment.

Changes made in this window are displayed as read only in the process dialog box, as shown in the following screenshot. They are the settings displayed in the **Batch Settings Summary** section:

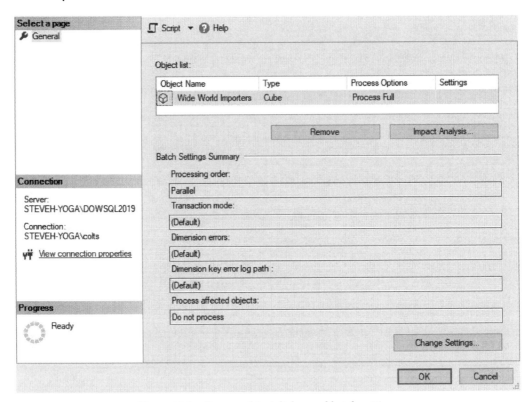

Figure 12.6 – Process object dialog and batch settings

This gives you a chance to review your changes before completing the process.

Other processing considerations

Besides the options and processing types supported, there are other ways to improve processing. One of the best options is to make sure that the source system is properly indexed for the processing operations. Besides tuning the source system, you have the options to manage the physical resources as well, such as CPU, RAM, and IO. We will review how to use **Performance Monitor** and **Dynamic Management Views** (**DMV**) in order to better understand processing demands and how to respond to them. Next, we will look at processing tabular model objects.

Processing tabular models and their components

Processing tabular models is not as complex with tabular models. There are three objects that can be processed in tabular models – databases, table, and partitions. Similar to multidimensional models, each object in a tabular models has a set of processing types available to them. The following table shows which processing type works with each object:

Process Type	Database	Table	Partition
Default	X	X	X
Full	X	X	X
Clear	X	X	X
Recalc	X		
Data		X	X
Defrag		X	
Add			X

Figure 12.7 – Tabular model processing types

The next sections dig into the details of each type of processing supported by tabular models.

Process Default

When using **Process Default**, Analysis Services determines the current state of the object to be processed and performs the appropriate action. This includes adding new data, calculating hierarchies, setting relationships, and populating calculated columns. As the name implies, **Process Default** is the default processing option for tabular model objects.

Process Full

Process Full replaces all data and recalculates hierarchies, relationships, and calculated columns. This is the most complete refresh of the data and structures.

Process Clear

Process Clear removes all the data from the selected object. This is ideal when you need to move the database and do not need to move the data with the structure.

Process Recalc

Process Recalc only works at the database level. This effectively recalculates hierarchies, relationships, and calculated columns without reloading the data in the tables. This option is typically used when there are performance issues with the model related to calculations created in the model. For example, if a calculated table is particularly slow or not returning data at all, processing with **Process Recalc** may resolve this issue.

Process Data

Process Data is the opposite of the **Process Recalc** option. However, it only works at the table level. This loads data into the table, but does not recalculate relationships, hierarchies, or calculated columns. When using **Process Full**, both **Process Data** and **Process Recalc** are run as part of the process. If you have a lot of calculations in your model, you may need to run **Process Recalc** to resolve calculation issues.

Process Defrag

Process Defrag is also for tables and is used to defragment the table after other operations have been used. For example, using **Process Add** and **Process Data** causes the tables to be out of sync. **Process Defrag** restructures the in-memory model to improve performance and reduce the model size. The only other way to perform this operation is to fully process the table.

Process Add

Process Add is used to incrementally add data to a table partition. Tables and databases are clearly visible in SSMS. However, unlike partitions in the multidimensional measure groups, there is no folder or other way to easily identify partitions in tabular models.

If you right-click on the table, there is a **Partitions** option that will display the partitions for the table. Check out the following screenshot to see the partitions we created in our tabular model in the `Sales` table:

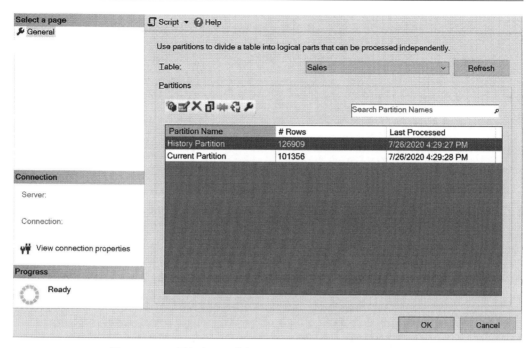

Figure 12.8 – Tabular model Partitions dialog for the Sales Table

The **Partitions** dialog will allow you to move between tables to see the partitions in each table. You can also manage the partitions by including add, remove, copy, and edit. All tables contain at least one partition – effectively the default partition. You can process one or more dimensions in this dialog as well.

Now that you have a good understanding of how to refresh the data in your models, we will move on to the techniques available to scale your models.

Scaling your models

There are two ways to scale in the database world – **scale up** or **scale out** – and they apply to Analysis Services models. Both options bring more compute, memory, and storage to support better performance or larger models.

Scaling up is a pure hardware play. This involves adding more resources to your environment such as RAM or CPUs. In this scenario, bigger is better. For example, you can choose to increase compute capacity by adding CPUs to a server, vCPUs to a virtual machine, and swapping in newer CPUs with more cores. In these situations, you typically leave the SSAS instance in place and it will consume the expanded resources. Scaling up has limits, as you would suspect. You can only scale so far.

The next option is to scale out. Relational databases in many cases do not natively support scale-out scenarios. However, SSAS scales out very well. Both tabular and multidimensional models are designed to scale out to support processing, model availability, and query optimization. One of the most common issues is that processing, which is resource-intensive, interferes with the query performance for end users. Scaling out is a great way to resolve this issue. Furthermore, SSAS works well with load balancers to further support heavy query loads for which SSAS is designed.

The following diagram is a common scale-out approach that has been used for years:

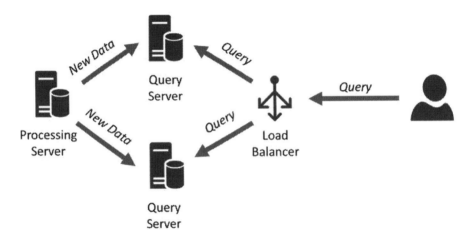

Figure 12.9 – Load-balanced Analysis Services architecture

This design allows for more scale out query servers to support more users. A good rule of thumb is to add query server nodes when concurrent user or query counts begin to exceed fifty per server. To be clear, these are concurrent users, not potential users. This is particularly true if users execute a large number of ad hoc queries, so caching is not as effective.

Understanding processing and query servers

The separation of processing and query operations can improve the customer experience when working with Analysis Services. Processing operations focus on loading and updating data. This often involves index rebuilds, aggregation rebuilds, and similar operations that will lock database objects when they are being performed. This means that users may experience queries fail or perform very poorly while processing is occurring.

By scaling out processing from querying, you allow users to keep querying without interference. When using a two-query node structure with a separate processing server, you are able to synchronize to a query node that is temporarily removed from the load-balanced pool.

If you have issues with processing performance, this configuration also allows you to tune the database servers differently. You can change the configuration on the processing server to better support writing data while the query servers are focused on returning data, including better caching for queries.

As your Analysis Services environment grows, understanding these configurations will allow you to support more users and queries while continuing to improve performance and availability.

Choosing scaling out versus clustering

One benefit of scaling out your cluster and using a load balancer is that you can remove the need to cluster SSAS. Unlike the database engine, Analysis Services does not natively support Windows clustering or Always On capabilities. The recommended approach to supporting a highly available SSAS solution is to scale out with a load balancer. If an SSAS server becomes unavailable, the load balancer can reroute traffic to the working server. This also allows for minimal downtime maintenance by taking one of the nodes offline at a time.

> **Note**
>
> The following section, *Synchronizing your databases*, requires multiple additional instances to complete the exercises. If you are running low on resources, it is not recommended that you execute the tasks set out in this section.

Synchronizing your databases

Now that we have reviewed the structure, let's look at the process to copy the new data to the query servers. In this section, we will install another instance for each server to show how each model type is configured. Because the amount of resources in your development environment will be significant, you may need to shut down instances you are not working with.

While the best practice is to use the three-server model as laid out in the preceding diagram (*Figure 12.8*), we will be using a two-server model for this exercise. In this scenario, we will not set up a load balancer, but we will set up a process server and a query server. You can use a two-server model if you have specific windows when the processing server can be unavailable for querying. This model uses the processing server as the additional query server. This may fit your needs and save you hardware and licensing costs if it meets the business **service level agreement** (**SLA**) on query performance during the processing window.

In the next two sections, we will walk through the steps to set up and configure synchronization for each model type.

Synchronizing multidimensional models

In this exercise, we will install another multidimensional instance and synchronize the data to the new server:

1. In *Chapter 1*, *Analysis Services in SQL Server 2019*, we walked through the instructions to install SSAS in multidimensional mode. Follow that process to add another SQL Server instance to your development environment. You do not need to install another SQL Server database instance, just the multidimensional instance.

2. In SSMS, connect to both multidimensional instances. The new instance should have no databases or other objects in it. We will be synchronizing the existing **WideWorldImportersMD** to this new instance.

3. On the new instance, right-click the Databases folder and choose **Synchronize**. This will open the **Synchronize Database Wizard**, shown in the following screenshot.

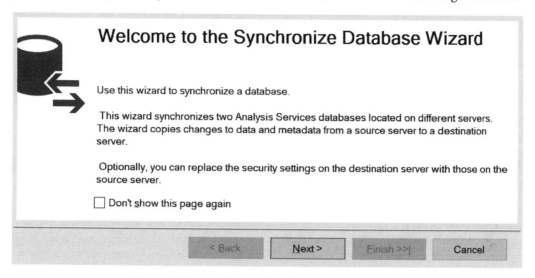

Welcome to the Synchronize Database Wizard

Use this wizard to synchronize a database.

This wizard synchronizes two Analysis Services databases located on different servers. The wizard copies changes to data and metadata from a source server to a destination server.

Optionally, you can replace the security settings on the destination server with those on the source server.

☐ Don't show this page again

< Back   Next >   Finish >>| Cancel

Figure 12.10 – Synchronize Database Wizard start page

4. Click **Next**.

5. On the next page, you will choose **Synchronization Source. Synchronization Destination** is already in the wizard. Use the server with the database deployed as the source and the new instance for the destination. You can change the folder for the data in the destination if you need to. We will leave the default in this exercise. Click **Next** when you are done.

6. This page will allow you to choose where to locate the partitions. We will use the defaults. Click **Next**.

7. **Synchronization Options** can be changed on this page. There are two key considerations here – security and compression. You have three options regarding security, as shown in the following screenshot. In most cases, we want to synchronize all the security as that will keep the query capability on the servers intact.

If you are synchronizing from the processing server to the query server, you may have different security models in place. In that scenario, you can use the **Ignore All** option to not synchronize any security operations. If you choose to not synchronize security, you will have to use a script operation for the synchronization, which will allow you to add the security back to the query servers via script as well.

8.   We will be using the **Copy All** option in our example here. This will bring all the security settings and permissions into the new database, which is the result we want:

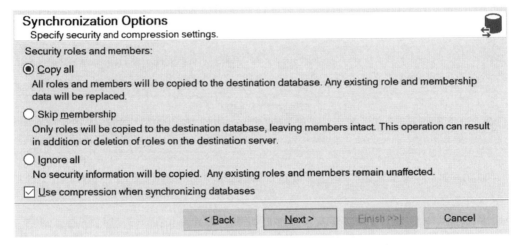

Figure 12.11 – Database synchronization options for security and compression

The other option on this screen concerns compression during synchronization. This is usually check marked as it reduces the size of the data being synchronized. It will have limited impact if the data is synchronized on the same hardware. However, if you are synchronizing across a network, this option will improve the performance of the synchronization process.

When you have the setting selected, which are the defaults in this case, click **Next** to move to the next page.

9.   Now the decision is made about whether to **Synchronize now** or **Save the script to file**. For our exercise, choose to save the file.

10. Enter a filename with an `.xmla` extension and click **Next**. Then, click **Finish** to create the script.

11. In SSMS, open the file we just created. If you did not give your filename a `.xmla` extension, you may want to rename the file, so it opens in the correct query editor in SSMS. Your script should look similar to the following script:

```
<Synchronize xmlns:xsi=name spaces removed">
   <Source>
      <ConnectionString>Provider=MSOLAP.8;Data
   Source=[server name removed];Integrated
   Security=SSPI;Initial Catalog=WideWorldImportersMD</
   ConnectionString>
      <Object>
         <DatabaseID>WideWorldImportersMD</DatabaseID>
      </Object>
   </Source>
   <SynchronizeSecurity>CopyAll</SynchronizeSecurity>
   <ApplyCompression>true</ApplyCompression>
</Synchronize>
```

As you can see, the destination server is not in this code. You need to execute this code that has a connection to the destination server.

> **Note**
>
> In the preceding script, namespaces and connection string information is removed for readability and security.

12. In SSMS, if you are not currently connected to the destination instance, change the connection of the query window to the correct server.

13. Before we execute the query, we need to make sure that the destination service account has access to the source server. For our exercise, we will add the service account to the **Server Administrators** group on the source server. (For details on making this change, refer to *Chapter 11*, *Securing Your SSAS Models*, which deals with security for servers.)

If you plan to use synchronization across multiple servers, we recommend that you use a single service account for all instances to simplify management and allow you to scale out in a standard pattern.

14. When you are connected to the correct server and you have security set up, execute the query. Be aware that this is a significant operation and may take a few minutes on your development system.

15. Once the process completes, refresh the destination server and you should now see the synchronized database and all the objects there.

If you want to test this further, make changes to the source database (either data or schema) and run the synchronize script again to see those changes populated in the destination. Remember to process the original cube after changes are made prior to synchronization.

> **Copying files with other tools**
>
> The synchronize option in SSAS is the simplest way to synchronize databases. However, if your database is very large, you may be able to improve performance by using Robocopy or similar file copy tools. Once the database has been processed, you can copy the files to the target server. This is effectively what synchronize does on your behalf. If you choose to use a different tool, you will have to stop and restart Analysis Services in order to see the new data. Synchronize is an online operation that permits querying during synchronization.

Synchronizing tabular models

In this exercise, we will install another tabular model instance and synchronize the data to the new server as follows:

1. In *Chapter 1, Analysis Services in SQL Server 2019*, we walked through the instructions to install SSAS in tabular mode. Follow that process to add another SQL Server instance to your development environment.

2. On the new instance, right-click the **Databases** folder and choose **Synchronize**. This will open the **Synchronize Database Wizard** shown in *Figure 12.10*. Click **Next**.

3. On the next page, choose **Synchronization Source**. **Synchronization Destination** is already in the wizard. Use the server with the database deployed as the source and your new instance for the destination. You can change the folder for the data in the destination if you need to. We will leave the default in this exercise. Click **Next** when you are done.

4. Leave the default settings on **Synchronization Options** and click **Next**. Refer to the multidimensional synchronize steps for details on these options.

5. Before we go to the next step, we need to make sure that the destination service account has access to the source server in order to synchronize the databases. For our exercise, we will add the service account to the **Server Administrators** group on the source server. For details on making this change, refer to *Chapter 11, Securing Your SSAS Models*, which deals with security for servers.

6. Now, a decision needs to be made about whether to **Synchronize now** or **Save the script to file**. On this occasion, let's opt for **Synchronize now**. Click **Next**, and then click **Finish** to create the synchronized database. While the synchronization process is running, you can see the files being copied in the **Database Synchronization Progress** window. When it completes, you can look at the file operations conducted in the wizard.

7. Once the synchronization completes, refresh the destination server and you should now see the synchronized database and all the objects there.

The synchronization code generated from the wizard is the same for both tabular and multidimensional models.

Before leaving this section, if you did perform the steps here, we recommend stopping the instances you created for synchronization as this will keep your resources at a better level. If you no longer need those instances, you should uninstall them. If you plan to keep them, but want to make sure they are disabled, we recommend disabling them in the Services application or updating the PowerShell scripts we created in *Chapter 1, Analysis Services in SQL Server 2019*, to manage them.

Discovering how your models are performing

Several open source tools are available to support monitoring and performance tuning in Analysis Services. When working with multidimensional models, many of the tools are many years old and may not have been updated recently. Multidimensional models are very mature and have experienced little change in the past few years. Tabular models have some key tools that can help you monitor and improve the performance of your models. While all the tools are not covered in this section, we will bring up some industry accepted tools in the topic list at the end of this chapter.

While those tools exist, you should be aware of out-of-the-box capabilities with SQL Server. This includes the maintenance views and even performance monitoring.

Using Dynamic Management Views

Dynamic Management Views or DMVs are available for both multidimensional and tabular models. While the entire list of DMVs is out of scope for this book, we will introduce you to how they are used and some common queries.

DMVs in Analysis Services are based on the data mining parser. While the syntax is similar to SQL, it has a limited set of functionality, such as SELECT (DISTINCT and TOP), FROM $System, <<some table or view name>>, WHERE, and ORDER BY. Aggregated queries are not supported. While the queries use the data mining parser, you can run the queries in an MDX or DAX query window as well. We recommend using the DAX query window because it works with both model types and does not open an object browser.

The following is a short list of some common queries you might use while troubleshooting your models:

- **Currently connected sessions – both models**: This query returns the session data for the server or instance you are connected to:

```
Select * from $System.discover_sessions
```

- **Tabular model table list**: This query is specifically for tabular models at 1200 compatibility level or higher(New DMV row sets were released specifically for 1200 and higher):

```
SELECT * FROM $System.TMSCHEMA_TABLES
```

- **Multidimensional model table list**: This query is designed for multidimensional models but works with tabular models as well. This will return a list of tables as defined in each model type:

```
SELECT * FROM $System.DBSchema_Tables WHERE TABLE_TYPE =
'TABLE' ORDER BY TABLE_NAME ASC
```

- **Memory consumption – both models**: When troubleshooting potential performance issues, you can use this query to ascertain memory consumption:

```
SELECT * FROM $System.DISCOVER_MEMORYUSAGE
```

- **Object activity – both models**: This is an interesting query. You can use this information to see activity performed on the object since the last time the service was started. It does not retain history:

```
SELECT * FROM $System.DISCOVER_OBJECT_ACTIVITY
```

This has been an introduction to DMVs. There is a wealth of documentation and examples available online (`https://docs.microsoft.com/en-us/analysis-services/ instances/use-dynamic-management-views-dmvs-to-monitor- analysis-services?view=asallproducts-allversions`). These are built into SSAS and are here to help you troubleshoot your solutions when needed.

Using SQL Server Profiler

SQL Server Profiler has been around for many years in SQL Server. While the information from this tool can be quite extensive, most data professionals refrain from using this as the first choice due to the impact on the performance of the systems it is profiling. However, it can provide a wealth of data for you when troubleshooting your server. Let's look at SQL Server Profiler with our tabular model as an example:

1. Open SQL Server Profiler by searching for `SQL Server Profiler` in Windows.

2. Click **File**, and then **New Trace** to start a tracing activity on your server. Choose your tabular model server in the server dialog.

3. This will open a **Trace Properties** dialog with two tabs. Give your trace a name, and then choose **Event Selection**.

4. Under **Event Selection**, you will see many different events already selected and ready. These events are for SSAS solutions and are the default set from SQL Server.

   i) If you click **Show all events**, you can see there are many more events to choose from.

   ii) In the **Query Processing** section, you can see events that target each model type, such as aggregations for multidimensional models and Vertipaq for tabular models. If you need to do some specific query tuning, these can help you dig into details.

   iii) By clicking **Show all columns**, you can also see that some data specific to model tuning will be exposed, such as **Calculation Expression**.

   For our purposes, deselect all the options from all event categories except **Queries Events**. This should leave **Query Begin** and **Query End** selected. Click **Run**. The trace will show no events at the moment.

5. Go to Management Studio and connect to your tabular model database. Right-click on the database and choose **Browse**.

6. In the model browser, add an attribute and measure (your choice) and execute the query. This should result in the two events in the profiler – **Query Begin** and **Query End**. Explore the various columns. For example, this shows you the MDX that was sent to the model for results. The SSMS browser uses MDX queries for both model types.

7. Now, open a DAX query window. We will use a query we created in *Chapter 8, Adding Measures and Calculations with DAX*:

```
DEFINE
MEASURE 'Sales'[Sales Total] = SUM('Sales'[Total
Excluding Tax])
EVALUATE(
    SUMMARIZECOLUMNS(
        'Date'[Calendar Year]
        , 'Item'[Color]
        , "Total Sales"
        , CALCULATE([Sales Total])
        ))
```

You should now see the same query in the trace. You can use the trace to determine query timings and resource consumption.

8. Stop your trace and close **Profiler**.

We only explored one set of events in SQL Server Profiler. This is a good tool for grabbing the code, which you can then use in SSMS for further testing.

Reviewing other maintenance tasks or tools

In this section, we have a number of tasks and tools that can support the operational needs of your SQL Server Analysis Server solutions. Let's look at each of them in detail.

Warming multidimensional models

One of the issues with multidimensional models is that they use caching extensively to improve query performance. When a cube is reprocessed, the cache is cleaned up. When users start to use the cube, they can experience significant performance issues because the data is being retrieved from disk as opposed to memory. While this can happen at any time, especially when uncommon queries are run, it can be frustrating if, every Monday morning, the CEO needs to wait for this query. Once it is cached, it performs great.

The solution to this issue is to warm the cache. This typically involves running several queries right after the cube has been processed to load common or key data into the cache, thereby improving the user experience (tabular models are all in-memory and do not have this issue).

Using usage-based optimization with multidimensional models

This technique collects several queries being executed in the cube and uses those queries to recommend new aggregations to build.

Add a database connection and table for query logs

If you don't have a connection in the `Log\QueryLog\QueryLogConnectionString` property of the server, you will not be able to complete these steps. We added a connection to our `WideWorldImportersDW` database for this example. If you plan to use this feature regularly, you should create a database to support it. Once you have this added, you can use the wizard. We created a new SQL login and user to create the table. You will also need to set the `Log\QueryLog\CreateQueryLogTable` setting to `true` in order to allow SSAS to create the query log table. You can change the name of the query log table if you wish to, but this is not required in order to continue. The table will be created when the system reaches the default sampling count of 10. If you want to increase the logging, you can reset this to 1. This value should never be set to 1 in production environments. Verify that the table has been created in the database before proceeding with the wizard. Run a few queries to give the wizard some data to work with.

Here is the process to set this up and collect the information:

1. Open your multidimensional model solution in Visual Studio.

2. Open the cube design window and navigate to the **Aggregations** tab.

3. In the buttons on the left of the tab, select **Usage Based Optimization** to open **Usage Based Optimization Wizard**.

4. Click **Next** on the opening page.

5. You can now see a list of partitions to modify. Choose a partition to optimize and click **Next**.

6. You can limit the queries you are planning to optimize. Click **Next**.

7. The next screen will describe the queries that will be optimized. If you see a query you don't want to optimize, deselect it here. Click **Next**.

8. Count the members and click **Next**.

9. Choose an aggregation option in the screen and click **Start**.

10. When the aggregation designer is complete, click **Next**.

11. Now you can create this as a new aggregation or add it to an existing design. This choice is about how you want to manage custom aggregations.

12. Once you are ready, click **Finish** to complete the design. Wrap this up by deploying the changes and reprocessing the cube.

This solution helps you to create targeted aggregations that can support specific query operations or users. Be sure to update these as usage patterns tend to change over time.

Removing unused fields from your tabular models

This may seem obvious, but it is a common issue in tabular models. Including fields in tabular models because you might need it later is a bad practice. Tabular models are loaded into memory and even if they are highly compressed, larger models can have performance issues. Removing unused fields reduces the memory load for the model and generally improves query performance.

Using open source tools to support tabular models

Tabular models continue to see a lot of support in the community. As a result, there are a few tools that have been released that support development and operations for tabular models. A few of the tools are described here:

- **DAX Studio** – `https://daxstudio.org`

  DAX Studio is a more elegant solution for creating, managing, and tuning DAX queries for your tabular models. This tool supports query performance investigations with more detail than you can find in SSMS.

- **Tabular Editor** – `https://tabulareditor.org`

  This tool allows you to edit tabular models without the workspace database. This is particularly helpful when working with large models and when you have to deal with development performance issues.

- **ALM Toolkit** – `http://alm-toolkit.com`

  ALM Toolkit allows model developers to compare data and schemas. It provides a clean method for seeing changes between models. This tool also supports advanced capabilities, such as partial deployments.

All these tools are open source products and have recently been integrated into Power BI Desktop as they all support Power BI as well.

Summary

With this chapter, we have come to the end of our journey with SQL Server Analysis Services 2019. This chapter covered a lot of maintenance and operational tasks and tools. When working with Analysis Services models, the tools are typically specific to the model type. While not an exhaustive list of tasks or tools, you now know how to back up, restore, synchronize, and performance tune your models. As you continue to work with Analysis Services, you will find these and other techniques valuable when moving to production environments.

The skills from this chapter wrap up the full life cycle when working with SQL Server 2019 Analysis Services. From install to backups, you now have a complete picture of the techniques and skills required to install and build out an analytic model on Analysis Services and deliver analytics to your customers and to your business.

Other Books You May Enjoy

If you enjoyed this book, you may be interested in these other books by Packt:

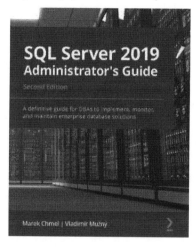

SQL Server 2019 Administrator's Guide- Second Edition

Marek Chmel, Vladimír Mužný

ISBN: 978-1-78995-432-6

- Discover SQL Server 2019's new features and how to implement them
- Fix performance issues by optimizing queries and making use of indexes
- Design and use an optimal database management strategy
- Combine SQL Server 2019 with Azure and manage your solution using various automation techniques
- Implement efficient backup and recovery techniques in line with security policies
- Get to grips with migrating, upgrading, and consolidating with SQL Server
- Set up an AlwaysOn-enabled stable and fast SQL Server 2019 environment
- Understand how to work with Big Data on SQL Server environments

SQL Server on Azure Virtual Machines

Joey D'Antoni, Louis Davidson, Allan Hirt, John Martin, Anthony Nocentino, Tim Radney, Randolph West

ISBN: 978-1-80020-459-1

- Choose an operating system for SQL Server in Azure VMs
- Use the Azure Management Portal to facilitate the deployment process
- Verify connectivity and network latency in cloud
- Configure storage for optimal performance and connectivity
- Explore various disaster recovery options for SQL Server in Azure
- Optimize SQL Server on Linux
- Discover how to back up databases to a URL

Leave a review - let other readers know what you think

Please share your thoughts on this book with others by leaving a review on the site that you bought it from. If you purchased the book from Amazon, please leave us an honest review on this book's Amazon page. This is vital so that other potential readers can see and use your unbiased opinion to make purchasing decisions, we can understand what our customers think about our products, and our authors can see your feedback on the title that they have worked with Packt to create. It will only take a few minutes of your time, but is valuable to other potential customers, our authors, and Packt. Thank you!

Index

V

W

X

Y

Made in the USA
Coppell, TX
04 March 2021